NCO Guide

10th Edition

CSM Dan Elder, USA (Ret.)

STACKPOLE BOOKS

0 11557 01402 0

NCO Guide and its predecessor, *The Noncom's Guide*, have been published by Stackpole Books since 1948. Tenth edition 2015.

Published by
STACKPOLE BOOKS
5067 Ritter Road
Mechanicsburg, PA 17055
www.stackpolebooks.com

Printed in the United States of America

10 9 8 7 6 5 4 3 2 1

This book is not an official publication of the Department of Defense or Department of the Army, nor does its publication in any way imply its endorsement by these agencies. The views presented are those of the author and do not necessarily represent the views of the Department of Defense or its Components.

Cover design by Tessa J. Sweigert
Cover photo © Program Executive Office Soldier/Flickr
All photographs courtesy of the US Army unless otherwise indicated

Library of Congress Cataloging-in-Publication Data

Elder, Daniel K., 1961–
    NCO guide / CSM Dan Elder, USA (Ret.). — 10th edition / revised by Dan Elder.
       pages cm
    Includes bibliographical references and index.
    ISBN 978-0-8117-1402-0
    1. United States. Army—Non-commissioned officers' handbooks.   I. Title.
II. Title: Noncommissioned officers' guide.
    U123.E53 2015
    355.00973—dc23
                                                                    2014048770

The NCO Creed

No one is more professional than I. I am a Noncommissioned Officer, a leader of soldiers. As a Noncommissioned Officer, I realize that I am a member of a time-honored corps, which is known as "The Backbone of the Army." I am proud of the Corps of Noncommissioned Officers and will at all times conduct myself so as to bring credit upon the Corps, the Military Service, and my country, regardless of the situation in which I find myself. I will not use my grade or position to attain pleasure, profit, or personal safety.

Competence is my watchword. My two basic responsibilities will always be uppermost in my mind—accomplishment of my mission and the welfare of my soldiers. I will strive to remain tactically and technically proficient. I am aware of my role as a Noncommissioned Officer. I will fulfill my responsibilities inherent in that role. All soldiers are entitled to outstanding leadership; I will provide that leadership. I know my soldiers, and I will always place their needs above my own. I will communicate consistently with my soldiers and never leave them uninformed. I will be fair and impartial when recommending both rewards and punishment.

Officers of my unit will have maximum time to accomplish their duties; they will not have to accomplish mine. I will earn their respect and confidence as well as that of my soldiers. I will be loyal to those with whom I serve, seniors, peers, and subordinates alike. I will exercise initiative by taking appropriate action in the absence of orders. I will not compromise my integrity, nor my moral courage. I will not forget, nor will I allow my comrades to forget, that we are professionals, Noncommissioned Officers, leaders!

Contents

PART II: TRAINING SOLDIERS AND SELF

Foreword

Stackpole Books has published the *NCO Guide* and its predecessor titles for over sixty years. We revise this book frequently so that it reflects the latest information needed by our Army's noncommissioned officers in the performance of their duties and for their own professional development. We seek the best-qualified senior NCO authors for this work, such as Command Sergeant Major Dan Elder, who revised this edition.

We believe the information in the *NCO Guide* represents virtually all the duties a noncommissioned officer is expected to perform, and we welcome comments and input from serving noncommissioned officers in all components.

One thing that impresses us each time we revise the *Guide* is the amount of knowledge, the numbers of skills, and quantity of information an NCO needs to effectively lead the soldiers in America's modern Army.

Given the very high reputation our Army has with the American public, a clear vote of thanks is due to our noncommissioned officers for the fine job they are doing leading and teaching America's young men and women who enter this ancient and honorable service.

Preface

The basic responsibilities of the US Army noncommissioned officer have changed little since this guide was first introduced in 1948. The all-encompassing nature of this handbook is not unlike one of the earliest military guides, the 1779 *Regulations for the Order and Discipline of the Troops of the United States* by Prussian officer Friedrich von Steuben. Called the "Blue Book" because of its appearance, von Steuben's instructions to sergeants and corporals noted that they would be "answerable for the squad committed to their care." He went on to teach that they "must pay particular attention to their conduct in every respect; that they keep themselves and their arms always clean; and that they have their effects always ready." On today's modern battlefield, the duties and responsibilities of the NCO may still be similar to the requirements in Washington's army at Valley Forge, but the battlefield has become much more complicated. This book is one way you can keep tips, lessons, and references right at your fingertips, in the tradition of von Steuben, no matter where you serve.

NCOs become good NCOs by using their time productively to study their profession and themselves. They read Army regulations, field manuals, military journals, and other official literature to hone their professional edge. They research military topics in sources ranging from on-post libraries to Army listings on the Internet. They spend many off-duty hours studying college texts or using alternative educational resources to pursue degrees to further develop their usefulness as leaders.

The *NCO Guide* is aimed at the corporals, sergeants, first sergeants, and sergeants major who will turn to it when they need self-help guidance or consolidated information that will benefit fellow soldiers. It is an educational resource and ready reference to key Army subjects, drawing on the education, experience, and training of myself and the other editors, as well as hundreds of sources. The *Guide* begins with a discussion of how and why the Army continues to change, and ends with how to make the most of a transition from service to civilian life—in essence, it follows a soldier life-cycle model. Readers will find information on the developmental aspects of soldiering, fitness, education, promotion, and dozens of other necessary topics relating to a noncommissioned officer's duties. The *NCO Guide* also serves as a desktop reference for when the reader or a fellow soldier has questions about pay, benefits, entitlements, personal appearance, uniforms, insignia, assignments, and personal or professional problems, and contains aids that quickly lead soldiers to official or other publications that may contain updates.

This tenth edition has been fully revised and includes topics all NCO leaders must understand. It contains new or updated information about our responsibilities: leading soldiers in combat; leadership and counseling; rigorous training; the Army values; personnel and property accountability; master fitness principles, weight control, and the Army Physical Fitness Test; the NCO Education System and civilian education; professional reading, writing, and multimedia; life, medical, and dental insurance; and the Thrift Savings Plan. It also addresses contemporary leadership issues such as professional ethics, PTSD, soldier behavior on the battlefield, fraternization, AIDS, discrimination, resiliency, and prevention of sexual harassment.

Readers will also find sections about the military justice system, including military discipline, the law of land warfare, command authority and soldier rights, nonjudicial punishment, the Manual for Courts-Martial, and its Uniform Code of Military Justice. Also provided is information about awards, decorations, and uniforms, with several pages of full-color photographs for your use.

This edition of the *NCO Guide* has reformed content and improved relevancy. It appears that everything in the Army has been subject to change over the last thirteen years of persistent conflict, and the team at Stackpole Books and I have done our best to bring you the latest in a very dynamic and changing time. Field manual numbers now reflect the DoD numbering system where appropriate, and we have converted our references to the Doctrine 2015 categorization of manuals to ADPs, ADRPs, and ATPs. Because of the large number of MOS-specific schools, discussion of these is restricted to the functional courses that apply the most, such as the NCO Education System, drill sergeant, airborne, recruiter, and so on.

As a career active-duty soldier who spent a lifetime serving my comrades and my nation, I am honored and humbled by the opportunity to continue to serve through this effort. It is through actions like maintaining this guide that "old soldiers" like myself continue to give back to our profession during times when others cannot. Though I am no von Steuben, it is in his tradition that we offer you this up-to-date and useful handbook that we believe will serve you for the many years ahead.

Daniel K. Elder
CSM, USA (Ret.)

Acknowledgments

I first touted the power of the Internet for soldiers in the Fall 1997 edition of the *NCO Journal*, and it still holds true today. The Internet is a source of so much information, and understanding how to use it efficiently is a critical task for today's noncommissioned officer because of the treasure trove of information at your fingertips. It is through the many sites and portals that we are able to provide the latest information and links to update this current handbook. Many sites contributed to this revision, including the following: USAPA, the Army's Publishing Agency, which lists many regulations and pamphlets; Army Knowledge Online; Department of Veterans Affairs; Defense Activity for Nontraditional Education Support; Army Family Advocacy Program; Army Community Services; TRICARE; Defense Media Activity; Human Resources Command; Enlisted Records and Evaluation Center; Soldier for Life and the Army Career and Alumni Program; Training and Doctrine Command; Army and Air Force Exchange Service; Army Training Support Center and the Army Training Network; Association of the United States Army; Office of the Chief of Public Affairs; Defense Finance and Accounting Service; Department of Education; and the Central Army Registry (formerly known as the Reimer Digital Library).

The following organizations also contributed: the Office of the Sergeant Major of the Army, Army News Service, *SOLDIERS* magazine, Army Continuing Education Services, Army Safety Center, Army Family Liaison Office, Judge Advocate General's Corps, Defense Imagery, the US Army Center of Military History, and the Army Community and Family Support Center.

I am indebted to my Stackpole editors for their professional support and guidance during production of the *NCO Guide: 10th Edition*. They are often the champions of projects like these. I also want to acknowledge all of the counsel I have received from my many friends and mentors—your advice and encouragement has been helpful and does not go unnoticed. Lastly, I must thank my wife and daughters, who always share the time that should be theirs with my many projects and efforts. It is only through their support, advice, and counsel that I am able to do half the things I do. I often say I am a lucky man and have been honored to serve the nation and as a soldier, none of which would have been possible without the strength of my family.

PART I

Leading Soldiers

1

America's Army

> The Army has been in a state of continuous war for the past twelve years, the longest in our Nation's history. More than 167,000 Soldiers are deployed or forward stationed in nearly 160 countries worldwide. The global security environment points to further instability, and the Army remains a key guardian of our national security.
>
> —Army Posture Statement (2013)

Our Army incorporates intellectual ingenuity, technological innovation, and the values that have always shaped America's Army throughout its more than two-hundred-year history. To be successful in this millennium, our Army needs skilled, versatile, and highly motivated NCOs who are capable of accomplishing their mission in changed environments; NCOs confident in their ability to train soldiers in individual through small-unit tasks relevant to their units' missions, using creative approaches to maximize their subordinates' full potential; and lastly, NCOs who can ably lead their soldiers in battle.

America's Army is the best land combat force in the world, serving the nation every day at home and abroad. It is often the commitment of our Army into trouble spots that makes the difference between the success and failure of America's defense policy. Land forces remain decisive and provide the most visible and sustained form of US commitment, and when ground troops deploy, the world knows the United States means business. Army forces are stationed overseas in places like Europe and the Pacific region, which allow the presence of US combatant commanders with military forces. This capability allows our soldiers to shape action, prevent conflicts, or, if all else fails, to fight and win.

Soldiers and the units they serve in are expected to accomplish whatever mission they are assigned, regardless of circumstances, location, funding, or priority. There are always challenges—and rewards.

The Army remains the best-led, best-trained, and best-equipped army in the world; however, it is beginning to suffer from overextension, with the operational tempo to Iraq and Afghanistan as well as to other areas of the world allowing insufficient recovery time for personnel, families, and equipment, and training resulting in just-in-time readiness for the next deployment. The next years will be as hard as the Army has faced. The priority will be four imperatives: *Sustain*, *Prepare*, *Reset*, and *Transform*.

READY AND RESILIENT: THE ARMY'S NCO CORPS

> My plans would have amounted to little had there not been trained NCOs available to build my decision. . . . Throughout my career, at every level of command to the position I now hold, I have relied on my NCOs. Whatever I entrusted them with, they accomplished to standard when given the full set of resources, including authority and responsibility to do so.
>
> —Lt. Gen. John P. Otjen, USA (Ret.), former commander, US First Army

Warrior Ethos

The Warrior Ethos is a set of guiding principles that defines the American soldier. It comes from the most basic document of every man and women who serves: the Soldier's Creed. The Warrior Ethos is developed and sustained through discipline, commitment to the Army Values, and pride in the Army's heritage as the foundation for the spirit of the Army.

Our ethos is a pledge all soldiers take to confirm their commitment that they will:

- Always place the mission first.
- Never accept defeat.
- Never quit.
- Never leave a fallen comrade.

The Warrior Ethos characterizes the fighting spirit and serves as a guide for soldiers. It is closely linked to the Army Values of loyalty to comrades, personal courage, and dedication to duty.

The Backbone of the Army

An NCO must be fully capable of fighting a war and transforming in an era of unpredictability. The Army's future vision of the NCO blends traditional duties with emerging future characteristics. The Army describes today's NCO as "an innovative, competent professional enlisted leader grounded in heritage, values, and tradition, who embodies the Warrior Ethos, champions continuous learning, and is capable of leading, training, and motivating soldiers; an

Staff Sgt. Elbert C. Walker, with the 1st Battalion, 8th Cavalry Regiment, participates in a Theater Assistance Force handover patrol on 10 November 2013 near Multinational Base Tarin Kowt, Afghanistan.

adaptive leader who is proficient in joint and combined expeditionary warfare and continuous, simultaneous full spectrum operations, and resilient to uncertain and ambiguous environments."

We have the finest noncommissioned officers corps in the world, and much of the Army's success is directly attributable to NCO leadership. Noncommissioned officers are famous for their abilities to get things done, whatever those might be. However, a leader must be concerned not only with the quality of unit achievements, but also with the process by which the achievements are attained. Many ethical conflicts occur when not in combat because some members of our profession forget that the real test occurs on the battlefield. Our Army's future has to be based on a solid foundation of moral-ethical values; any lessening of this standard compromises and corrupts our ability to lead soldiers and, in the long run, diminishes the support of the American public.

Army leaders speak of maintaining the Army as a military profession by its soldiers and leaders who meet the Army's certification criteria of competence, character, and commitment. No matter how intellectually or technologically advanced we become, we can never forget these fundamental truths. The Army way of life should inspire us to a sense of purpose that will sustain us in the brutal realities of combat and the ambiguities of operations other than war. Our values of fairness and concern for the individual are supported by our national values, but they also contribute to unit loyalty and cohesiveness. These values are also useful. They create standards of behavior that we, as members of a professional Army, need to hold to in order to be successful. These values then become the standards of the unit.

Standards are those principles or rules by which behavior is measured as acceptable and tasks are measured as successfully accomplished. Once the standard becomes a criterion for acceptance into a section, company, or battalion and all share the values and understand the standards that flow from them, soldiers will measure other soldiers and the result will be a more cohesive organization, a real team.

Army Doctrine Reference Publication (ADRP) 1, The Army Profession, expresses its guiding beliefs, standards, and ideals succinctly in one word—professional. A profession is a type of job or vocation that requires special education and training, but being *professional* means fulfilling your obligations while adhering to the highest standards of the Army Ethic. It is behavior guided by moral obligation, demanded by custom, or enjoined by feelings of rightness. It requires the impartial administration of standards without regard to friendship, personality, rank, or other bias.

Ethics are your personal set of values. They are the thread that weaves throughout the fabric of the professional Army Ethic. *Ethical* means honesty, uprightness, the avoidance of deception, and steadfast adherence to standards of behavior. Ethical means that personal standards are consistent with professional values and demands a commitment to act according to the other Army Values. Ethics are the most important character trait of any leader, and we all make decisions based on the ethics of those reporting to us. Ethics can be ordered, but they can only be achieved by encouragement and example. As NCO leaders, we must not only be tactically and technically competent, but also commit ourselves to the highest standards of ethical conduct and foster soldier commitment to the values of the profession.

How many times have commanders and senior NCOs "blinked" at how an objective was accomplished? At how, for the "no one falls out" division run, the less fit are culled from the ranks during the first formation? Soldiers see and understand these shenanigans for what they are: ethical lapses by their leaders. We must eliminate the mindset that produces directives such as "I don't care how you do it, just do it."

If a leader puts a positive spin on a report in garrison, what happens during battles and operations? There is no time in combat to verify reports, question the accuracy of information, or wonder about the reliability of equipment or someone's word. When leaders initial a safe as being checked without actually checking it and then punish a soldier for not having checked the motor pool, all credibility is lost. Soldiers know the difference between right and wrong and no matter how much is said to justify something wrong, they lose respect for the unethical leader. However, leaders who make it clear that they will not tolerate ethical ambivalence and who demonstrate by their actions that they hold themselves to the same standard promote mutual confidence and understanding among their soldiers. There is no senior-subordinate difference when it comes to doing what is right.

NCOs play a key role in influencing "command climate." Every organization, whether a squad, company, brigade, or higher echelon, has only so much energy to expend to accomplish a given mission. That energy can be wasted or it can be used wisely. In a unit with a positive, healthy climate, that energy can be even more than the sum total of the energy of its members. The energy of an organization can be wasted as well. If you are forced to expend energy looking over your shoulder, preparing to cover yourself for some inspection, building a wall of numbers and statistics to look good, you will have little energy left to teach your soldiers, be innovative, or accomplish your mission. It is only through steadfast, ethical leadership that soldiers and units can reach their full capabilities and be most effective. Soldiers in units with a good moral climate understand right from wrong.

All soldiers make mistakes. Errors of omission (such as not knowing how to do something and doing it wrong) should receive little notice outside additional training. However, errors of commission, such as submitting a doctored report or lying to protect oneself, should result in immediate punishment. If we make a decision that is contrary to what is expected of us, then we must also take responsibility for our actions.

ADRP 1 highlights *trust*, which is defined by the core qualities of *character*, *competence*, and *commitment*. Trust is much more than a cursory interest in others. It means sincere involvement in helping to find solutions to problems and improving welfare; talking with and listening to subordinates, not simply talking at them; doing something about hardships or problems, not paying lip service to them; and teaching individuals by counseling, not by abusing them. Trust develops and sustains confidence among soldiers as they do their day-to-day missions.

The most basic and essential characteristics of the Army profession are:

- *Trust*. We must maintain trust and respect between soldiers and with the people of the nation we serve. We accomplish this through the shared purpose of service.
- *Military expertise*. Our professional expertise comes from nearly 240 years of service by our Army to the country, and from the organization, training, and employment of our land forces.
- *Honorable service*. In performing our national duties, we are expected to always respect the dignity of others.
- *Esprit de corps*. It takes dedicated professionals in order to persevere and win our nation's wars. We do so through our bonds in a common goal and purpose to maintain our nation.

- *Stewardship of the profession.* Expertise is created and grown in the Army through high standards of excellence and disciplined experience, which are grounded in the professional Army Ethic.

Caring means fostering a climate that challenges people, convinces them that their contributions make a difference, and allows them to feel good about themselves and the Army they serve. We have to take the time to see, hear, and resolve problems before they affect our units and our soldiers.

What do Soldiers Expect of NCO Leaders?

Throughout our Army's history, NCO duties have centered around maintaining good order and discipline within units; serving as small-unit and/or technical skill leaders; training soldiers in individual skills; and ably leading teams, squads, and sections in combat and in support of combat. All leaders are responsible for accomplishing the unit's mission; ensuring subordinates' physical, moral, personal, and professional welfare; setting and exemplifying the highest professional and ethical standards; and treating subordinates with dignity, respect, fairness, and consistency.

Good senior NCOs, along with officers, will foster a moral climate in which leaders teach, individual character has the opportunity to mature, and recognition of achievement and tolerance of honest mistakes fosters personal and professional growth. They show their soldiers what right looks like. Leaders must nurture a human relations environment in which all soldiers, regardless of race, creed, color, gender, religion, or national origin, are treated as soldiers. NCO leaders who deal daily with soldiers affect values and behavior by establishing day-to-day procedures, practices, and working norms; by their personal example; and by building discipline, cohesion, motivation, consistency, and fair play.

NCOs ensure that a soldier behaves as a soldier, both on and off duty. The NCO takes immediate action when a soldier's conduct affects good order and discipline. Soldiers who infringe on other soldiers' rights need to be told to modify their behavior or go elsewhere. There is no substitute for observing for oneself what is going on at the muddy-boots level. No PowerPoint presentation listing everything, right down to boot sizes and numbers of shoelaces, will ever come close to "eyes on the target." We expect all noncommissioned officers, regardless of rank, to form the habit of getting down in the trenches with the soldiers, of seeing what is taking place, of measuring it against one's own scale of values, and ordering changes as necessary.

We expect our small-unit leaders to lead by example and to practice the professional Army Ethic; to enforce Army standards of appearance and conduct; to supervise maintenance of equipment, living areas, and work places; to instill discipline; and to take care of subordinates. Those NCOs serving in staff positions must never forget their responsibilities to train, mentor, and look out for the well-being of other soldiers in their sections.

A critical task for NCOs is to assist in the creation and development of expertise and experience of ourselves and our squads, sections, and platoons. It takes study and practice to develop that expertise, but it defines one of our primary roles. It is more than just tactical and technical expertise—it also includes moral, cultural, and human experience. We must develop in our soldiers and ourselves the ability to take appropriate action on our own initiative in the absence of orders, while ensuring it is still in support of the commander's intent. Lifelong learning is expected of all Army professionals.

In such an environment, *competence* is vitally important. Competence is your ability to perform your duties successfully and to accomplish the mission with discipline and to standard. Competence comes from how you combine your character with your knowledge, skills, and behaviors that define you as a leader.

Your *character* defines your dedication and adherence to the Army Values and Ethic. You display character by consistently showing it in all your decisions and actions. These are the qualities that are shared between you and your comrades and what distinguishes military service from other professions. Though they may have other values and ethics, it is Army Values and Ethics you adhere to.

By your *commitment*, you strive to serve honorably and to perform your duties with discipline and to standards while working to be successful and accomplishing each mission with high ethical values, no matter the adversity or challenge.

If we can trust a corporal with a color guard to render proper respect to the flag when no one is watching, then we can also trust that corporal to do what he or she believes is right when faced with an ethical dilemma. If properly trained and understanding of what is right and what is wrong, our soldiers will invariably do what is right. But if they observe their senior leaders bending the rules for one reason or another, they will find it more difficult to justify the harder right. Moral character develops out of repeating good actions; it cannot be learned from orders, but it can be learned by imitation. The best discipline is self-discipline, when you do what you know is right because you want to do the right thing. It is especially important for young soldiers to learn this immediately. As former Chief of Staff of the Army (CSA) Gen. John Wickham once said:

> During the initial tour the young soldier's life is lived mainly at the squad level with his primary chain of command ranging up through platoon and company/battery/troop level. Therefore the brand of leadership that is exercised by the soldier's squad leader, platoon sergeant, platoon leader, first sergeant and company commander is absolutely critical.

NCOs must *motivate* soldiers, help them grow, develop them personally and professionally, and inspire them to achieve their maximum potential. We have to allow our subordinates to learn from honest errors, while ensuring that they correct their mistakes. Not correcting mistakes breeds mediocrity. If you walk by a deficiency and say nothing, it becomes the standard.

When told of a soldier not performing to standard, many senior leaders question how effective the immediate leader is in counseling, mentoring, or teaching the soldier his or her job. We must make soldiers want to excel; those soldiers who do not strive for the highest rungs and who are content to reside at the lowest level of performance can do so elsewhere.

Everyone tells us we have the best soldiers in the world. Let us treat them as the professionals they are. They are beyond the stage of requiring babysitters. We must foster their faith in us by ensuring that we give them the respect and confidence they deserve. Anything else will result in compromise and will impair our ability to lead soldiers into the next century. If we and our subordinate leaders foster strong *esprit* in our soldiers by being personal and professional examples of excellence and by treating them as professionals, there is no doubt they will act professionally. Again, this does not mean that we look the other way when soldiers are not performing to standard.

You do not have to stop soldiers who have pride in themselves and their unit. You just need to steer them. Former US Army Forces Command (FORSCOM) CSM Richard Cayton once said, "Your soldiers will walk a path and they will come to a crossroads; if you are standing at the crossroads, where you belong, you can guide your soldiers to the right path and make them successful."

I have found no soldier—Active, Guard, or Reserve—who wants to fail. But many do, not for lack of effort (we expend a lot of that) but for lack of knowing how. Some NCOs are unfamiliar with their training responsibilities, and some officers are reluctant to let their NCOs have their piece of the training pie. We should all consider the following:

- No soldier should ever have to do his or her duty ill-trained or ill-prepared to do it.
- NCOs are responsible for the proper conduct of individual, crew, squad, and section-level training.
- No NCO should ever stand before his or her soldiers unconfident or incompetent to lead or train them.
- All soldiers should hold their NCOs in high regard and want to follow their lead and example.
- Each NCO must accept full responsibility for his or her soldiers' success and failure.

Leading in the Twenty-first Century

When we entered the mechanized age at the turn of the twentieth century, our Army found an increasing need for a different type of noncommissioned officer—one who was familiar with the technical aspects of the field as well as basic soldiering skills. Today, the NCO Corps again sits at the crossroads of a complex environment. As the Army transitions from over a decade of war and looks to the future, we are leaning toward an increased reliance on the small-unit leader. A smaller force requires NCOs to shift from some of the more traditional roles and to become skilled in developing and training NCO leaders who have direct responsibility for teaching our soldiers in these new technologies.

A senior NCO's primary duty is much like that of the master guildsman of old: It is to ensure that subordinate leaders are trained as skilled professionals and future leaders. If a sergeant is unconfident and unfamiliar with the task he or she is to train soldiers in, several things happen. First, the noncommissioned officer loses credibility with his or her soldiers, and the training is not learned or accomplished. Second, training resources and time are wasted and the task is either rescheduled or, more commonly, listed as unsatisfactory and collective training is begun.

Let us now look at the relationship between the commander and senior NCOs concerning training. ADP 7-0 and ADRP 7-0 specify that senior non-commissioned officers—sergeants first class through sergeants major—are an integral part in the planning and execution of soldier, team, and squad training, and that they should be made responsible for how well their soldiers are trained.

Some compare senior commanders to architects who design the Mission Essential Task List (METL) for their organizations. Subordinate officers take the METL and extract those collective tasks necessary for successful completion at their level. Senior NCOs at each echelon take the collective tasks and determine which individual soldier tasks are necessary to be completed in order for the unit to complete its mission. Just as the architect relies on the contractor to transform the design into a building, the officer must rely on the NCO to put his or her intent into effective individual and leader training programs that make up the building blocks for the collective tasks that support the unit METL.

In a 1994 *Military Review* article, Gen. Gordon Sullivan wrote: "Concentration on basics will mean that we reduce the number of tasks on a unit's mission essential task list, not increase them. Football has six basics—run, pass, catch, block, tackle, and think. We must look to the same type of basics. Without excellence in the basics, versatility is impossible." The same holds true today.

Some leaders believe that making important collective, leader, and individual tasks nondiscretionary robs the leader of creativity and initiative. The fact is that senior leaders have to provide sufficient structure to ensure superior performance from leaders newly introduced into their position, by defining the ever-talked-about box. It is only when the boundaries are clear that creativity and initiative become free from timidity rooted in uncertainty. NCOs who know they have to build a mousetrap will look for better ways to build it.

The NCO Creed states that officers will be given time to accomplish their duties and that they will not have to do ours. We give officers that time by ensuring that soldiers are trained to standard in individual tasks before we attempt training them in collective tasks. This development of training not only occurs at the beginning and end but also is ongoing throughout. Since both the commander and the senior NCO are involved with the development of the training plan at different levels, collective and individual, each must sequence and talk through the different stages. Too much reliance on either collective or individual tasks will result in failure to meet the overall objective. Tankers will never get to Tank Table XII if everyone concentrates only on Tank Table VIII. Without this corporate "buy-in" by both officers and NCOs, training in units becomes little more than a list of discrete, nonrelated, often poorly resourced events. However, when everyone buys into the plan, training will be successful.

The following chapters cover many areas, from the uses of military history to the history of the role of the NCO to the "master trainer" concept for identifying individual training needs and conducting After Action Reviews (AARs). How-to's for conducting NCO induction ceremonies, marksmanship ranges, and physical fitness programs are also addressed. The unifying factor in all is the noncommissioned officer and your responsibilities to soldiers. Much of the book consists of quick reference guides regarding promotion, assignments, the Uniform Code of Military Justice, and other topics that will assist in your role as a noncommissioned officer. Officers expect you to provide your soldiers with the best training possible, so that when the time comes, they will know that they are competently trained and well led and will have confidence that they can fight and win in combat. A soldier dying for lack of training is nothing less than criminal. Your job and responsibility is to ensure that this does not happen.

So where do you go from here? If you are serious about leading in the twenty-first century with all its technology, and are still expecting your soldiers to fight and—if necessary—die, you must focus your efforts on training, leading, and mentoring your soldiers and supporting your fellow noncommissioned officers so they can perform the same duties for the men and women in their charge. I am certain that noncommissioned officers will continue to produce a quality force that will serve the Army and this nation in this century as well as it did in the last century.

Today, as the Army wrestles with fundamental changes in the way it operates and is organized, an array of disconcerting issues face soldiers and the NCOs who lead and train them. With the nation at war, members of the Army have had to deal with seemingly ever-increasing deployments and assaults on their character because the bad behavior of a few of their fellow soldiers sullied the Army's reputation.

Perhaps. But selfless service calls for personal sacrifice and dedication to duty, regardless of the circumstances. No one gets rich on Army pay. If elements of the nation seem less than caring, well, that's just how it is—so don't sweat it. According to the annual national polls, the military is still the highest-rated institution in the nation. And in the Army family, plenty of good people do care and go about their business because it must be done. The Army's 13th Sgt. Maj. of the Army Kenneth O. Preston commented:

> Today's global environment challenges us to be a Culture of Innovation. Our operational Army is adapting to its threats on the battlefield daily. So too must our Institutional Army adapt to ensure our training and processes move at the speed of an Army at war, supporting a nation at war. I always encourage Soldiers to collaborate, think out of the box, and find innovative solutions to today's toughest problems. Phrases like "that's the way we've always done it" or "if it ain't broke, don't fix it" are unacceptable excuses today.

This is excellent advice for anyone. Sergeants and their soldiers have enough to concern themselves with on a daily basis. Mission tasks, seemingly endless deployments, leading soldiers in combat, maintaining good order and discipline, keeping fit, appearance, meeting the standards of service, upholding their sworn or affirmed oath to defend the Constitution and obey the orders of superior officers—these are some of the unchanging principal requirements of soldiering in a changing Army, in a dangerous world.

Remember that "the strength of our Nation is our Army," coupled with "the strength of our Army is our Soldiers" and "the strength of our Soldiers is our Families." Nothing could be truer.

ARMY ROLES, MISSIONS, AND FUNCTIONS

The Army exists to serve the American people, to protect enduring national interests, and to fulfill national military responsibilities. The Army is charged with providing forces able to conduct timely, continued combat on land as well as stability and reconstruction operations, when required. The Army provides the Joint Force with capabilities required to prevail in the protracted Global War on Terrorism and sustain the full range of its global commitments. The Army's primary mission is "to fight and win our Nation's wars by providing prompt, sustained land dominance across the full range of military operations and spectrum of conflict in support of combatant commanders." We do that by accomplishing missions assigned by the president, secretary of defense, and combatant commanders, and by transforming for the future.

When it comes to fighting and winning a major regional conflict, no one is in our league. The Army has demonstrated both in operations in Afghanistan and Iraq that we own the battlefield, day and night. But ownership can be slippery. To win the next battle, the Army will have to get to trouble spots quickly with a sustainable fighting force. It will have to dominate the information war, acting promptly on incoming data to strike targets deep in enemy territory with a new generation of indirect-fire weapons. And commanders at all levels will have to maneuver quickly and decisively, leaving an enemy with no options except withdrawal or surrender.

The roles, missions, and functions of the military are defined as follows: *Roles* are the broad and enduring purposes for the services that are established by Congress in law; *missions* are the tasks assigned by the president or secretary of defense to combatant commanders (CCDR); and *functions* are specific responsibilities assigned by the president or secretary of defense to enable the services to fulfill their legally established roles. Simply stated, the primary function of the services is to provide forces that are organized, trained, and equipped to perform a role—to be employed by a CCDR in the accomplishment of a mission.

Hundreds of thousands of soldiers are involved in vital roles, missions, and functions on a daily basis. In 2014, approximately 450,000 soldiers were serving on active duty, while men and women from all components are deployed or forward-stationed in more than 120 countries to support operations in Iraq, Afghanistan, and other overseas locations to deter aggression while securing the homeland. Soldiers from the Army National Guard and the Army Reserve are making a vital contribution, with more than 800,000 Reserve Component personnel activated since September 2001 and performing a diverse range of missions worldwide. In addition to their duties overseas, soldiers from all components, including the Guard and the Reserve, are supporting civil authorities during disaster relief operations, such as hurricane and winter storm relief.

Assigned Army missions affect how the military is structured, trained, and employed. The Army's new regional focus, combined with major troop reductions overseas, puts enormous emphasis on strategic mobility. Airlift and sealift mobility improvements being made today will enable deployment of an Army light division and a heavy brigade to any crisis area in about two weeks, and two heavy divisions in about a month.

Regardless of how roles, missions, functions, and force structures change with the era of persistent conflict, NCOs play a vital role in the effort. The effort is worth making because the objective, as always, is safeguarding our country while maintaining and improving combat readiness for twenty-first-century Army missions.

CURRENT TRENDS IN THE ARMY

As the Army wraps up its participation in the longest war of our nation's history, we must understand that we live in an uncertain international security environment and face uncertainty around every corner. No one can predict where the next call for the American soldier will come, as our recent response to the Ebola crisis in the continent of Africa showed. Not only must our leaders have confidence that the Army is trained, equipped, and ready for most any mission, we must also be prepared to meet a combatant commander's strategic requirements. With that, our challenge is to change into a smaller—but still capable—force with less money, while downsizing is still in high demand. Some of the immediate risks to Army stability include:

- We have learned that the cost of unpreparedness causes failure for those asked to respond to the next crisis.
- Our country needs a strong Army that is trained and ready to face uncertainty.
- There is an enormous pool of potential combatants armed with irreconcilable ideas.
- Our adversaries seek adaptive advantage through asymmetry.
- We have near peer competitors in niche areas of military science.
- Conventional force-on-force conflicts are still possible.
- Our homeland is part of the battlespace.

Army Modernization

Transformation was a process that recognized the changing nature of military competition and cooperation, which the Army addressed through new combinations of operational doctrine, military capabilities, people, and organizations. As a result, the Army pursued the most comprehensive modernization of its forces since the early years of World War II.

Transformation was intended to produce evolutionary and revolutionary changes to improve both Army and Joint Force capabilities to meet current and future full-spectrum challenges. Prior to 2007, the Army unit strength was forty-two Brigade Combat Teams (BCTs) and seventy-five modular support brigades; by 2013 that had increased to forty-five BCTs and eighty-three modular support brigades. However, by 2014, the Army chief of staff announced a reduction of thirteen BCTs and that end strength would reduce by at least eighty thousand soldiers, with additional future cuts anticipated.

The modular BCT was a standalone, self-sufficient, and standardized tactical force of between 3,500 and 4,000 soldiers; recent changes have increased personnel strength to 4,500. Infantry and armored BCTs are listed to receive a third maneuver battalion because of budget cuts, which will also include added engineering and artillery units. A restructure of National Guard BCTs is also planned to reflect the changes made to the active component. These units are more capable of independent action than current division-based organization, with greatly improved strategic responsiveness.

There are three common organizational designs for ground BCTs, which include:

- A heavy BCT with two armor-mechanized infantry battalions and an armored reconnaissance battalion.
- An infantry BCT with two infantry battalions and an armored reconnaissance and surveillance battalion.
- A Stryker BCT with three Stryker battalions and a reconnaissance and surveillance battalion.

Plans also now exist for additional fires and engineering units to be assigned to each armor and infantry brigade combat team to make them more lethal.

Each support brigade performs a single function: aviation, fires, sustain, and battlefield surveillance. Modularity increases each unit's capability by building in the communications, liaison, and logistics capabilities needed to permit greater operational autonomy and support the ability to conduct joint, multinational operations—capabilities that previously were at much higher organizational echelons.

The Army's goal is to generate forces in a rotation while enhancing soldier stability. The modular force structure should allow active component soldiers to spend at least two years at home following each deployed year, Reservists at least four years, and National Guardsmen five years.

Divisions, Corps, and Armies

A decade ago, the Army considered creating new command and control units for the transformed Army, but in the end decided to retain current division and corps names. Both the transformed division and corps headquarters, with about eight hundred and a thousand soldiers respectively, can function as a joint task force and a joint force land component command. Nine of the ten active division headquarters are now based in the United States.

Field army headquarters will also continue to exist, modified for Army transformation needs, primarily as joint forces land component commands. US First, Second, Third, Fifth, Sixth, and Seventh Army have been designated to date. US Eighth Army continues to serve in Korea and the US Ninth Army was aligned to Africa Command.

Transformation Stationing Plan. The active corps, division, and BCT designations were influenced by a desire to preserve the lineage and honors of the units and divisions to which they are assigned. The following table shows the current stationing of the corps, division, and brigade combat teams.

Numbered Corps. I Corps is headquartered at Fort Lewis, Washington; III Corps is headquartered at Fort Hood, Texas; and XVIII Airborne Corps is headquartered at Fort Bragg, North Carolina.

ACTIVE DIVISIONS AND BRIGADE COMBAT TEAMS

1st Armored Division	Headquarters Fort Bliss, Texas 1, 4, 5 (Heavy) BCT at Fort Bliss 2 (Heavy) BCT at White Sands Missile Range 3*, 6 (Infantry) BCT at Fort Bliss Combat Aviation Brigade at Fort Bliss
1st Cavalry Division	Headquarters Fort Hood, Texas 1, 2, 3, 4* (Heavy) BCT at Fort Hood Combat Aviation Brigade at Fort Hood
1st Infantry Division	Headquarters Fort Riley, Kansas 1, 2 (Heavy) BCT at Fort Riley 3* (Infantry) BCT at Fort Knox, Kentucky 4* (Infantry) BCT at Fort Riley Combat Aviation Brigade at Fort Riley
2nd Infantry Division	Headquarters Camp Red Cloud, South Korea 1 (Heavy) BCT at Camp Casey, South Korea 2, 3, 4* (Stryker) BCT at Fort Lewis, Washington Combat Aviation Brigade in South Korea
3rd Infantry Division	Headquarters Fort Stewart, Georgia 1, 2* (Heavy) BCT at Fort Stewart 3 (Heavy) BCT at Fort Benning, Georgia 4 (Infantry) BCT at Fort Stewart, Georgia Combat Aviation Brigade at Hunter Army Airfield, Georgia

4th Infantry Division	Headquarters Fort Carson, Colorado
	1, 2, 3* (Heavy) BCT at Fort Carson
	4, 5 (Infantry) BCT at Fort Carson
	Combat Aviation Brigade at Fort Carson, but
	    reflagging to CAB, 1st Armored Division,
	    and moving to Fort Bliss

7th Infantry Division	Headquarters Joint Base Lewis-McChord
10th Mountain Division	Headquarters Fort Drum, New York 1, 2, 3* (Infantry) BCT at Fort Drum 4 (Infantry) BCT at Fort Polk, Louisiana Combat Aviation Brigade at Fort Drum
25th Infantry Division	Headquarters Schofield Barracks, Hawaii 1 (Stryker) BCT at Fort Wainwright, Alaska 2 (Stryker) BCT at Schofield Barracks

(continued)

ACTIVE DIVISIONS AND BRIGADE COMBAT TEAMS *continued*

	3 (Infantry) BCT at Schofield Barracks
	4 (Airborne) BCT at Fort Richardson, Alaska
	Combat Aviation Brigade at Schofield Barracks
82nd Airborne Division	Headquarters Fort Bragg, North Carolina
	1, 2, 3, 4* (Airborne) BCT at Fort Bragg
	Combat Aviation Brigade at Fort Bragg
101st Airborne Division	Headquarters Fort Campbell, Kentucky
	1, 2, 3, 4* (Infantry) at Fort Campbell
	Combat Aviation Brigade at Fort Campbell
	159th Combat Aviation Brigade at Fort Campbell

2nd Cavalry Regiment (Stryker)
BCT at Vilseck, Germany

3rd Cavalry Regiment (Stryker)
BCT at Fort Hood, Texas

11th Armored Cavalry Regiment
(multi-compo Heavy BCT) at
Fort Irwin, California

173rd Airborne (Airborne)
BCT at Vicenza, Italy

*BCTs scheduled to be cut between FY 2013 and FY 2017. These reductions will leave the Army with twelve armored BCTs, fourteen infantry BCTs, and seven Stryker BCTs.

SUPPORT BRIGADES*

	Active Component	Army National Guard	Army Reserve
Combat Aviation Brigades	11	8	0
Battlefield Surveillance Brigades	4	6	0
Maneuver Enhancement Brigades	4	16	3
Fires Brigades	6	7	0
Engineer Brigades	5	4	3
Sustainment Brigades	16	11	8

*The Army noted that it would reduce and reorganize numerous non-BCT units as part of a drawdown.

Army Force Generation (ARFORGEN)
To manage its forces with the dollars available, the Army spreads out unit readiness, deployment, and soldier stability through the following stages.

Reset Force Pool. Units enter the Reset Force Pool after returning from a deployment. Their mission is to reconstitute, reset equipment, receive new equipment, assign new personnel, and train to achieve the required capabilities necessary to enter the Ready Force Pool. Units in this pool are available to support civil authorities for national emergencies.

Train/Ready Force Pool. Units in the Train/Ready Force Pool conduct mission preparation and collective training for anticipated future missions. Units in this pool are eligible for deployment to unanticipated contingencies or other operational requirements.

Available Force Pool. Units in the Available Force Pool are available for worldwide deployment.

As a part of restructuring, the Army transitioned from an individual replacement manning system to a unit-focused system, with soldiers over the long term being stabilized at the same post for extended periods to increase combat readiness and cohesion, reduce turnover, and eliminate many repetitive training requirements.

NEW THREATS
The end of the Cold War had three key strategic events: the collapse of international communism, the demise of the USSR, and an end to bipolar competition. These events, in turn, affect power and security relationships throughout the world. One result is the relative dispersal of power away from the states of the former Soviet Union toward regional power centers. Another is the potential struggle within regions as the dominant states vie for position within the emerging power hierarchy. A third is that in many regions the "lid has come off" long-simmering ethnic, religious, territorial, and economic disputes.

Terrorism
The United States continues to face a variety of threats from terrorist organizations such as Islamic State of Iraq (ISI) and Muslim extremist groups. The primary threat for the foreseeable future is a network of Islamic extremists hostile to the United States. The network is transnational and has a broad range of capabilities, which include mass-casualty attacks.

We face an al Qaeda–associated movement of likeminded groups who interact, share resources, and work to achieve common goals. Some of the groups in the movement provide safe haven and logistical support to extremist members, others operate directly with them, and still others fight in the Afghanistan–Pakistan region.

Terrorists hit the Pentagon on September 11, 2001.

The Global Jihadist Movement

The global jihadist movement predates al Qaeda's founding and was reinforced and developed by successive conflicts in Afghanistan, Bosnia, Chechnya, and elsewhere during the 1990s. As a result, it spawned several groups and operating nodes and developed a resiliency that ensured that destruction of any one group or node did not destroy the larger movement. Since 2001, extremists—including members of al Qaeda and affiliated groups—have sought to exploit perceptions of the US-led global war on terrorism and, in particular, the war in Iraq to attract converts to their movement. Many of these recruits come from a large and growing pool of disaffected youth who are sympathetic to radical, anti-Western, militant ideology. At the same time, these extremists have branched out to establish jihadist cells in other parts of the Middle East, South Asia, and Europe, from which they seek to prepare operations and facilitate funding and communications. Foreign fighters appear to be working to use the insurgency in Iraq to turn the country into what Afghanistan was to the earlier generation of jihadists—an international melting pot, a training ground, and an indoctrination center. In the months and years ahead, a significant number of fighters who have traveled to Iraq could return to their home countries, where they might strengthen existing extremist networks with their new skills and experience. Terrorists consider information operations a principal part of their effort. Use of the Internet for propaganda, recruiting, fundraising, and, increasingly, training, has made the Internet a virtual safe haven.

Another goal of the jihadist movement is the overthrow of "apostate" Muslim governments, those which do not promote Islamic values or support or are friendly to the United States and other Western countries. The goals also call for withdrawal of the United States and other Coalition forces from Muslim countries, the destruction of Israel, the restoration of a Palestinian state, and re-creation of the caliphate, a transnational state based on Islamic fundamental tenets.

Underlying the rise of extremism are political and socioeconomic conditions that leave many, mostly young male adults, alienated. There is a demographic explosion or "youth bubble" in many Muslim countries. The portion of the population under age fifteen is 40 percent in Iraq, 49 percent in the Gaza Strip, and 38 percent in Saudi Arabia.

Educational systems in many nations contribute to the appeal of Islamic extremism. Some schools, particularly the private *madrasas*, actively promote it. School textbooks in several Middle East states reflect a narrow interpretation of the Koran and contain anti-Western and anti-Israeli views. Many schools concentrate on Islamic studies focused on memorization and recitation of the Koran and fail to prepare students for jobs in the global economy. Unemployment rates in these countries are as high as 30 percent in Saudi Arabia and about 50 percent in the Gaza Strip. Groups like al Qaeda capitalize on the economic and political disenfranchisement to attract new recruits. The State Department's *Country Reports on Terrorism* states that even historically local conflicts involving Muslim minorities or fundamentalist groups such as those in Indonesia, the Philippines, and Thailand are generating new support for al Qaeda and present new al Qaeda–like threats.

COUNTRY AND REGION REPORTS

Although terrorism is our most important challenge today, both Iran and North Korea are potential threats to the United States. The future of Russia and China—two major powers undergoing great change—also remains uncertain, plus other issues such as the dynamics on the Korean peninsula; the prospects for lasting peace or continuing conflict in the Middle East; genocidal, ethnic, religious, and tribal conflict in Africa; the global impact of the proliferation of military technology; and an array of upcoming leadership changes.

Afghanistan

Afghanistan has struggled to build a stable, democratic, and tolerant government in the face of vicious attacks by the Taliban and related groups on Coalition Forces, civilians, international non-governmental organizations (NGO), and other soft targets, most notably through suicide bombings. That said, Afghanistan's central government is perceived by many of the populace as a weak and corrupt government that is failing to halt the spread of Taliban control. A resurgent Taliban, a still-flourishing drug trade, and a border with

Pakistan—believed to be the home base for al Qaeda—are doing much to undermine successes gained in Afghanistan. In June 2011, President Obama announced his plan to begin the withdrawal of US troops from Afghanistan, and our mission there has changed from combat to support. The process of transition was to have been completed by 2014 to allow the Afghan people to be responsible for their own security, but the end date has been extended.

Iraq

American military forces were mandated to withdraw from Iraq by 31 December 2011 under the terms of a bilateral agreement signed in 2008 by President Bush; the last US troops left on 18 December 2011. The Iraqi government, with support from Coalition Forces, made significant progress in combating al Qaeda in Iraq (AQI) and affiliated terrorist organizations, emphasizing national reconciliation and passing key pieces of related legislation. There was great success in taking practical steps that helped to advance reconciliation at the provincial and local levels. Coalition and Iraqi forces made their gains against AQI and like-minded extremists with much help from the grassroots engagement of Sunni and Shiite tribal leaders and Concerned Local Citizens (CLC)/Sons of Iraq (SOI) groups. With the rise of the Islamic State of Iraq (ISI), its militants took part in the 2011 Syrian uprising known as the Arab Spring and attacked into the bordering countries. The Iraqi government took no outward actions to stem the militias, and in some locations US-trained Iraqi Army units were overrun. At this time, up to three thousand American noncombat forces have returned to Iraq to train and advise; American involvement will continue to be in flux.

Iran

Iran is important to the United States because of its size, location, energy resources, military strength, and hostility toward US and Western interests. It actively supports terrorist groups in the region, such as Hezbollah, and could encourage increased attacks in Israel and the Palestinian Territories to derail progress toward peace. Iran also aids insurgents in Iraq in their drive to oust the United States from that country and ultimately the Middle East. In the near term, Iran's goal is a weakened, decentralized, and Shiite-dominated Iraq that is incapable of posing a threat to Iran. The country's mullah-dominated government will also continue its weapons of mass destruction and ballistic missile programs. Its drive to acquire nuclear weapons is a key test of international resolve and the nuclear nonproliferation treaty.

The government in Tehran has the only military in the region that can threaten its neighbors and Gulf stability. Its expanding ballistic missile inventory presents a potential threat to states in the region. As it fields new longer- and medium-range ballistic missiles, Iran will have missiles with the ability to reach many of our European allies. Although the country maintains a sizable conventional force, it has made limited progress in modernizing its capabilities.

Air and air defense forces rely on out-of-date US, Russian, and Chinese equipment. Ground forces suffer from personnel and equipment shortages. In addition, the equipment is poorly maintained. Intelligence services estimate that Iran could briefly close the Strait of Hormuz, relying on a layered strategy using predominately naval, air, and some ground forces.

As of this writing, American leaders are in discussion with Iran, but the country may remain a threat to the national security interests of the United States for the foreseeable future.

Syria

The Syrian conflict has been growing in intensity and scope since 2011 and has deteriorated to civil war. The uprising is mostly between forces loyal to the government and those seeking to oust it. The United Nations reports over 190,000 people have died since its beginning. Syria continues to support Lebanese Hezbollah and several rejectionist Palestinian groups, which its government argues are legitimate resistance groups. While the country is making minor improvements to its conventional forces through purchases of modern antitank guided missiles and overhauling of some aircraft, it cannot afford major weapon systems acquisitions.

North Korea

After more than a decade of declining or stagnant economic growth, Kim Jong-un's military capability has significantly degraded. The North's declining capabilities are even more pronounced when viewed in light of the significant improvements over the same period of the Republic of Korea (ROK) military and the US-ROK Combined Forces Command (CFC). Nevertheless, the North maintains a large conventional force of over 1 million soldiers, the majority of which may be deployed south of Pyongyang.

The North Korean People's Army remains capable of attacking South Korea with artillery and missile forces with limited warning. Such a provocative act, absent an immediate threat, is highly unlikely, counter to Pyongyang's political and economic objectives, and would prompt a US-ROK CFC response it could not effectively oppose.

North Korea has sought to develop nuclear weapons; its regional neighbors and the United States are seeking to forestall this development diplomatically.

China

Beijing's military modernization and buildup is tilting the balance of power in the Taiwan Strait. Improved Chinese capabilities could threaten US forces in the region should a major reason for hostilities emerge.

China remains keenly interested in Coalition military operations in Afghanistan and Iraq and is using lessons from those operations to guide the People's Liberation Army (PLA) modernization and strategy; however, it will take several years before these lessons are incorporated into the armed forces.

China continues to develop or import modern weapons. Priorities include submarines, surface combatants, air defense, ballistic and antiship cruise missiles, and modern fighters. The government, however, also faces technical and operational difficulties in many areas. The PLA continues with its plan to cut approximately 200,000 soldiers from the army to free resources for further modernization, an initiative that began in 2004.

China is increasingly confident and active on the international stage, trying to ensure it has a voice on major international issues, secures access to natural resources, and counters what it sees as US efforts to contain or encircle the country.

Russia

Despite an improving economy, Russia continues to face endemic challenges related to its post-Soviet military decline. Seeking to be a great power, the Russian government has made some improvements to its armed forces but has not addressed difficult domestic problems that will limit the scale and scope of military recovery. Defense should continue to receive modest real increases in funding, unless Russia suffers an economic setback. Budget increases will help Russia create a professional military by replacing conscripts with volunteer servicemen and focus on maintaining, modernizing, and extending the operational life of its strategic weapons systems, including its nuclear missile force.

On 6 March 2014 the United States authorized sanctions on individuals and entities responsible for violating the sovereignty and territorial integrity of Ukraine in response to Russia's illegal intervention in the country.

The Balkans

International peacekeeping forces in Bosnia and Kosovo continue to operate in a complex environment that poses significant challenges to the establishment of a stable and enduring peace. The Bosnian factions should continue to generally comply with the military aspects of the Dayton Accords. Montenegro's potential drive for independence from Serbia presents the next possible crisis. Kosovo has since gained its independence from Serbia, and under five thousand troops from the NATO-led Kosovo Force (KFOR), provided by thirty-one countries, remain deployed in Kosovo to help maintain a safe and secure environment. US and allied forces expect to be involved in stability operations for the mid-term.

South Asia

The tense rivalry between India and Pakistan over Kashmir is our most important security concern on the South Asian subcontinent. While neither side wants war, both see their security relationship in zero-sum terms. India's larger economy and more robust military is balanced by Pakistan's threat to retaliate with nuclear weapons if the two nations go to war. With frequent low-level clashes, the potential for miscalculation and rapid escalation is constant.

The South Asian drug trade presents another serious regional concern, with many production and trafficking areas outside effective government control. Afghanistan and Pakistan will remain significant opium producers, with Pakistan and Iran also serving as key drug transit nodes. Destabilized governments as well as other economic and political imperatives will continue to limit the effectiveness of regional counterdrug efforts.

Latin America

The scourge of narcotics trafficking, money laundering, weapons and contraband smuggling, and insurgency all combine to provide threatening conditions for some countries and governments of the Latin American region and for US interests. The potential for more serious insurgency and widespread terrorism and crime in several areas of Central and South America and the Caribbean continues to demand our vigilance.

In summary, the threats facing the United States remain high, although we will not likely see a global "peer competitor" within the next ten years. On the other hand, the world remains a very dangerous and complex place, and there is every reason to expect US military requirements to be at about the same level of the past several years, and that use of our forces will be required along the full spectrum of operations.

2

The Role of the NCO

An NCO Corps, grounded in heritage, values and tradition, that embodies the warrior ethos; values perceptual learning; and is capable of leading, training and motivating soldiers.

—NCO Vision, FM 7-22.7

Much of the following overview of NCO history has been extracted from the Center of Military History's *The Story of the Noncommissioned Officer Corps*, written in 1989 for the Year of the NCO and reissued with updates and additional chapters in 2010. It is a valuable resource for anyone desiring a more in-depth lesson on the uniquely American army noncommissioned officer. Further information can be found at the Center of Military History website, www.history.army.mil.

BRIEF HISTORY OF THE NCO CORPS
Throughout our Army's history, NCOs have performed vital functions as small-unit leaders, technical experts, trainers, and, perhaps most important, guardians of the Army Corps standards. The history of the US Army and of the noncommissioned officer began in 1775 with the Continental Army. The men who faced the opening rounds of the American Revolution exemplified the ideal of citizen-soldiers. However, patriotism alone was not sufficient to ensure victory in an age when linear tactics dominated the battlefield. There was little that was systematic about NCO duties until Gen. Friedrich Wilhelm von Steuben standardized them at Valley Forge. With the publication of his now famous "Blue Book," he described the duties of sergeant major, quartermaster sergeant, first sergeant, sergeant, and corporal, and their corresponding responsibilities. A truly unique American NCO emerged from that war with the blending of traditions of the British, French, and Prussian armies.

The lessons of the Revolutionary War battlefields, especially the value of sergeants and corporals, had to be relearned the hard way during the War of 1812. In 1825, the first attempt was made to establish a systematic method for noncommissioned officer selection, with the appointment of regimental and company NCOs the duty of the regimental commander. In 1829, instructions were published for training NCOs so that they had "an accurate knowledge of the exercise and use of their firelocks, of the manual exercise of the soldier, and of the firings and marchings." In 1840, an effort was made to give the NCO Corps greater prestige by adopting a distinctive sword. The model 1840 NCO sword remains the sword of the NCO Corps and is still used on special ceremonial occasions. During Mexican War battles, an outnumbered American force gained victory by applying the concept of combined arms operations. These tactics succeeded in part because career NCOs within the ranks of infantry, artillery, engineer, and dragoon regiments mastered the necessary skills of working together.

The Civil War was the last major use of linear fighting tactics. Much deadlier weapons and horrible casualties added emphasis to the sergeant's role in holding units together. As both sides shifted to more open formations, NCOs took on added leadership responsibilities. This experience and the new tactics served the Army well in operations against Native Americans after the war. Although short in duration, the Spanish-American War tested the ability of both regular and National Guard NCOs to make a swift transition from peace to combat. Overcoming disease and tropical heat, these troops captured Santiago, Cuba.

The United States entered the twentieth century as a new world power. NCOs soon faced duty on foreign shores including the Philippine Insurrection and China's Boxer Rebellion. On the eve of World War I, sergeants and corporals from the active and reserve components experienced excellent training when troubles along the border with Mexico prompted a temporary mobilization. Sergeants and corporals deployed to France as part of the American Expeditionary Forces (AEF). Massing a huge army and deploying it overseas taxed the abilities of the nation—but the NCOs came through. Many were real heroes, and their roles in the trenches of the first modern war spanned the widest array of technical and tactical specialties to that date. After WWI, in a cost-cutting move, Congress reorganized the NCO ranks into five grades: master sergeant, technical sergeant, staff sergeant, sergeant, and corporal. Until the 1930s, NCOs usually stayed with their regiment; to leave meant giving up their stripes, which belonged to the regiment.

World War II made more demands upon the noncommissioned officer corps and had a greater impact upon the NCO's role and status than any previous conflict in American history. By the end of the war, there were 23,328 infantry squads in 288 active infantry regiments. More than 70 separate battalions, including armored infantry and rangers, raised the total number of such squads to over 25,000, all needing noncommissioned leaders. Drafted, trained, and promoted during the hectic months of the early war years, these citizen-soldiers carried out their duties as noncommissioned officers superbly in countless engagements on every front during World War II, but especially those areas where small-unit leadership was at a premium.

The 1950–53 "police action" in Korea sent NCOs into combat as part of a United Nations (UN) force when the Cold War heated up. Despite the onrush of technology, some fundamental NCO functions had to be performed in a time-honored fashion. The United States and the Soviet Union, each armed with nuclear weapons, spent the decades after World War II engaged in a new kind of rivalry. The Cold War placed different demands on the NCO Corps than did conventional combat. Education became essential to the development of a professionally competent soldier. Although formal instruction for officers began with the establishment of West Point [in 1802], peacetime leadership programs for NCOs began only after World War II. The precedent was set when the garrison forces in Germany established a school at Sonthofen, which soon spread across the Army. Two senior grades, E-8 and E-9, were created in 1958, and the rank of sergeant major reappeared.

Eight years of fighting in Southeast Asia provided a challenge to the corps. Beginning with small-scale deployments of advisors to help the Army of the Republic of Vietnam, the American presence grew to over a half-million men. The Vietnam era's heavy requirement for small-unit tactical leaders, technical specialists, and trainers strained the available pool of NCOs. At the same time, the 365-day tour of duty disrupted the traditional ability of the NCO Corps to provide the Army with continuity and experience in the field. In 1966, the chief of staff created the position of sergeant major of the Army.

In the last half of 1971, the Army implemented the Noncommissioned Officer Education System (NCOES). This progressive system was designed to educate NCOs in subjects and skills needed to enhance their performance and abilities. The results of the NCOES were prominent during the liberation of Grenada in 1982 and during operations in Panama and Kuwait in 1989 and 1992, respectively, and, presently, in places such as the Middle East and Africa. Today, NCOs' presence is felt across the battlegrounds and upon the parade grounds, as well as in countless countries and in units training in the United States. It is to these small-unit leaders and soldiers who had trained so hard and well during the late 1980s through the early 1990s that the laurels of victory fell. Brig. Gen. John S. Brown, USA (Ret.), Chief of Military History, wrote: "The characteristic that most distinguished Americans from their late-twentieth-century adversaries was the caliber of their NCOs. No army exceeded and few approximated the combination of experience, leadership, and technical knowledge represented by sergeants through command sergeant major. This does not diminish the roles that officers and other ranks played; it just highlights what has made the US Army what it is today."

Except for short periods of national emergency, the Army has normally had to operate with limited funds. Training continued during lean periods because NCOs knew how to improvise. Looking back over the more than two centuries that have passed since the creation of the US Army, it is clear that the evolution of the NCO's role and status to a modern, professional identity was not always smooth, as the Army leadership and Army doctrine tried to keep pace with these developments. Today's NCO retains the duties and responsibilities established by von Steuben in 1778 and has added to this rich heritage the roles of small-unit leader, trainer, technician, and guardian of Army standards.

MILITARY HISTORY AND NCO LEADERSHIP
What NCOs do today is not new. Despite profound changes in the outward appearance of noncommissioned officers during the last century, the mission "to protect and defend" remains. From the stand-up battles of the Civil War and enforcement of peace in the American West to the war of maneuver in the Gulf, peacekeeping in Bosnia and Kosovo, and the war on terrorism in Afghanistan, Iraq, and other regions of the world, the essentials of small-unit leadership and, therefore, the duties of the NCO have remained the same. Although many NCOs have an active interest in the "big picture" of military history, the true applicability of military history for the NCO lies in relating the big picture to the basic NCO duties of soldier accountability, reconstituting small units, and the unit cohesiveness built by NCOs through small-unit training.

Senior noncommissioned officers traditionally have been the keepers of their organization's lineage and traditions. Serving as role models and mentors, they pass on and inculcate the traditions and organizational ethos into newly arrived soldiers.

The staff ride is an important leader development technique that analyzes battles on the actual terrain where historic events took place. Illustrating the complexity of human conditions during combat, military history can help NCOs bridge the gap between peacetime training and war. Although most unit staff rides study decision-making at the higher levels, including maneuver, logistics, and politics, some units integrate the different perspectives of officers and NCOs. When staff rides incorporate the human conditions under stress of battle, such as why and how soldiers fought, and the combat duties and responsibilities of the different ranks, as well as the equally important and necessary lessons learned regarding casualty evacuation and reporting, resupply, and training and integration of replacements, NCOs learn more about their present-day duties. When NCOs can make comparisons between past and present—when they realize, for example, that instead of moving as members of a fire team, soldiers were moving as members of a company in line—they had better understand the greater role that NCOs of all branches and occupational specialties play in achieving victory on the decentralized battlefield.

The Story of the Noncommissioned Officer Corps also includes portraits of NCOs in action. It views NCO leadership responsibilities and addresses them through extracted documents, including Baron von Steuben's historic *Regulations for the Order and Discipline of the Troops of the United States*, published in 1789. The book also presents an evolution of NCO rank insignia and a gallery of noncommissioned heroes. Here is an extract of one such noncommissioned officer fighting in Afghanistan:

> The platoon sergeant surveyed his soldiers as they debarked the CH-47 helicopter after their days of trudging up and down the ridges of Shah-I-Kot fighting the Taliban and al Qaeda. His soldiers were finally relaxed after days of pumping adrenaline. They were light infantrymen who took pride in their craft, their buddies, and their organization. There was nothing flashy or fancy about them. They were like every other doughboy, dogface, grunt, or crunchy who fought with his boots on the ground and today they were bearded, dirty, and tired, but their weapons gleamed. As infantrymen, they lived under the stars and got wet when it rained, shivered when it was cold, were excited when moving to contact, exhausted when moving to daylight, and felt the adrenaline rush when shot at.
>
> The platoon sergeant submitted the daily status, ensured that his soldiers were fed and kept their equipment serviceable. When the packing list for the upcoming operation arrived, he had all of the soldiers repack their rucks and then he and his squad leaders inspected each. The rucksacks were loaded with ammunition, batteries, night vision and communications gear for the operation itself and "hawk" gear consisting of Gortex, fleece liners, and polypropylene underwear to keep warm when the big heat tab in the sky went down, water, and food.
>
> When they boarded the CH-47 for the flight into combat, the platoon sergeant checked each man's name against the manifest as they quietly filed by, each lost in his own thoughts and mortality. During the long flight soldiers dozed to the drone of the engines, heads bouncing against their chests, back against the cabin wall, or leaning on another soldier's shoulders. The signal came to get ready five minutes out and soldiers shuffled and arranged their equipment. The platoon sergeant made his final check and received the thumbs up from his squad leaders. He could see the stress on the faces around him and hoped that his own did not reveal his last thoughts before landing. The nose of the CH-47 rose abruptly and the crew chief yelled one minute. A load whine and shock on landing, the ramp drop, and soldiers spilled into the whirlwind of gravel and dust kicked up by the rotors.
>
> They landed in what appeared [to be] an onion patch high up on one of the ridgelines so they would now have to fight 2,000 meters straight up. The rough terrain was more an obstacle than

the elevation, although breathing was a task. They were above 9,000 feet and it was a real effort to hump the rucksack or even just to move around at that altitude. Although warned to expect altitude sickness, there was none in his company and no cold weather injuries, due to the watchful eyes of the junior NCOs.

Throughout the combat operation the platoon sergeant kept daily accountability, arranged for [MEDEVAC] of those soldiers wounded, and kept them resupplied with ammunition, water, and rations, and then ensured that everyone ate. On the tenth day, he and the other members of his platoon boarded helicopters for the return flight to their initial staging area. As the platoon sergeant watched his soldiers move toward their tents at Bagram Air Base, he knew they had accomplished the mission assigned them.

First combat.

History has been recorded in many ways during the US military's existence. Official museums operate throughout the Army and benefit thousands of interested soldiers. At Fort Bliss, Texas, soldiers can visit the United States Army Heritage Center of the Noncommissioned Officer. At Fort Knox, Kentucky, they can visit the Patton Museum of Cavalry and Armor, and at Fort Benning, Georgia, they can visit the Infantry Museum. In North Carolina, Fort Bragg's 82nd Airborne Division Museum is chock-full of paratrooper and glider infantry history, and Fayetteville boasts the Airborne & Special Operations Museum. Soldiers interested in the history of women in the Army can visit the Women's Army Corps Museum at Fort Jackson, South Carolina. The Finance Museum is also located there. Visitors to the Pentagon should visit a small alcove called the Hall of Heroes to read the names of the nation's Medal of Honor recipients. Virtually all major installations and many minor ones have some kind of history facility, and all are worth visiting. Locations and hours of operation for Army museums can be found at www.history.army.mil/museum.html.

NCO INDUCTION CEREMONY

For many years, senior noncommissioned officers have upheld the induction ceremony tradition, yet there are no official documents that capture what it should consist of or how it is to be conducted. Ideas have been shared and passed on from one senior sergeant to another.

The importance of crossing over from an enlisted soldier to a noncommissioned officer is a milestone in an enlisted soldier's career and should not be taken lightly. It is the responsibility of senior NCOs to ensure we continue this tradition for many years to come.

Promotion Ceremony

The importance of recognizing the transition from "just one of the guys or gals" to a noncommissioned officer should be shared among the superiors, peers, and subordinates of the newly promoted. This action allows the commanders, the ultimate approving authority for the promotion of enlisted soldiers within their charge, to serve their role in the process. The induction ceremony should be held separately and serve as an extension of the promotion ceremony. Typical Army promotion effective dates occur on the first day of a month, and when possible, so should the induction ceremony.

Induction Ceremony Purpose

The induction ceremony is a celebration of the newly promoted joining the ranks of a professional noncommissioned officer corps, and emphasizes and builds on the pride we all share as members of such an elite corps. The ceremony should also serve to honor the memory of those men and women of the NCO Corps who have served with pride and distinction.

Induction ceremonies should in no way be used as an opportunity for hazing, but more as a rite of passage. They allow fellow NCOs of a unit to build and develop a cohesive bond, support team development, and serve as a legacy for future NCO induction ceremonies.

The NCO induction ceremony is typically conducted at the battalion (or equivalent) level. Though it can be held at higher or lower levels, this text, based on the *1998 Unofficial Guide for Newly Inducted NCOs* written by the author, will focus on the principles for executing a Battalion NCO Induction Ceremony. By changing the titles of key NCO leaders to meet your own needs, you can tailor this document to your own organization.

Induction Ceremony Location. Though the location of the ceremony is not as important as the content, there are some considerations that should be acknowledged. As part of the socialization process of newly promoted non-commissioned officers, the induction ceremony should be held in a social meeting area, such as an NCO, community, or all-ranks club. Alternately, a well-equipped gymnasium, post theater, or, for smaller ceremonies, a unit day-room could be used. Chapel use is discouraged for concerns of "ritualistic" or "mystic" overtones that may be perceived, which go directly against the intended result (see Induction Ceremony Purpose).

Timing. As part of the socialization process for new noncommissioned officers, the induction ceremony should be scheduled as a training event on the training calendar. The formal portion should take place during the duty day, prior to retreat. By making it a training event during duty hours, you not only get maximum participation, but also command support (commanders approve training schedules). The optimum time is 1630–1700 for the formal portion (the ceremony), and 1700–1730 for the informal portion (greetings, congratulations, and socializing).

Key Personnel. As the senior NCO of the command, the battalion command sergeant major serves as the host of the NCO Induction Ceremony. The unit first sergeants are the command sergeant major's assistants, and they compose the "official party." If desired, a guest speaker for the ceremony may be included and is a part of the official party. A narrator will serve as the Master of Ceremonies.

Invited Guests and VIPs. As a wholly noncommissioned officer sponsored event, guests and VIPs should be limited to current and former US Army NCOs. Certain situations may warrant an officer or civilian to attend and would not detract from the nature of the occasion. Typical invited guests could include higher-echelon command sergeants major (brigade, division, regimental, commandant), installation or base support battalion (BSB) command sergeants major, or even lateral (battalion-level) command sergeants major. Additionally, special guests serving as motivational speakers should be included (though not required) as part of an induction ceremony.

Equipment. Each ceremony should be as different as the people it recognizes but share some commonalities. The following items should be available for each:

1. A passage of a citation for bravery or valor in the face of difficulty demonstrated by a noncommissioned officer. Citations are easily accessed and printed from sites such as army.mil or www.awod.com/gallery/probono/cmhs, or from various books.

2. Copies of the NCO Creed, one per inductee (available through many sources).
3. Army Training Circular 7-22.7, Noncommissioned Officer Guide, dated 7 April 2015, one per inductee. This book can be dedicated to the new NCOs who will carry the torch passed on to them and is available through normal publication channels.
4. Sound system (*optional*). Requirement based only on the number present and the "command voice" of the participants.
5. Programs (*optional*). Include the words to the NCO Creed.

Ceremony

This ceremony is a "living" process, which means it was developed to grow and mature with the different users. The intent is to give a common basis from which to begin, and then tailor it to suit your specific needs. The ceremony is not *the* correct ceremony; rather, it is *a* ceremony, one based on the intent of presenting a professional NCO Induction Ceremony.

PLACES:

Official party—Waiting outside the ceremony room.

Narrator—At the sound system/podium.

Inductees—Formed in advance at an appropriate location. Each should have a copy (or portion) of the NCO Creed.

(Two minutes before ceremony begins)

NARRATOR: Ladies and gentlemen, the ceremony will begin in two minutes.

(At the predetermined time)

NARRATOR: Please rise for the official party.

(Official party arrives, marches to designated location. Stops, then takes appropriate positions.)

NARRATOR: Welcome to (this month's) (month name) NCO Induction Ceremony, where we recognize the passing of the group before you (the inductees) into the ranks of the time-honored United States Army Noncommissioned Officer Corps. Today's official party consists of (names).

The tradition of commemorating the passing of a soldier to a noncommissioned officer can be traced to the Army of Frederick the Great. Before one could be recognized in the full status of an NCO, he was required to stand four watches, one every four days. At the first watch, the private soldiers appeared and claimed a gift of bread and brandy. The company NCOs came to the second watch for beer and tobacco, and the first sergeant reserved his visit for the third watch, when he was presented with a glass of wine and a piece of tobacco on a tin plate. Today, we commemorate this rite of passage as a celebration of the newly promoted joining the ranks of a professional noncommissioned officer corps, and emphasize and build on the pride we all share as members of such an elite corps. We also serve to honor the memory of those men and women of the NCO Corps who have served with pride and distinction. Today, we remember one of our own, one whose courage should not go unremembered: (Read citation. Include name, unit, etc.)

Since the earliest days of our Army, the noncommissioned officer has been recognized as one who instills discipline and order within a unit. In his instructions for the "Sergeants and Corporals," Baron Friedrich Wilhelm von Steuben, the US Army's first "Drill-Master," listed in his *Regulations for the Order and Discipline of the Troops of the United States*, the Blue Book, that: "Each Sergeant and Corporal will be answerable for the squad committed to his care. He must pay particular attention to their conduct in every respect and that they keep themselves and their arms always clean. In dealing with recruits, they must exercise all their patience, and while on the march, the noncommissioned officers must preserve order and regularity."

Today, we continue that tradition. (Name), our (guest speaker) (CSM) now will share his/her instructions with our newest sergeants and corporals.

SPEAKER: (Motivational speech)

NARRATOR: The Creed of the Noncommissioned Officer has served as a guiding document for noncommissioned officers since its inception in 1973, though its concepts have been always been a part of our Corps. Each major paragraph begins with three letters: N, C, and O. These words have inspired noncommissioned officers and have served as a compass to guide us down the right paths that we encounter. Today, our newest noncommissioned officers will affirm their commitment to the professionalism of our corps and become a part of the "backbone" of the Army.

(Inductees rise)

Option 1: Inductees all simultaneously read the NCO Creed.

Option 2: Divide the NCO Creed into equal parts, based on the number of inductees. Have each inductee read his or her portion in sequence.

Option 3: Have all present read the NCO Creed together (*note*: provide copies in advance to all present).

CSM/HOST: (Moves to each inductee, issues them a copy of TC 7-22.7, Noncommissioned Officer Guide, then shakes their hand and congratulates them.)

ALL PRESENT: (Applause)

NARRATOR: As we conclude today's ceremony, we ask you to greet our newest inductees and join us in welcoming them to the Corps. Please rise for the exit of the official party.

OFFICIAL PARTY: (Departs. Ceremony ends. Informal portion begins—socializing.)

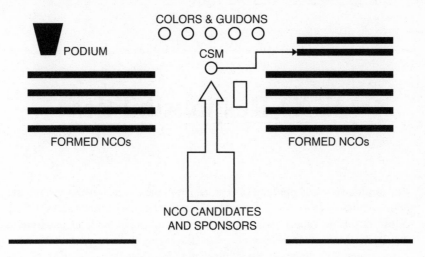

NCO Induction Ceremony

Streamer Ceremony—Preserving the Tradition
Organizations should use the following paragraph as part of the ceremony awarding campaign and battlefield honors:

In October 2005, The Secretary of the Army authorized award of campaign participation credit to eligible US Army units that served or are serving in the Theater of Operations in support of the Global War on Terror. In recognition of [unit's name] participation in Operation [ENDURING or IRAQI] FREEDOM, the campaign streamer—with the colors of the [Afghanistan or Iraq] Campaign Medal and inscribed "[Afghanistan or Iraq]"—is authorized to be flown from its organizational colors.

3

NCO Responsibilities

Army culture is a consequence of customs, traditions, ideals, ethos, values, and norms of conduct that have existed for almost 240 years. This culture promotes certain norms of conduct; the moral and ethical tenets of the US Constitution, the Declaration of Independence, and the Army Values characterize the Army's professionalism and culture and describe the ethical standards expected of all Army leaders.

Command responsibilities are those of the unit—such as at the squad, company, or battalion level—and include how well the unit performs its missions. These responsibilities come with duties tasked from higher command and may also include many factors, for example the mission, unit position, the subordinates' willingness to accept the responsibilities, and the superiors' faith that orders will be carried out.

Individual responsibility means each soldier is responsible for his or her own personal conduct. You are held accountable for your actions toward your fellow soldiers, leaders, unit, and the army. As a leader, it is your duty to ensure that your soldiers understand their responsibilities as team members and soldiers.

An NCO leads by example, trains and enforces standards, maintains discipline, takes care of soldiers, and adapts to a changing world. NCO responsibilities are divided into twelve broad categories:

1. Individual training of soldiers in military occupational specialties (MOS) and in basic soldiering skills.
   * Train soldiers to fight, win, and live.
   * Teach soldiers the history and traditions of the Army, military courtesy, personal hygiene, appearance standards, and drill and ceremonies.
2. Personal and professional development of soldiers.
   * Fix responsibility. Give soldiers tasks they can do based on their abilities, experience, and know-how. Train soldiers to take on increasingly difficult or complex tasks.
   * Train soldiers to replace you, just as you trained to replace your superiors.
   * Hold soldiers responsible for their actions.
   * Ensure that required publications are available and convenient.

- Help soldiers cope with personal and professional problems. Until the problem is resolved, you have a soldier with a problem in your unit, so it is your problem, too.
- Counsel soldiers on their strengths and weaknesses; build on strengths and help them strive to overcome weaknesses.
- Recommend promotions and awards through the NCO support channel, but do not promise them.
- Recommend that good soldiers attend service school specialist or career development courses as needed and as appropriate.

3. Accountability for the squad, the section, or the team.
- Know what each soldier in the unit that you lead is doing during duty hours (and off-duty hours as well when a problem spreads from off duty to on duty).
- Know where your soldiers live and how to contact them.
- Know why a soldier is going on sick call or other appointments, how he or she is treated, and what is wrong.
- Use the unit to accomplish as many missions as possible, but never volunteer troops for missions to make yourself look good in the eyes of superiors. Know your team's limitations.
- Know the readiness status or operating condition of unit weapons, vehicles, and other equipment.

4. Military appearance, physical fitness, and training.
- Make corrections when you see something wrong, wherever you may be and to whomever is concerned. Be polite and diplomatic.
- Supervise the physical fitness training and development of your soldiers in accordance with FM 7-22, Army Physical Readiness Training.
- Ensure that you and your soldiers meet the Army's weight and body fat standards in accordance with Army Regulation (AR) 600-9, The Army Body Composition Program.

5. Physical and mental well-being of the soldier and his or her family.
- Know your soldiers' family situations and help them if they have problems.
- Make sure your soldiers know what services and benefits they and their families are entitled to. Your personnel service NCO can provide this information.

6. Supervision, control, motivation, and discipline of subordinates.
- Counsel soldiers and maintain counseling records.
- Support subordinate NCOs. Similarly, when they are wrong, tell them so, but do it privately.
- Teach your soldiers about the Uniform Code of Military Justice.
- Recommend commendations and passes.
- Recommend bars to reenlistment, or elimination actions, if appropriate. Weeding out the bad soldiers will encourage good soldiers to stay.

- Conduct corrective training when required.
- Keep soldiers informed—do not let them be surprised by details, field training exercises, inspections, or other events.
- Enforce the Army Equal Opportunity Program.

7. Communication between the individual soldier and the organization.
   - Use, and insist that soldiers use, the chain of command and support channels.
   - Listen and act on soldiers' suggestions and complaints, but be able to distinguish between bellyaching and real concerns.
   - Support and explain reasons for current policies.
   - Try to develop a feeling of loyalty and pride in your team and unit.
   - Do not complain to, or in the presence of, your soldiers.

8. Plan and conduct day-to-day unit operations.
   - Provide input to the training NCO for individual skill training.
   - Conduct team training.
   - Supervise events as required by training schedules.

9. Maintain established standards of performance.
   - Treat all soldiers with the respect they deserve, and ensure that your soldiers do the same.
   - Explain clearly what you expect from soldiers.
   - Conduct special training to correct weaknesses.
   - Train soldiers to standards set by soldiers' manuals and other literature.
   - Provide up-to-date information for appropriate levels of self-development tests.
   - Be professional.

10. Maintenance, serviceability, accountability, and readiness.
    - Inspect soldiers' equipment often. Use the manual or approved checklist. Hold soldiers responsible for repairs and losses.
    - Learn how to use and maintain the equipment that soldiers use. Be among the first to operate new systems, whether unit equipment or rapidly fielded gear.
    - Enforce maintenance and supply system procedures.
    - Encourage economy and deal with soldiers who abuse equipment.
    - Keep up-to-date component lists and conduct inventories. Know what is on hand and turn in excess or unserviceable equipment.

11. Appearance and condition of unit billets, facilities, and work areas.
    - Ensure that decorations in soldiers' rooms and common areas do not have an impact on good order and discipline of the organization.
    - Conduct fire and safety inspections and drills.
    - Set and enforce cleanliness standards.
    - Eat in the mess hall and observe mess operations.

12. Advise on, support, and implement policy established by the chain of command.

PRINCIPAL NCO DUTIES

An NCO leads by example, trains and enforces standards, maintains discipline, takes care of soldiers, and adapts to a changing world. NCO duties generally fall into two categories: taking care of soldiers and accomplishing the mission. Of those most basic responsibilities, noncommissioned officers have three formal types of duties:

- *Specified.* Duties that come with jobs and position assignments and are described in regulations and manuals; see Army Regulation 600-20, Army Command Policy, for a number of specified duties for NCOs.
- *Directed.* Written or spoken orders, not typically written down and not listed as part of a job description; they may be short-lived or mission specific.
- *Implied.* Duties often done solely through the initiative of the individual; implied orders may not be written in manuals or instructions or issued verbally, but they are assumed to be required due to their nature.

PRINCIPAL NCO AUTHORITY

Knowing the source of authority, as well as the amount of authority you have, is key to exercising good judgment when performing your duties. Principal NCO authority is the source of legitimate power that noncommissioned officers are granted to perform their duties and follows the fundamental lines of authority that emanate from the Constitution and through Congress and the president. *Command authority* is the authority an individual has over another, relevant to rank or position. It is inherent for noncommissioned officers by virtue of their position to direct or control soldiers. *General military authority* extends to all soldiers and authorizes them to take action in the absence of orders or a designated unit leader. This type of authority comes from law, rank, oaths of office, regulations, and tradition, and is what allows leaders to make on-the-spot corrections in and out of uniform.

Both command and general military authority come from the Constitution and are further defined by Congress. Additional sources include Army Regulations, the Manual for Courts-Martial, and the chain of command and NCO support channel. Leaders may delegate any or all of their authority to their subordinate leaders, provided that no restrictions apply and they do not delegate or assume authority they do not have.

THE CHAIN OF COMMAND

The importance of the chain of command to success is nothing new in military affairs. How well any institution works depends upon how effectively orders and information are passed from top to bottom and back. The role of the NCO in making the chain work is vital.

The chain is defined as the succession of commanders from a superior to a subordinate through which command is exercised. There is only one chain of command in the Army, but it is paralleled and complemented by the NCO support channel. Both are communication channels used to pass information up and down. Neither is a one-way street, nor are the two entirely separate. In order for the chain of command to work, the NCO support channel must be operating.

THE NCO SUPPORT CHANNEL

The NCO Support Channel begins with the command sergeant major and ends with the junior-ranking NCO. This channel functions orally through the command sergeant major or first sergeant and normally does not involve written instructions; however, either method may be used, and both are considered directive in nature. In addition to passing information, this channel is used for issuing orders and getting jobs done. The channel leaves the commander free to plan, make decisions, and program future training and operations.

Some of the tasks the NCO support channel assists the chain of command with are planning and conducting day-to-day unit operations; training soldiers in individual and small-unit collective tasks; caring for soldiers and their families on and off duty; accounting for and maintaining individual and unit equipment under their control; and ensuring that soldiers meet the standards for physical training (PT), height, and weight.

Sergeant Major of the Army

The sergeant major of the Army is the senior sergeant major rank and designates the senior enlisted position of the Army. The individual who occupies this office serves as the senior enlisted advisor and consultant to the chief of staff of the Army in the following areas: problems affecting enlisted personnel and solutions to these problems; professional education, growth, and advancement of NCOs; and morale training, pay, promotions, and other matters concerning enlisted personnel.

Command Sergeant Major (CSM)

The command sergeant major (CSM) is the senior NCO of the command at battalion level or higher. He or she executes policies and standards and advises the commander on training, appearance, and conduct of enlisted soldiers. Activities of the local NCO channel emanate from him or her. The command sergeant major administers the unit Noncommissioned Officer Development Program (NCODP).

First Sergeant

The position of the first sergeant is similar to that of the command sergeant major in importance, responsibility, and prestige. The first sergeant is in direct and daily contact with sizable numbers of enlisted personnel, requiring of him or her outstanding leadership and professional competence. The first sergeant is the senior NCO in companies, batteries, and troops. Although heavily involved in company administration, the first sergeant's principal duty is the individual training of enlisted members of the unit.

Platoon Sergeant

The platoon sergeant is the principal assistant and advisor to the platoon leader and, as such, is second in command. It is normal for a platoon sergeant to become the platoon leader during the absence or disability of commissioned officers of the platoon.

Section, Squad, and Team Leaders

Section, squad, and team leaders are responsible for the personal appearance and cleanliness of their soldiers, for property accountability and maintenance, for the whereabouts of their soldiers at all times, and for the ability to perform the primary mission at all times.

THE NCO AND THE OFFICER

There is no such thing as NCO business and officer business. It is all Army business. Officers and NCOs in units determine the exact division of responsibilities by considering the mission, the situation, and the abilities and personalities of the leaders. Officers and their principal NCO should complement one another, i.e., if one walks around with a dark cloud overhead, the other should be a ray of sunshine, or if one focuses on training, the other may focus on maintenance. The following are general types of tasks for officers and NCOs:

- Officers command, plan, establish policy, and manage the Army; NCOs conduct the daily business of the Army within established policy.
- Officers focus on collective training leading to mission accomplishment; NCOs focus on individual training, which leads to mission capability.
- Officers are primarily involved in units and unit operations; NCOs place their major focus on individual soldiers and team leading.
- Officers concentrate on unit effectiveness and readiness; NCOs ensure that all subordinate NCOs and soldiers are individually ready and functioning as effective unit members—and that equipment in their possession is also ready and functioning.

The division of these functional areas of responsibilities between officers and NCOs does not imply that they operate in separate, compartmentalized manners. The functional areas of responsibility of the officer and NCO are interlocking and interdependent.

PRECEDENCE AND RELATIVE RANK

The determination of rank and precedence for enlisted personnel is used when determining, among two or more individuals of equal rank, which one will be responsible for functions within the enlisted support channel. Date of rank is also used as the first determinant in computing standing on DA promotion boards.

Among enlisted personnel of the same grade of rank in active military service, including retired personnel on active duty, precedence or relative rank is determined as follows:

1. By date of rank.
2. When dates of rank are the same, by length of active service in the Army.
3. When 1 and 2 above are the same, by length of total active service.
4. When the foregoing tests are not sufficient, by age.

ENLISTED INSIGNIA OF GRADE

AIR FORCE	ARMY	MARINES	NAVY
Chief Master Sergeant of the Air Force (CMSAF)	Sergeant Major of the Army (SMA)	Sergeant Major of the Marine Corps (SgtMajMC)	Master Chief Petty Officer of the Navy (MCPON)
Chief Master Sergeant (CMSgt) / Command Chief Master Sergeant	Command Sergeant Major (CSM) / Sergeant Major (SGM)	Sergeant Major (SgtMaj) / Master Gunnery Sergeant (MGySgt)	Fleet/Command Master Chief Petty Officer / Master Chief Petty Officer (MCPO)
Senior Master Sergeant (SMSgt) / First Sergeant (E-8)	First Sergeant (1SG) / Master Sergeant (MSG)	First Sergeant (1stSgt) / Master Sergeant (MSgt)	Senior Chief Petty Officer (SCPO)
Master Sergeant (MSgt) / First Sergeant (E-7)	Platoon Sergeant (PSG) or Sergeant First Class (SFC)	Gunnery Sergeant (GySgt)	Chief Petty Officer (CPO)
Technical Sergeant (TSgt)	Staff Sergeant (SSG)	Staff Sergeant (SSgt)	Petty Officer First Class (PO1)
Staff Sergeant (SSgt)	Sergeant (SGT)	Sergeant (Sgt)	Petty Officer Second Class (PO2)
Senior Airman (SrA)	Corporal (CPL) / Specialist (SPC)	Corporal (Cpl)	Petty Officer Third Class (PO3)
Airman First Class (A1C)	Private First Class (PFC)	Lance Corporal (LCpl)	Seaman (Seaman)
Airman (Amn)	Private E-2 (PV2)	Private First Class (PFC)	Seaman Apprentice (SA)
Airman Basic (AB) (no insignia)	Private E-1 (PV1) (no insignia)	Private (Pvt) (no insignia)	Seaman Recruit (SR)

OFFICER INSIGNIA OF GRADE

AIR FORCE	ARMY	MARINES	NAVY
General of the Air Force	General of the Army	(None)	Fleet Admiral
General	General	General	Admiral
Lieutenant General	Lieutenant General	Lieutenant General	Vice Admiral
Major General	Major General	Major General	Rear Admiral (Upper Half)
Brigadier General	Brigadier General	Brigadier General	Rear Admiral (Lower Half)
Colonel	Colonel	Colonel	Captain
Lieutenant Colonel	Lieutenant Colonel	Lieutenant Colonel	Commander
Major	Major	Major	Lieutenant Commander

OFFICER INSIGNIA OF GRADE

AIR FORCE	ARMY	MARINES	NAVY
Captain	Captain	Captain	Lieutenant
First Lieutenant	First Lieutenant	First Lieutenant	Lieutenant Junior Grade
Second Lieutenant	Second Lieutenant	Second Lieutenant	Ensign

ARMY

SILVER AND BLACK

W-5 · Chief Warrant Officer
W-4 · Chief Warrant Officer
W-3 · Chief Warrant Officer

SILVER AND BLACK

W-2 · Chief Warrant Officer
W-1 · Warrant Officer

MARINES

SCARLET AND SILVER

W-5 · Chief Warrant Officer
W-4 · Chief Warrant Officer
W-3 · Chief Warrant Officer

SCARLET AND GOLD

W-2 · Chief Warrant Officer
W-1 · Warrant Officer

NAVY

W-4 · Chief Warrant Officer
W-3 · Chief Warrant Officer

W-2 · Chief Warrant Officer
W-1 · Warrant Officer

AIR FORCE (None)

COAST GUARD

Coast Guard officers use the same rank insignia as Navy officers. Coast Guard enlisted rating badges are the same as the Navy's for grades E-1 through E-9, but they have silver specialty marks, eagles and stars, and gold chevrons. The badge of the Master Chief Petty Officer of the Coast Guard has a gold chevron and specialty mark, a silver eagle, and gold stars. For all ranks, the gold Coast Guard shield on the uniform sleeve replaces the Navy star.

4

Leadership

The process of influencing people by providing purpose, direction, and motivation to accomplish the mission and improve the organization.

—The Army definition of leadership

To be a noncommissioned officer is to be a leader. In order to be an NCO, you must continually *develop* and *exhibit* certain behaviors, skills, and knowledge. Above all, an NCO's performance must be in accordance with Army Values.

Regardless of where, when, under what circumstances, or by whom it is exercised, leadership boils down to getting soldiers to willingly carry out orders and accomplish the mission. The more expert the leader, the more likely that soldiers will follow. NCOs must be able to motivate and inspire soldiers to carry out missions for the greater good of the Army. Good leaders acquire leadership attributes through a never-ending process of individual study, education, training, and experience. Although many principles of leadership exist, the ability to lead by example has stood the test of time and the rigors of battle and has shown itself to result in correct performance of duty.

ADP 6-22, Army Leadership, speaks of leaders as those who inspire and influence people to accomplish organizational goals through their roles and responsibilities, whether assigned or assumed. According to the ADP, "Army leaders motivate people both inside and outside the chain of command to pursue actions, focus thinking, and shape decisions for the greater good of the organization." Innovative and adaptive leaders are always aware of the situation around them. They demonstrate character in everything they do, are experts in the profession of arms, boldly confront uncertainty, and solve complex problems. They are decisive and prudent risk takers who effectively manage, lead, and change organizations and are able to operate independently in an ambiguous, dynamic, and politically sensitive environment. NCO leaders must reinforce the view that actions counter to Army Values and the standards of conduct can compromise the nation's strategic objectives; "We don't do that in this organization" is sometimes the case.

NCO leaders should perform the following:

1. Set and exemplify the highest ethical and professional standards as embodied in the Army Values.
2. Accomplish the unit mission.
3. Ensure the physical, moral, personal, and professional well-being of subordinates.
4. Effectively communicate vision, purpose, and direction.
5. Build cohesive teams and empower subordinates.
6. Teach, coach, and counsel subordinates.
7. Build discipline while inspiring motivation, confidence, enthusiasm, and trust in subordinates.
8. Develop their own and their subordinates' skills, knowledge, and attitudes.
9. Anticipate and manage change and be able to act quickly and decisively under pressure.
10. Use initiative to assess risk and exploit opportunities.
11. Treat subordinates with dignity, respect, fairness, and consistency.
12. Foster a healthy command climate.

DISCIPLINE

Military discipline relies for the most part upon self-discipline, respect for properly constructed authority, and commitment to the Professional Army Ethic with its supporting individual values. Maintenance of discipline is a function of command and the first responsibility of the NCO leaders. Leaders must ensure that all soldiers present a neat and soldierly appearance and must take action in cases where conduct is prejudicial to good order and military discipline.

NCOs also must take action to quell any quarrel, fray, or disorder among persons subject to military law and to apprehend the participants. In order to fulfill your duty, you may have to risk physical injury, so proceed with judgment and tact, but *take action*. In public, you may request the civilian police to take an offender into custody when no military police are available.

You must exercise your military authority with promptness, firmness, courtesy, and justice. Make on-the-spot corrections of uniform or courtesy violations wherever possible and handle minor infractions as much as possible through the NCO support chain. One of your most effective nonpunitive disciplinary measures is extra training or instruction. Training or instruction given to an individual to correct deficiencies must be not only directly related to the deficiency observed but also oriented to improving performance. For example, soldiers with dirty weapons can be required to clean their own weapons, as well as other soldiers' weapons. This requirement reinforces the standard that weapons must be clean, and it gives soldiers additional practice at cleaning weapons, so that in the future they will understand the standard.

NEW DIRECTIONS IN LEADERSHIP DOCTRINE

The Army defines leadership as "the process of influencing people by providing purpose, direction, and motivation, while operating to accomplish the mission and improve the organization." Leadership, despite the great strides in technology, remains the same—influencing and motivating people to get a job done. ADRP 6-22 discusses character-based leadership, clarifies values, establishes attributes as part of character, and, most importantly, focuses on improving people and organizations for the long term. It places additional emphasis on the role of leader teams and the importance of the leadership requirements model as a universal mindset. Leaders must empower subordinates to use their critical-thinking skills instead of allowing subordinates to become overly dependent on checklists or seeking clear guidance before taking action. Noncommissioned officers have a basic responsibility to lead others, which they do by developing themselves, others, and their profession. According to newly developed Army doctrinal guidance in ADRP 6-22, "Leadership is a reciprocal influence process between leaders and followers. . . . Effective leadership and leader development require mutual recognition and acceptance of leader and follower roles."

Leader Attributes

Attributes influence how people act and learn in their environment. Army leader attributes include character (values and identity), presence (appearance, demeanor, actions, and words), and intellect (mental and social skills).

Your character, which includes your personal identity, has an effect on your leadership abilities. If you are a leader with a strong sense of integrity—doing what is right, both legally and morally—you will set a high standard for your soldiers to emulate by adhering to the values that make up your personal identity. If you do not have a strong grasp of personal identity, you will be uncertain.

The impression you make on your soldiers will affect your ability in getting them to follow you. Build a positive impression by being aware of your outward appearance, attitude, words, and actions and by maintaining high standards of character and intellect. Soldiers will look to and respect a leader with a strong presence, especially in high-pressure situations.

Your intellect will determine how well you consider problems, find creative solutions, make decisions, and lead others. While everyone has different intellectual strengths and ways of thinking, as a leader you must be conscious of your own strengths and weaknesses and how they will affect your problem solving. Maintaining sound judgment will result in the best decision for any situation.

Core Leader Competencies

Competencies provide a clear and consistent way of conveying expectations for Army leaders and apply across all levels of the organization leader positions and throughout one's career. These are demonstrated through behaviors that can be readily observed and assessed by a spectrum of leaders and followers—superiors, subordinates, peers, and mentors. This makes them a good basis for leader development and focused multisource assessment and feedback. The competencies categories take on new challenges as noncommissioned officers move from direct leadership positions into those at organizational and strategic levels.

Leads

- *Leads others.* Leaders motivate, inspire, and influence others to take the initiative, work toward a common purpose, accomplish tasks, and achieve organizational objectives.
- *Extends influence beyond the chain of command.* Leaders must extend their influence beyond direct lines of authority and chains of command. This influence may extend to joint, interagency, intergovernmental, multinational, and other groups and helps shape perceptions about the organization.
- *Leads by example.* Leaders are role models for others. They are viewed as examples and must maintain standards and provide examples of effective behaviors. When Army leaders model the Army Values, they provide tangible evidence of desired behaviors and reinforce verbal guidance by demonstrating commitment and action.
- *Communicates.* Leaders communicate by expressing ideas and actively listening to others. Effective leaders understand the nature and power of communication and practice effective communication techniques so they can better relate to others and translate goals into actions. Communication is essential to all other leadership competencies.

Develops

- *Develops the environment.* Leaders create a positive organizational climate. They are responsible for establishing and maintaining positive expectations and attitudes, which produce the setting for positive attitudes and effective work behaviors.
- *Prepares self.* Leaders are prepared to execute their leadership responsibilities fully. They are aware of their limitations and strengths and seek to develop and improve their knowledge. Only through preparation for missions and other challenges, awareness of self and situations, and the practice of lifelong learning and development can individuals fulfill the responsibilities of leadership.
- *Develops others.* Leaders encourage and support the growth of individuals and teams to facilitate the achievement of organizational goals. Leaders prepare others to assume positions within the organization, ensuring a more versatile and productive organization.

Achieves
- *Achieves organizational goals.* Achieving focuses on accomplishing the mission. Leaders provide guidance and manage resources and the work environment, thereby ensuring consistent and ethical task accomplishment.
- *Gets results.* Getting results embodies the actions taken to complete a job on time and to standard. These actions include providing clear priorities with direction and guidance on what needs to be done and how, and evaluating how your organization performs so you can effectively identify strengths and correct weaknesses. This will ensure consistency and effective application of the professional Army Ethic.
- *Monitors performance.* Leaders must identify strengths and correct weaknesses in organizations, groups, and individuals to allow for accomplishing missions consistently and ethically.

Rather than provide a one-size-fits-all leadership model, Army leadership doctrine now outlines three levels of leadership—*direct, organizational*, and *strategic*—and identifies leader intellect that apply at all levels: *mental agility, sound judgment, innovation, interpersonal tact*, and *expertise*. The discussion of actions outlines for each level what leaders do—what turns character into leadership.

Direct leaders build cohesive teams, empower subordinates, and develop and execute plans that implement policies and accomplish missions. Besides communicating, team building, supervising, and counseling, NCOs need to think analytically and creatively, considering multiple perspectives and the intended and unintended consequences of their decisions. They also must be able to operate independently—within the limits of the commander's intent, assigned missions, task organization, and available resources. Just as NCOs train technically and tactically, they must now develop this ability to handle ideas, thoughts, and concepts.

Organizational leadership occurs at levels from battalion through corps. Here, because of increased unit size and complexity, organizational leaders influence, operate, and improve their outfits through programs, policies, and systems. At this level, failure or success is more often due to one of these procedures than to an individual's success or failure. Senior NCOs must concern themselves with the higher organization's needs—as well as those of their subordinate units and leaders—learn to filter information, and decide how best to gather, analyze, and evaluate it.

Strategic leadership occurs at the highest military levels, whether in institutional settings stateside or in operational contexts around the world. Here, the strategic leader provides the vision that focuses the force, from which flow the goals, plans, and benchmarks that shape the Army of the future. To support their vision, strategic leaders continually emphasize the Army's core messages to soldiers, their families, and their elected leaders.

Army Values

Each soldier comes to the Army with his own set of personal values developed in childhood, but upon enlisting he agrees to follow a new set—the Army Values. These principles, standards, and qualities are considered the most important for the success of the Army. Army Values help soldiers make the right decision in any situation, and teaching values is an important NCO responsibility.

The Army recognizes seven values that all members must develop. When read in sequence, the first letters form the acronym "LDRSHIP."

- *Loyalty*. Bear true faith and allegiance to the US Constitution, the Army, your unit, and other soldiers.
- *Duty*. Fulfill your obligations.
- *Respect*. Treat people as they should be treated.
- *Selfless service*. Put the welfare of the nation, the Army, and your subordinates before your own.
- *Honor*. Live up to Army Values.
- *Integrity*. Do what is right, legally and morally.
- *Personal courage*. Face fear, danger, or adversity (physical and moral).

LEADING SOLDIERS IN THE TWENTY-FIRST CENTURY

Most of the qualities and skills required to lead soldiers today will also be necessary in the future. Look to FM 7-27.7, Noncommissioned Officer Guide, and ADRP 6-22, Army Leadership, to determine what it takes to lead soldiers today. Understand what your organization expects of you, learn who your immediate leader is and what he or she expects of you, and assess the level of competence and the strengths and weaknesses of your subordinates. Identify the key people outside your unit whose willing support you need to accomplish the mission.

Demonstrate tactical and technical competence; that is, know your business. Teach your subordinates. Be a good listener. Treat your soldiers with dignity and respect. Stress the basics, including courage, candor, confidence, commitment, and compassion. Set the example through selfless service and abide by Army Values. Set and enforce the standards. Lead by example.

ADP 6-22, Army Leadership, states why leadership is extremely important today and will be tomorrow:

> In an era when technological advantages have narrowed, and access to information of all kinds is relatively limitless, the most effective and efficient way for the Army to maintain its competitive edge is by enhancing the effectiveness of people and organizations. Good leadership can facilitate this goal. Whether preparing for war, fighting a war, or supporting a war, leadership skills, knowledge, and behavior must be consistent with the war-fighting doctrine of the U.S. Army.

Teaching Army Values

Soldiers learn and draw strength from leaders who encourage the development of values as inalienable professional attributes. Leaders, in turn, are expected to live by and exemplify those values. Internalizing these values—living by them—is what builds professional soldiers in America's Army. Values and traditions are the soul of the Army. As an institution, we must be unwavering in upholding them.

As noted earlier, the Army has seven bedrock values to which all soldiers must adhere: loyalty, duty, respect, selfless service, honor, integrity, personal courage, and discipline. These values are the baseline, core, and foundation of every soldier. They define all soldiers: who they are, what they do, and what they stand for. They drive soldiers internally (their beliefs) and externally (their actions) at home and work, in peace and war.

You must teach and stress to your soldiers the values of the professional. Your role is not to change their long-held personal values; we all have individual differences. But development of the seven basic soldierly values is vital as well. Also develop their *candor*, which is honesty and faithfulness to the truth. Teach them to be *competent* so that their working knowledge and abilities contribute directly to mission success. Develop in them a sense of the mental and moral strength—*courage*—that they will need to enable them to retain control and continue the mission when they are in harm's way. And make them understand that *commitment* to unit accomplishment takes priority over personal wishes, wants, pleasures, and, perhaps, needs.

Warrior Ethos

The Warrior Ethos is defined as the professional attitudes and beliefs that characterize the American soldier. It involves selfless commitment to the nation, mission, unit, and fellow soldiers. Servicemembers demonstrate the Warrior Ethos through their discipline, commitment to the Army Values, and pride in the Army's heritage. The *Soldier's Creed*, to which the Ethos is linked, best encapsulates the contract between the soldier, the leader, and the Army.

The Soldier's Creed

I am an American soldier.
I am a warrior and a member of a team. I serve the people of the
United States and live the Army Values.
I will always place the mission first.
I will never accept defeat.
I will never quit.
I will never leave a fallen comrade.

I am disciplined, physically and mentally tough, trained and
proficient in my warrior tasks and drills. I always maintain my
arms, my equipment, and myself.
I am an expert and I am a professional.
I stand ready to deploy, engage, and destroy the enemies of the
United States of America in close combat.
I am a guardian of freedom and the American way of life.
I am an American soldier.

The four emphasized lines constitute the Warrior Ethos, sustained through discipline, realistic training, commitment to the Army Values, and pride in the Army's heritage.

SOLDIER TEAM DEVELOPMENT

When you talk to soldiers in good units, you will usually hear the words "us" and "we," rather than "I" and "me." Unit members look out for and take care of one another. The unit has developed its own workable ways of accomplishing missions to standard, rather than relying heavily on being guided by outsiders and regulatory material. The excellent unit has a steady high-performance rhythm, and members have effective skills for coping with stress and pressure. The unit has high standards, ethical values, and its own way of expressing how well it is performing. Members will voluntarily work however hard and long is necessary based on unit operational needs.

Building strong soldier teams is critical in the Army. Readiness is the goal. An outnumbered and overpowered team can achieve its mission goal when it has a strong desire—the spirit—to do so. Spirited soldiers believe in their cause. Your leadership should produce a winning spirit; it is critical to building a cohesive team. You should build cohesion in numerous other ways as well. Respect your soldiers and help them develop physically, socially, emotionally, and spiritually. Doing so will give them the stamina necessary for sustained performance under stress and will teach them to mature, work together, and face danger with hope and purpose. Signs of self-discipline, initiative, effective judgment, and confidence will be positive indicators of your effort.

Do a mental assessment of your soldiers' willingness and ability to work as a cohesive unit. Listen, observe, and monitor. In each new situation, you must reassess and correct to retain and build teamwork. Practice verbal and nonverbal communication. Encourage development of your unit's "vocabulary"—short-cut words and terms—to communicate complex messages. *Ensure that those words and terms always comply with the commander's intent.*

Teach your soldiers to use the chain of command so that decisions are made at the right level. Give them their own planning and decision-making responsibilities as well so that they know the mission and operate within the commander's guidance. Combat teamwork requires training so that soldiers think on their feet and communicate effectively.

Every new soldier in your unit will go through a formation stage, the process of checking out other soldiers and his or her leaders. As trust develops, the soldier will participate more actively in unit missions. You must help by answering a new soldier's questions about your team, its work, and the soldier's personal concerns. Develop the soldier's strengths into unit strengths.

Put the new soldier to work as soon as possible. Afterward, watch for signs that he or she is trying to exert independence. The soldier will be trying to find his or her range and limits as a unit member. You will know this is happening when you begin to feel resistance to your leadership. Share with the soldier your thoughts and feelings about the unit and ask him or her to do likewise, to teach the soldier to pass information back and forth. This will help dissolve a communication barrier before it can form. You want the soldier to depend on you and others on the team, and vice versa, to build cohesion.

. Constantly guide your developing team. Retain control. Listen. Establish lines of authority and develop individual and team (squad, section, platoon, battery, company, troop) goals.

Operational deployments, when having trained soldiers counts.

Training is paramount. Train your soldiers as a unit during peacetime. Focus your team on training to standard. Treat each job, task, or detail as a training opportunity. Use mission opportunities to motivate and challenge soldiers while you train them in their wartime missions. With the world as it is today, your company might be in garrison one day and in a distant country the next week.

Training in combat is different. Time will be critical. Soldiers' lives will be at stake. The field manual and experienced combat veterans emphasize that the NCO leader must use every available opportunity to sharpen survival skills. In combat, you must teach your soldiers to know the enemy and what the threat is, and how to respond to hostile activity. Training is conducted during real operations, which causes extreme stress, so you must help your soldiers use coping skills. (Turn to FM 6-22.5, Combat and Operational Stress Control Manual for Leaders and Soldiers, for more information.) Realistic training during peacetime and the ways you demonstrate your ability on the battlefield will contribute to your soldiers' self-confidence.

LEADING SOLDIERS IN COMBAT

In a combat zone, noncommissioned officers continually train their soldiers for what lies ahead, ensure they are rehearsed and inspected before operations commence, and lead by example when under fire. It is training and discipline—instilled by pride and training and maintained by good leadership—that keeps soldiers alive.

A story about a squad of military police from the 617th MP Company, Kentucky National Guard, demonstrates this well. The squad defeated more than three times their number, killing and capturing most of the insurgents in a battle that occurred at a time and place of the enemy's choosing. The squad's soldiers believed even before this fight that their NCOs were the best in the Army and that they have the best squad in the Army.

On this Sunday afternoon, on the southeastern outskirts of Baghdad, forty to fifty heavily armed Iraqi insurgents attacked a convoy of thirty civilian tractor-trailer trucks that were moving supplies for the coalition forces. The MP squad had been following the convoy from a distance behind the last vehicle, and when the convoy halted in the kill zone, the squad sped up, paralleled the convoy up the shoulder of the road, and moved to the sound of gunfire.

Leadership under Fire. The squad was committed to the fight when the three noncommissioned officers stepped out of their vehicles. Several of the squad fell wounded during the first moments of contact. The squad leader dismounted and grabbed the team leader out of the first vehicle after she had radioed the contact report to higher. The squad leader staff sergeant and team leader sergeant rushed the nearest ditch about twenty meters away and began clearing it of the enemy. The fire of the two NCOs plus that from the high mobility multipurpose wheeled vehicles (HMMWVs) turned the ambush into a killing ground for the ambushers.

Combat Loading. One of the sergeants ran low on ammo and double-timed back to a vehicle to reload. She moved to her squad leader's vehicle and blindly reached her arm into it to find ammo, because each vehicle was packed the same way. The day before, the squad had taken the recently issued new type bandoliers and experimented with mounting them in their vehicles. Once they determined how, they preloaded a second basic load of ammo into magazines, put them into the bandoliers, and mounted them in their vehicles—the same exact way in every vehicle—with load plans enforced and checked by leaders.

Training for the Unexpected. With an AT-4 antitank rocket, the medic destroyed insurgents firing out of a building at the wounded. The past week his squad leader had forced him to train on it, though he did not think that, as a medic, he would ever use one.

Discipline and Training. These are what make the difference, and it is up to NCOs to ensure standards are maintained. On a battlefield, you must ensure that your soldiers remain informed. The soldier wants to know all he or she can about the situation. Keep the news flowing as regularly as the situation permits. Do not speculate or allow rumors to grow. The unit's supporting Army Public Affairs team or detachment, American Forces Radio and Television Service, and the chain of command will all be able to provide pieces of accurate information. As you are informed, and especially when the bits and pieces form a complete picture of some sort, pass along the news as quickly and as objectively as possible. Avoid distractions, however; keep your soldiers focused on their mission. Suppress fearful behavior, because it can spread.

Teamwork. The best results on and off the battlefield come from teamwork. You will be the key to sustaining cohesion among your soldiers. Focus on teamwork, training, and weapons and gear maintenance. Do everything within your power to ensure timely supply of needed items, and learn the supply system.

PROFESSIONAL ETHICS

Of the general principles of ethical government conduct, one is listed first for a reason—"Public service is a public trust, requiring [soldiers] to place loyalty to the Constitution, the laws, and ethical principles above private gain"—because it goes to the heart of selfless and ethical service. Developing, achieving, maintaining, and teaching high ethical standards is NCO business.

Noncommissioned leaders and supervisors frequently face ethical problems that, if not handled properly, can damage—or destroy—unit cohesion, discipline, and effectiveness. You must do what is right and enforce correct conduct and behavior standards. And you must always set the example.

No Middle Ground

Nothing says more and nothing says less about an NCO than the way he or she acts or behaves on and off duty. The honorable corporal, for example, is not the one whose conduct is exemplary on duty but despicable off duty when he or she mentally or physically abuses family members. An honest sergeant is not the one who accomplishes a key task, then later falsely reports sick-in-quarters because of a hangover. A loyal staff sergeant is not the one who tells his soldiers how good they are and then turns around and badmouths them in front of others for incompetence.

The Professional Army Ethic

Fortunately, most NCOs do not fit into the portraits illustrated above; instead, they try to live the Professional Army Ethic.

Most NCOs are aware of the Department of Defense (DoD) Standards of Conduct. All NCOs have attended periodic common military training based on the DoD Joint Ethics Regulation. Basically, the law and regulations address proper and improper ways to accept gifts, handle financial matters, seek part-time employment, use position or rank, raise funds, teach, speak in public, and write for compensation. The law also compels soldiers to always act with integrity, to use Army property and soldiers for government business only, to never use official position for personal gain, and to never coerce a soldier to help pay for a gift for a superior. These are easy requirements to meet, really, when you look at larger ethical issues.

When faced with an ethical matter, tackle it with the following reasoning process: Identify the problem, know the relevant rules, develop and evaluate courses of action, and choose the one that best represents Army Values. Ethical choices may be between right and wrong, shades of gray, or two rights. Some problems center on an ethical dilemma requiring special consideration of what is *most* ethical, and leaders must apply multiple perspectives to determine the most ethical choice. One perspective comes from the view that desirable virtues such as courage, justice, and benevolence define ethical outcomes. A second comes from the set of agreed-upon values or rules, such as the Army Values or rights established by the Constitution. A third perspective is based on the consequences of the decision: Whatever produces the greatest good for the greatest number is the best choice. NCOs may also turn to FM 7-27.7, The Army Noncommissioned Officer Guide, which makes this point: "If the NCO is the 'backbone' of the Army, then the Professional Army Ethic is the 'heart' of the NCO Corps, and from that heart springs our pride."

NCOs, if they must, may lead with the full legal force of general military or delegated command authority under the provisions of AR 600-20, Army Command Policy. NCOs rarely need to lean on regulations, however. Instead, they instinctively do what is right, for the right reasons, when necessary, no matter how hard it may be to do so. NCOs earn their stripes every day. An NCO who is reported and placed under the scrutiny of command or the public embarrasses and discredits the Army, whether the problem involves personal conduct or a more serious breach of ethics, as described in the following section. And more importantly, a soldier who has or causes ethical problems distracts his or her leaders from mission accomplishment.

The Cost of Unethical Conduct

The abuses at Abu Ghraib prison and other instances of unethical and un-soldierly conduct committed by a few soldiers have done much to embarrass and severely damage the credibility and morale of the majority of US soldiers who serve with honor and distinction. These acts of unethical, criminal conduct accelerated the loss of public support for the war effort and in the long run made it harder for the Army to successfully accomplish its mission.

NCOs must uphold and enforce ethical behavior and conduct standards to retain the trust and confidence of superior officers, including commissioned troop leaders who may face extremely hard ethical decisions on a future battle-field. The effort on your part, at your level, will help enable the Army to main-tain the unwavering support of the nation.

PERSONAL CONDUCT

NCOs should be above reproach at all times. This does not mean that a slip automatically spells disaster. Keep this in mind when your subordinates err.

Money

Never lend money to other soldiers for interest. Be careful about lending money to anyone based only on a verbal agreement, no matter how much is involved. Of course, if a friend or coworker asks for a small sum occasionally, to tide him or her over on a heavy date or to buy lunch, give it if you can afford to. But never telegraph through the outfit that you are an "easy touch." If you do, every freeloader in the unit will hit you up for small loans, which they will seldom repay. Young soldiers are particularly vulnerable to this sort of thing. Guard against it yourself and advise your subordinates to do the same. Be alert for soldiers who are habitual borrowers. They are heading for trouble, and if they are your subordinates, soon their trouble will be yours.

If a friend is really in trouble and you can help with a loan, then do so—what are friends for? But have him or her back it up by signing a promissory note. This is merely insurance against the unexpected, not an indication of dis-trust; the note will enable you to claim any unpaid debt against his or her estate, should your friend die. If your friend cannot pay you back all at once, be sure to give him or her receipts for each payment he or she does make. This will help you both later on if there is any disagreement.

Gambling

NCOs should never gamble with subordinates, no matter the circumstances. Gambling can be as addictive and as ruinous to some people as alcohol and drugs are to others. When you acquire financial responsibility for other people, such as your family, they must always come first. Don't allow what can be an innocent and pleasant pastime to develop into a compulsion that will wreck your family. Never allow sharks—card, pool, loan, or otherwise—to operate in your unit.

Adultery

Adultery is punishable under the Uniform Code of Military Justice (UCMJ). The best advice you can receive in regard to this subject, and the best you can give someone else about it, is this: Don't do it. If you do, and are found out, take responsibility for your actions.

At some point in your career, though, the temptation to err will be strong, especially where alcohol and sex are readily available, the idle hours are long, and diversions are few. Remember, what you do in the heat of passion may come back to haunt you in years to come. Precisely how a person deals with this problem depends on the individual. Keep up an active correspondence with your spouse. Go easy on the intoxicants. Concentrate on your military duty, and cultivate your hobbies.

Should you succumb, you will have to live with your indiscretion. Repeated unfaithfulness becomes general knowledge in a small, tightly knit military community. Your soldiers will lose respect for you, and if continued, someone in the chain of command will tell you to straighten up, or else. Adultery hurts everyone—you, your spouse, your family, and your friends. A single person who enters into an adulterous relationship with a married man or woman is not much better off than the married person who is unfaithful. The single person's career (and life) can be as easily ruined by adultery as that of a married person.

Lying

Society would crumble if it were not for the accepted social lie. We all know that nobody wants to listen to someone else's personal problems. And nobody in his or her right mind tells everyone exactly what he or she thinks of them. Military life is no different from civilian life in this regard.

Never lie to cover up mistakes, however, whether yours or those of your subordinates. Lying to anyone in the line of duty is wrong. Once those in your unit lose faith in you because of a lie discovered, no matter how small that lie may be, you may never be able to recover that confidence. And once you get away with a lie, it sometimes becomes necessary to tell more and more of them to cover up the initial one, until you create a tissue of lies that sooner or later will tear and expose the truth.

Indebtedness

Ensure that you pay off your debts. Keep tight control of your budget. Do not allow yourself to fall behind on credit payments. This will require restraint and self-denial at times. A letter of indebtedness from a creditor will harm your career as well as damage your reputation in the business world and make it harder for you to get credit when you really need it.

Our whole economy operates on indebtedness, and most of us are in debt for something: homes, cars, credit card services, and so on. You will, from time to time, counsel your soldiers on their indebtedness. Help them to learn to budget and overcome a vicious cycle.

Self-perception

NCOs have always been important. In units in which the NCOs are enthusiastic, mission oriented, and supportive of one another, things click. In units where NCOs put themselves before their men and their organization, things go clunk. May you always serve in units that click, but should you have the misfortune to be assigned to one that clunks, turn things around. Don't wait for the officers to catch on; clue them in. Rise to the occasion and do what has to be done. Do not try to find ways to get out of doing things. Do not look back. Get the job done. You represent the NCO Corps at its finest.

5

Contemporary
Leadership Issues

The war on terrorism is a different kind of war, a world war, where deployments take soldiers from the United States to the mountains of Afghanistan, the desert of Iraq, the streets of Baghdad, the jungles of the Philippines, Bosnia, Kosovo, and any other location where terrorism is located and must be rooted out. Battles may range from a 10,000-foot peak in Afghanistan to the streets of Baghdad where foot soldiers search for the hard-to-pin-down insurgent.

THE LAW OF WAR
The Army has been tarnished by a few soldiers operating outside the bounds of military discipline and law. Although their misdeeds have been exposed by fellow soldiers and investigated by the chain of command, their actions have brought great discredit to not only themselves but also the Army and our nation.

The United States and its Armed Forces abide by the laws of war. Soldiers are expected to comply with both the spirit and intent of these laws in all of their actions. Army officers and NCOs are the main safeguard to ensure that its soldiers abide by these laws in both peace and war. It is only this respect for, and obedience to, the rule of law that differentiates our Army from savages. Nevertheless, the very nature of war can lead some of the fighting forces to fall prey to violence and disorder and to participate in unlawful actions. Such actions, at whatever level and for whatever reason, cannot be permitted. Only when all members understand that everyone in the Army must be absolutely opposed to any unlawful conduct—and that any such conduct will be met with immediate action—will the United States be living up to its national goals. If leaders accept an unlawful order or permit unlawful actions by any member of their organization, it is no different than if they themselves committed the act. If something feels wrong, question it. If you walk by, you may be acquiescing to establishing a standard for patterns of abuse. Consider "But sir, Sergeant Jones saw us doing this and said nothing, so we assumed it was OK" versus "Is this correct, Sergeant Jones?"

The September 11, 2001, al Qaeda attacks against the United States were more than crimes—they were acts of war. However, al Qaeda, without regular armed forces, territory, or citizens to defend, also presented unprecedented military challenges. The Geneva Conventions legally do not apply to acts of terrorism because al Qaeda is not a nation-state and has not signed the treaties. Insurgents and lone-wolf attackers also do not qualify as legal combatants because they hide among peaceful populations and launch surprise attacks on civilians, violating the fundamental principle that war is waged only against combatants. As such, the US administration has concluded that groups like ISI and the Taliban are not legally entitled to the protections of the Law of War, such as treatment afforded those who have POW status.

That said, US forces comply with the Law of War during the conduct of military operations and related activities in armed conflict as well as during peacekeeping and peace enforcement. Because of the broad applicability of these legal principles, commanders are responsible for both their own conduct as well as the actions of troops under their command. The rules of engagement generally embody the command guidance governing the use of force to accomplish a given mission. Commanders will develop rules of engagement that are taught to soldiers and followed during operations. Noncommissioned officers enforce the rules of engagement.

Attacking noncombatants and protected property is illegal. You must be able to distinguish "noncombatants" from "combatants" and distinguish "protected property" from "military objectives." Combatants are defined as anyone engaging in hostilities in an armed conflict on behalf of a party to the conflict. Combatants are lawful targets unless "out of combat." Military objectives are lawful targets. Commanders must ensure that any use of force, even if directed against what would be a lawful military objective under the Law of War, complies with the mission statement. Military objectives are defined as combatants, defended places, and those objects that by their nature, location, purpose, or use make an effective contribution to military action (FM 27-10, The Law of Land Warfare, paragraph 40; Geneva Protocol [GP] I, article 52[2]).

RULES OF ENGAGEMENT

The DoD *Dictionary of Military Terms* defines rules of engagement (ROE) as "Directives issued by competent military authority that delineate the circumstances and limitations under which United States forces will initiate and/or continue combat engagement with other forces encountered." Army training about ROE envisions two general circumstances for using weapons: in self-defense and to accomplish the mission. Whether ROE are "permissive" (allowing more use of force) or "restrictive" (limited use of force) depends on the anticipated conditions extant in the mission: for example, the presence or absence of quantities of small arms and light weapons; existing, organized opposition groups, armed and unarmed; and the competency of local security forces.

Some ROE are included in unit standing operational procedures (SOP) and form the basic structure from which changes are made to develop operational-specific ROE issued to forces just prior to the start of an operation.

Remember that in all cases and regardless of ROE, a soldier always has the inherent right of self-defense.

SECURITY

The US Army in its past has been unusually careless about security when in combat theaters. Analysts believe that in past wars this resulted in almost a quarter of our casualties. And it is not very different today. Use alternate routes if possible; never react exactly the same for similar situations, even though you achieve success the first few times. The enemy will soon discern your techniques and design workarounds.

FRATERNIZATION

The Army has always had policies concerning senior-subordinate relationships. This is nothing new, and it is not just a problem relating to gender.

Army policy states that relationships between soldiers of different rank that involve or give the appearance of partiality, preferential treatment, or the improper use of rank or position for personal gain and that are prejudicial to good order, discipline, and high unit morale, will be avoided. Leaders must counsel those involved or take other action, as appropriate, if relationships between soldiers of different rank cause actual or perceived partiality or unfairness; involve the improper use of rank or position for personal gain; or create an actual or clearly predictable adverse impact on discipline, authority, or morale.

Unprofessional relationships can be between persons of different ranks in the same chain of command, the same unit, or a closely related unit, and include dating and close male-female friendships and frequently spending off-duty time together, regardless of gender. Because of the possible repercussions of dating, courtship, and marriage between persons of different ranks, whether or not in the same unit, guidance should be sought from the first sergeant, the commanding officer, or the staff judge advocate.

This policy is based on the principles of good judgment and common sense. An association between an officer and an enlisted soldier or relationships between enlisted soldiers might not be considered fraternization yet may still be inappropriate. Just because a certain relationship does not break the law does not mean it is acceptable or appropriate, and leaders have the responsibility to articulate what is improper. When a relationship between soldiers violates this policy, the Army is firmly committed to corrective action.

The above does not negate a leader's responsibility in the professional development of their soldiers. Leaders cannot stop mentoring, coaching, and teaching soldiers because they fear being accused of fraternization or worse. They must continue to encourage individual study and professional development, and mentor the continued growth of their subordinates' military careers. If they are professional and treat each soldier as a soldier instead of as a male, a female, or a member of a minority, then many of the problems will disappear.

EQUAL OPPORTUNITY

The policy of the Army is to provide equal opportunity and treatment for soldiers without regard to race, color, religion, gender, or national origin, and to provide an environment free from sexual harassment both on and off post. To execute this, commanders often turn to their senior noncommissioned officers to provide advice and assistance on equal opportunity (EO) matters. To achieve the Army EO goal of ensuring fair treatment of all soldiers, NCO leaders must develop, establish, and maintain a climate of discipline that corrects those who exhibit inappropriate social behavior that could affect the unit's work environment. When commanders and their subordinate leaders remain too focused on the next mission and not enough on the behavior of their soldiers, and when NCOs fail to keep the problem away from an already overworked leadership, then the threats to the Army posed by sexual harassment, extremism, racial separatism, and gender discrimination can become major issues that detract from readiness and our ability to accomplish the mission.

There is a direct correlation between behavior in an organization and its human relations environment. A poor climate can foster stereotyping and hate, and a unit with poor human relations can become a breeding ground for inappropriate behavior and unhealthy attitudes. Likewise, a strong human relations climate fosters open communications, promotes tolerance of diversity, encourages dialogue, and is reflective of Army Values.

The Army has placed responsibility for equal opportunity in the hands of unit commanders and has articulated the connection between equal opportunity and unit readiness by enforcing the policy through the traditional chain of command. AR 600-20, Army Command Policy, is the starting point to learn about the Army Equal Opportunity Program; chapter 6 establishes the program and is explicit in affixing responsibility for equal opportunity to the chain of command. It states:

> The chain of command, whether military or civilian, has the primary responsibility for developing and sustaining a healthy climate. This responsibility entails, but is not limited to, promoting positive programs that enhance unit cohesion, esprit, and morale; communicating matters with EO significance to unit personnel and higher headquarters; correcting discriminatory practices by conducting rapid, objective, and impartial inquiries to resolve complaints of discrimination; encouraging the surfacing of problems and preventing reprisal for those who complain; and taking appropriate action against those who violate Army policy.

Under current regulations, commanders have the legal authority to deal with cases of unlawful discrimination or sexual harassment. AR 600-20, paragraph 4-4, "Soldier Conduct," provides that ensuring proper conduct of soldiers is a function of command. Commanders rely on all leaders in the Army to "Take action against military personnel in any case where the soldier's conduct violates good order and discipline." Although chapter 6 is not punitive, the commander's inherent authority to impose administrative sanctions and the specific offenses under the UCMJ provide commanders with the authority sufficient to enforce Army policy on discrimination and harassment. Figures 4-7 and 6-1 in Department of Army Pamphlet (DA PAM) 350-20, Unit Equal Opportunity Training Guide, list sexual harassment behavior and EO violations subject to UCMJ violations.

Sexual Harassment/Assault Response and Prevention (SHARP)

The Department of Defense defines sexual harassment as a form of gender discrimination that involves unwelcome sexual advances, requests for sexual favors, and other verbal or physical conduct of a sexual nature between the same or opposite genders. These apply when:
- Submission to, or rejection of, such conduct is made either explicitly or implicitly a term or condition of a person's job, pay, or career.
- Submission to, or rejection of, such conduct by a person is used as a basis for career or employment decisions affecting that person.
- Such conduct has the purpose or effect of unreasonably interfering with an individual's work performance or creates an intimidating, hostile, or offensive working environment.

For military personnel, the working environment pertains twenty-four-seven, on or off post, and on or off duty. This definition emphasizes that workplace conduct, to be considered "abusive work environment" harassment, need not result in concrete psychological harm to the victim, but rather need only be so severe or pervasive that a reasonable person would perceive—and the victim does perceive—the work environment as hostile or offensive. Any person in a supervisory or command position who uses or condones any form of sexual behavior to control, influence, or affect the career, pay, or job of a military member or civilian employee is engaging in sexual harassment. Similarly, any military member or civilian employee who makes deliberate or repeated unwelcome verbal comments, gestures, or physical contact of a sexual nature in the workplace is also engaging in sexual harassment.

Sexual harassment can include verbal abuse, profanity, off-color jokes, sexual comments, threats, barking, growling, oinking, or whistling at passersby to indicate a perception of their physical appearance. It also includes nonverbal abuse such as leering, ogling (giving a person the "once-over"), blowing kisses, licking lips, winking, leaving sexually suggestive notes, and displaying sexist cartoons and pictures. Unwanted physical contact such as touching, patting, hugging, pinching, grabbing, cornering, kissing, blocking a passage-way, and back and neck rubs may also constitute sexual harassment.

Sexual harassment can lead to sexual assault. To encourage a good climate of sexual assault prevention, it is important to address inappropriate behavior before it can escalate. Following are some techniques to help address sexual harassment:

- Confront and tell the harasser that the behavior is not appreciated or welcomed and must stop immediately.
- Prepare and send a letter or memorandum to the harasser. State the facts and include your personal feelings about the inappropriate behavior and what you expect as a response.
- Request help from a trusted person.
- Ask someone else to talk to the harasser for you. You can also ask someone to accompany you or to intervene on your behalf with the harasser to resolve the issue.
- Report the behavior to your direct supervisor (or others in the chain of command) to ask for assistance in resolving the situation.
- Soldiers may file an informal or formal complaint. Instructions are listed in appendix D of Army Regulation 600-20 and follow the same steps as those for an EO complaint.

Soldiers can also contact the Sexual Harassment Assistance Line:

Phone: (703) 695-4711

DSN: (312) 225-9964

Help Line: (800) 267-9964

Gender Discrimination

Gender discrimination is defined as discrimination based solely on an individual's gender in a subgroup "female" or "male." It is distinguished from sexual harassment because it does not have a sexual component. Discrimination based on gender is often linked to a set of assumptions based on sex role stereotypes concerning the abilities, competence, status, and roles of the particular subgroup. These assumptions result in a disparate treatment or impact on those groups. Operations in Afghanistan, Iraq, and other parts of the world have changed many of the peacetime perceptions of women in combat, and taboos about the "other" sex have gone by the wayside. One of your duties as a noncommissioned officer is to ensure that your soldiers are treated fairly. If it affects your soldiers, it affects you. It all hurts unit cohesion.

SUICIDE PREVENTION

The loss of any American soldier's life is a great tragedy, regardless of cause. In the case of suicide, the Army is committed to providing resources for awareness, intervention, prevention, and follow-up necessary to help our soldiers, civilians, and their families overcome difficult times. Effective suicide prevention requires everyone in the unit to be aware of the risk factors for suicide and know how to respond.

Suicide prevention, like all leadership challenges, is every leader's responsibility at all levels. The success of the Army Suicide Prevention Program rests upon proactive, caring, and courageous people who recognize the imminent danger and then take immediate action to save a life. Active engagement of everyone can help to minimize the risk of suicide within the Army to stop this tragic and unnecessary loss of human life. *Suicide prevention is everybody's business in the Army.* In any situation, if a soldier threatens suicide, take him or her very seriously. You may have very limited time and only one chance to intervene. The most important thing to do is take action.

Distress can lead to the development of unhealthy behaviors. People closest to the soldier (fellow soldiers, family, and friends) are in the best position to recognize changes because of distress and to provide support. Look for:

- Comments that suggest thoughts or plans of suicide.
- Rehearsal of suicidal acts.
- Giving away possessions.
- Obsession with death, dying, and so on.
- Uncharacteristic behaviors (e.g. reckless driving, excessive drinking, stealing).
- Significant change in performance.
- Appearing overwhelmed by recent stressor(s).
- Depressed mood; hopelessness.
- Withdrawal from social activities.

Following are some of the resources available to help leaders respond to soldiers who may be at risk for suicide. Leaders can also contact their unit chaplain or mental health provider.

Defense Suicide Prevention Office (DSPO), www.suicideoutreach.org

Military Crisis Line, www.militarycrisisline.net

Army G1, www.armyg1.army.mil/hr/suicide

If you or one of your soldiers are experiencing a crisis, call (800)-273-TALK (8255) and press 1 for the Military Crisis Line, or text 838255.

EXTREMISM

Although the Constitution guarantees freedom of speech and association, soldiers do not have the right to use these freedoms to infringe upon the rights of others.

Policy

Chapter 4-12 of AR 600-20 makes it clear that participation in extremist organizations or activities is inconsistent with the responsibilities of military service. It defines extremist organizations and activities as those "that advocate racial, gender, or ethnic hatred or intolerance; advocate, create, or engage in illegal discrimination based on race, color, sex, religion, or national origin; [or] advocate the use of or use force or violence or unlawful means to deprive individuals of their rights under the United States Constitution or the Laws of the United States, or any state, by unlawful means."

By regulation, soldiers are prohibited from the following actions in support of extremist organizations or activities:

- Participating in a public demonstration or rally.
- Attending a meeting or activity with knowledge that the meeting or activity involves an extremist cause when on duty, when in uniform, when in a foreign country (whether on or off duty or in uniform), when it constitutes a breach of law and order, when violence is likely to result, or when in violation of off-limits sanctions or a commander's order.
- Fund-raising.
- Recruiting or training members (including encouraging others to join).
- Creating, organizing, or taking a visible leadership role in such an organization or activity.
- Distributing literature on or off a military installation when the primary purpose and content concern advocacy or support of extremist causes, organizations, or activities and it appears that the literature presents a clear danger to the loyalty, discipline, or morale of military personnel; or if the distribution would materially interfere with the accomplishment of a military mission.

Penalties for violations of these prohibitions include the full range of statutory and regulatory sanctions, both criminal (UCMJ) and administrative.

Any soldier involvement with or in an extremist organization or activity, such as membership, receipt of literature, or presence at an event, could threaten the good order and discipline of a unit. In any case of apparent soldier involvement with or in extremist organizations or activities, whether or not in violation of the prohibitions above, commanders must take positive actions to educate soldiers and make them aware of the potential adverse effects that participation in violation of Army policy may have upon good order and discipline in the unit and their military service. This includes educating soldiers regarding the Army Equal Opportunity Program. Commanders should advise soldiers that the goals of extremist organizations are inconsistent with Army goals, beliefs, and values concerning equal opportunity, and that any participation in extremist organizations or activities will be taken into consideration when evaluating soldiers' overall duty performance, including appropriate remarks on evaluation reports and making selections for positions of leadership and responsibility.

Command Authority

Commanders have the authority to prohibit military personnel from engaging in or participating in any other activities that the commander determines will adversely affect good order and discipline or morale within the command. This includes but is not limited to the authority to order the removal of symbols, flags, posters, or other displays from barracks; to place areas or activities off-limits (see AR 190-24, Armed Forces Disciplinary Control Boards And Off-Installation Liaison And Operations). Commanders can also order soldiers not to participate in those activities that are contrary to good order, discipline, or the morale of the unit or that pose a threat to health, safety, and security of military personnel or a military installation.

HUMAN IMMUNODEFICIENCY VIRUS (HIV)

Military readiness, medical, and personnel policies associated with Human Immunodeficiency Virus (HIV) look to protect the Army's ability both to fulfill its Constitutional role and to confidentially identify, evaluate, and provide an appropriate level of care for infected members.

Active-duty soldiers are tested biennially for HIV and Reserve Component servicemembers every five years. Soldiers who are HIV-positive will not be deployed outside the continental United States (CONUS); Alaska, Hawaii, and Puerto Rico are considered CONUS in this definition. The fact that HIV-positive soldiers are nondeployable does not preclude their assignment to deployable units, except for Ranger and Special Forces units, which are totally closed to HIV-positive soldiers. Servicemembers who are HIV-infected are eligible for all military professional development schools and may also attend formal military training to qualify them for reclassification, provided the schooling does not exceed twenty weeks.

Mandatory testing and HIV prevention awareness are being emphasized Army-wide. You must teach your soldiers—and implore them to teach their families—how to avoid the spread of the disease. For more information, review Army Regulation 600-110, Identification, Surveillance, and Administration of Personnel Infected with Human Immunodeficiency Virus.

THE ENVIRONMENT

Leaders must protect resources, including land used for training. Soldiers must understand that they are stewards of our environmental resources. At a minimum, abide by the following rules, which will do much to assist in keeping you and your organization out of trouble:

- Avoid maneuver damage and report observed damage as soon as possible.
- Do not dig, cut down or "dismember" trees, or otherwise alter the environment unless you have approval from proper military authority (usually your commanding officer).
- Do not contaminate the soil or water with petroleum, oil, or lubricants (POL). Report POL leaks or spills immediately to your chain of command.
- Do not burn or bury garbage, refuse, or rubbish.

- Do not use tracers during training, do not set off pyrotechnics, and do not allow open flames in areas that are likely to catch fire.
- Obey posted environmental signs.
- Include environmental preservation in training plans.

MEDIA

NCOs have a role to play in teaching soldiers about the media. If your soldiers see unescorted members of the press—newspaper, magazine, radio, or television reporters and crewmembers—they should inform their chain of command.

Members of the press provide a service to the nation. Still, commanders often shun coverage because mission security and soldiers' lives come before the media's "right to know." Animosity between the military and the media does a disservice to both and to the nation. For years, annual national polls have shown that citizens rate the military at the top of lists of the most credible of all vital national institutions. The press nevertheless is entitled under the First Amendment to investigate military activities and report news to the nation. The military–media relationship continues to be marked by a contest of wills regarding the right to know versus operational security.

When approval is granted, soldiers must guard against making comments about troop strength, position, direction, condition, tactics, strategy, or other factors an enemy may use to gain an advantage. Giving operational information will result in operations security (OPSEC) leaks—the kind that compromise the mission and destroy units.

Here are some important tips to keep in mind if you are asked to speak with the media:

- Think first before you answer.
- Tell the truth. Never lie or intentionally mislead members of the media.
- Discuss only the facts that you have direct responsibility for or personal knowledge about. Speak at your level—don't speak for those above your position.
- Don't answer "what if" or hypothetical questions.
- Avoid acronyms, jargon, slang, and technical terms.
- When asked multiple questions, answer the one with which you feel most comfortable.
- Keep your remarks short and concise.
- Assume everything you say will be printed or broadcast.
- Use "I"—not "we"—when giving your opinion.
- If you don't know the answer to a question or cannot discuss something, say so. You should never say "no comment."

Social Media

The widespread use of social media represents a shift in the way we communicate as a culture. Internet platforms like Facebook, YouTube, Twitter, and others are a new way to connect and interact. The Army has recognized that social media gives soldiers and families a way to communicate with larger audiences faster and in new ways. Because of that, it has become an important tool for Army messaging and outreach. Social media affords a place to speak freely about activities and interests, but soldiers must remember that they are subject to Army punishment even when off duty. Talking negatively about supervisors or releasing sensitive information can result in punishment, and a soldier's actions or photographs may come back to haunt him or her. It is important that servicemembers remember that even on a social media platform they still represent the Army. Self-portrait photographs ("selfies") showing one or more soldiers in compromising positions should be considered as in the public domain once they are loaded to a social media site, no matter the controls taken to protect them.

For more information about media training, contact your servicing Army public affairs office.

6

Problem Solving
and Counseling

Counseling is a standardized tool used to provide feedback to a subordinate. Counseling focuses on the subordinate by producing a plan outlining actions he or she can take to achieve individual and organizational goals. It is central to leader development and should be part of a comprehensive program for developing subordinates. A consistent counseling program includes all subordinates, regardless of the level of each one's potential.

HELPING YOUR SOLDIERS SOLVE THEIR PROBLEMS

Extended overseas deployments, marital strife, substance abuse, failure to comprehend or to comply, inability to perform duties, a medical condition, weight control, failing or a low score on the Army Physical Fitness Test, no pay due, nonpayment of just debts, spouse or child abuse, poor self-management skills—the kinds of problems that soldiers can encounter go on and on. Small problems often are easily resolved without assistance. Some problems, though, are bigger than the individual, who may require our assistance with them before they spiral out of control.

Recognizing Soldiers with Problems

Some soldiers will come to you, explain their problem, and seek your guidance or assistance. Others will not. Those who do not may be hard to spot unless you know what to look for during daily contact. Watch for signs when you speak with or observe your soldiers.

If a soldier who is normally on time to work begins to show up late, he or she might be losing sleep for any number of innocent reasons. However, sleep loss can also be caused by partying late into the night or substance abuse. Observe the soldier's appearance. Is it neat? Does he or she look disheveled? Do you smell alcohol on the soldier's breath? If married, is the soldier getting along well with his or her spouse? Does the soldier have teenage children who stay out late, and does the soldier wait up?

Something is wrong when a soldier who usually has a good attitude and behaves properly suddenly develops an improper attitude or exhibits irrational behavior. If deployed overseas, did he or she receive unpleasant news from home? Does the soldier feel unfairly treated? Is the soldier lashing out or venting because emotional release is needed? Or is there some other cause of the problem?

The only effective way to identify and deal with the myriad problems that crop up in Army units is to stay tuned in to your soldiers. Try the following tactics to promote healthy ways of handling problems:

- Anticipate stressful events.
- Stress the value of problem-solving and conflict-resolution skills, respect, self-accountability, walking away when emotions are at a peak, and being in control of a situation.
- Encourage soldiers to be open about their concerns and problems at the first signs of stress.
- Be supportive and nonjudgmental.
- Listen—not only to what is being said, but also to how it is said.
- Balance a leadership approach with a supportive response to a soldier's or family's explanation of their problems.
- Teach soldiers that it is their personal obligation to take responsibility for their actions and to seek help before a problem becomes a crisis.
- Be aware of the unit grapevine and alert to concerns and rumors.

Obtaining Information and Assistance

The table on page 74 shows some of the staff office and support agencies that can help soldiers with advice and assistance in their personal affairs. In all cases, personnel should first contact the right person in their chain of command for guidance: immediate supervisors, squad leaders, first sergeants, or unit commanders. A 1 in the table indicates primary or key contacts; a 2 indicates other contacts, as applicable.

LEADERSHIP COUNSELING

Counseling is central to leader development. Leaders who serve as designated raters have to prepare their subordinates to be better soldiers or civilians. Good counseling focuses on the subordinate's performance and problems with an eye toward tomorrow's plans and solutions. The subordinate is expected to be an active participant who seeks constructive feedback. Counseling cannot be an occasional event but should instead be part of a comprehensive program to develop subordinates. With effective counseling, no evaluation report—positive or negative—should be a surprise. A consistent counseling program includes all subordinates, not just the people thought to have the most potential.

Effective counseling helps subordinates develop personally and professionally. In the past, many soldiers perceived counseling as bad because the

	YOUR CHAIN OF COMMAND	PERSONNEL NCO OR OFFICER	REENLISTMENT NCO	JUDGE ADVOCATE	INSPECTOR GENERAL	FINANCE OFFICER	CHAPLAIN	HOUSING OFFICER	TRANSPORTATION OFFICER	AMERICAN RED CROSS	ARMY COMMUNITY SERVICES	ARMY EMERGENCY RELIEF	EDUCATION OFFICER/ADVISOR
Appeals	1	2		2	2		2						
Assignment, reassignment, MOS, and proficiency pay	1	1				2							
Reenlistment	1		1										
Personnel matters: promotion, reduction, discharge, retirement Veterans' benefits	1	1	2	2									
Complaints (requests for assistance)	1	2	2	2	2	2	2	2	2	2	2	2	
Debts and civilian creditors	1	1		2		2	2				2		
Dependents' schools	1	1									2		
Family and religious affairs	1	2					1			2	2		
Travel of dependents, shipment of POV and household goods	1	2				2			1		2		
Medical service (individual and dependents)	1	1											
Pay, allowances, and incentive pay	1	2				1							
Leaves and passes	1	2											
Insurance, all types (SGLI and commercial)	1	1				2							
Legal assistance, including US and foreign law, wills, and powers of attorney	1			1									
Military education	1	2	2										
Nonmilitary education	1	2											2
PX, commissary, QM sales store	1				2								
Government quarters, off-post housing	1	2						1					
Registration/operation of privately owned vehicle (POV), registration of firearms	1												
Entry into U.S., passport, visa, naturalization, immigration, birth certificate (children born in foreign country)	1	2		1							2		
Home conditions and emergency leave	1	2					2			2	2	2	
Emergency financial assistance	1	2				1				2	2	2	
Postal service	1												
Drug and alcohol rehabilitation program	1						2				1		

1. Primary source
2. Other sources as appropriate

Guide for Obtaining Information and Assistance

only time their leaders spoke to them was to correct deficiencies or to check the block for the mandatory monthly counseling. Now there is a different reason to counsel. The Army Values of loyalty, duty, and selfless service require that we counsel subordinates, while the values of honor, integrity, and personal courage require us to be honest and straightforward with our feedback. Lastly, the value of respect requires that we find the best method in which to convey that feedback so that our subordinates understand it. The new doctrine mandates two-way communication and encourages the development of a plan of action (if required).

This is pretty clear guidance—and for good reason. Effective leadership is the Army's key to success, not only in training and combat but also in developing soldiers. Soldiers watch leaders very carefully, and your competence, candor, and evenhandedness will help establish and maintain their faith in you. As a leader, you can suggest alternatives, persuade, urge, advise, direct, punish, and reward using directive, nondirective, or combined approaches. Counseling can range from a few words of praise or guidance with a hand on a shoulder to long, structured sessions.

What was once described as formal counseling is now known as *developmental counseling*, which in essence means that it should progress toward some type of conclusion. The two major categories are event-oriented and performance-oriented (professional) growth. *Event-oriented counseling* focuses on a specific event or situation, such as instances of superior or substandard performance; reception and integration counseling, crisis counseling, referral counseling, promotion counseling, or separation counseling all fit into this category. You should use Department of the Army (DA) Form 4856, Developmental Counseling Form. *Performance-oriented counseling* is required under the NCO Evaluation Report (NCOER) system and consists of a review of past performance over a given period as well as the joint establishment of performance objectives and standards for the next period. In *professional growth counseling*, which focuses on the future, you assist subordinates in establishing short- and long-term goals and objectives to achieve organizational and personal goals.

The counseling approach you use will depend on the circumstances and how well you know the soldier and his or her duties. The directive approach is good for immature or insecure soldiers, while the combined and nondirective methods encourage open communication. The directive and combined approaches give the counselor an opportunity to use his or her experience, while the nondirective approach develops the soldier's personal responsibility. All three methods require you to listen, observe, and respond appropriately.

ATP 6-22.1, The Counseling Process, goes into more detail about developmental counseling as well as the different counseling approaches, effective communication, how to be an active listener and keep the dialogue moving, what to interpret from silence at various points during counseling, and how to respond under friendly and hostile circumstances.

The Directive Approach

The directive approach is the quickest method but does not encourage maturity and is often suited to "I talk, you listen" situations in which the counselor must correct a soldier who is the problem. The directive approach is commonly used when making on-the-spot corrections. You give advice, offer solutions, and tell the soldier what must be done. This approach may also be used to praise on the spot.

The directive approach is simple, quick, and provides immediate solutions, but it has shortcomings. Your dominant influence may cause resentment because the soldier may feel that you are taking the ability to solve the problem away from him or her. The approach may address only symptoms of the real problem. And decisions are made by the leader, not the soldier, so the soldier may later blame the leader if the solution did not fix the problem. Sometimes, regardless of its shortcomings, you must use the directive approach to counsel an unresponsive soldier who will not connect bad behavior or conduct with the consequences.

The Nondirective Approach

The nondirective approach encourages maturity but takes considerable time and requires the greatest counseling skill. NCOs using the nondirective approach to counseling will find that it is more relaxed and focused on the soldier's self-discovery toward finding a solution. The soldier can verbalize and work out solutions through personal insight, judgment, and realization of the facts. The counseled soldier must understand, however, that he or she must be willing to openly discuss the subject and take responsibility for the solution.

Often, a soldier will come to you with a problem, a concern, or perhaps a good idea. This is the time, if it is convenient, to use the nondirective approach. If it is not a convenient time, you should set a better time and appropriate place. During counseling, avoid offering solutions; let the soldier work it out, if possible. Certainly, you must guide the conversation to keep it focused on the subject, but make the soldier realize that the session is on his or her time. This way, the soldier may be less inclined to become defensive or to feel guilty.

Try to establish rapport. Display sincere interest. Give the soldier an opportunity to state the problem. Don't interrupt. Ask leading, open-ended questions to clarify the nature and scope of the problem. Let the soldier respond. Listen for responses that indicate the soldier is approaching a resolution. Approve the soldier's solution if it is honest and may work.

If you are unable to help the soldier, refer him or her to someone who can, such as the local chaplain, finance officer, legal officer, or whoever else is appropriate. If time permits, go with the soldier. Briefly tell the official about the problem, then depart. After the soldier returns to your control, follow up to ensure the problem has been or will be resolved. As far as possible, keep superiors informed about the situation, your actions, the soldier's actions, and the resolution.

Mentoring is leading. SGT. DUNCAN BRENNAN, WWW.ARMY.MIL

The Combined Approach

The combined approach is moderately quick but may take too much time in some situations. Using the combined approach, you apply parts of the directive and nondirective approaches to adjust your counseling style as the tone of the conversation and the requirements of your role as counselor change. You can adapt to emphasize what is best for the soldier.

This approach assumes that the soldier will eventually take charge of solving the problem but needs some help along the way. Use the ethical decision-making process and related problem-solving process in ADRP 6-22 to help guide the soldier. If you work from directive to nondirective, listen for information that defines the problem and allow the soldier an opportunity to suggest his or her own solutions. You may add your own suggestions as well. But remember, the counseling goal is to get the soldier to "own" or resolve the problem.

Lastly, when you counsel a member of the opposite sex, ask the person whether he or she would mind if another person of his or her gender were present during counseling. You must show that you care—avoid violating the soldier's confidence—but maintain a professional distance. To avoid an allegation of harassment or other wrongdoing, you may decide that it is in your and the soldier's best interest to have a third party present. Use your judgment, but err on the side of caution.

ALCOHOL AND DRUG ABUSE

Abuse of alcohol or the use of illicit drugs is inconsistent with Army Values and the standards of performance, discipline, and readiness necessary to accomplish the Army's mission. As an NCO, you will at some time in your service encounter soldiers who depend on or abuse alcohol and other drugs. A drug is defined as "any substance which by its chemical nature alters structure or function in the living organism." This definition includes alcohol, glue, and aerosols, among many other potential sources. The harm and misery done to soldiers by substance abuse are incalculable. Soldiers should be proud of their service, job, and uniform. They should strive to maintain their own individual fitness and live a healthy lifestyle free of drugs or substance abuse.

Soldiers who use or sell drugs do not belong in the US Army. Any soldier who relies on alcohol to make it through the day or who feels he or she must turn to some drug to get by or get high should have the personal courage to quit or to seek help from the local Army Substance Abuse Program. Command referral is an almost-sure ticket out of the Army.

Alcohol Abuse

It is Army policy to maintain a workplace free from alcohol. At all levels, alcohol will not be glamorized or made the center of attention at any military function. It should not become the purpose for, or the focus of, any military social activity. Impairment due to alcohol use while on duty is no longer tolerated. AR 600-85, The Army Substance Abuse Program, stipulates no alcohol consumption during duty hours (unless approved by a general officer) and that soldiers on duty will not have a blood alcohol level equal to or greater than 0.05 grams of alcohol per 100 milliliters of blood. So watch the benders from the night before!

Drug Abuse

AR 600-85 also makes it clear that drug abuse in today's Army is unacceptable: Abusers "have violated the special trust and confidence that the Army has placed in them." Several years ago, the Army introduced a stricter policy about substance abuse that basically says "zero tolerance," and in 2001 the separations policies in effect for drug-using officers and NCOs were expanded to include all soldiers.

Treatment issues in the Army Substance Abuse Program do not affect command administrative or disciplinary decisions made in the best interest of the Army, meaning that command referral of a soldier into a treatment plan in no way prevents disciplinary action or separation processing.

Urinalysis testing is commonplace and random. Soldiers prescreening positive for substance abuse will have their samples verified by a supporting forensic laboratory. Discharge for misconduct under AR 635-200, Active Duty Enlisted Administrative Separations, Chapter 14 (for enlisted), will be initiated and processed to the separation authority for all soldiers involved in illegal traf-ficking, distribution, possession, use, or sale of illegal drugs, with the exception of self-referrals. Soldiers could face the consequence of a court-martial and the punishment it may direct, including confinement, loss of all pay and allowances, and a less than honorable (e.g., bad conduct or dishonorable) discharge. Note that the separation authority is not required to approve the discharge.

Prevention and Control

The Army Substance Abuse Program (ASAP) is a command program that emphasizes readiness and personal responsibility—one in which alcohol, other drug abuse, and all related activities are addressed as a single program. The programs are generally short-term and conducted in a manner that supports the military organization. Even when a soldier is enrolled in the program, unit commanders retain their authority to make personnel decisions such as initia-tion of separation from service, bar to reenlistment, and extension on active duty to permit reenlistment; they can also require soldiers to attend field train-ing or deployments, even when such actions may interfere with the treatment plan. The ultimate decision regarding separation or retention of abusers rests with the NCO's chain of command.

You can help, too, by educating your soldiers. Motivate any abuser to rec-ognize the advantages of self-referral. Otherwise, it is your responsibility to ensure that identified abusers receive command referral to the program. Abusers who do not cooperate and who are not rehabilitated will be separated.

ASAP and Efficiency Reports

A soldier's voluntary participation in the ASAP is not normally mentioned in an NCO Evaluation Report, but raters may make note of incidents of alcohol or drug abuse not derived from ASAP records. Once a soldier has been identified in a report as having a substance abuse problem, his or her voluntary entry into the ASAP or successful rehabilitation may be mentioned in subsequent reports.

FAMILY ABUSE

Frequent moves and deployments guarantee that military families will spend a lot of time in transition. This perpetual change can lead to individual and family strain, financial pressure, and the loss of valuable support networks. Transitions also lead to shifts of control as spouses endure frequent or long separations and learn to survive independently. Soldiers also face greater work demands and longer workdays, which inevitably add pressure to family relationships.

A soldier's spouse and children should be the most important people in his or her life. Nothing about service, no family issue at home or in quarters, and no external pressure or stress can justify abusive treatment of loved ones. This applies not only to our own home lives, but also to those of our soldiers. Every leader is responsible for acting upon known or suspected cases of family violence. As leaders, we must learn to detect such cases. We must create an environment of support and caring that encourages victims to come to us for assistance. As leaders, we must be familiar with the Family Advocacy Program and other resources locally available. If our families are in trouble, so too is the soldier and unit readiness. We must be advocates of family well-being by linking soldiers with services that can help their families work together through stress and change. It is crucial that we connect soldiers with these services at the first signs of stress—before a problem evolves into a violent crisis.

When soldiers and families get involved in violent incidents, their behaviors often suggest that they are trapped in a "cycle of violence": *Tension building*—increased demands, stress buildup, "walking on eggshells," or put-downs—leads to *explosion*—hitting, threatening, pushing, humiliating, controlling—which is followed by *honeymoon*, or denial of the problem. The honeymoon period gives the spouse hope for change—"It's over now"; "It won't happen again"; "It only happened because . . . "; "Everything is OK now"—when the abuser makes promises, cries, declares love, and gives presents. But with the onset of stress, the cycle begins again.

It is wrong to verbally abuse (curse, defame, intimidate, belittle, embarrass, malign), inflict physical pain on (slap, hit, punch, kick, or otherwise harm), or neglect (omit necessary care for) the people who rely on you for their support, welfare, and safety—and who probably love you very much. Deal with the problems leading to the abuse. Do not vent frustration on family members. Cool off. Regroup your emotions. Refocus your attitude. Ask for forgiveness and show loved ones that they come first. If you cannot do so, or if you have tried to avoid an abusive nature but failed, call the local Army family advocacy office to get help. If you supervise an abusive soldier or know someone else who is an abuser, follow the guidance in this section.

Prevention and intervention in family violence is a community responsibility: No single individual, agency, or organization can implement an effective and comprehensive program. Teamwork is the key. NCOs are major team members for the success of this mission because they are frequently on the "front line" when it comes to assisting soldiers and families.

If a dependent of a soldier reports abuse to you, it is your duty to immediately report the matter to your chain of command. Your superiors, acting within command channels, may take it upon themselves to investigate the allegation. If you know that the abuse victims need protection, you should also inform the military police or local civilian authorities. Take care of the soldier and the family.

Child and spousal abuse are extremely sensitive matters. Senior leaders throughout the Army take a grim view of abusive soldiers. It is important to stress to an abusive soldier that most reported incidents of abuse or neglect lead to treatment and assistance, not to prosecution. Family advocacy officials will work to preserve and protect the family unit. Program officials can verify whether a soldier is an abuser, and then treat and rehabilitate both the abuser and the victims. A soldier's participation in the program is not intended to harm a military career; it is designed to be supportive and offer needed assistance. If abuse continues, however, officials may make recommendations regarding criminal or administrative actions. In cases where violence continues and persons refuse to cooperate, command involvement must be initiated.

(The Lautenberg Amendment addresses domestic violence and firearms. As such, this amendment may or may not apply.)

For further information, check the Army OneSource Family Advocacy Program resource at www.myarmyonesource.com/familyprogramsandservices/familyprograms/familyadvocacyprogram and AR 608-18, The Army Family Advocacy Program.

ABSENCE WITHOUT LEAVE (AWOL) AND DESERTION

Absence Without Leave (AWOL) is not the serious problem that it once was; however, it is still a problem, especially with younger soldiers. Numerous factors influence a soldier to go AWOL: job dissatisfaction, personality clashes, deployment stress, and family and financial problems, to name just a few. First-line NCOs are usually the first to notice changes in attitudes and performance and can do much to alleviate a soldier's urge to go AWOL by using the same preventive measures that work well in other situations: Stay attuned to soldiers' needs and problems and conduct regular professional and personal counseling. As the saying goes, "An ounce of prevention is worth a pound of cure."

After a soldier goes AWOL, unit leaders must store the soldier's personal belongings and turn in organizational issue items. Leaders change the soldier's status on unit manning documents and the duty roster, report the matter to higher authority, conduct an immediate inquiry to determine the soldier's location, notify the provost marshal (within forty-eight hours), and mail a notification letter to next of kin (on the tenth day). All of these steps are described in DA Pam 600-8, Management and Administrative Procedures; the official next-of-kin letter can be found in AR 630-10, Absence without Leave, Desertion, and Administration of Personnel Involved in Civilian Court Proceedings.

On the thirty-first day of a soldier's absence, the unit commander drops the member from the unit rolls, known as dropped from rolls (DFR). If considered a "special category" absentee, the soldier may be dropped sooner. A special category soldier is one with access to top-secret information during the last twelve months or a current assignment to a special mission unit, which also covers defection to another country. When placed into a DFR status, the former member is declared a deserter or defector.

When the soldier is dropped, the unit commander prepares a Department of Defense (DD) Form 458, Charge Sheet, for desertion or defection, and any other military infractions under the UCMJ. Next, the commander prepares DD Form 553, Deserter/Absentee Wanted by the Armed Forces. These two documents, along with DA Form 4187, Personnel Action (entering the soldier into DFR status), constitute a deserter packet. The packet is necessary for a warrant to be entered into the FBI National Crime Information Center for apprehension.

If the soldier returns to military control prior to submission of the DFR packet, the soldier will be carried only as AWOL and remain assigned to the unit. DFR packets submitted after a soldier has returned to the unit could put the commander and the Army at risk of erroneous arrest and lawsuits. Be sure to follow proper reporting procedures to the letter.

If your commander is unsure about what to do in a particular case, the Army Deserter Information Point (ADIP) operates a twenty-four-hour information line that can be contacted at DSN 536-3711, or commercial (502) 626-3711 or 3712 or 3713. The ADIP, located at Fort Knox, Kentucky, can also be accessed online at www.knox.army.mil/Garrison/des/spc.aspx. *Note:* The department can no longer release DFR status to individuals.

PART II

Training Soldiers and Self

7

Leader Development

The Army Leader Development Strategy provides a comprehensive roadmap to prepare Army leaders for the challenges that our
nation will face. In this strategy, leader development is defined as
the deliberate, continuous, and progressive process that grows soldiers into confident, committed, professional leaders of character.
—Gen. Raymond T. Odierno, Chief of Staff of the Army

Developing future leaders is a deliberate and continuous process grounded in
the Army Values. Leader development enables soldiers to grow into competent
and confident noncommissioned officers capable of leading their teams and
units to accomplish the assigned missions. This process is accomplished
through the knowledge, skills, and abilities gathered from education, training,
and experience.

LEADER DEVELOPMENT PROCESS
Noncommissioned officers learn new skills and gain knowledge and experience through a combination of formal training and education, operational
assignments, and self-development. The Army's leader development process
was designed to ensure the growth of soldiers through training and education,
field experience, counseling and feedback, and evaluations and selection. This
progression happens in Army units, at military schools, and at civilian education institutions across the globe.

Confident leaders who are technically and tactically competent are integral
to maintaining a combat-ready force. Commanders are responsible for arrang-
ing leader training and leader development programs for their units, and for
providing a climate that encourages and facilitates learning. As part of their
overall unit training program, commanders must prepare and plan, execute, and
then assess leader training and leader development.

Noncommissioned officers also have an important role in the development
of their subordinates. The Army leadership assessment process "measures

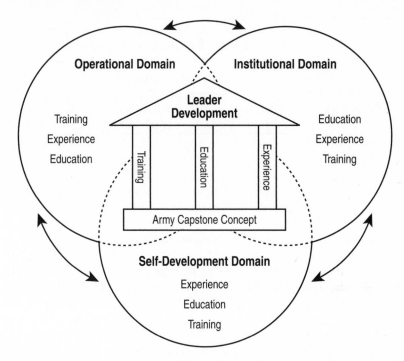

Army Leader Development Model

subordinates' leadership values, attributes, skills, knowledge, and potential to lead" at higher levels. An NCO is always being evaluated, whether formally by his or her leaders or informally by peers and subordinates. Formal assessments give feedback or numerical ratings based on individual or team performance and encourage development to improve potential. For both of these steps to be effective, the NCO's performance is rated against specific standards that are understood by both the individual and supervisor conducting the assessment.

The Army has identified seven leader development non-negotiable principles that guide policy and actions in order to develop leaders with the required qualities and characteristics:

1. Demonstrate commitment to the Army profession, lifelong learning, and development.
2. Balance the Army's commitment to the training, education, and experience components of leader development.
3. Manage military and civilian talents to benefit both the institution and the individual.
4. Select and develop leaders with positive leader attributes and proficiency in core leadership competencies for responsibility at higher levels.

5. Prepare adaptive and creative leaders capable of operating within the complexity of the operational environment and the entire range of military operations.
6. Embed Mission Command principles in leader development.
7. Value a broad range of leader experiences and developmental opportunities.

NCOs gain the most experience during assignments to operational units, just as soldiers gain their technical skills and junior NCOs further develop their ability to lead small sections and teams at this stage. These assignments also enable senior NCOs to develop expertise and contribute to the progression of more advanced tactical, operational, and strategic skills. All of the education and self-development activities conducted during the process of training, planning, preparing, executing, and assessing Army operations are essential to the development of noncommissioned officers. After Action Reviews, coaching, counseling, sharing, and mentoring also should be given equal consideration.

Institutional assignments consist of all organizations and activities in the Army as well as the Army staff, agencies, centers, and schools that provide initial training and professional education for soldiers. Assignments to the institution include attending college, training with industry, and fellowships, each of which supplements leader education. The use of technology allows soldiers a real-time link to facilitators, peers, leaders, and mentors. Those institutions offer knowledge to develop the leadership attributes and competencies necessary for advancement.

Self-development includes planned, goal-oriented learning that builds on and expands the soldier's knowledge and self-awareness. It connects training and education gaps between the operational and institutional areas and helps soldiers to better achieve development and growth. There are three types of self-development:

- *Structured.* Mandatory learning modules to meet specific or directed learning objectives, typically performed during periods between education systems-directed courses.
- *Guided.* Recommended but optional learning, such as professional reading lists or branch journals.
- *Personal.* Self-initiated learning to meet personal training, education, and experience goals, such as attending trade schools or colleges or earning industry certifications.

ARMY LEADER DEVELOPMENT STRATEGY

The purpose of Army leader development is to "educate, train, and provide experiences to progressively develop leaders to prevail [in full-spectrum operations] in a 21st Century security environment and to lead the Army." The Army Leader Development Strategy (ALDS) is an outline of the Army's goals and plans for conducting leader development for service professionals. The strategy includes development through lifelong training and education and experiences from assignments and opportunities in the operational, institutional, and self-development areas.

ARMY CAREER TRACKER (ACT)

Army Career Tracker (ACT) is an information system that incorporates training and education into a personalized website. Soldiers can search multiple education and training resources, monitor their career development, and receive personalized advice from leadership. The ACT is also an effective tool for leaders and supervisors. In addition, the ACT enables soldiers to:

- Identify training and requirements based on their career management field, their career field, and their individual career program maps.
- Track progress of their individualized development plan (IDP) goals.
- View multiple skill and competency career progressions across the various career maps.
- Search training catalogs.
- Connect with their peers through the My Journal collaboration tab. ACT will eventually include a supervisor and career program manager dashboard as well.
- Provide an unofficial "lifelong learning transcript" that gathers all assignments, training, and education accomplishments into one comprehensive document.

Individual Development Plan (IDP)

The ACT can help soldiers create individual development plans (IDP) in just a few steps. Soldiers start by entering their long- and short-term goals into the database. They can then opt to select degree programs and certifications to add.

To create a new IDP, visit the ACT website, https://actnow.army.mil, and click on the IDP tab. Next, click on the Create New IDP button located under the IDP portlet and select a start date. The end date will automatically populate. The IDP will automatically be filled in with some established goals. Refine and submit the IDP for approval and print copies to keep and for your supervisor to sign.

8

Training in
Operational Assignments

In no other profession are the penalties for employing untrained
personnel so appalling or so irrevocable as in the military.
—Gen Douglas MacArthur (1933)

Since 1896, when Rudyard Kipling coined the phrase in his poem "The
'eathen," noncommissioned officers have been referred to as the "backbone of
the Army." It was not just because of their ability to train soldiers, but also
because they maintain good order and discipline within their units. It has only
been within the past hundred years that sergeants and corporals have assumed
the individual training role from officers, and only in the last thirty years that
senior noncommissioned officers have been given the responsibility by regulation to plan and conduct training of soldiers, sections, squads, teams, and
crews. Today we have the world's best NCO Corps, and the Army leadership
entrusts us with what was once considered "officers' business." The difference
between our Army and every other army in the world is that we have a professional NCO Corps that takes pride in, and accepts responsibility for, the care
and individual training of soldiers. It is up to the NCO Corps to uphold that
trust and execute the responsibility. Our soldiers' lives, the success of Army
missions, and strength of our nation depend on it.

All leaders are trainers, and training is a primary leadership mission of
noncommissioned officers. Every enlisted soldier has an NCO. It is that NCO's
responsibility to ensure not only that the soldiers get that training, but also that
the training is presented in a professional manner, by expert, qualified trainers,
and that the soldiers' proficiency at duty performance is increased and sustained as a demonstrated result of that training. Soldiers in transportation units,
supply operations, signal units, and higher staff sections need training in combat, technical, and professional duty skills just as much as soldiers in front-line
combat units.

The NCO Corps is also responsible for helping officers to train the unit in collective tasks, developing and conducting training for subordinates, mentoring other NCOs and junior officers, and advising senior leaders.

What follows is a detailed look at today's noncommissioned officers and their role in training soldiers. Along with describing Army training doctrine, this section provides thoughts on senior NCOs and their training responsibilities, as well as techniques on how to determine collective, leader, and individual tasks for the small-unit leader; what an After Action Review should "feel like"; and some thoughts on running marksmanship ranges.

TRAINING FOR UNIFIED LAND OPERATIONS

The most fundamental role of Army forces is to deter or defeat enemy threats on land, and the goal of all training is to achieve the Army standard. Within the confines of safety and common sense, NCO leaders must be willing to accept less than perfect results initially and must demand realism in training.

Tough, realistic, and intellectually and physically challenging training excites and motivates soldiers and leaders. NCOs must develop training that will be recent and relevant yet still rigorous enough to challenge soldiers and the unit. Realistic training should:

- Be well resourced at the appropriate level to ensure success.
- Build competence and confidence by developing and honing skills.
- Instill loyalty and dedication to the unit through a shared sense of accomplishment.
- Inspire excellence by fostering initiative, enthusiasm, and eagerness to learn.
- Develop aggressive, well-trained, disciplined soldiers.

Make conditions in training as close to wartime conditions as possible. Seize every opportunity to increase training challenges for your soldiers. Successful completion of each training event increases the capability and motivation of your team for more sophisticated and advanced training.

Unit Training Management

The training management cycle begins with an understanding of the unit's wartime mission and the establishment of mission-essential tasks. According to Army doctrine, a mission-essential task (MET) "represents a task a unit could perform based on its design, equipment, manning, and table of organization." The MET should not be confused with a collection of mission-essential tasks, known as a mission-essential task list (METL).

The commander begins planning for unit training by determining the mission, reviewing the METL, and determining and analyzing the necessary support tasks the unit must perform. He is then able to decide how the unit will train for those specific tasks.

When selecting which collective tasks to train for, commanders seek those that support the primary mission as well as unexpected missions. During mission analysis, the commander also considers:

- The unit's current readiness assessment of the collective tasks.
- The higher commander's guidance.
- The time available to train.
- The expected operational environment.
- Risks involved in not training for collective tasks that the mission might require.
- Any resources needed for training that are not readily available at the home station.
- Input from subordinates.

Development of a Unit Training Plan

While reviewing the list of approved collective tasks, the unit commander develops the training events, which may include field training exercises, situational training exercises, and terrain walks. The final result is the creation of the unit training plan (UTP). The commander should make sure to allot enough time for subordinates to also plan their own training events.

The UTPs developed for company-sized units are created using the eight steps of troop leading procedures (TLP). These steps provide small-unit leaders with an outline for planning and preparing for operations and are the basic fundamental process of the crew, team, or squad-level leader. The TLPs spread the military decision-making process out to squad- and platoon-level leaders. Once the company UTP is approved, and when appropriate, TLP are also used for planning training events.

Leaders begin TLP for unit training when they receive the initial warning order (WARNORD) from their next higher unit. The steps of TLP are as follows:

Step 1—Receive the mission
Step 2—Issue a warning order
Step 3—Make a tentative plan
Step 4—Initiate movement
Step 5—Conduct reconnaissance
Step 6—Complete the plan
Step 7—Issue the order
Step 8—Supervise and refine

To be effective trainers, NCOs must know their unit's mission and the individual, leader, and collective tasks that support the wartime mission. They also must understand the roles that other units—combat, combat support, and combat service support—play in the overall scheme.

LEADER DEVELOPMENT PLANNING

Commanders, along with noncommissioned officers and other leaders, plan, execute, and assess leader development objectives. As commanders develop their UTPs, they also plan how they intend to develop subordinate leaders. These plans can be detailed and formal or broad and informal, but they always list specific objectives and often include:

- Leadership's expectations of subordinate leaders.
- Leader individual training and certification programs by position.
- Leader development objectives in scheduled unit training events.
- Opportunities for leaders to experience positions of higher responsibility in training.
- Subordinate unit leader development plans.
- Leader professional training and education.
- Retraining until leader achieves task standards.

Pre-deployment training is vital to mission accomplishment.

Techniques and Tips for Training at Unit Level

Force Leaders at All Echelons to Make Decisions. Push the decision-making process down to the lowest level that has the knowledge to make the decision. Set down objectives, but don't dictate how to perform the task. Let the NCOs make the hard choices. There will be errors in judgment, but in peacetime those can be readily corrected. Give NCOs the freedom to make mistakes, but not the freedom to fail. A task is repeated until it is done to standard, whether once or twenty times. The chain of command should identify any errors to the NCO to preclude him or her from making the same mistake twice, but control of the problem should not be taken away.

Mentor Development of Aspiring NCOs. Mentoring usually occurs two levels down and usually outside the mentored NCO's chain of command, i.e., the command sergeant major mentors platoon sergeants, and first sergeants mentor squad leaders. This helps both the mentor and mentored; one gets the advice and counsel from someone who is senior and reasonably distant, and the other gets the view from the trenches. This day-to-day training and mentoring allows a solid senior-subordinate relationship and enables the senior NCO to take charge of the development of those who are junior in grade and experience. The senior NCO can begin the molding process that establishes a foundation for further development.

Lead Subordinates in Execution of the Activities of the Day. Such leadership is exemplified in understanding the instruction or task before beginning; in giving clear, concise instruction; and in being a demanding, willing teacher and an aggressive role model. No school can duplicate the example that a good unit NCO leader makes on a young soldier.

Conduct Unit Instruction. An often-neglected area, unit instruction is possibly the most important tool used in developing NCOs. To be effective, the instruction has to be meaningful, well planned, and professionally presented. Design the classes to be progressive and to fill the needs of both the NCO and the unit. Match the training to the echelon that is getting the training (i.e., platoon sergeants receive training from the first sergeant on how to maintain duty rosters, or platoon sergeants teach their squad/team leaders how to supervise construction of a fighting position).

Use Unscheduled Time. An NCO may be given a requirement to read a book, view a lesson, or write a report when things get quiet, when on staff duty, during charge of quarters (CQ), or when without troops.

Complete Pre-execution Checks. The training plan must allocate time for pre-execution checks to ensure that equipment is ready and serviceable and that trainers are prepared. They also verify that training support resources are coordinated and available, and that leaders have conducted their initial risk assessment checks.

Perform Rehearsals. A rehearsal of a concept drill helps leaders see events as they will unfold in real time. Rehearsals are great tools for both soldiers and their leaders to understand how an event is scheduled to progress and what their duties are during the event.

SUBORDINATE TRAINING MANAGEMENT

One of the hardest, yet most important, tasks for an NCO to accomplish is determining what is important to train. There is not enough time in a year to train all the tasks and battle drills or to know all the collective tasks for every MOS, whether Active, Guard, or Reserve. When commanders develop their training plans, they allocate adequate time for subordinates to plan their own training events. By allowing time for each level, training can be conducted down to individual tasks.

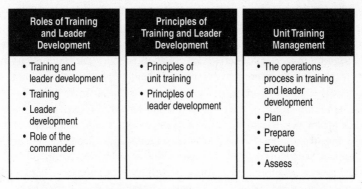

Roles of Training and Leader Development	Principles of Training and Leader Development	Unit Training Management
• Training and leader development • Training • Leader development • Role of the commander	• Principles of unit training • Principles of leader development	• The operations process in training and leader development • Plan • Prepare • Execute • Assess

Basic Principles of Unit Training and Leader Development

Using Lanes to Integrate Tasks

Once training tasks have been defined, use lanes to certify the individual, collective, and leader tasks as shown in the figure below. Lanes are drills designed to teach each unit task and to test collective, leader, and individual proficiency. Note the input to the design of the lanes.

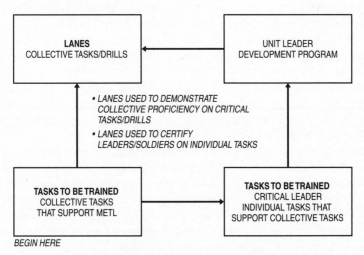

**Lane Development and Relationship between
Collective and Individual Tasks**

Lanes enable NCOs to train both themselves and their subordinates before going into the field. It is important to certify individual and leader skills prior to field exercises because soldiers react differently under stress. For example, a squad leader may demonstrate proficiency in determining which movement techniques to use with his or her squad on a sand table, but on a lane, when tired and thinking about the next hill, he or she may not be as proficient.

IDENTIFYING AND PRIORITIZING COLLECTIVE TASKS

There is nothing more important than a solid foundation in the leader and individual tasks. Collective tasks and missions fail because leader and individual tasks were not accomplished to standard. Fortunately, many of these tasks apply to more than one collective task, such as preparing a fragmentary order or navigating from one point to another. If a leader can control organic fires in a defense, then chances are he or she can do the same in an ambush.

A standardized list of mission-essential tasks (METL) are those that a unit could be asked to perform based on its organization or type of equipment. Units given a nonstandard mission will not change their standardized essential tasks but will decide what additional collective tasks they must train on before the mission.

The lowest echelon that can have an METL is a company. Platoons have supporting tasks that support the company METL (see figure). Leaders can use this flow chart to determine platoon supporting tasks. Using the company METL and commander's guidance, a collective task list can be developed that supports the company METL. Squad leaders, acting together and using the platoon tasks and the platoon leader's guidance, will then develop their own supporting tasks.

For example, the task *defend* is on the company METL. To support this mission-essential task, one of the platoon supporting tasks is *ambush*. There are thirty-one collective tasks in the MTP that support this task. Given competing requirements, this is probably too many to train. This means that the platoon leader, using the commander's intent and input from the other leaders in the platoon, must reduce the list to critical tasks to be accomplished when preparing the platoon training plan. It is far easier to evaluate a small number of critical tasks during an exercise than a laundry list that looks good but is impossible to execute. In this instance, the platoon leader selects *prepare for combat*, *move tactically*, and *consolidate and reorganize*, all of which apply to almost every mission the platoon does; and *occupy objective rally point* and *perform point ambush*, which apply to the mission itself.

Once one of the tasks is rated T (trained), establish a program to sustain the task and move on to another that is either untrained or needs practice. Some of the tasks, such as *prepare for combat* and *move tactically*, as well as the battle drills, have such an impact on other tasks that they must not be allowed to slip in proficiency. Depending on the training to be achieved, add or delete from the list as necessary. Some of the other tasks, such as the military operations in urban terrain (MOUT) tasks, are dependent upon the situation and might wait until all of the primary tasks are trained, unless they apply to the company METL.

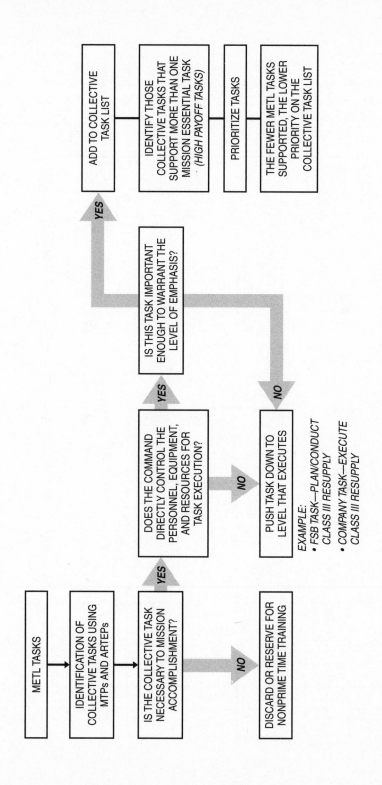

Identification of Tasks for the Collective Task List

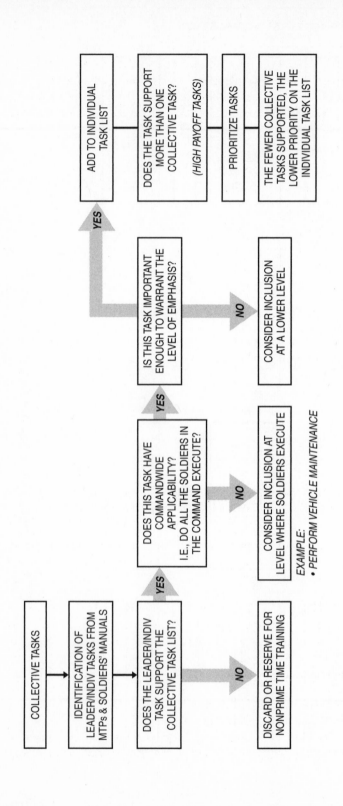

Identification of Tasks for the Leader/Individual Task List

PRINCIPLES OF UNIT TRAINING AND LEADER DEVELOPMENT

According to ADP 7-0, "Unit commanders are responsible for ensuring their units are capable of accomplishing their missions." NCOs must ensure that their soldiers are proficient at their required individual and collective tasks.

Principles of Unit Training

- Commanders and other leaders are responsible for training.
- Noncommissioned officers train individuals, crews, and small teams.
- Train to standard.
- Train as you will fight.
- Train while operating.
- Train fundamentals first.
- Train to develop adaptability.
- Understand the operational environment.
- Train to sustain.
- Train to maintain.
- Conduct multiechelon and concurrent training.

Principles of Leader Development

- Lead by example.
- Develop subordinate leaders.
- Create a learning environment for subordinate leaders.
- Train leaders in the art and science of mission command.
- Train to develop adaptive leaders.
- Train leaders to think critically and creatively.
- Train your leaders to know their subordinates and their families.

Principles of Unit Training and Leader Development

The leader development process was discussed in Chapter 7. Now we bring it all together to see how it applies to unit training. The principles of unit training in the table above describe leader responsibilities and how effective leaders will conduct training.

Commanders and Other Leaders are Responsible for Training. The unit commander is responsible for training and proficiency and for ensuring his units can perform the assigned missions. Subordinate leaders handle the proficiency of their units.

Noncommissioned Officers Train Individuals, Crews, and Small Teams. NCOs train enlisted soldiers, crews, and small teams; assist officers in training units; develop and conduct soldier training that supports the UTP; advise senior leaders; and coach and mentor other NCOs and junior officers.

Train to Standard. Individual and collective tasks each have an established Army standard, and leaders must always train to and enforce them.

NCOs must first know and understand the standards and strive to ensure their soldiers and units meet those requirements. If there is not an existing standard, then it is up to commanders to establish one and seek approval from the next higher command.

Train as You Will Fight. NCOs should train soldiers in an environment similar to that expected for the mission, including aspects such as terrain and culture. Training to fight should include role players or actual mission partners.

Train While Operating. Units should continue training while deployed or when conducting daily or routine operations. Both formal and informal After Action Reviews will help units improve performance and make necessary changes in tactics, techniques, and procedures that affect the operation.

Train Fundamentals First. Basic fundamentals include warrior and common tasks, battle drills, marksmanship, and fitness. All units must master and maintain these technical skills before they can accomplish mission assignments. Units that have mastered the fundamentals are in a better position to take on higher-level or more complex tasks that support the missions of other units.

Leaders Train to Develop Adaptability. Factors can change quickly in any operational environment. Developing the ability to adapt quickly requires training under complex, changing conditions, with minimal information available from which to make decisions. Leaders continue to mature during operational and field assignments and learn how to better adapt to new situations. Operational assignments enable leaders to develop on the job, and commanders often see improvements in confidence and maturity firsthand.

The figure above also lists the Army's principles of leader development. They are:

Lead by Example. Great leaders know and understand that they are role models for others and should reflect the desired leader characteristics embraced by the Army.

Develop Subordinate Leaders. An Army leader's primary responsibility is to develop subordinate leaders and train them to be successful tactically and technically and to be prepared to assume positions of greater responsibility.

Create a Learning Environment for Subordinate Leaders. Leaders establish an environment that allows subordinates to try different solutions to problems. Subordinates need to know that they can try new or innovative solutions to problems without fear of retribution. The environment should allow for honest mistakes instead of repeated or careless mistakes.

Train in the Art and Science of Mission Command. Effective leaders conduct operations while using mission command. They work to improve their ability to communicate intent, end-state, concept of operation, and understanding of the situation so that subordinates can take initiative consistent with the mission.

Train to Develop Adaptive Leaders. Training must allow leaders to respond to unexpected conditions in a positive and constructive way. Units cannot train on every task for every condition, so they must excel at a few tasks and be able to adapt to new ones.

Train Leaders to Think Critically and Creatively. Leaders must be able to analyze challenging problems, keep an open mind to different perspectives, and find unconventional solutions. Soldiers are not necessarily born with critical thinking and creativity; however, these skills can be developed.

Train Your Leaders to Know Their Subordinates and Their Families. Leaders should know their subordinates at least two levels down: their strengths, weaknesses, and capabilities. The Army trains leaders to understand and assist not only subordinates but also their families.

Digital Training Management System (DTMS)

The Digital Training Management System (DTMS) is a customized Web-based software application based on Army Field Manual 7-0, Training for Full Spectrum Operations. DTMS was developed for use at brigade level and below and is where the unit commander publishes the approved unit training plan. DTMS is used to plan, resource, and manage unit and individual training. The application collects and displays consolidated unit training, enabling leaders to track weapons qualification, physical fitness tests, mandatory training, and individual deployment tasks from enlistment to retirement. The system includes entries for collective and individual tasks, combined-arms training, the Army Universal Task List, and the Universal Joint Task List.

NCO Responsibilities

These regulations are important to NCOs in their roles as trainers. AR 600-20, Army Command Policy, prescribes policy on basic responsibilities of command, military discipline and conduct, and enlisted aspects of command. Paragraph 2-18 states that NCOs via the NCO Support Channel will support the chain of command by:

1. Transmitting, instilling, and ensuring the efficacy of the professional Army Ethic (see ADRP 1 for an explanation of the Army Profession and the Army Ethic).
2. Planning and conducting the day-to-day unit operations within prescribed policies and directives.
3. Training of enlisted soldiers in their military occupational specialty (MOS) as well as in the basic skills and attributes of a soldier.
4. Supervising unit physical fitness training and ensuring that unit soldiers comply with the weight and appearance standards of AR 600-9, The Army Body Composition Program, and AR 670-1, Wear and Appearance of Army Uniforms and Insignia.
5. Teaching soldiers the history of the Army, to include military customs, courtesies, and traditions.
6. Caring for individual soldiers and their families both on and off duty.

7. Teaching soldiers the unit mission and developing individual training programs to support the mission.
8. Accounting for and maintaining individual arms and equipment of enlisted soldiers and unit equipment under their control.
9. Administering and monitoring the NCO professional development program and other unit training programs.
10. Achieving and maintaining courage, candor, competence, commitment, and compassion.

ADP 7-0, Training Units and Developing Leaders, is the Army's standardized training document and along with ADRP 7-0 (see next paragraph) provides the necessary guidelines on how to plan, execute, and assess training at all levels. It lists the eleven Principles of Unit Training, which state that while commanders are responsible for all training, NCOs are the primary trainers of individuals, crews, and small teams. NCOs are responsible for "the proficiency of their respective organizations and subordinates."

ADRP 7-0, Training Units and Developing Leaders, assists commanders in planning, executing, and assessing unit training programs. Paragraph 2-3 states:

> Noncommissioned officers (NCOs) are the primary trainers of enlisted Soldiers, crews, and small teams. NCOs take broad guidance from their leaders; identify the necessary tasks, standards, and resources; and then plan, prepare, execute, and assess training. They ensure their Soldiers demonstrate proficiency in their individual military occupational specialty (commonly known as MOS) skills, warrior tasks, and battle drills. NCOs instill in Soldiers discipline, resiliency, the Warrior Ethos, and Army Values. In their assessment, NCOs provide feedback on task proficiency and the quality of the training.

Leaders allow enough time and provide the right resources to empower NCOs to plan and prepare, execute, and evaluate soldier training based on the NCO's evaluation of strengths and weaknesses.

TC 7-22.7 (FM 7-22.7), Noncommissioned Officer Guide, 7 April 2015, says that NCOs conduct the daily operations of the Army. Noncommissioned officers are trainers, mentors, advisors, and communicators, and as such they are expected to:
• Conduct complex tactical operations.
• Make intent-driven decisions.
• Operate in joint, interagency, and multinational environments.

NCOs are responsible for maintaining and enforcing standards as well as for installing a high degree of discipline. NCOs also perform the following duties:
• Process soldiers for enlistment.
• Teach basic soldier skills.

- Account for the care of soldiers.
- Set the example.

AR 350-1, Army Training and Leader Development, provides doctrine and guidelines for the synchronization of the Noncommissioned Officer Development Program (NCODP) into the Army's leader development program. The goal of the NCODP is to increase and sustain NCO combat readiness and complement the overarching Army NCODP.

A unit's NCODP is tailored to the unique requirements of the unit and supports the unit commander's leader training and leader development (LT/LD) program.

1. As with all LT/LD, the NCODP is a command responsibility, reflecting command priorities and expectations for leader training and leader development, and is typically managed by the command sergeant major or senior NCO in the organization.
2. The program is equally applicable to both TO&E and TDA units.
3. The NCODP consists of training programs—formal and informal, one-on-one or in groups—involving coaching as well as instruction, and will be fully integrated into the unit's overall training program.
4. The NCODP builds upon the contributions of the Army's Enlisted Personnel Management system (EPMS) and the sequential and progressive design of the NCOES. These two systems provide a valuable foundation for the development of NCOs; however, it is through the application of skills, knowledge, and abilities in the unit that soldiers become quality NCOs.

The objectives of the NCODP are:

- To develop and strengthen the skills, knowledge, and abilities to train, deploy, and lead soldiers in combat through battle-focused training.
- To develop NCOs who are self-aware, adaptive, competent, and confident.
- To realize the full potential of the NCO support channel.
- To foster a unit environment that enhances continued NCO leader development and encourages self-development as part of a lifelong learning process.

AR 350-1, Army Training and Leader Development, outlines essential training functions accomplished in units and complements ADP 7-0 and ADRP 7-0. The regulation explains training requirements and strategy that relate directly to unit training and the METL development process. Chapter 4, section 2, addresses noncommissioned officers as part of leader development. Section 3 of the same chapter covers Army policy on the following: soldier training programs, including weapons proficiency; physical fitness; nuclear, biological, chemical (NBC) training; the combat lifesaver program; code of conduct; personal recovery (PR) training; law of war training; and modernization training.

The Senior NCO as Master Trainer

Emerging prominently from current Army training doctrine is the relatively new role of senior NCOs as "master trainers." With fifteen to twenty-five years of service and the benefits of the Army's advanced NCO schools, our senior NCOs are the equivalent of the guild masters of the olden days.

Masters once trained midlevel journeymen in the more advanced skills of the craft and taught them how to train apprentices. Above all, the masters set the standards and enforced them within the trade. Those who did not meet the masters' standards were dismissed from the trade.

The commander can be viewed as the architect who designs the master blueprint for the organization. The subordinate officers take the blueprint and extract those parts necessary for successful completion of their parts of the operation. The senior noncommissioned officers at each echelon take the blueprints and determine which individual tasks are necessary to successfully complete the project and then, while they are at it, look to see whether there is an easier, more cost-effective way to achieve the same goals. Sometimes the best plans in the world are never accomplished because someone doesn't know how to lay the foundation.

The NCO master trainer must know exactly what is needed to meet the officer's "architect" specifications. Just as a master of masonry did not care whether he was building a cathedral or a post office—his only concern was to ensure that the blocks of stone were cut exactly to the architect's standards—the NCO ensures that standards are met on the individual tasks that contribute to mission accomplishment. Just as the architect relies on the contractor to transform the design into a building with doors, walls, and windows, the officer must rely on the noncommissioned officer to put his or her intent into tangible individual and leader training that will build the collective tasks and ultimately the unit METL.

As the Army's master trainers, senior NCOs at the battalion and company level have a responsibility for planning and executing to standard all individual and most small-unit training in a manner that is supportive of, and synchronized with, collective and leader tasks. This is why it is important for the commander and leaders to sequence their work and talk through each stage of their unit's training plan.

Basic NCO roles and responsibilities for each echelon must be well understood within the NCO support channel, as well as the organization's collective mission essential tasks during unit training. The entire NCO support channel, consisting of command sergeant majors, first sergeants, platoon sergeants, squad leaders, and other key NCOs, provides input on squad, section, team, and individual soldier proficiency for essential tasks for the commander's assessment.

Command Sergeant Major and Sergeant Major

The command sergeant major (CSM) is the senior NCO of the command at battalion level or higher. He or she executes policies and standards and advises the commander on the training, appearance, and conduct of enlisted soldiers.

Activities of the local NCO channel emanate from the command sergeant major, who administers the unit Noncommissioned Officer Development Program (NCODP).

The sergeant major (SGM) is typically the senior enlisted advisor and technical expert on a staff in operational and institutional units, as a Special Forces Team sergeant major, or as a staff member at the Sergeants Major Academy. Sergeants major often have the same experiences as command sergeants major and fill the role in the command sergeant major's absence.

First Sergeant and Master Sergeant

The position of first sergeant (1SG) is similar to that of the command sergeant major in importance, responsibility, and prestige. The first sergeant is in direct and daily contact with sizable numbers of enlisted personnel, requiring of him or her outstanding leadership and professional competence. The first sergeant is the senior NCO in companies, batteries, and troops. Although heavily involved in company administration, the first sergeant's principal duty is the individual training of enlisted members of the unit.

The master sergeant (MSG), like the sergeant major, is often the senior enlisted advisor and subject matter expert on a staff in operational and institutional units.

Platoon and Section Sergeants

Platoon and section sergeants are the primary enlisted assistant and advisor to the platoon or section leader. They work closely with squad, team, and crew leaders, and are responsible for individual training and caring for soldiers. At their levels, they are the first senior NCOs involved in the company METL development.

The platoon sergeant assists the commander with coaching the platoon leader, and therefore has an enormous effect on how that officer will perceive NCOs for the rest of his career. The platoon sergeant also takes charge of the platoon in the absence of the platoon leader.

Squad, Crew, and Team Leaders

Squad, crew, and team leaders are critical links in both the chain of command and the NCO support channel; they are the only enlisted leaders who serve that role. These noncommissioned officers work and live among their soldiers daily and are responsible for the training, welfare, and safety of their personnel. It is their job to ensure their soldiers meet Army standards and to train them to perform their assigned individual tasks. These NCOs enforce standards and professionally develop soldiers in their military specialty as well as in unit tasks.

Training

Commanders may use a number of techniques or events to ensure their units are trained to the specified standards. They use their knowledge of the assigned mission, the time available, and an understanding of their unit's capabilities to choose the best courses of actions (COA). Once the COA is selected, the commander seeks approval from the next higher commander during a training briefing. Once approved, it becomes the unit training plan (UTP).

The training briefing focuses exclusively on unit training and leader development planning and is a contract between commanders. The unit commander agrees to train as described in the plan, and the higher commander approves the plan and agrees to provide the resources necessary to execute it. The resulting written plan is the UTP. After the training briefing and the higher commander's approval, the unit commander publishes the plan via the Digital Training Management System (DTMS).

The training plan is created to assist the unit in reaching training proficiency and leader development within a given period. It lays out a series of training events that will lead the unit to that proficiency in select collective tasks. The plan often includes a unit training calendar that depicts major training events and the sequence in which they will be executed.

CONDUCTING THE AFTER ACTION REVIEW

After Action Reviews (AARs) help to provide soldiers and units with feedback on mission and task performances in training and in combat. After Action Reviews are one of the best times for a unit to use analysis to the fullest with a goal of developing critical thinking skills in soldiers and leaders. These types of critical looks are often led by facilitators and can be great tools for improving a unit's overall performance. When conducted at the end of a training event, the objective should be improvement of performance for future training or operations. AARs identify how to correct deficiencies, sustain strengths, and focus on specific METL training objectives. The spirit in which the AAR is given is key. The environment and climate surrounding an AAR must be one in which the soldiers and leaders openly and honestly discuss what actually transpired, in sufficient detail and clarity that everyone not only will understand what did and did not occur and why but also, most importantly, will have the strong desire to seek the opportunity to practice the task again.

The Squad After Action Review
A One-Act Play[*]

The rifle squad files quietly into the AAR tent—soldiers' eyes squint as they adjust to the change in light. Everyone shuffles around as they find chairs and drink water. Yellow keys are in all but three soldiers' multiple integrated laser engagement simulation (MILES) harnesses. The squad has just completed a tactical exercise in which it sustained heavy losses in an ambush.

Moments later the observer/controller enters the tent and walks to the front of the squad between the terrain table and charts.

---

[*]Published by Sgt. Maj. Robert S. Rush in *Army Trainer*, January 1994.

Observer/Controller (OC): "Welcome to the After Action Review for the Squad React to Ambush Lane. I am Sergeant First Class Hall and I walked with you on the lane as your observer/controller. Before we begin the AAR, let me orient you to the sand table. The top of the table is north, the blue string on the left is the Snake River, and the white powder is the primary trail through the area. The vegetation represents the wooded area, and the red string represents your start point and your direction of travel. Any questions on the sand table? No questions? Then let's begin.

If you look at the butcher paper, you will see the sequence for the AAR. Although your mission did not specify React to Ambush, the lane was set up for you to be ambushed while you were performing your mission. Okay! Squad leader, what was your mission?"

AAR BRIEFING SEQUENCE

Introduction
- Training objectives: Evaluate squad on drill *react to ambush* and supporting collective, leader, and individual tasks
- Map orientation

Planning
- Squad mission
- Higher intent
- Squad leader's plan
- OPFOR plan

Execution
- What happened?
- How it happened?
- Why it happened?
- Specific leader and individual tasks that affected mission accomplishment

Summarization

Squad leader (SL): "Sergeant Hall, my mission was to conduct an area recon along the river to detect OPFOR [opposing forces] infiltration routes in the area and destroy any enemy units of fewer than four men."

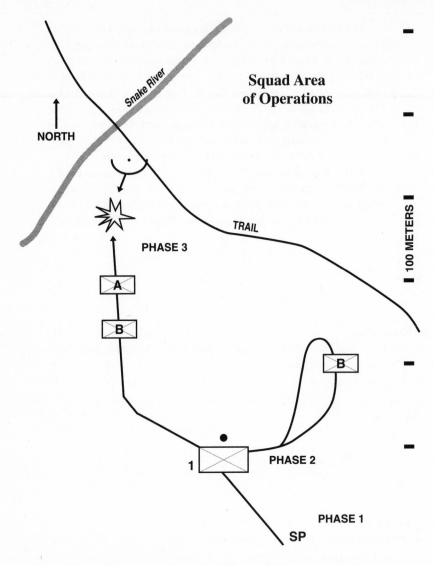

Squad Area
of Operations

OC: "What was your commander's intent?"

SL: "The commander wanted us to recon our zone's crossing sites and report all enemy in the area and destroy those elements that contained fewer than four men."

OC: "What was your plan?"

SL: "I planned to move my squad using traveling overwatch along the river. If I found a crossing site that was recently used, I'd set up an ambush along the trail the OPFOR was using."

OC: "OK, OPFOR commander, your plan."

OPFOR: "I had two four-man teams in the area—one walking along this trail and one in an ambush position by our previous crossing site. That team had an M60 machine gun. I hoped that the BLUFOR [blue forces, friendly forces] squads would find the trail used by the roving patrol and follow it back to the crossing site, where they would be ambushed. Since our maneuver area was small, each of the teams had the additional task of moving to the other's assistance if contact was made."

OC: "All right, squad leader, what happened?"

SL: "Well, we crossed the friendly forward lines about 0900."

OC: "What formation were you in?"

SL: "Traveling overwatch."

OC: "Really! B-Team leader, how close were you to A-Team?"

B-Team Leader (BTL): "About 20 meters."

OC: "Squad leader, what formation were you in?"

SL: "Traveling."

OC: "Continue with execution."

SL: "We had moved about 100 meters when the lead fire team saw movement to its 11 o'clock."

OC: "A-Team leader, what did you see?"

A-Team Leader (ATL): "I didn't really see soldiers, but the bushes were moving and there was no wind."

OC: "Good observation. Squad leader, what were your actions?"

SL: "I had the A-Team leader select a good overwatch position and then I had B-Team move right."

OC: "B-Team leader, what did the squad leader tell you?"

BTL: "He didn't really tell me. He pointed out where the enemy was and signaled that he wanted me to take my team into the trees on the right."

OC: "What did you do?"

BTL: "I brought my team into the trees and tried to turn to the left to get behind the enemy."

OC: "A-Team leader, could you follow the B-Team's movement?"

ATL: "No, I lost them as soon as they went into the woods."

OC: "Squad leader, did the B-Team do what you wanted them to do?"

SL: "Not really. I wanted Sergeant Charles to go to the woods and set up an overwatch so that I could move A-Team."

OC: "Everyone, what is the arm and hand signal for bounding overwatch or cover me?"

The squad members begin patting the top of their heads with their right hands.

OC: "What happened when the team disappeared into the woods?"

SL: "Well, I changed my plan and tried to follow their movement through the woods by the noise they made, but after about five minutes everything was quiet."

OC: "B-Team 203 Gunner, talk to me."

B-Team Gunner: "The woods were really thick; I had a hard time watching the team leader. I couldn't see Smith, the rifleman, on my left. I tried to signal the team leader that Smith was missing, but he wouldn't turn around. The team leader finally stopped and signaled that he heard noises to the front. We all froze. The noise got louder as whatever it was moved toward us, and then Smith broke out of the woods. He was lucky we didn't shoot him."

OC: "Smith, what happened?"

Smith: "I was having a hard time following Maxwell. Then I came to a small trail and followed it. It was a lot easier than breaking brush. After a couple of minutes I couldn't hear anyone, so I decided to double back through the woods. It was really quiet and I started to get nervous. Finally, I broke through the thicket and saw everyone pointing their weapons at me."

OC: "OK, OPFOR commander, what was happening on your side?"

OPFOR: "My team on the trail did not know they had been detected until we heard noises on our left flank. It sounded like they were coming close so my trail team moved back to the ambush site."

OC: "Squad leader, you now have your A-Team in an overwatch position, and your B-Team somewhere in the trees. What were your actions?"

SL: "I hoped that the B-Team would pop out of the woods where we could see them."

OC: "What would have happened if they had popped out in front of A-Team? How were you planning to control your organic fires?"

The A-Team rifleman speaks up: "We would have waited to identify them positively as the enemy."

OC: "Sounds good. Now, what would have happened if B-Team had engaged enemy in the woods? Could you have supported them?"

A-Team Rifleman: "Not from where we were."

OC: "B-Team leader, what happened then?"

BTL: "I went back to where we had entered the woodline, then SSG Thomas signaled me to bring my team back."

OC: "All right, squad leader, your squad is together again, what were your actions?"

SL: "I didn't want to go down the trail or through the thick woods on the right. On our left, where the river was, there looked like an area that was reasonably open but still offered some concealment."

OC: "Let's back up a bit. Were you in radio contact with your platoon leader?"

SL: "Yes, I had called him when we crossed the LD [line of departure]."

OC: "Not after?"

SL: "No, I didn't think it was necessary."

OC: "Don't you think that the platoon leader would want to know that you modified your route? He might find it difficult to support you if he doesn't know where you are."

SL: "I should have called the platoon leader with the change."

OC: "OK, let's continue. What movement formation were you in?"

SL: "Traveling overwatch."

OC: "Again, B-Team leader, what was the distance between you and A-Team?"

BTL: "About 20 meters."

OC: "Same mistake as before. Continue, Staff Sergeant Thomas."

SL: "We moved ahead another 200 meters toward the river. I could see the river through the trees to our front and a big trail on our right."

OC: "What was the terrain like?"

SL: "It was pretty much flat with thick trees and brambles along the river itself. On the right across the trail was a gentle rise into thicker trees."

OC: "What happened then?"

SL: "When the A-Team was about 50 meters from the edge of the woodline, we were ambushed. The enemy had a machine gun."

OC: "A-Team SAW [squad automatic weapon] gunner, what were your actions?"

A-Team SAW Gunner: "As soon as they started firing, I fired a couple of rounds and got down."

OC: "I see a yellow key in your harness. What happened?"

A-Team SAW Gunner: "I didn't get down fast enough."

OC: "A-Team leader, were you in grenade range?"

ATL: "No."

OC: "Squad leader, what were your actions?"

SL: "I wanted to break contact because they had a machine gun. I tried to maneuver B-Team to the flank so that they could support A-Team's withdrawal."

OC: "B-Team leader, what happened?"

BTL: "We were also in the kill zone. Two others and I were hit when we tried to move to the right."

OC: "OPFOR commander, tell me about your ambush."

OPFOR: "The squad basically paralleled the trail into our ambush site. We could see them for about 250 meters. I was able to reposition the ambush to where they were walking right into us. We held fire until they were just out of grenade range."

OC: "What did the friendly squad look like?"

OPFOR: "There was good dispersion among the team members but it seemed like the teams were right up on one another. I had the machine gun shoot from the left, where there was cover, to the right. I directed my rifleman to shoot at the leaders."

OC: "Good plan. Squad leader, how effective was the OPFOR plan?"

SL: "Well, just after I had told the B-Team to maneuver, I was hit."

OC: "Where were you located?"

SL: "Up by A-Team."

OC: "A-Team leader, looks like you were in charge. What did you do?"

ATL: "I knew that my SAW gunner was down. I called to Jones and Murphy to cover me. I crawled over, checked the gunner, and got his SAW. I then yelled out for everyone to bound back by buddy teams, A-Team first, while I covered them. I don't know how many were left in B-Team.

My two guys went back about 20 meters and set up another position. I was hit when I got up to pull back."

OC: "Sergeant Adams, you did a good job! A-Team 203 grenadier, what happened then?"

A-Team Grenadier: "Brown in B-Team pulled back past us and began supporting us from a small depression in the ground. Jones and I pulled back to that location also. Then you stopped the exercise."

OC: "Let's look at the next chart and talk about some of the collective/leader and individual tasks that applied to this mission. Some of the leader and individual tasks identified on the chart were not accomplished because of the way the lane went. Squad leader, how do you think you did analyzing the terrain?"

TASK: REACT TO AMBUSH

	Trained	Practice	Untrained
Collective Tasks			
React to ambush	T	P	U
Move tactically	T	P	U
Overwatch, support by fire	T	P	U
Leader Tasks			
Analyze terrain	T	P	U
Implement movement techniques	T	P	U
Control organic fires	T	P	U
Direct fire movement against an enemy position	T	P	U
Control fire team movement	T	P	U
Reorganize following contact	T	P	U
Individual Tasks			
Move as a member of a fire team	T	P	U
Move under direct fire	T	P	U
Select temporary fighting position	T	P	U
Engage targets	T	P	U
Employ hand grenades	T	P	U
Report enemy information	T	P	U

SL: "I thought it was OK at the beginning, but I sort of lost it when I had the problems with controlling B-Team."

OC: "We'll address that later. You told me earlier that you did not go through the woods for control reasons. But tell me, why didn't you use that slight high ground on the right to overwatch with?"

SL: "I didn't think that we would make contact when we did. I wasn't expecting an ambush."

OC: "OK, your mission is now to set up an ambush. Given that area, where would you put it?"

SL: "Probably where the OPFOR put it."

OC: "Squad leader, when do you use traveling, traveling overwatch, bounding overwatch?"

SL: "Not expected, possible, expected."

OC: "How long prior to the ambush had you seen the enemy?"

SL: "About ten minutes."

OC: "So contact was . . . "

SL: "Expected."

OC: "But you kept in traveling overwatch. Where were you in the formation?"

SL: "Just behind the A-Team, so I could control movement."

OC: "OK, B-Team leader, how far behind the squad leader were you?"

BTL: "Pretty close, I guess about 20 meters."

OC: "What formation have we just described?"

BTL: "Traveling."

OC: "Squad leader, when contact was made, how easy was it to control B-Team?"

SL: "Control was pretty easy. I could yell at him and he could hear. My only problem was that I was getting near misses from the ambush."

OC: "So you were suppressed along with A-Team?"

SL: "Yes."

OC: "Had you been back with B-Team and the interval about 50 meters, what do you think could have been different?"

SL: "It would have been a lot easier to maneuver my B-Team where they could support A-Team's pullback."

OC: "B-Team leader, how hard was it to control your fire team's movement?"

BTL: "It wasn't hard. My men followed where I went."

OC: "Grenadier, how about it?"

B-Team Grenadier: "The team leader needs to turn around more; some of the brush was really thick."

OC: "Valid point. Team leader, how far apart are you supposed to be from A-Team in traveling overwatch?"

BTL: "50 meters."

OC: "Why were you so close?"

BTL: "So I could hear the squad leader."

OC: "Squad leader, why where you so close to A-Team?"

SL: "So that I could control them better."

OC: "What kind of guidance did you give the A-Team leader?"

SL: "I would use my hand to point the direction that I wanted him to go."

OC: "No specific instruction?"

SL: "I guess not. I wanted to be up front in case something happened."

OC: "Do you trust the A-Team leader?"

SL: "Absolutely."

OC: "Then let him do what he's paid to do—lead a team. You lead a squad."

SL: "Roger."

OC: "B-Team leader, why did you go off into the woods with your team?"

BTL: "I believed that was what the squad leader wanted."

OC: "Are you sure?"

BTL: "Well, Staff Sergeant Thomas is new and I was trying to help him out."

OC: "Where did your expanding on his intent get the squad?"

BTL: "We lost contact with the enemy and forced the squad leader to change his plan."

OC: "The moral of the story is . . ."

BTL: "Let the squad leader plan for the squad."

OC: "OK, good. Now let's carry the discussion one step farther. What were your thoughts when the squad leader directed you to move to the right flank when contact was made?"

BTL: "I knew that we wouldn't make it, but decided since I hadn't really done what he wanted me to do earlier, that I would execute no matter what."

OC: "What should you have done?"

BTL: "What the squad leader wanted me to do was right. He didn't dictate *how*, but *what*. I should have bounded by buddy team in rushes to the flank. It probably would have taken a little longer, but we might have gotten out with fewer casualties."

OC: "The moral to this story is, work within the leader's intent—don't read into it more than there is. Leaders, what leader tasks do you need to relook before you go back out on the lane?"

SL: "I need to put myself in the enemy's place when I analyze terrain to determine better what movement techniques and formation to put my squad in. I also have to watch both teams to ensure that they are in the movement technique I want them in. I will also let the team leaders do their job."

OC: "Good critique. A-Team leader?"

ATL: "I should have thought to throw smoke before we began breaking contact. That probably would have stopped some of the casualties."

OC: "Good comment and good job. You really played heads-up out there today. B-Team leader?"

BTL: "Try not to second-guess the squad leader, and maneuver my team within his intent. I have also got to look back more often at my team to see if there are any problems."

OC: "Good. Now from left to right, how do you think you did on individual tasks?"

B-Team Rifleman: "Move as a member of a Fire Team—I need to stay in my lane and watch the team member on my right."

B-Team Grenadier: "Engage targets—the M203 is just extra weight when using MILES. We would have had a better chance of breaking the ambush if I could use TP [training practice] rounds or there was a laser device for the grenade launcher."

OC: "You're right, the problem with duplicating MILES kills with the grenade launcher makes it hard for the squad leader to use all of his systems properly. The squad leader has the same combat systems as the company commander: where the company has mortars, the squad leader has 203s; for direct fire the company has M60s and the squad SAWs; for maneuver the company has platoons and the squad fire teams. While there are fire markers for mortar fire, there is no system for 203s, and though using 203 TP is one solution to the problem, I don't consider it the approved one. As accurate as you gunners are, someone would get hurt fast. Enough said. Next man."

B-Team SAW: "I don't know what task this falls under, but we need to keep the team leader informed."

OC: "Bad news does not get better with age." (*Points to next soldier.*)

A-Team Rifleman: "Move as a member of a Fire Team—I thought our distance between members and control was good in A-Team."

A-Team Grenadier: "Engage targets—I agree with Maxwell, the B-Team grenadier. From my last position, I could have pasted the ambush site with 203 rounds without getting return fire."

A-Team SAW: "Move under direct fire—I need to get down quicker."

OC: "Those are all good comments. You all did a good job in identifying the critical tasks. Now, let's see how the leader and individual tasks affected the collective tasks.

"React to ambush—untrained; both fire teams were in the kill zone and the squad was unable to react. The squad suffered more than 30 percent casualties. Move tactically—untrained; the squad did not employ the movement technique ordered by the squad leader. The squad leader did not select the proper movement technique based on the likelihood of enemy contact. Initial contact with the enemy was made with the entire squad rather than with a team.

"SSG Thomas, although I rated your squad untrained for the two collective tasks observed, there were sparks of brilliance. Your plan was well thought out, and your squad showed enthusiasm and determination even when everything began to go wrong. I did not observe any systemic problems and those problems that were identified should be easily correctable. Are there any further comments from anyone? (*Pause*)

"If not, this concludes the AAR. I enjoyed walking with you and wish you good luck on the next mission. May the Force be with you."

MARKSMANSHIP

Every noncommissioned officer, regardless of MOS, must know how to train soldiers in basic rifle marksmanship skills. Marksmanship proficiency is critical and basic to soldiering and is required for any unit deployed to a wartime theater. There is nothing else as important to a soldier, or as important for teaching NCOs how to train soldiers, than conducting marksmanship training.

The unit's combat mission must be considered when establishing training priorities. This not only applies to the tasks selected for the unit's METL, but also to the conditions under which the tasks are to be performed. If a unit may be employed in an urban environment, the effects of range, gravity, and wind may not be too important, but automatic or burst fire, quick fire, and assault fire would be. The reverse may be true of a unit that expects to engage the enemy at long ranges with rifle fire.

Marksmanship training is an individual task, and as such should be led by NCOs to the greatest extent possible. Each echelon of NCO leadership has a different piece of the planning and training pie. The command sergeant major is primarily responsible for the collective individual weapons training of his or her unit. At the company level, the first sergeant is responsible for the collective individual weapons training of his or her company. Platoon sergeants train the trainer in the fundamentals of rifle marksmanship and ensure that the training is executed to standard, and the section/squad/team leaders, knowing their soldiers better than anyone else, are the primary trainers of their units.

Sergeant Major	First Sergeant	Platoon Sergeant	Section/ Squad Leaders
Plan/Resource	Resource/Evaluate	Evaluate/Train	Train

Scenario 1

"First Sergeant, we are having problems zeroing some of our soldiers. We may have to change the rotation times for the firing orders so that we can train the soldiers on how to achieve tight shot groups."

Dry firing is becoming a lost art within the US Army. The term "dry fire" means to simulate the firing of live rounds with an empty weapon. Soldiers given proper dry-fire training move to the firing line and assume good, comfortable firing positions. They fully understand the aiming process, and breath control and correct trigger squeeze are second nature. Dry fire is an excellent training technique to use as concurrent training, opportunity training, or as a primary technique to maintain marksmanship proficiency.

While initial dry-fire training should focus on establishing a steady position, each phase should involve the full simulation of firing a shot—establishing a steady position, aim, breathing, and trigger squeeze.

If the firer, who is the best judge of position, can hold the front sight post "rock" steady through the fall of the hammer, this indicates a good position. Once the supported position has been mastered, the firer should work on the various unsupported positions.

Some of the other exercises that can be used during dry fire are the shadow box method (used to verify proper aiming), the dime/washer exercise (used to practice trigger squeeze), and the use of the Riddle sighting device (used to determine proper sight picture), all of which are explained in FM 3-22.9, Rifle Marksmanship, M16-/M4-Series Weapons.

Scenario 2

"Sir, we don't have enough time to run all the soldiers through the qualification course on the EST 2000. We need more time!"

The Engagement Skills Trainer (EST) 2000 provides initial and sustainment marksmanship training, static unit collective gunnery and tactical training, and shoot/don't shoot training. The EST 2000 is a computerized training device that very closely approximates the live firing of an M16A2 rifle and the M4 carbine, and a host of other military weapons. It's an excellent marksmanship training device that can be used for skill development, problem diagnosis, remedial training, and evaluation. However, it's not a cure. Overreliance on the EST 2000 or other simulators while avoiding more conventional means of preparatory marksmanship training wastes good marksmanship training time. Use the EST 2000 or other computerized systems as diagnostic devices, letting each soldier spend a few minutes on them to determine shooting problems and then relying on more conventional methods to help correct those problems.

Scenario 3

"Specialist Jones is missing the farthest target. He's the best shot. There must be something wrong with the target mechanisms."

For many years, the Army's primary marksmanship program meant zeroing at 25 meters and practicing and qualifying on pop-up targets that provided only hit-or-miss data. This, coupled with the simplified approach to training that taught that the M4 bullet had a flat trajectory not influenced by wind and gravity, made it difficult for leaders to learn about bullet trajectory. Without knowledge of where bullets were hitting, target misses were blamed on bad rifles, bad shooting, or bad target mechanisms.

Scenario 4

"Sergeant Jones, look at my shot group. What am I doing wrong?"

Training is more effective when leaders are directly involved in training their soldiers. First-line leaders, assisted by—if not one themselves—marksmanship trainers (in FM 23-9 known as instructor trainers), must teach and coach their own soldiers during basic rifle marksmanship and on the firing line. A good instructor-trainer must understand the training phases and techniques for developing marksmanship skills. FM 3-22.9, Rifle Marksmanship, M16-/M4-Series Weapons, says that the instructor-trainer must possess the following qualifications:

1. *Knowledge.* Have a thorough knowledge of the rifle, proficiency in firing, and a thorough understanding of FM 3-22.9 and supporting manuals.
2. *Patience.* Relate to the soldier calmly, persistently, and patiently.
3. *Understanding.* Enhance success and understanding by emphasizing close observance of rules and instructions.
4. *Consideration.* Enhance soldier enthusiasm for firing by encouraging firing abilities.
5. *Respect.* Soldiers respect technical expertise, especially those who are alert for mistakes and patiently make needed corrections.
6. *Encouragement.* Encourage soldiers by convincing them to achieve good firing performance through practice.

An added benefit to marksmanship training is that it is one of the best methods with which to train subordinate leaders in how to train soldiers.

Scenario 5

"The Commanding General is going to visit us at the qualification range Friday."
"Oh no, another dog-and-pony show!"

Many believe that "dog-and-pony" shows are a waste of time, and they are when it comes to pretty charts, designated parking areas, and briefing NCOs whose primary mission is to brief the VIPs. However, there are good points to such shows.

NCOs are prepared to teach classes, and teach them well, because they have done their homework. Soldiers get more out of training because sound training was conducted. We should consider soldiers the VIPs.

Other methods could be used to get better training out of the meager time and resources we have available for marksmanship training. Remember that an effective marksmanship program will reflect the interest that we place in it. We should provide the necessary refresher training to maintain standards, while conducting new and more advanced training to continue the improvement of individual shooting skills. A good program will focus on the tasks most important for mission accomplishment and will advance the soldier from more basic skills to those that are more complex. This will result in all soldiers being able to perform all shooting skills required in combat, the ultimate live-fire range.

SERGEANT'S TIME TRAINING
NCOs develop and conduct training for their subordinates and assist officers in training units. They are training advisors as well as teachers. According to ADRP 7-0, Training Units and Developing Leaders, paragraph 2-4, "Sergeant's time training (known as STT) is a common approach to NCO-led training events. NCOs conduct sergeant's time training to standard, not time."

Soldier's Manual of Common Tasks Warrior Skills
Soldier Training Publications (STPs) are Army field manuals that guide and support individual soldier training. The primary manuals that commanders and trainers use are STP 21-1-SMCT and STP 21-24-SMCT. Consult them any time you intend to plan, conduct, sustain, and evaluate individual or warrior task training. STP 21-1-SMCT, Soldier's Manual of Common Tasks, Warrior Leader, Skills Level 1, includes the Army Warrior Training Plan for warrior skills level (SL) 1 and task summaries for SL 1 critical common tasks that support unit wartime missions. STP 21-24-SMCT, Soldier's Manual of Common Tasks, Warrior Leader, Skill Levels 2, 3, and 4, is for noncommissioned officers.

Warrior Tasks and Battle Drills (WTBD)
Warrior Tasks and Battle Drills (WTBD) were initially identified from the STPs to focus unit and individual training on tasks required on the battlefield. Warrior Tasks are individual skills that are critical to a soldier's survival. The tasks are grouped by subject areas such as shoot-move-communicate, weapons training, or first aid. Battle drills are groups of skills intended to teach a unit to react and survive in typical combat situations. Examples include how to react to an ambush or how to evacuate injured personnel.

WTBDs focus training on combat expectations and increase training difficulty. Lessons learned are a large factor in changes to WTBDs—commanders must be aware that the enemy adapts quickly. Individual soldier task training will change more rapidly because of observations in fluid operational environments.

Leader Book
Unit commanders identify critical soldier tasks that support the unit's mission-oriented tasks. It is important that noncommissioned officers fully understand those collective tasks and how the individual tasks support them. Because of limited training time, unit leaders normally cannot train and stay proficient at

every task, so training must focus primarily on those important to the soldier's duty position. According to TC 25-30, A Leader's Guide to Company Training Meetings, a leader book is a tool maintained by leaders at all levels to record and monitor soldier proficiency. Noncommissioned officers should use it to record MOS-specific tasks that support the unit METL and to keep track of each of their soldiers' proficiency.

The design and makeup of leader books vary by unit and mission but they usually contain information such as administrative data, common task training status, and a crosswalk of individual training tasks and how these support the unit's METL. A leader book also records personal information that leaders need to know about what affects soldiers' training performance to tailor training to meet their soldiers' personal needs. The information recorded can also be adapted to meet each unit's specific needs. With a leader book, NCOs can quickly identify weaknesses and plan and conduct training to improve overall proficiency. Example leader books are available at https://atn.army.mil/dsp_template.aspx?dpID=450.

9

Training at Service Schools

America's Army is the envy of the world. Other nations look to model our tanks, our helicopters, our equipment, but the one area they wish they could model most is our NCO Corps. Those nations recognize the depth and maturity of our corps and the value of our education system. We look at our past heritage for inspiration, to today's heroes for motivation, and then look to the future warrior and ask "what if." Sergeants continue to pass the torch of training, education, values, and ethos from our Greatest Generation to today's Next Greatest Generation.

—former Sergeant Major of the Army Kenneth O. Preston

THE ARMY SCHOOL SYSTEM

The Army School System (TASS) is a multipart organization made up of Active and Reserve Component institutions that conduct soldier and leader training. For enlisted soldiers, TASS conducts initial military training, reclassification training, NCO professional development training and education, and functional training through both in-school resident training and distributed-learning courses. In the Reserve Components, TASS units and schools are aligned and linked to appropriate branches and training proponents.

Noncommissioned Officer Education System (NCOES)

The Noncommissioned Officer Education System (NCOES) is an integral part of the Enlisted Personnel Management System (EPMS) and provides the Army with trained leaders and technicians. The NCOES applies to all enlisted personnel of all components of the Army and is an integrated system of resident training—service school and NCO academy—that, combined with supervised on-the-job training, individual study, and on-the-job experience, provides job-related training for NCOs throughout their careers. The NCOES is designed to provide progressive, continuous training from the primary through the senior level.

NCOES and Structured Self Development
Centralized Promotions

YEARS OF SERVICE

| 2 | 5 | 8 | 2 | 14 | 17 | 20 | 23 |

GUIDED SELF-INITIATED	GUIDANCE SELF-INITIATED	GUIDANCE SELF-INITIATED	GUIDANCE SELF-INITIATED	GUIDANCE SELF-INITIATED		GUIDANCE SELF-INITIATED
SSD-I	SSD-II	SSD-III		SSD-IV		SSD-V

SELF DEVELOPMENT

B
C
T
//
A
I
T

ASSIGNMENT EXPERIENCES /// DEPLOYMENTS /// REAL-WORLD PROBLEM SOLVING

WLC	ALC	SLC	MLC*	SMC
	MOS/Mission Functional Courses	Drill SGT // Recruiter // OC // AC/RC	TT // PRT	
		BSNCOC		CSMD ELC

OPERATIONAL

INSTITUTIONAL

| BASIC | SENIOR | CAREER | C SEL KEYSTONE |

MOS Competency → MOS Mastery/CMF Competency → CMF Mastery/Operational Competency

* At the time of this writing, a Master Leader Course is in development.

Six skill levels representing progressively higher levels of performance capability, experience, and grade characterize the EPMS, and six levels of training have been established in support of these skill levels. Completion of initial entry training provides the soldier with the foundation of professional and technical knowledge needed to perform at the first duty station; with subsequent individual training in the unit, the soldier qualifies at skill level 1. The next four levels (eventually five) of training (primary, basic, advanced, master, and senior) are taught through the NCOES.

As an NCO you, as well as your soldiers, must realize the importance of NCOES to professional development and career progression. Do not look at attendance as "a break" from routine duties. Most soldiers can easily pass any phase of NCOES, but to score in the top 20 percent is an achievement. Graduation from the school and having board members see that you were among the best are both discriminators. While in school, help those around you who need it, as you are all working together toward a common goal: graduation.

Graduation from the appropriate level NCOES school is a prerequisite for promotion. Full linkage of NCOES to promotions ensures that NCOs acquire the appropriate skills, knowledge, and duty performance needed to assume the duties and responsibilities of the next higher grade. The connection aligns NCO professional and leader development with the Army philosophy of "select, train, promote."

Commanders and their senior NCOs at every level understand that NCOES training must receive high priority and that soldiers must attend school when scheduled. A strong, competent, and highly motivated NCO Corps is every leader's responsibility, and promotion linkage ensures training the right soldier at the right time for the next level of leadership. Keeping a soldier away from school because he or she is needed hurts both the unit and the soldier— one because the unit never learns to do without its hard chargers, and the other because the soldier stagnates in rank.

Command sergeants major, in concert with Army selection boards, ensure that soldiers who need NCOES training receive it. Soldiers who are not otherwise qualified will not be sent for training merely to fill a quota. In the past, the Army's NCO academies were plagued by soldiers who did not want or deserve to be there. The following guidelines apply in the selection of noncommissioned officers for training:

1. The NCOs must meet course prerequisites and have demonstrated high levels of performance, mental capacity, aptitude, and self-discipline that clearly indicate potential for continued development.
2. They must be fully qualified to perform tasks at their current skill level, be recommended by their chain of command, have their personal and financial affairs in order, have required clothing and equipment, and be mentally and physically prepared for all course requirements.

Enlisted soldiers who have been selected for promotion and are performing in, or pending assignment to, duty positions for which the training is designed will be scheduled to attend NCOES courses. Attendance will be on a priority basis as allocations become available. The following training priorities ensure that the NCOES meets the needs of the Army and the development needs of the NCO:

1. The first priority is for soldiers who have been selected for promotion and are performing in duty positions for which the training is established.
2. The second priority is for soldiers who have been selected for promotion and are pending assignment to a duty position in their primary MOS for which the training is established.

Human Resources Command (HRC) schedules soldiers for resident training at Advanced Leader Course (ALC), Senior Leader Course (SLC), and the US Army Sergeants Major Course (SMC), while local selection authority governs attendance at Warrior Leader Course (WLC). At the time of this writing, the Army was developing a Master Leader Course.

Soldiers are selected for WLC based on a battalion-level (or equivalent) order of merit list. To be eligible, a soldier must accomplish the following:

- Have trained on 70 percent of all MOS tasks in his or her individual soldier's job book within the past six months.
- Have passed the Army Physical Fitness Test within the past six months.
- Meet the weight standards.
- Be eligible for reenlistment.
- Be recommended by his or her unit commander.

Time Remaining in Service

Regulatory guidance on the service remaining requirements (SRR) obligation incurred after attending military schools is found in AR 614-200, Enlisted Assignments and Utilization Management, Chapter 4. Soldiers who are selected for and attend service schools incur an SRR obligation based on the length of the course, which begins upon completion of the course. Soldiers selected for special training programs must meet the SRR obligation prescribed for the program selected; the maximum obligation is thirty-six months. NCOES courses require an obligation of six months, except the Sergeants Major Course, which incurs a twenty-four-month obligation. For example, to attend the Advanced Leader Course (ALC), soldiers must have six months remaining on their enlistment from the time they graduate. Soldiers with insufficient time remaining in service (TRS) to meet the prescribed SRR obligation must reenlist or extend before attending training. Voluntary retirements will not be approved for soldiers until after they have completed all SRR obligations, including those resulting from school attendance.

Profile Policy (NCO Course Attendance)

Soldiers may not attend NCOES courses with a temporary profile. If they are scheduled for an NCOES course and are on a temporary profile, or if the recovery period of the profile overlaps with their course report date, they should immediately notify their unit school's NCO and their installation training office, who will in turn notify the HRC NCOES section to cancel the reservation. Soldiers may attend NCOES courses with a permanent designator 2 (P2) physical profile with a copy of DA Form 3349 as long as they can meet the minimum course graduation requirements. A soldier's doctor must provide written documentation that the soldier can participate in and perform all physical training within the course, including an Army Physical Fitness Test, marching, and field training. Soldiers may attend NCOES courses with a permanent designator 3 (P3) or permanent designator 4 (P4) physical profile with a copy of DA Form 3349 that has been reviewed by a medical screening board. Soldiers who have not been medically screened and classified with appropriate limitations may not attend NCOES courses. Soldiers who have been before a medical screening board, awarded medical limitations, and allowed to retain their MOS or reclassified will be eligible to attend NCOES and will be required to meet course prerequisites up to the limits of their profile.

Structured self-development (SSD) is required studying that helps soldiers supplement their development when they are between two leader development courses, during assignments in operational units, and during attendance at learning institutions. Soldiers are automatically enrolled in the appropriate SSD upon completion of select NCOES courses and generally are allowed up to three years to complete each level. For more discussion on self-development and SSD, see Chapter 10.

Pre-execution Checklist

TRADOC Form 350-18-2-R-E, The Army School System (TASS) Unit Pre-Execution Checklist, is a pre-enrollment requirement for all TASS courses and institutions except the resident Sergeants Major Course. The first-line leader and soldier attending training both must initial each line item no earlier than ninety days before the start of the class. The unit then fills in all information, after which the soldiers attending sign and date, followed by the commander or designated signature authority.

This checklist is found in US Army Training and Doctrine Command (TRADOC) Regulation 350-18, The Army School System (TASS).

NONCOMMISSIONED OFFICER ACADEMIES

Noncommissioned Officer Academies (NCOA) conduct training in challenging and leadership-intensive environments. First created in the 1950s, they have matured over time but have always been designed to reinforce leadership and professional skills as part of student academic training. While enrolled in these institutions, attending studies and training is the soldier's primary daily routine. The mission of NCO Academies is to provide NCOES training to qualified soldiers, to train them in the fundamentals of leadership, to prepare them to train subordinates, to offer them increased educational opportunities, to prepare them to work in all kinds of environments, to instill them with increased self-confidence and a sense of responsibility, and to provide selected personnel with specific critical MOS training. To ensure that soldiers are provided equal opportunity to attend NCOES courses, the NCOA network has been divided into geographic training regions. If certain NCOES training is not available within a region, that region's student population may receive its training at the nearest NCOA that offers the training. Appendix E of AR 350-1 lists the NCOA regions.

NCOA courses do not award an MOS, an additional skill identifier (ASI), or a higher skill level. Leadership courses offered in academies emphasize training management and leadership skills that focus on senior and subordinate relationships, the needs of the soldier, discipline, counseling, and techniques of soldier motivation. While NCOAs ensure that students maintain high standards of military courtesy, conduct, and fitness, the level of discipline should not detract from the learning environment.

Overweight soldiers who report to any of the NCOES courses are tape-tested by instructors to determine body fat content. If they are over the limit for their age, gender, and height, they are denied enrollment and sent home. Overweight soldiers returning to the unit may be barred from reenlistment for failing an Army school, be removed from any promotion list, and might ultimately be separated if they fail to make satisfactory progress in the weight-control program. Almost as important, the funds wasted on the round-trip airfare could have been used for another soldier.

Listed below are the Army's NCO academies (listed by location) with their courses and websites, which contain welcome letters and provide packing lists, directions, phone numbers, and mailing addresses.

NCO Academy Location	Courses Taught
Fort Bliss, TX (NCOA)	
https://usasma.bliss.army.mil/page3.asp?id=43	WLC
East Fort Bliss, TX (USASMA)	
https://usasma.bliss.army.mil	SMC
Fort Benning, GA	
www.benning.army.mil/tenant/whinsec/ncoAcademy.html	WLC/ALC/SLC
Fort Bragg, NC	
www.bragg.army.mil/18abc/ncoa/Pages/default.aspx	WLC
Fort Campbell, KY	
www.campbell.army.mil/units/ncoa/Pages/home.aspx	WLC
Fort Drum, NY	
www.drum.army.mil/NCOAcademy/Pages/Home.aspx	WLC
Fort Eustis, VA	
www.eustis.army.mil/ncoa	ALC/SLC

(*continued*)

NCO Academy Location	Courses Taught
Fort Gordon, GA	
www.signal.army.mil/index.php/signal-units/rncoa	ALC/SLC
Fort Hood, TX	
www.hood.army.mil/ncoa	WLC
Fort Huachuca, AZ	
https://www.ikn.army.mil/apps/IKNWMS/Default.aspx?webId=2244	ALC/SLC
Fort Jackson, SC	
www.ssi.army.mil/ncoa	ALC/SLC
Fort Lee, VA	
www.alu.army.mil	ALC/SLC
Fort Leonard Wood, MO	
www.wood.army.mil/newweb/mncoa	WLC/ALC/SLC
Fort Lewis, WA	
https://jbextra.lewis-mcchord.army.mil/NCOA	WLC
Fort Meade, MD	
www.signal.army.mil/index.php/nco-academy-detachment-welcome	ALC/SLC
Fort Polk, LA	
http://sill-www.army.mil/polkncoa	WLC
Fort Rucker, AL	
www.rucker.army.mil/usaace/ncoa/index.html	ALC/SLC
Fort Sam Houston, TX	
www.cs.amedd.army.mil/ncoa.aspx	ALC/SLC
Fort Sill, OK	
http://sill-www.army.mil/usancoa	WLC/ALC/SLC
Fort Stewart, GA	
www.stewart.army.mil/units/home.asp?u=NCOA	WLC
Fort Richardson, AK	
www.usarak.army.mil/ncoa	WLC
7th Army NCO Academy	
www.eur.army.mil/jmtc/Organization/NCO_Academy/NCOA.html	WLC
8th Army NCO Academy	
http://8tharmy.korea.army.mil/NCOA	WLC
JAG Legal Center and School	
https://www.jagcnet.army.mil	ALC/SLC
NCOA Hawaii	
www.usarpac.army.mil/NCOA	WLC

Updates can be found at https://www.hrc.army.mil/Enlisted.

Warrior Leader Course (WLC)

The Warrior Leader Course (WLC) is a branch-immaterial, basic leadership course that provides soldiers with an opportunity to acquire the skills, knowledge, and experience needed to lead a team-size element and serves as the foundation for further training and development. This four-week course is conducted at NCOAs worldwide. Training focuses on self-discipline; professional skills; leading, disciplining, and developing soldiers; and caring for soldiers and their families. It culminates with an extensive field environment situational training exercise (STX). Other areas include the planning, executing, and evaluating of individual or team training, and the planning and executing of missions or tasks assigned to a team-size unit. Successful completion of WLC establishes the foundation for further training and leader development. Small-group leaders assess the students' leadership potential and evaluate their ability to apply lessons learned and effectively lead their classmates in a tactical environment. On 1 April 2013 SSD I completion became a course prerequisite to enroll in the WLC.

There are abbreviated two-week versions of this course offered to Army Reserve and National Guard soldiers and to support rapid deployments of active-duty soldiers. Sergeants are required to attend this course before consideration for promotion to staff sergeant, or are given a temporary waiver.

Attendance at WLC is mandatory for promotion to sergeant. Priority of attendance goes to sergeants who have not previously attended, E-4 promotable (P), and E-4 serving in leadership positions. Soldiers may appear before promotion boards, but they cannot be promoted until they complete WLC. Conditional promotions may occur when a soldier meets the cutoff score while operationally deployed.

Noncommissioned Officer Education System Equivalency for WLC. US Army Human Resource Command (HRC) is authorized to grant equivalent credit for the WLC based on completion of sister service courses listed below.

Any of the several Marine Corps NCO courses above the Corporal's Course
Officer Candidate School (AC/RC OCS from any service)
Officer Basic Course from any service
Officer Advanced Course from any service
CAS3 from any service
Command and General Staff Officer's Course from any service
Reserve Officers Training Corps Advanced Camp from any service
Warrant Officer Candidate School (Army or USMC only)

The following courses, among many others, are not equivalent to AC WLC: any nonresident corresponding study programs, courses taught at the USMC institute in Washington, D.C., or any US Air Force or US Navy NCO training.

Individuals requesting equivalent credit must submit the request through command channels to Human Resources Command via email to usarmy.knox .hrc.mbx.epmd-ncoes-operations@mail.mil.

WARRIOR LEADERS COURSE PACKING LIST
WLC 600-C44

ALL OTHER PACKING LISTS DATED BEFORE 1 October 2013 ARE OBSOLETE

Mandatory Uniform Items
*See AR 670-1 Proper wear and appearance of Army uniforms and insignia.
___1 Each—Military Common Access Card (CAC) ID **Know Your Pin#
___2 Each—IPFU, Short Sleeve
___2 Each—IPFU, Shorts
___1 Each—IPFU, Sweat Pants
___1 Each—IPFU, Jacket
___1 Pair— Running Shoes
___1 Each—Reflective Belt (Orange)
___4 Pairs—White Socks (Ankle-length / No Logos or Strips)
___1 Each—ACU, Patrol Cap w/ Rank and Name Plate
___4 Each—ACU Coat w/ Minimum Required Patches
___4 Each—ACU Trousers
___1 Each—Rigger Belt (Tan w/ Black Buckle)
___4 Pairs—OD Green or Black Socks
___2 Pairs—Combat Boots
___5 Each—Tan Undershirt
___5 Each—Undergarments

Mandatory TA50 Items
* Military issued TA50 only.
___1 Each—Duffle Bag
___1 Each—Set—Ear Plugs w/ Carrier
___1 Each—Red/White Lens Flashlight
___1 Each—Field Pack w/ Frame LCI (Rucksack)
___2 Each—1qt Plastic Canteen w/ Cover
___1 Each—Cup, Water Canteen
___1 Each—Camelback or Similar Hydration System (100oz)
___1 Each—Advanced Combat Helmet (ACH) w/ ACU Cover and Band
___1 Each—First Aid (IFAK) Case w/ Pressure Bandage
___1 Each—Small Arms Ammo Case (M-16) MOLLE Equivalent
___1 Each—Belt, Pistol, Individual, MOLLE Equivalent
___1 Each—Ballistic Eye Protection
___1 Pair— Gloves Tactical
___1 Each—Cleaning Kit, Weapon
___1 Each—Poncho
___1 Each—Poncho Liner
___1 Each—Lensatic Compass w/ Case
___7 Each—Weapon Magazines, 30 Rounds M16
___1 Each—IBA or IOTV (DCU Unauthorized)
___1 Each—Assault Pack (ACU, OD Green, or Black NO LOGOS)
___1 Each—Entrenching Tool w/ Carrier Case

(continued)

WARRIOR LEADERS COURSE PACKING LIST *continued*

___1 Each—Mat, Sleeping
___1 Each—Modular Sleeping System
___1 Each—Bag, Waterproof

Mandatory Classroom Equipment Items
___1 Pack—Map Pens Permanent w/ Correction Pen
___1 Each—Protractor (GTA 5-2-12)
___1 Each—Note Book (Standard Size)
___1 Each—Note Pad (Pocket Size)
___2 Each—Black Ink Pens
___2 Each—Pencils #2 or Mechanical
___2 Each—Permanent Black Pen
___1 Each—STP 21-1-SMCT, 9/11/2012 SOLDIER'S MANUAL OF COMMON
TASKS WARRIOR SKILLS LEVEL 1

Mandatory Personal Items
___2 Each—Pad Lock (Key or Combination)
___22 Day Supply—Personal Hygiene Kit (Toothbrush, Soap, Shaving, etc.)
___1 Pair— Shower Shoes
___2 Each—Towel
___1 Each—Wash Cloth
___5 Each—Wire Hangers
___22 Day Supply—Laundry Soap
___1 Each—Laundry Bag
___1 Each—Whistle, Ball

Optional Items
Multi-Tool or Leatherman
Sunscreen
Lip balm
Index Cards (5X7)
Post-it Notes
Blank CD-RW/DVD-RW (Virus Free)
Highlighters

Advanced Leader Course (ALC)
Combat Arms (CA)/Combat Support (CS)/Combat Service Support (CSS) Advanced Leader Course (ALC) is conducted at proponent service schools. Successful completion of ALC is a prerequisite to be considered for promotion to sergeant first class. Training lengths vary from two to nineteen weeks; with an observer/controller (OC), attendance is currently aligned with Army Force Generation (ARFORGEN). ALC is hands-on, performance-oriented training with instruction in the MOS-specific areas as well as in troop-leading procedures, physical fitness, and safety training. Priority for ALC goes to a staff sergeant by date of rank, and then to a sergeant (P) by promotion points.

All soldiers attending ALC are scheduled via the Army Training Requirements and Resources System (ATRRS). The system provides HRC with an order of merit listing of soldiers eligible to attend ALC. This listing comes from criteria established by Headquarters, Department of the Army. The report enables HRC to identify the best-qualified soldiers for training and nominate them to their commander for verification that the soldiers are qualified to attend ALC. Commanders have the option of canceling the nomination if the soldier is unqualified. If the commander cancels the nomination, HRC will then select a replacement.

ATRRS has a history file showing every soldier scheduled; whether the soldier arrived for training or was a no-show; and if the soldier was released, failed, or graduated. It is better to be a cancellation than a no-show; if there is a cogent reason you cannot attend, make sure your chain of command notifies the NCOES section.

You get out what you put into it. STAFF SGT. JASON STADEL, *NCO JOURNAL*

Senior Leader Course (SLC)

The Senior Leader Course (SLC) is a branch-specific course that provides an opportunity for soldiers selected for promotion to sergeant first class to acquire the leadership, technical and tactical skills, knowledge, and experience needed to train and lead platoon-size units. Training builds on experience gained in previous training and operational assignments, with emphasis on technical and advanced leadership skills and knowledge of military subjects. Branch schools and selected training battalions conduct this course in a live-in learning environment, where possible, with soldiers attending in a temporary duty status.

HRC centrally manages SLC selection through the Sergeant First Class/Senior Leader's Course Selection Board. HRC announces the zone of consideration before each board convenes. In keeping with "select, train, promote," the Army sends NCOs to SLC only after selection for promotion to sergeant first class, with soldiers normally attending SLC within a year after the release of the appropriate sergeant first class selection list. Scheduling is done by the soldier's career branch, with the priority for SLC attendance given to sergeants first class and staff sergeants (P) who have not already attended. All soldiers selected for promotion to sergeant first class who have not previously attended SLC are automatic selectees. Additionally, there may be an alternate SLC selection list based on the number of NCOs selected for promotion to sergeant first class. Commanders may defer NCOs scheduled to attend SLC only once for operational reasons; other than this one operational deferment, the only deferment requests considered are for medical or compassionate reasons. No-shows at SLC for any reason other than those mentioned above result in the NCO losing his or her promotion status.

An NCO must be an SLC graduate to be considered for promotion to master sergeant. All sergeants first class must successfully complete SLC in order to be considered for promotion to master sergeant.

Master Leader Course (MLC)
The Army currently is developing and piloting a Master Leader Course (MLC) designed to prepare newly promoted master sergeants for their anticipated positions and assignments.

US Army Sergeants Major Course (SMC)
The Sergeants Major Course (SMC) is the only senior-level NCOES course and the capstone of NCO education. It is a ten-month, task-based, performance-oriented, scenario-driven course of instruction designed to prepare promotable master sergeants for sergeants major within a force projection Army. Only the most qualified NCOs attend this capstone course; selection for attendance is a large step forward in an NCO's career because course completion is mandatory for promotion to sergeant major and command sergeant major. The curriculum design broadens the senior NCO's already acquired knowledge and is quite different from the MOS-related training accomplished at the basic and advanced levels of the NCOES. The SMC provides education and training to develop critical reasoning, creative thinking, and decision-making skills; further develop character; enhance self-expression; and strengthen the ability to work as a member of a team. The course integrates the learning objectives

from the Battle Staff NCO Course, the Master Fitness Trainer Course, and facilitator training. Emphasis is on the skills, knowledge, and attitudes required for sergeants major to excel in positions of greater responsibility throughout the defense establishment.

Attendance at the SMC is a permanent change of station to Fort Bliss, Texas. Spouses and families are an essential and vital part of the academy experience, and they are included in many educational, social, and recreational activities, many of which will assist students and their spouses in their new assignments.

Nonresident Sergeants Major Course (NRC)

The US Army Sergeants Major Academy Nonresident Course (NRC) is an eighteen- to twenty-four-month program that uses both distributive learning and resident educational technologies that parallel the resident course curriculum. It is available only to soldiers who are selected by the CSM/SGM/SMC Board. Graduates of both the resident and nonresident courses receive identical consideration for all personnel management decisions. The course assists students in developing logical and practical thought, as well as the reasoning skills necessary for problem solving. Participation in this program is highly selective and consists of senior noncommissioned officers in the ranks of master sergeant, first sergeant, sergeant major, command sergeant major, and the equivalent ranks from sister services and allied nations.

Much like the resident course, the NRC provides an intellectually broadening educational experience as well as a detailed study of contemporary leadership subjects. Phase 1, the correspondence phase, consists of six modules with six to twelve lessons each, for a total of fifty-three lessons. There is a comprehensive exam at the end of each module to validate knowledge of the material learned for each lesson. Phase 2 is conducted in residence at the Sergeants Major Academy, Fort Bliss, Texas. Those students satisfactorily completing Phase 1 requirements are eligible to attend the 120-hour resident phase, during which period they complete the final graduation requirements and become graduates of the SMC.

Dismissal from Courses

Camp commandants may remove students from NCOES courses before course completion for disciplinary reasons, lack of motivation, academic deficiencies, or other valid reasons, such as illness or injury. Failure to maintain established academic, physical fitness, conduct, and weight-control standards at any time during a course is cause for elimination and may constitute an infraction of the UCMJ or indicate a lack of motivation or aptitude. Students whose actions during training constitute a probable violation of the UCMJ may be suspended, dismissed, or reported to a commander exercising court-martial jurisdiction. Students who show a probable lack of motivation will be counseled.

If disenrollment is determined to be appropriate and adequately documented, the commandant notifies the student in writing of the proposed action, the basis for the action, and the consequences of disenrollment. The student has the right to appeal but must submit any appeal within two days after receipt of written notification. A disinterested command sergeant major reviews the appeal.

Soldiers eliminated from the SMC are not eligible for reentry. Those eliminated academically from other NCOES courses will not be eligible for further NCOES training for a period of six months.

NCOs dismissed for cause from an NCOES course face a mandatory bar to reenlistment or separation proceedings. "For cause" can mean for lack of discipline or motivation, or for other problems such as insubordination or alcohol abuse.

FUNCTIONAL COURSES FOR NCOS

Unlike NCO academy courses, functional courses are not generally mandatory, but they are quite important to day-to-day activities and mission-critical operations. Specifically identified senior NCOs—such as command sergeants major, first sergeants, battle staff, operations, and intelligence position selectees— either must or should attend the associated functional course. Additionally, NCOs who currently serve in one of these positions should voluntarily seek enrollment in the associated functional course. Functional courses are both career enhancing and beneficial from a professional viewpoint. The better armed you are with the skills, knowledge, and behaviors derived from such courses, the better prepared you will be on the job.

Command Sergeants Major Course (CSMC)

Command Sergeants Major Course (CSMC) is conducted simultaneously with the Pre-Command Course at Fort Leavenworth, Kansas. This twelve-day course assists battalion and brigade command sergeants major in their preparation for assignment, with a focus on leader development, Army policy and programs, and items of special interest as determined by the Chief of Staff of the Army. The purpose of the course is the development of senior-level leadership skills, creative and strategic thinking, communicating strategically, and effective influence. The course emphasizes self-awareness as a leader and corporate-level strategic planning and implementation. The CSMC provides selected command sergeants major the chance to participate in small-group discussions on key and emerging leadership trends and to reflect on where they are in their own personal and professional competence levels. It is highly recommended that spouses attend the Command Team Spouse Development Program, which runs concurrently.

Immediately following the CSMC is the Command Sergeants Major Development Program, a five-day course designed to assist command sergeants major selects in their preparation for the direct level of leadership within a battalion. The course covers leading and managing soldier training; growing and developing leaders at the operational level; providing practical advice to the commander and staff officers; and instilling the heritage and traditions across the battalion. It consists of graduate-level seminars facilitated by currently serving senior nominative and brigade command sergeants major. These courses must be completed consecutively.

Battle Staff NCO Course (BSNCOC)
The Battle Staff NCO Course (BSNCOC) is designed to educate NCOs on how to be successful members of a battalion or higher staff. The BSNCOC is conducted in one phase as a branch immaterial functional course for staff sergeants through sergeants major who are on or have been selected for staff assignments at the battalion level and above. BSNCOC encompasses the key land and joint operations in the day-to-day tasks of battalion- and brigade-level staff and provides soldiers with insight into the processes of tactical planning and operations. BSNCOC graduates are able to perform many of the responsibilities found in a tactical operations center.

Graduates of the BSNCOC are identified by the additional skill identifier (ASI) code 2S. Attendance is mandatory for those soldiers assigned to positions coded ASI 2S. Major subjects of study include plans, orders, and annexes; graphics and overlays; military intelligence; and combat service support operations. The resident course can be attended at either USASMA (Fort Bliss, Texas) or at the NCOAs in Fort McCoy, Wisconsin; Fort Indiantown Gap, Pennsylvania; or Camp Williams, Utah.

Drill Sergeant Course (DSC)
The Drill Sergeant Course (DSC) is a functional course providing qualified NCOs with specialized training, earning them the ASI X skill qualification identifier. The nine-week resident course is conducted at Fort Jackson, South Carolina, in three phases to provide candidates with firsthand experience in the phase training concept employed in Initial Entry Training (IET) and knowledge of training techniques for the skills drill sergeants must teach in basic combat training. Tasks include human relations, leadership, counseling, physical fitness training, weapons training, drill and ceremonies, methods of instruction, hand grenades, combatives, general subjects, gender integrated training management, and initial entry tactical training. The major emphasis of the course is on how drill sergeants can best train initial entry soldiers to become highly motivated, skilled, and physically fit soldiers who live the Army Ethic.

Army Recruiting Course (ARC)
The purpose of the Army Recruiting Course (ARC) is to provide the recruiter with the skills and techniques required to enlist qualified men and women into the Army. The six-week course is designed to teach the interpersonal,

conceptual, administrative, technical, and tactical skills necessary to succeed in the contemporary recruiting environment. The curriculum is divided into nine major segments, with the largest devoted to the application of all leadership skills during prospecting and the Army interview. This course is held at Fort Jackson, South Carolina.

Equal Opportunity (EO) Courses

The Defense Equal Opportunity Management Institute (DEOMI) curriculum consists of two resident courses: a twelve-week EO Advisor Course (EOAC) and a five-day Leadership Team Awareness Seminar (LTAS). A two-phase Equal Opportunity Advisors Reserve Component Course (EOARCC), consisting of one four-week resident phase and one online module, is conducted for Army National Guard (ARNG) and US Army Reserve (USAR) personnel.

Master Resilience Trainer Course (MRT)

The Master Resilience Trainer (MRT) Course is a program used to reduce behavioral health problems. It produces leader-trainers with the necessary skills to teach techniques that enhance soldiers' performances and increase their resilience. Students learn about the science of the factors that predict behaviors. Graduates serve in many noncommissioned officer leader roles in units and in training centers and are expected to train other soldiers in their unit on these learned skills. MRTs serve as subject matter experts for their commanders and may be assigned as a unit, post, or geographical area MRT, based on need.

Combatives Course

The Combatives School trains students in close-quarters combatives skills to ensure soldiers are better prepared to defeat an enemy in hand-to-hand combat. They currently offer Basic Combatives, Tactical Combatives, and Instructor courses. As of this writing, the Army is piloting a Combative Master Trainers course that will combine Combatives Level III and IV training.

SPECIALIZED COURSES FOR NCOS

Soldiers may apply for a number of additional qualification training courses. For example, soldiers are sometimes directed to take certain language training courses in connection with special assignments.

Air Assault Course

Obstacle courses, physical training, aircraft safety, Pathfinder operations, combat assaults, sling-loading operations, rappelling from UH-60 Black Hawk helicopters, 12-mile road marches with rucksack and rifle—this ten-day course is packed with challenges. To attend, soldiers must receive permission from their commander and pass the Army Physical Fitness Test (in the seventeen-to twenty-one-year-old age group).

Airborne Course

Airborne training is available on a voluntary basis for enlisted personnel, without regard to current assignment, who will be assigned to an airborne unit after training. This functional training is conducted by the US Army Infantry School and is designed to qualify volunteers in the use of the parachute as a means of deployment. Mental and physical training is intended to develop leadership, self-confidence, and an aggressive spirit. Graduates receive an additional skill identifier (P). Eligible personnel volunteering for airborne training should submit applications according to the instructions contained in AR 614-200 and should be physically qualified for parachute duty in accordance with AR 40-501, Standards of Medical Fitness.

Language Training

The Defense Language Program is designed to provide personnel the minimum essential professional linguistic skills needed to meet specific Army Foreign Language Program requirements. Basic language training is provided through the Defense Language Institute, Presidio of Monterey, California. Training requires full-time attendance. Nonresident training is conducted in education centers, units, or established language training facilities using approved materials. Details of the management of the program are set forth in AR 350-20, Management of the Defense Foreign Language Program; AR 11-6, Army Foreign Language Program; and AR 621-5, Army Continuing Education System (ACES). An additional skill identifier (L) is usually awarded to graduates of the program.

Ranger Training

This voluntary training conducted by the US Army Infantry School, Fort Benning, Georgia, is designed to develop leadership skills and provide a knowledge of Ranger operations involving direct combat with the enemy. Nonairborne enlisted graduates receive a special qualification identifier (G) for their MOS code, while those who are airborne qualified receive a V. Ranger training is available on a voluntary basis for soldiers who hold an MOS and grade that is authorized in the 75th Ranger Regiment. Submit applications according to the instructions contained in AR 614-200.

Special Forces Training

Special Forces soldiers undertake missions ranging from counterterrorism to unconventional warfare and rely on stealth to complete their missions. Special Forces (SF) teams are generally organized into small groups, called Operational Detachment Alphas (ODA). A typical ODA contains twelve team members, each with his own specialty: weapons sergeants, communications sergeants, medical sergeants, and engineering sergeants; commander and assistant commander; operations/intelligence sergeant; and a noncommissioned officer-in-charge (NCOIC). However, these teams often change according to the type of mission. Each soldier in an ODA is specially trained and cross-trained in different disciplines. SF units are designed to operate either independently or in support of and combined with native military and paramilitary forces.

The Special Forces Assessment and Selection (SFAS) program assesses and selects soldiers to attend the Special Forces Qualification Course (SFQC). This program allows school leadership to review each soldier by testing his physical, emotional, and mental stamina. The SFAS also gives soldiers the opportunity to make an educated decision about SF and their career plans. Soldiers attend SFAS on a temporary duty status at Fort Bragg, North Carolina, for up to thirty days. The course involves individual cross-country land navigation and covers distances from 18 kilometers up to 50 kilometers, with the distances and weight carried increasing during the course. Being prepared mentally and physically for the events cannot be emphasized enough.

DISTRIBUTED LEARNING
The Army has entered the digital age with soldiers attending classes at their posts, where they attend courses presented by schools and instructors located at far-off institutions through digital and video teleconferencing links. The Army's Distributed Learning (DL) program delivers training and educational opportunities to soldiers using a variety of new technologies. Army DL supports the Army assignment policies by ensuring leaders have the right training available when needed. Technology allows soldiers and leaders to learn at their home station so they can spend more time with their families instead of long-term temporary assignments to schools. Army DL also facilitates a balance between soldiers' needs and Army requirements.

Soldiers attending courses—whether through a resident school, a Total Army Schools System (TASS) Training Battalion, or a digital training facility—receive the same credit for successfully completing training as soldiers attending the regular classes. The Army Distributed Learning Program (TADLP) delivers training and education to soldiers, leaders, and units using the most appropriate methods to help develop leaders. TADLP uses new technology and lessons designed to provide cost-effective and efficient learning material, and even allows learning through Web- and mobile device-enabled applications, where available.

The Army Learning Management System (ALMS)
The Army Learning Management System (ALMS) is a Web-based information system that manages training information and enables collaboration, scheduling, and career planning in either resident or non-resident training environments. Army personnel can access ALMS from anywhere with access to a computer and the Internet.

10

Self-development

The Army defines self-development as "planned, goal-oriented learning that reinforces and expands the depth and breadth of an individual's knowledge base, self-awareness, and situational awareness." Self-development is complementary to classroom learning and on-the-job experience and increases soldiers' confidence and competence. The Army has defined the three types of self-development as:

- *Structured self-development*. Required learning that continues for an entire career and is closely aligned with classroom training and on-the-job experience.
- *Guided self-development*. Recommended but optional learning that prepares soldiers and leaders to adapt to changing technical and functional responsibilities throughout their career.
- *Personal self-development*. Self-initiated study in which the soldier defines the objective, speed, and process.

NCO SELF-DEVELOPMENT
Self-development links operational assignments, training, and education, and prepares soldiers for continuous learning and growth. Self-development activities might include completing a self-assessment and seeking feedback on a periodic basis or using tools such as the Travel Risk Planning System (TRiPS) or the Multi-Source Assessment and Feedback (MSAF).

Structured Self-development (SSD)
Structured self-development (SSD) was designed to link operational assignments with Army schools to ensure constant learning during the periods between NCO educational programs. It is required study outside the classrooms and during operational assignments. SSD ensures learning is ongoing for soldiers from private to command sergeant major and supplements the NCOES system. SSD is both an individual and first-line leader responsibility and is completed at the individual's pace, supervised by the first-line leader. It is centrally managed and must be completed at specified career points as a prerequisite for attendance to NCOAs.

Guided Self-development

NCOs should enroll in the Army Correspondence Course Program and encourage their soldiers to do so as well. It is clear that MOS-related courses build on battle competencies desired in NCOs and increase confidence. Taking these types of courses broadens NCOs professionally and increases their knowledge as a whole. Self-development helps soldiers move through the ranks and demonstrate to promotion boards that they have the initiative to improve their military education. The unit NCO Development Program should be based on the long-term education of an NCO, and individuals should maximize their participation in these activities. A great way to create analytical and leadership skills is through an individual reading program; books like the *NCO Guide* are helpful for learning. Self-guided programs can extend knowledge and nurture an interest in reading. Taking the time to read and understand helps foster analytical skills and planning for the future by understanding the past.

Army Correspondence Course Program. The Army Correspondence Course Program (ACCP) offers a number of self-study correspondence courses that are each specific to an MOS or a career field. General courses in leadership and training management are geared toward directed professional development opportunities. Proponent schools develop the courses, many of which are sub-courses that provide soldiers with promotion points upon completion. The Army Institute for Professional Development (AIPD) is the Army's virtual institution for administering and managing the ACCP; soldiers can enroll online at www.atsc.army.mil/tadlp/accp.

Army e-Learning. Army e-Learning is computer-based training on the Army Training Requirements and Resources System (ATRRS) Self-Development Center that is available to soldiers for free. To use Army e-Learning, soldiers must log in and complete their registration through ATRRS at https://www.atrrs.army.mil/selfdevctr. Not to be confused with ACCP (above), the Army's eLearning Program provides over five thousand courses to every active-duty soldier and member of the National Guard or Army Reserve through the commercial Skillport application, which provides access to information technology, business skills, foreign language, and interpersonal skills courses. Visit http://usarmy.skillport.com to learn more.

Double-dipping. There are some ACCP and Army e-Learning/Skillport courses that have been evaluated by the American Council on Education (ACE) and could also be worth college credits. As of this writing, they have approved forty Army e-Learning Courses for credit. Soldiers who enroll and complete those courses may be entitled to military education credit and civilian education credit when competing for promotion to sergeant or staff sergeant. These points can be used for both categories on the promotion point worksheet. According to the HRC Enlisted Promotions Branch, promotion points can be applied under military education with completion certificates from Army e-Learning/Skillport courses. Course completion documentation that lists credit hours must be reflected in ATRRS before any promotion points will be awarded. Promotion points are awarded under the same rules as correspondence courses (5 training hours = 1 promotion point). Log into AKO, go to My Education, and click on the Army e-Learning link to find information on how to receive ACE credit.

Personal Self-development

While this guide does not advocate making college graduates of the NCO Corps, collegiate-level education helps noncommissioned officers accomplish day-to-day tasks. If all NCOs can comprehend what is being written, then there will be less confusion in determining which tasks are to be accomplished. This allows NCOs to better understand organizational priorities, the implied tasks, and the commander's intent.

There are thousands of years of NCO experience in each brigade or group, and hundreds in each company. NCOs should tap into that experience and use it to help them create the best-possible personalized self-development programs.

SETTING PROFESSIONAL GOALS

Weapon systems superiority is not the only bedrock of American Army success; leadership development also is a core component, and everything you do should focus in that direction.

Self-development means both the development of oneself as a leader and the development of oneself as a person. Unlike the bygone days, no one remains at one rank forever—the retention control points force you to move up or get out. Promotion in any MOS has certain elements applicable to all. With promotions being competitive, you must do the best you can at whatever you do. Identify yourself to the chain of command (and the board) through your good actions and as a soldier who shoulders more than his or her share of the work, whether holding a table of organization and equipment (TO&E) position or a table of distribution and allowance (TDA) position.

Seek leadership positions as early as possible within your career management field (CMF). You should be performing duties in your primary MOS at the authorized or next higher grade. Take advantage of any opportunity to serve in a leadership position at the next higher grade, as you might not get the opportunity again. Physical fitness is also essential for soldiers; nothing more need be said. Additionally, it is important to round out your career with duty in both TO&E and TDA units. A number of high-priority assignments—drill sergeant, recruiting, ROTC, and Active and Reserve Components—provide unique professional development opportunities and a chance to catch your breath and reflect.

Finally, you should take advantage of every opportunity to attend military and civilian schools. Begin taking Army correspondence courses early in your career. Take college courses if you are in a position to do so. The additional military and civilian education that you achieve on your own shows the chain of command that you are a self-starter seeking to improve yourself. Additionally, it will improve your chances for promotion by converting educational credit into promotion points. Remember, however, that your leaders recommend you for promotion because of your duty performance.

THE NCO ROAD MAP TO SUCCESS

Rank	Assignments	Positions	Military Schools	NCOES	Promotion
Sergeant	The focus during this stage of your career should be on developing your leadership skills, technical expertise, and tactical knowledge.	Almost all positions held while a SGT should be in TOE organizations so that you can develop your skills in leading soldiers and improve your MOS knowledge. Leadership positions you can hold are team leader (TL) and squad leader (SL).[1]	There are many MOS-specific schools available to you at this grade.[2] Non-MOS-specific schools available to you are air assault and airborne.	The Basic NCO Course (BNCOC) is a requirement for promotion to the rank of staff sergeant. BNCOC is an MOS-specific course that provides SGTs (P) with the technical, tactical, and leadership training necessary to prepare them to lead and train soldiers.	

[1] A very small number of exceptionally qualified SGTs may be DA selected for recruiting duty. Recruiting duty is vital and necessary to ensure an accession of highly motivated men and women into our Army. Recruiting duty is a stabilized three-year tour. Twelve months before completing your tour you must contact your career advisor and request to return to a TOE unit.

[2] For more information regarding prerequisites and availability of these schools, see your battalion school's NCO and the *Army Formal Schools Catalog*, DA Pam 351-4.

THE NCO ROAD MAP TO SUCCESS

Rank	Assignments	Positions	Military Schools	NCOES	Promotion
Staff Sergeant	The critical assignment at this stage of your career is squad leader. In order for you to be considered "branch qualified" at this grade level you should have at least 18 to 36 rated months of squad leader time.	It is during this stage of your career that you may start serving in other TOE assignments. However, before requesting a TDA position you should ensure that you have built a solid base of troop time. There are many different positions you can hold as a SSG, including squad leader, platoon sergeant, drill sergeant, reserve component duty, observer/controller, recruiter, TRADOC instructor.	Non-MOS-specific schools available to you are Recruiting School, Drill Sergeant School, Battle Staff Course.	The Advanced NCO Course is a requirement for promotion to SFC. ANCOC prepares SSGs (P) to become technically and tactically proficient at skill level 4 and 5 tasks. Currently SSGs selected for promotion to SFC will automatically attend ANCOC.	A DA centralized board selects SSGs for promotion to SFC. The board relies entirely on your Official Military Personnel File (OMPF), your Personnel Qualification Record (DA Forms 2-1 and 2-A), and your military photograph. The condition of your OMPF and the quality of your photo are the basis for promotion.

THE NCO ROAD MAP TO SUCCESS

Rank	Assignments	Positions	Military Schools	NCOES	Promotion
Sergeant First Class	The critical assignment at this stage of your career is platoon sergeant. More than any leadership assignment, platoon sergeant is the assignment you must have and excel in if you want to advance to MSG and SGM/CSM. You should attempt to hold this assignment for 18 to 30 months.	The primary positions you can hold as a SFC are platoon sergeant and first sergeant. TDA positions include reserve component duty, recruiter, drill sergeant, ROTC instructor, TRADOC instructor.	Schools available to you at this level are Ranger, Pathfinder, Battle Staff, Recruiter, First Sergeant, Drill Sergeant, and EO.	Upon completion of ANCOC you have completed all necessary levels of NCOES until selected for promotion to SGM; then you must attend the Sergeants Major Academy (SMA).	As with the DA centralized board for promotion to SFC, there is a DA centralized promotion board for selection to MSG.
Master Sergeant	The critical assignment for a master sergeant is first sergeant. Demonstrated superior performance while serving in a first sergeant position (strive for 24 months) is the best message to the SGM/CSM selection board.	The primary positions you can hold are first sergeant, detachment sergeant, and operations sergeant. TDA positions at this level are reserve component duty, ROTC instructor, TRADOC instructor.	Schools at this level are limited to the following: Battle Staff, First Sergeant, Ranger, and EO.	The final level in this NCOES is the Sergeants Major Academy, which is a requirement for promotion to SGM/CSM.	A DA centralized board selects soldiers for attendance at the SMA. A DA centralized board selects MSGs for promotion to SGM/CSM.

NCO Road Map for Success

The career development guide above uses a standard format for each grade covered. It includes rank, key leadership assignments, duty positions, military schools, and the NCOES. Much is extracted from enlisted newsletters at the G1 website, https://www.hrc.army.mil/site/Active/enlist/ENLIST.htm.

You should actively seek information and guidance from your chain of command, mentors, and career advisor. You must play an integral part in the decision and assignment process in order to achieve the goals you have set for yourself. The bottom line is if you do not help make the decisions, someone else will make them for you.

Your career branch is there to assist you in determining what is right for you, both professionally and personally. You should maintain communication with your branch to inquire about your next move, school, or promotion. For further information or assistance, review our Branch Manager contacts in Chapter 13 (page 200).

DA Pam 600-25, Noncommissioned Officer Professional Development Guide, was revised in 2008 to better provide noncommissioned officers with more robust career development guidance. The new pamphlet specifically identifies the duties, prerequisites, required institutional training, and recommended self-development for NCOs in each MOS by career management field and skill level. The pamphlet is available online at www.apd.army.mil/pdf files/p600_25.pdf.

Professional development models (PDMs) establish a standardized framework and all-inclusive career-enhancing information to soldiers, leaders, and personnel managers for the professional development of NCOs. The PDM serves as the professional reference for a successful military career while supplying information and guidance on assignments, education, and training. PDMs are created for each MOS and are available at the Army Training (and Education) Network (ATN) at www.train.army.mil. They are Web-based and interactive, based on the three core domains that shape the critical learning experience throughout the soldier's career: the operational domain, the institutional domain, and the self-development domain.

New technologies are allowing the Army to more rapidly develop and update career development models; one of these tools is the Army Career Tracker (ACT). The ACT integrates training and education into one personalized, easy-to-use website. Users can search multiple leadership development resources, monitor their own career progression, and receive personalized advice from their leadership. PDM career maps are also available in the ACT and on the AKO My Training page. To get more information click the Gadget button on the Army Training Network (ATN) page.

Individual Study: Enhancing Your Leadership Abilities

The learning process is an individual endeavor and is not just about more schooling. Develop yourself by *observing* both good and bad leaders in action; listening to your subordinates' comments, aspirations, and frustrations to gain their perspective; and reading about wartime leaders to obtain a perspective that few experience but all should study. Analyze your experiences and think about how you can be better. Soldiers who do not think about their experiences will stagnate, continue to live with their existing mental models, and never fully develop their potential.

Remember, however, that you cannot evaluate your own effectiveness with total objectivity; consider others' perceptions and attempt to reconcile the differences between their perceptions and your own. Seldom formal, these talks might take place over the hood of a Humvee, sitting against a tree in the field, in the motor pool, through emails with someone you seldom meet, or even over a cold drink at a social event.

The Self-development Process

Noncommissioned officer self-development is an individual responsibility and the only leader development phase over which NCOs have direct control. Every NCO has the professional responsibility to continually seek self-improvement and self-development wherever the soldier is and no matter what the soldier is doing. Self-development focuses on maximizing leadership strengths, minimizing weaknesses, and achieving individual goals.

Just as having an accurate understanding of friendly and enemy unit strengths and weaknesses is paramount to successful military operations, having an accurate understanding of individual strengths and weaknesses is paramount to the development of an effective leader training and leader development action plan. Follow your assessment with frank discussions with those you trust to identify what makes you strong in some areas and weak in others. Develop your action plan to highlight and prioritize the specific actions that you should take to achieve your self-developmental goals.

Job training is continuous. Here, soldiers in Kuwait conduct battle drills to maintain proficiency.

Your leader training and leader development action plans should emphasize the following activities that categorize your goals over time:
- Immediate goals concentrating on accomplishing tasks related to the current job that are therefore very specific.
- Near-term goals that are somewhat broader in scope and develop you for responsibilities at the next operational assignment.
- Long-term goals for the activities that have the broadest scope, focusing on tasks that prepare you for duties and responsibilities beyond your next operational assignment.

Focus on Where You Want to Be in Five Years
Noncommissioned officer self-development activities are the broadest in nature and are limited only by your imagination. These include attending military and

civilian education courses, participating in professional organizations, reading professional materials, seeking challenging assignments, practicing critical leader technical and tactical tasks, and participating in leadership activities in both the military and civilian communities.

ARMY CONTINUING EDUCATION SYSTEM

Through its many programs, the Army Continuing Education System (ACES) promotes lifelong learning opportunities and sharpens the competitive edge of the Army. Today's soldiers can take advantage of numerous educational programs. The comprehensive website for Army education is https://www.hrc .army.mil/site/education/index.html.

Your DA Form 669, Army Continuing Education System Record, can serve a very important purpose during your military career—or it can collect dust. DA Form 669 contains information used by education counselors to document your pursuit of higher education. Semester after semester throughout your career, you should (whenever the mission allows) contribute course completion slips to your record. Consider it as making regular deposits to an intellectual savings account that earns enormous interest—the kind that Army promotion boards and civilian employers will offer as your educational value increases.

View your record online by logging into your AKO account, going to Self Service, and clicking on the MyEducation link, or by going directly to the GoArmyEd portal. Open or create an account, and then click on My Education Record link and select DA 669. From there you can either view or print your form.

Leaders can use the planned, progressive individual development program supported by ACES to enhance and sustain their leadership plans discussed earlier. Under the guidelines of AR 621-5, Army Continuing Education System, NCOs and their soldiers should meet the following educational objectives:

- Master academic skills needed to perform duties of their primary MOS and meet prerequisites for the NCOES.
- In cases of exception to the enlistment rule regarding having a high school diploma, earn a high school diploma and begin postsecondary studies during the first five years of enlistment.
- Earn an associate's degree or complete education goal between the fifth and fifteenth year of service.
- Establish a lifelong learning professional and personal plan by seventh year of service and/or complete a bachelor's degree by twentieth year of service.

Invest in yourself. The Army does, and benefits in the process. The Army Continuing Education System's mission is intended, in part, to improve the combat readiness of the Army by planning, researching, and implementing educational programs and services to support the professional and personal development of quality. ACES programs and services are designed to expand soldiers' skills, knowledge, and behavior. Programs and services discussed later in this chapter contribute to the three pillars of leader development: institutional training, operational assignments, and self-development.

Army Education Center Counselors

Counselors are wonderful people who are critical to the success of the ACES mission. They help soldiers establish realistic education goals and continue to provide counseling through attainment of the goals. They also help soldiers get the maximum benefit from limited tuition assistance and other resources.

Soldiers should not need a regulatory push to receive counseling; they should virtually run to get the valuable advice and assistance that counselors provide. That said, AR 621-5 requires that soldiers new to an installation receive education counseling within the first thirty days of their arrival and then receive follow-up counseling as needed. Counselors help with school selection, application procedures (which can be lengthy and complex), prerequisite assessments, and financial aid. When they cannot locate financial aid for formal courses of instruction, counselors can recommend free alternative methods of obtaining educational credit (see Defense Activity for Nontraditional Education Support, College Level Examination Program, and Graduate Record Examinations below). Nevertheless, soldiers must take the first step and go online to https://goarmyed.com/login, or call the local Army Education Center, make an appointment, and speak with a counselor.

Army Learning Center (ALC)

The Army Learning Center (ALC) is designed to meet the unique mission of the command being served. The ALC provides educational services with direct training support and academic services and maintains publications to support training in the assigned MOSs. In addition, a wide variety of study programs are available, including basic and advanced academic skills, Army Forces Classification Test or General Technical improvement, college-level examination programs review, preparation for college entrance exams, effective study skills programs, and other topics. The goal is to provide a "One-Stop Training Support Facility" for commanders and their soldiers. Education centers are staffed with specialists who can coordinate the unique education and training requirements of the unit leaders and soldiers in support of combat readiness. Additionally, the full-time facilitator can work directly with the command and soldiers in identifying and accessing appropriate training materials, conducting training, and coordinating facilities and other resources for specific training needs.

Army learning centers provide a variety of independent study materials, computer-based instruction, language three labs, tutorial services, and a military publications library. These centers support self-development, unit, and individual training. Materials recommended on PDM reading lists can generally be found in Army learning centers.

High School Completion Program (HSCP)

The High School Completion Program (HSCP) is an off-duty program that provides soldiers and adult family members the opportunity to earn a high school diploma or equivalency certificate. Tuition assistance is authorized for soldiers for up to 100 percent of the costs of courses, provided soldiers take them through accredited institutions. ACES will not pay fees covering items such as books, matriculation, graduation, and parking.

The General Education Development (GED) exams are an alternative to receiving a high school diploma (equivalency certificate) for those who have not graduated high school. In many cases, a high school diploma or GED is either required or highly encouraged before a soldier is allowed to reenlist in the Army. The GED test is available at no cost to military personnel on all major Army installations at the post Education Center.

Montgomery GI Bill enrollees must finish a high school completion program or earn an equivalent certification during their first enlistment. The HSCP is open to all non-high school graduates.

Functional Academic Skills Training (FAST)

Functional Academic Skills Training (FAST) is an on-duty commander's program to ensure soldiers possess the necessary reading and writing skills to succeed in their occupational specialty. The program offers instruction in reading, mathematics, and communication skills to help soldiers function on the job, prepare for advanced training, and meet prerequisites for continued education. The courses assist selected soldiers in achieving the current recommended reading grade levels and the Army's recommended writing standard and assist in General Technical (GT) score improvement; General Education Development (GED) test preparation; or reading, math, and language skill development. Basic Skills Education Program (BSEP) courses, a component of FAST, offer soldiers instruction in reading and math during the workday. Unit leadership allows soldiers to attend BSEP during duty hours to improve job performance and to prepare for more advanced schooling.

Credentialing Opportunities On-Line (COOL)

What we do as soldiers often requires certification as a civilian. The Credentialing Opportunities On-Line (COOL) website, https://www.cool.army.mil, explains how soldiers can meet civilian certification and license requirements related to their MOSs. You can locate information on a specific credential by searching under an MOS, the name of a specific credential, or credentialing agency. Related certifications and licenses are also listed if they are linked to an MOS. Once on the site, soldiers can learn how to fill gaps between Army training and experience and civilian credentialing requirements, as well as learn about resources available to assist them in obtaining civilian job credentials.

COLLEGE DEGREE PROGRAMS

Postsecondary programs are academic, vocational, technical, and occupational courses of study leading to a credential. Colleges and universities have developed certificate programs allowing students to "build" courses toward an overall certification program—often understood as capstone. Postsecondary program courses may be offered through modules or under the capstone concept but should not be confused with certificate courses or programs offered through proprietary institutions at the postsecondary level. Postsecondary programs include the GoArmyEd, SOCAD -2/-4, and SOCGuard (career/occupational, certificate, associate's, bachelor's, and master's degrees) programs.

Thousands of degree programs are available to soldiers—too many to list here. But you may use dedicated resources to find out more information about obtaining an Associate in Arts or Associate in Science degree, a Bachelor of Arts or Bachelor of Science degree, a Master of Arts or Master of Science degree, or even a Doctorate.

If you want to take college courses but are concerned about your ability to comprehend course material, use the Army Training (and Education) Network (ATN) at www.train.army.mil. It contains numerous courses covering practically every MOS in the Army, as well as courses in basic math, English, and science. For example, suppose you want to earn an electrical engineering degree. You could sign up for the basic electricity course listed in the online catalog. This course is open to "any student who meets the basic qualifications for correspondence study" and has a Common Access Card (CAC) and a CAC-enabled computer. After successfully completing seventeen sequential electricity subcourses, you should be fully prepared to enroll in a college course that deals with the subject of electricity. Apply this method to other subjects and you will see the value of "boning up" through correspondence studies.

Servicemembers Opportunity Colleges (SOC)

The Servicemembers Opportunity Colleges (SOC) is a network of schools across the country and overseas that have recognized and responded to soldiers' expectations for postsecondary education. They must have liberal entrance requirements, allow soldiers to complete courses through nontraditional modes, provide academic advising, offer maximum credit for experiences obtained in service, have residence requirements that are adaptable to the special needs of soldiers, have a transfer policy that recognizes traditional and nontraditional learning obtained at other schools, promote the SOC, and provide educational support to servicemembers.

A subgroup of the SOC, the Servicemembers Opportunity Colleges Army Degree (SOCAD) Program offers degree and certification programs through which soldiers are normally awarded degrees or certificates for an academic or technical course of study, with the programs developed to provide common curricula in disciplines related to Army MOSs. Coursework taken from colleges and universities to complete an Army Career Degree does not substitute for military training core courses of the NCOES; however, it should be complementary and supportive of soldiers' career development.

The SOCAD student agreement gives soldiers a one-time evaluation of everything they have done that can be credited toward the college degree and lists what they must take to graduate. The SOCAD colleges require soldiers to take no more than 25 percent of their coursework with that college to receive their degree—not necessarily on campus, but from their offerings, credit for non-traditional learning, and guaranteed course transfer. Once soldiers complete residency, future courses taken at other colleges will be accepted and applied toward the original degree plan.

GoArmyEd
GoArmyEd is the Web application and pathway for eligible Active, Guard, and Reserve soldiers to gain access to Tuition Assistance (TA) education benefits. The GoArmyEd portal automated many of the paper-based processes and now allows soldiers to better manage their education records, as well as track college classes, credentialing, and testing and gain Army Education Counselor support. The website offers soldiers a streamlined approach to a variety of postsecondary degrees and technical certificates. All courses allow soldiers to study on their own schedule. Highly motivated soldiers can complete degree and certification requirements regardless of work schedules, family responsibilities, and deployments.

College Credit for Military Experience
Army Education Center counselors can help you complete DD Form 295, Application for the Evaluation of Learning Experiences during Military Service. The completed form is used to inform institutions, agencies, and employers about in-service educational achievements. Schools use the form to determine how many and what kinds of college credits to award to soldiers based on military education, training, and experience. Your pursuit of a degree should include completing and forwarding DD Form 295 to the college or university of your choice.

The American Council on Education evaluates Army service school courses and recommends the number of semester hours of credit that civilian schools may award based on a soldier's military training and experience. Vocational credits, credits toward associate's degrees, lower- and upper-level baccalaureate credits, or graduate-level credits may be awarded. These recommendations are published in the *Guide to the Evaluation of Educational Experiences in the Armed Services* (ACE Guide).

The College of the American Soldier (CAS) consists of two education pathways: the Career NCO Degrees Program and the Enlisted Education Program. It works in conjunction with the Army Career Tracker and colleges whose degrees participate in the two pathways. The Career NCO Degrees program builds upon current civilian degree plans in a variety of majors that offer career NCOs college credit for attending noncommissioned officer education courses throughout their career. The Enlisted Education Program is a degree path for entry-level soldiers in Combat Arms MOSs in Career Management Fields (CMFs) 11 Infantry, 13 Field Artillery, 14 Air Defense Artillery, and 19 Armor to obtain an associate's degree during their first term of enlistment. Degrees selected for the two programs are all SOCAD degrees and available through the GoArmyEd portal.

Joint Service Transcripts (JST)

The Joint Service Transcripts (JST), formerly known as AARTS, is a free online portal that produces official transcripts for eligible soldiers to document military experience. The system combines the soldier's military education and job experience with descriptions and college credit recommendations developed by the ACE. The Military Evaluations Program evaluates service school and military education courses and occupational specialties to ensure servicemembers can earn college credit for their military training and on-the-job experience. The JST can be used similar to college transcripts and is available online at https://jst.doded.mil for Active, Guard, and Reserve members, as well as veterans and retirees.

Independent Study and Examination Programs for College Credit

If you are working on an undergraduate (associate's or bachelor's) degree, you should know about independent ways to earn credit through the following programs: Defense Activity for Non-traditional Education Support (DANTES), including the College Level Examination Program (CLEP); DSST Exams, (formerly known as Defense Subject Standardized Tests); the Excelsior College Examinations (ECEs); and the Graduate Record Examinations (GRE).

The DANTES, CLEP, DSST, ECEs, and GRE offerings all require independent study. Many subject packets include texts, workbooks, and audio or videotapes used in conjunction with the paper materials. Most of the for-credit tests offered by these programs and agencies are worth 3 or 4 semester hours of credit each. The GRE, which includes a general exam and subject exams, is worth much more. The GRE sociology examination, for example, is worth 30 semester hours of undergraduate credit, 15 hours of lower division (100- and 200-level) courses, and 15 hours of upper division (300- and 400-level) classes.

DANTES independent study and examination program services are available to all eligible active-duty soldiers. One important aspect of DANTES is the College Level Examination Program (CLEP), which also enables students to earn credit by examination. CLEP examinations are a free option that you and your soldiers should consider as a way to receive college credit for what you already know. You can earn college credit for knowledge acquired through coursework, self-development, cultural pursuits, travel, special interests, and military service schools. The examinations measure knowledge of the basic concepts and applications involved in courses that have the same or similar titles. The thirty-three different subject areas are divided into two types: general examinations and subject examinations.

The general examination measures college-level achievement in five basic areas of the liberal arts: English composition, social sciences and history, natural sciences, humanities, and mathematics. The test material covers the first year of college, often referred to as the general or liberal education requirement. Subject examinations measure achievement in specific college courses and are worth course credit. Examples of test titles include Introduction to Business Management, General Psychology, Western Civilization, and American Literature.

Each civilian educational institution has its own evaluating criteria for using CLEP test scores to determine credit. You should have official transcripts forwarded to the registrar of the college or university at which you desire to receive credit (some institutions require that a minimum number of semester hours of class work be completed before CLEP credit will be accepted). Another type of subject test that, like CLEP, substitutes for college classroom work are the nationally recognized DSST Exams, which help you receive college credits for learning acquired outside the traditional classroom. DSST offers thirty-eight exams in college subject areas of social sciences, math, applied technology, business, physical sciences, and humanities. DSST Exams are recommended for credit by the American Council on Education, offer a variety of subject-level tests, and may be accepted for credit toward an associate's or bachelor's degree. These exams help soldiers save time and money while reducing the amount of time it takes to earn a degree.

TUITION ASSISTANCE PROGRAM

The Tuition Assistance (TA) Program provides financial assistance for voluntary off-duty education programs in support of a soldier's professional and personal self-development goals. All soldiers (officers, warrant officers, and enlisted) on active duty, and Army National Guard and Army Reserve on active duty pursuant to US Code Title 10 or Title 32, may be authorized to participate in the TA program. Before obtaining TA, active-duty soldiers must request tuition assistance by registering at the GoArmyEd portal at https://www.GoArmyEd.com. Once registered, soldiers must declare a specific degree or credential as an educational goal and obtain a degree map. TA is available for ground campuses or those that are online delivered through distance learning methods. The courses must be offered by schools that are registered in the GoArmyEd portal and are regionally or nationally accredited by agencies recognized by the Department of Education.

TA covers tuition, fees, books, academic advising, library resources, and administrative and technical support. All eligible soldiers receive 100 percent tuition as well as authorized fees up to a cap of $250 per semester hour for a maximum of 16 semester hours each fiscal year. Current policy is constantly under review. As of this writing, it limits TA to 130 semester hours of undergraduate credit or a baccalaureate degree, whichever comes first; and 39 semester hours of graduate credit or a master's degree, whichever comes first. The 39-hours-per-semester limit applies to all credits taken after completion of a baccalaureate degree.

Soldier Eligibility. Soldiers in the Active and Reserve Components will not be eligible to use TA until one year after graduating from initial entry training. Desired classes must be listed by the school in the GoArmyEd portal and be from the soldier's approved degree plan, which was created with the soldier's education counselor and home school. TA cannot be used for a second, equivalent degree or for a "first professional degree" (PhD, MD, and JD). Soldiers flagged for adverse action, for failure of the Army physical readiness test, or for failing to meet weight standards cannot use TA. Soldiers must request TA through the GoArmyEd portal before they start any courses.

Tuition Assistance Top-up. In some cases TA won't cover the entire cost for a course. Top-up benefits may be an option if soldiers are working to complete a degree while on active duty and do not plan to continue their education after service. Soldiers eligible for the Montgomery GI Bill can use it as a top-up to Tuition Assistance to cover the remaining charges. Top-up can also be helpful for just taking a few courses with TA while on active duty and saving the remainder of the GI Bill benefits for after service is completed.

THE GI BILL

Valuable education benefits offered under the GI Bill are available today for would-be college graduates and for soldiers who wish to pursue certain kinds of training. Originally named the Servicemen's Readjustment Act of 1944, which was signed into law by President Franklin D. Roosevelt on June 22 of that year, the GI Bill is now called the Montgomery GI Bill after its latest champion, Congressman G. V. "Sonny" Montgomery. It takes the following forms: the Post-9/11 GI Bill, the Montgomery GI Bill–Active Duty, and the Montgomery GI Bill–Selected Reserve. The Post-Vietnam Veterans Educational Assistance Program (VEAP) is also covered by the Montgomery GI Bill. Types of training that can be taken under current GI Bill benefits include college (undergraduate and graduate), certificate programs, on-the-job training, apprenticeship training, flight training, and non-college degree courses. Valued at hundreds of dollars a month for up to thirty-six months, a wide range of benefits at various levels are available. I cannot emphasize enough that you should take full advantage of the benefits to which you are entitled.

The variety of different entitlements and the appropriate time to use them are important decisions and should not be taken lightly. These valuable benefits should be discussed with an educational counselor and an appropriate education specialist. In considering which program to use, it is important to understand the differences between them. Managed by the Veterans Administration (VA), some of the major program descriptions include:

Montgomery GI Bill–Active Duty (MGIB–AD). For active-duty members who enroll and pay $100 per month for twelve months and are then eligible for a monthly education benefit upon completing a minimum service obligation.

Montgomery GI Bill–Selected Reserve (MGIB–SR). For Reservists with a six-year obligation in the Selected Reserve who are actively drilling.

Post-9/11 GI Bill. For servicemembers with at least ninety days of aggregate active-duty service after 10 September 2001 and who are still on active duty; or for honorably discharged veterans or soldiers discharged with a service-connected disability after thirty days.

Transfer Post-9/11 GI Bill to Spouse and Dependents. Eligible servicemembers may transfer all thirty-six months or a portion of unused Post-9/11 GI Bill benefits to a spouse, children, or possibly both.

Yellow Ribbon Program. Yellow Ribbon Program schools agree to make additional funds available for coursework without reducing servicemembers' GI Bill entitlement. The school agrees to the Yellow Ribbon rules in conjunction with the VA and chooses the amount of tuition and fees that will be contributed. VA matches that amount and issues payments directly to the institution.

Post-Vietnam Veterans Educational Assistance Program (VEAP). VEAP is available for servicemembers who made contributions from their military pay to take part in this education benefit program. The government matched their contributions on a 2-for-1 basis.

Reserve Educational Assistance Program (REAP). REAP provides educational assistance to members of the Reserve components called or ordered to active duty in response to a war or national emergency declared by the president or Congress. Certain Reservists who were activated for at least ninety days after 9/11 may be eligible for REAP benefits.

The Post-9/11 GI Bill

The Post-9/11 GI Bill provides money for soldiers with at least ninety days of aggregate service on or after 11 September 2001, or for those discharged with a service-connected disability after thirty days. This benefit is payable only for training at an institution of higher learning (IHL) and became effective for training 1 August 2009; it provides up to thirty-six months of education benefits. If you were a member of the Armed Forces on 1 August 2009, the DoD may offer you the opportunity to transfer benefits to your spouse or dependent children. The GI Bill can pay you for more than one degree, as long as you have remaining entitlement on your GI Bill.

If enrolled exclusively in online training, or still in the military, you may not receive the housing allowance or books and supplies stipend. Once you elect to receive benefits under the Post-9/11 GI Bill, you will no longer be eligible to receive benefits under the program from which you elected the Post-9/11 GI Bill. You are only eligible for GI Bill benefits for other types of training if you have eligibility under other GI Bill programs such as the GI Bill–Active Duty, Reserve GI Bill, REAP, or VEAP. The rules for the Post-9/11 GI Bill change regularly and you should contact your education service officer or the VA for more information on this valuable benefit.

The monetary issue is most likely a very important factor you will consider before selecting a benefit. While you may think you will receive more money under the Post-9/11 GI Bill, that will not always be the case.

The Montgomery GI Bill–Active Duty (MGIB–AD)

The Montgomery GI Bill–Active Duty, Chapter 30, US Code (USC), provides up to thirty-six months of benefits. Soldiers covered by Category I of this program entered active duty for the first time after 30 June 1985 and contributed a nonrefundable $100 a month for the first twelve months of service. Active-duty members may begin using their benefits after completing two years of service. Members of the National Guard who are in the Active Guard and Reserve Program also are covered by this contributory program, but they must have entered service after 29 November 1989 and must not have previously served on active duty (see Category IV).

Soldiers with remaining benefits under the Vietnam Era GI Bill (Chapter 34, USC) are entitled to benefits through an automatic conversion to Category I of the MGIB–AD. A Vietnam–era soldier who never used his or her benefits is today eligible for up to thirty-six months of entitlements under the Montgomery Program. Vietnam–era soldiers do not have to contribute to the program to receive benefits, which include an additional allowance paid for dependents. Soldiers in Category II can verify their benefits by contacting the local or regional Department of Veterans Affairs (DVA) office. Category IV covers those soldiers on active duty on 9 October 1996 with money remaining in a Veterans Educational Assistance Program (VEAP) account on that date who elected MGIB by 9 October 1997.

In any instance, all must have had their military pay reduced by $100 a month for twelve months or have made a $1,200 lump-sum contribution.

The Montgomery GI Bill–Selected Reserve

The Montgomery GI Bill–Selected Reserve (Chapter 106, USC) is available to members of the Army Reserve and the Army National Guard. It applies to members who entered Selected Reserve status after 30 June 1985. To receive up to thirty-six months of entitlements under this program, members must have a six-year commitment that began after 30 September 1990. Members must also have completed initial active duty for training, be high school graduates or have equivalent certificates, and serve in an Active Reserve or National Guard unit and remain in good standing. Soldiers entering the National Guard or Army Reserve on or after 1 October 1992 have their eligibility end fourteen years from their beginning date of eligibility or on the day they leave the Selected Reserve. Soldiers entering service prior to 1 October 1992 lose their eligibility ten years after their beginning date of eligibility, or on the day they leave the Selected Reserve.

The Veterans Educational Assistance Program (VEAP)

The VEAP (Chapter 32, USC) was a program in which a soldier made contributions from his or her military pay, which were matched on a $2 for $1 basis by the US government. The program was for soldiers who entered service between 1 January 1977 and 30 June 1985 and who opened a VEAP account before 1 April 1987. Changes to the law in 1997 allowed soldiers who had at least $1 remaining in their VEAP account to transition to the MGIB–AD. See your education counselor for details if you were a participant in VEAP.

Monetary Value of the GI Bill

As indicated above, the monetary value of the benefit program you qualify for will depend on various factors, including the date you entered the military, your status in the military, how long you have been or were in service, and the character of a previous discharge or separation. Also, if you are in a contributory program, the amount of money the government will pay depends on how much you contribute, up to a maximum matching amount.

In-service benefits are worth less, monetarily, than postservice benefits and normally cover only tuition and fees. But here is the kicker: Under current federal law, if you receive a college or university assistantship, fellowship, or grant that pays or offsets part or all of your tuition and fees or research expenses, you may still be entitled to receipt of education benefits—meaning that monthly entitlements received from the DVA are yours to keep.

Entitlement retention applies to serving, separated, and retired soldiers who compete for and receive school assistantships and the like, and who can work at the school a specified number of hours—normally at least twenty—per week.

Other Financial Aid

The US Department of Education's *The Student Guide* will inform you and your family members about federal student aid programs and how to apply for them. Its advice is to contact the financial aid administrator at the school that you, your spouse, or your children are interested in and ask about the total cost of education. Ask the state higher education agencies about state aid. Check the local library for state and private financial aid information. Check with companies, foundations, religious organizations, fraternities or sororities, and civic organizations such as the American Legion. Also ask about aid through professional associations. *The Student Guide* is free and may be available at your local Army Education office.

You may have earned valuable education benefits under more than one educational program, or if you have a service-connected disability you may be eligible for vocational training. Regardless, you should be sure to consult with a local VA counselor and discuss your education plans. If local counselors are unavailable, contact VA regional offices. VA toll-free telephone service is available in all fifty states, Puerto Rico, and the US Virgin Islands. Call (800) 827-1000.

SAVINGS BONDS AND EDUCATION

Buy bonds. Series EE savings bonds may be entirely tax-free when used for education. If you have children and are considering the rising cost of education, purchasing bonds on a regular basis is a smart way to invest in their future and protect your financial security. For example, assuming an annual interest rate of 6 percent, putting just $50 a month into bonds for a one-year-old child who will begin college at age eighteen will yield $17,356. Investing $100 a month will yield $34,712. If you are an NCO with an older child, for example one who is twelve and who will begin college in six years, putting $50 a month into bonds will provide $4,227; $100 a month will yield $8,454, minimum!

If you are a junior NCO, say a sergeant with five or six years in service, you may purchase bonds for yourself, hold them five years or so, then use them to augment other financial aid you or your family members will apply toward a college degree.

Beginning with Series EE bonds purchased after 1989, the interest earned can be excluded from federal income tax if you pay tuition and fees at colleges, universities, and qualified technical schools during the same year the bonds are cashed. The exclusion applies not only to your own educational expenses but also to those of your spouse and any other dependents. Some restrictions apply. Visit the Treasury website, https://www.treasurydirect.gov/indiv/planning/plan _education.htm, for more information.

PROFESSIONAL READING AND WRITING

NCOs must read to remain abreast of changing events and policies, and soldiers rely on their leaders to keep them informed. Writing ability is critical for similar reasons. To keep up, NCOs need to be able to comprehend what they read, be clear in their writing, and know how to use the software products on their computer. The ability to read, rapidly understand, and respond in writing to memorandums, letters, reports, and other documents hinges on command and comprehension, grammar, vocabulary, and related skills. To write clearly and efficiently, NCOs must organize their thoughts, put them in order of precedence, and tell readers up front what they should get from the paper.

NCOES Contribution to Literacy

The Army considers reading comprehension so important that soldiers attending primary, basic, and advanced NCOES courses must read at the tenth-grade level and at the twelfth-grade level for the Sergeants Major Course. Were this policy not in effect, soldiers who could not read at a high level would be at a disadvantage against those who could, and would fare poorly during the course.

This requirement carries over to duty performance. Senior leaders, both officers and NCOs, routinely read inches-high piles of official documents that flow through local mail distribution systems, and junior leaders pore over field manuals or memorandums of instruction while preparing classes for their soldiers.

Writing is as important as reading. NCOs who have a hard time putting thoughts on paper—even if they are otherwise excellent leaders—limit their influence to those they directly supervise. Some intended meanings get through to the busy readers, but too many remain buried because of poor writing skills. Largely due to formal training provided by NCOES, thousands of NCOES graduates understand that the Army writing standard puts the bottom line up front, which means placing the intended meaning of their writing in the first sentences or paragraph.

Write and Read to Succeed

Write directly and to your audience. If you can convey an idea with a single understood word instead of a series of words or one that no one understands, do so, rather than flashing how erudite you might be. If you are writing to sell a program or an idea, put it into as few words as possible. Senior leaders look at hundreds of documents every day; those not concise or clear fall by the wayside—even if they represent the day's best idea—because they were too long to read, confusing, or had the main point buried somewhere in the text. Any person able to read and summarize a ten-page paper in two or three paragraphs that convey the meaning of the longer paper is a cherished asset in any organization.

When writing, watch your sentence structure, grammar, punctuation, mechanics, usage, tense, subject-verb agreement, and jargon, which can all contribute to reader confusion. The easier your writing is to understand, the better chance you have of making your point. Remember that those who have a difficult time comprehending what they read will have even more difficulty if what they read is poorly written.

PERSONAL REFERENCE LIBRARY AND RECOMMENDED READING

Whatever your literary pursuits, you need basic reference books to be an adept communicator. Make sure you have *Webster's New Collegiate Dictionary* in your personal reference library, as well as the *Army Dictionary and Desk*

Reference by Maj. Tim Zurick (Stackpole Books), and the *Guide to Effective Military Writing* by William A. McIntosh (Stackpole Books).

Also read *The Story of the Noncommissioned Officer* and *The Sergeants Major of the Army*, which are both available through the Government Printing Office (GPO). Write to Superintendent of Documents, US Government Printing Office, Washington, D.C. 20402, or visit the US Government Bookstore at http://bookstore.gpo.gov.

The US Army Chief of Staff's Professional Reading List

Historically, one of the most important, distinguishing characteristics of outstanding soldiers has been a challenging personal professional development program based largely on reading. On 14 June 2000, in coordination with the Army's 225th birthday, the Chief of Staff established a professional reading list to represent his personal commitment to self-study as a critical aspect of professional development. Subsequent chiefs have upheld that tradition and created their own reading lists. As of this printing, the current US Army Chief of Staff's Professional Reading List is divided into three categories: Armies at War: Battles and Campaigns, the Army Profession, and Strategy and the Strategic Environment. By using sublists, the books are grouped so that readers of any rank or position can select the titles that they are most interested in.

The reading list includes only some of the many books relating to the military profession. They are specifically selected for their value in helping readers learn more about the Army as well as better understand the service's long and distinguished history. These books are great for anyone interested in the military and work well to demonstrate the decisive role played by armies in conflicts across the centuries. The list can be found at www.history.army.mil/reading.html.

What follows are the books and poetry that most affected my attitudes toward service as an NCO and that I have recommended that my NCOs read. Most lend a historical perspective and deal with issues we have all faced or will face in the future: soldier motivation and morale, ethics, training, and leadership, most especially that of the small unit in extreme circumstances. Lastly, many look at leaders who are looking at themselves.

Nonfiction Books

American Military History, Richard Stewart
Brave Men, Ernie Pyle
Common Sense Training, Arthur S. Collins
Gettysburg: A Testing of Courage, Noah Andre Trudeau
GI: The US Infantryman in World War II, Robert S. Rush
Hell in Hürtgen Forest, Robert S. Rush
Homeward Bound: American Veterans Return form War, Richard H. and
     Sandra Wright Taylor

Long Hard Road: NCO Experiences in Afghanistan and Iraq, US Army
   Sergeants Major Academy
Long Hard Road II: NCO Experiences in the Surge, US Army Sergeants
   Major Academy
On Point: The United States Army in Operation Iraqi Freedom, Gregory
   Fontenot, E. J. Degen, and David Tohn
Sgt. York: His Life, Legend & Legacy, John Perry
The Shake 'n Bake Sergeant: True Story of Infantry Sergeants in Vietnam,
   Jerry S. Horton, PhD
Small Unit Leadership, Dandridge (Mike) Malone
The Three Meter Zone: Common Sense Leadership for NCOs, J. D. Pendry
Top Sergeant, William G. Bainbridge
The U.S. Army's Transition to the All-Volunteer Force, Robert K. Griffith Jr.
We Were Soldiers Once . . . and Young, Harold G. Moore and Joseph L.
   Galloway
Taming the Fire Within: Life After War, Anne Freund, PhD

Fiction Books
   The Centurions, Jean Larteguy
   Forgotten Soldier, Guy Sager
   Once an Eagle, Anton Myrer
   Starship Troopers, Robert A. Heinlein

Poetry
   "If," Rudyard Kipling
   "The 'Eathen," Rudyard Kipling
   "The Quitter," Robert W. Service

Blogs and Forums
   DODLive, www.dodlive.mil
   NCO Journal, ncojournal.dodlive.mil
   RallyPoint, www.rallypoint.com
   Small Wars Council, council.smallwarsjournal.com

I would also recommend the following books: *The Forgotten War: Amer-*
ica in Korea 1950–1953 by Clay Blair for his detailed research on the Korean
War, and *Until the Last Trumpet Sounds: The Life of General of the Armies*
John J. Pershing by Gene Smith.

The US Army Center of Military History has hundreds of books available
at no cost to units with publication accounts through the Government Printing
Office. Stackpole Books, the *NCO Guide*'s publisher, offers more than a hundred other titles of interest to the military reader. *Army Times* is also a useful
source of military news, features, and other information, although not as vital

now that the Army has most information on its websites. The print editions of the *NCO Journal* and *SOLDIERS* are now published online and are recommended sources of current information on units and people in the Army.

Journals of professional associations are another good resource. The Noncommissioned Officers Association (NCOA) and the Association of the US Army (AUSA) publish *NCOA Journal* and *AUSA News*, respectively. The AUSA also mails its monthly *Army* magazine to members. More on these associations will follow in respective sections below.

Read the trade magazines and Army professional journals that apply to your MOS to keep up with trends, changes, and other matters related to your specialty. Combat arms soldiers may read the *Infantry*, *Armor*, and *Field Artillery* Professional Bulletins. Other combat arms, combat support, and combat service support publications are available as well, including *Army Sustainment* magazine. Check with your first sergeant or command sergeant major for other recommendations.

If you are stationed overseas, read the *Stars and Stripes*, which is published in several editions to provide daily news, sports, features, columns, and other information to soldiers and their families. Daily offerings from *USA Today*, the *Wall Street Journal*, the *Herald Tribune*, and certain other major newspapers serve soldier-readers stationed at major installations abroad. Most newspapers also have websites that you can access to remain abreast of world developments.

WRITING FOR PROFESSIONAL DEVELOPMENT

Your professional development should be shared. Writing will develop your professional skills and your writing abilities through the discipline of writing for publication. Other factors being equal, an NCO who writes well is more valuable and is promoted faster than one who doesn't. As you learn, share your knowledge by writing about it. Submit material to the following:

- *NCO Journal.* The editor is always on the hunt for good material. Here are the guidelines: Keep the reader in mind, address the subject to a wide audience, write conversationally, keep it simple and short (four double-spaced pages fill a magazine page), and include photos or other illustrations. The editor also wants letters from NCOs who agree or disagree with what they read in the journal, or who have a better idea about aspects of NCO business. Book reviews are also welcomed. Include the title, author, publisher, date published, price, whether it is hardbound or softbound, and number of pages. For more information, contact the editor and ask for a reprint of "Wanted: Writers." The address is *NCO Journal*, ATTN: Editor, USASMA, Fort Bliss, TX 79918.

- *The AUSA Institute of Land Warfare (ILW).* The ILW wants to hear from you. Request a copy of "Manuscripts Wanted" from the institute at 2425 Wilson Blvd., Arlington, VA 22201, or call (800) 336-4570. The

AUSA needs land warfare papers, essays, and books. You may also submit material to *Army* magazine at the same address. Write and ask for a copy of the magazine's style requirements.
- Center for Army Lessons Learned (CALL). If you have learned a valuable professional lesson, relate it in writing to the CALL. Send material to Commander, Combined Arms Command, ATTN: ATZL-CTL, Fort Leavenworth, KS 66027-7000. Lessons shared help drive doctrinal and force structure improvements.
- The different branch journals.

Regulations about For-profit Writing

Before you try to make money selling what you write, consult the *Department of Defense Ethics Guidelines*. Visit your local ethics counselor at the Judge Advocate General's office to discuss your topic, research methods, data resources, commercial intention, and proposed business relationship with your publisher. Let the counselor be your guide. If you get the nod to proceed, then go for it. If the counselor recommends that you not publish, then discuss alternatives—for example, switching from nonfiction to autobiographical fiction—but do not twist sound guidance into an illegal framework based on a profit motive. Put the Professional Army Ethic first.

If you are on active duty, do not allow a publisher to print your official rank before your name on a cover or to use your rank to solicit for sales, because doing so is a conflict of interest in most for-profit cases; it could make potential customers believe that, contrary to federal law, the government endorses your work.

The Department of Defense (DoD) ethics guidelines give potential enlisted soldier-authors a lot of leeway. Officers in procurement and acquisition positions have much more restrictive guidance to follow. Just remember, however, that certain restrictions apply, some of which will depend on your subject matter and your own position. Further—and it should go without saying—do not disclose classified information. Again, you are strongly encouraged to visit your local ethics counselor before selling a manuscript.

THE ARMY ONLINE

The Army is transitioning much of its printed materials and automating processes using Web-enabled tools and sites, with thousands currently online and more being published daily. Casual awareness or use of computers alone is not enough in this era; noncommissioned officers must become technologically savvy and have a deeper understanding of how to use and employ these tools. Commercial, public, and government communications have spread across vast electronic networks in public or encrypted forms. You no longer have to thumb through old copies of the *Army Times* or look for the latest Human Resources Command (HRC) message to find information vital to your career. Just enter the HRC home page and view the most up-to-date information concerning your MOS. Entire field manuals and regulations are online from the Army Training (and Education) Network's home page. Need to prepare a class on the most current techniques to breach a minefield? Try the Center for Army Lessons Learned. It's all there—you just have to look.

The Internet, intranets, Web pages, electronic mail, and remote access are all mainstream methods of transmitting and receiving information to and from the digital platforms that we use every day. These forms of communication were practically unheard of fifteen years ago; now they are essential for doing business. Nearly all companies and organizations throughout the world have their own websites that are used both to advertise and to make available vast quantities of information. With computers, smartphones, and tablets, NCOs can reach out and communicate with—or retrieve information from—anyone, anywhere in the world.

The Internet
The Internet is the worldwide free enterprise network of computers that links distant sites together. It is a combination of tens of thousands of computer servers linked to computer users via telephone lines or direct circuits. Each server is a separate "site" with a unique name. Although the US DoD originally developed the Internet as a means of transmitting research data, it uses the "net" to transmit routine electronic mail (email) as well as to post great quantities of current information. The Nonsecure Internet Protocol Router Network (NIPRNet) is used to transmit unclassified information between government computers, and to allow government users access to the Internet. The Secret Internet Protocol Router Network (SIPRNet) and other networks are a part of the Defense Information Systems Network and allow for the transfer of classified information.

Intranets
Intranets or portals are simply proprietary internal versions of the Internet within a large organization. Intranets are primarily used as graphical bulletin boards where current information and commonly used text reference materials are posted. This greatly enhances document access and information flow between workers.

Web Pages
A Web page is the visual presentation of a document on the Web. Usually each page contains one type or grouping of information with links to other subpages or to other Web pages at different sites. Web pages can be as simple as text pages or as complex as pages with pictures, animated images, video clips, and attached sound files.

Electronic Mail (Email)

Email is the electronic transmission of messages and documents across one or more networks, computer to computer. This form of communication has literally exploded in the past few years. Email is generally a standalone system or a separate module within a software package that uses any one or more of the following to transmit data: local area networks (LANs), wide area networks (WANs), telephone connections, or the Internet. The Army's intent is for every soldier (Active, Guard, and Reserve) and DA civilian to have a transportable email account that they can use in any organization to which they belong.

Social Media Considerations

Social media has become a major factor in our culture, and its use has been known to help and improve the sharing of information between units and soldiers and their families. In this day and age we depend on social media, but its use can be extremely dangerous if you're not careful, especially when deployed. Operations security (OPSEC) and protecting your personal privacy should be a concern whenever you use social media. It does not matter whether you are at home or deployed, or whether you are only using it to stay in touch with close friends and family. Social media is a rewarding communication tool but must be used smartly. Never post online what you wouldn't want your mother or first sergeant to see.

Soldiers are personally responsible for all content they publish on social media sites, blogs, or other websites. NCO leaders need to continuously remind them of the perils of bad behavior online. Clear-cut lines between a soldier's personal and professional life often get blurred when spending time online or using social media applications, so soldiers should always be mindful about mission-related and non-military-related content when posting. The bottom line is that soldiers who violate Federal law, regulations, or policies through inappropriate personal online activity are subject to discipline under the UCMJ.

US Army Online

Listed below are some of the more popular websites that deal with military issues. At the time of writing, all of the listed links worked.

Adjutant General Directorate	https://www.hrc.army.mil/TAGD
APFT Score Converter	http://apftcalculator.com
Army and Air Force Exchange Service	www.shopmyexchange.com
Army Capabilities Integration Center	www.arcic.army.mil
Army Continuing Education System	https://www.armyeducation.army.mil
Army Correspondence Course Program	www.atsc.army.mil/accp
Army electronic forms	http://armypubs.army.mil/eforms
Army home page	www.army.mil

Army Housing	https://www.housing.army.mil
Army Knowledge Online access page	www.us.army.mil
Army National Guard	www.arng.army.mil
Army Public Affairs	www.army.mil/info/institution/publicAffairs
Army Publishing Directorate (USAPA)	www.apd.army.mil
Army Reserve	www.usar.army.mil
Army Retirement Services	http://soldierforlife.army.mil/retirement
Army Strong Bonds	www.strongbonds.org
Army Substance Abuse Program	http://acsap.army.mil
Army Suggestion Program	https://asp.hqda.pentagon.mil/public
Army Training Network (ATN)	www.adtdl.army.mil
Army Training Requirements and Resources System (ATRRS)	https://www.atrrs.army.mil
Assignment Satisfaction Key (ASK)	https://www.ask.army.mil/ask
Association of the United States Army	www.ausa.org
CALL (Center for Army Lessons Learned)	http://usacac.army.mil/CAC2/call
Center of Military History (CMH)	www.history.army.mil
Comprehensive Soldier and Family Fitness (CSF2)	http://csf2.army.mil
Defense Activity for Non-Traditional Education Support (DANTES)	www.dantes.doded.mil
Defense Finance and Accounting Service	www.dfas.mil
DefenseLink	www.defense.gov
Defense Travel System (DTS)	www.defensetravel.osd.mil/dts/site/index.jsp
Department of Veterans Affairs	www.va.gov
DoD Dictionary	ww.dtic.mil/doctrine/dod_dictionary
Enlisted National Guard Association	www.ngaus.org
Enlisted Personnel Management Directorate (HRC)	https://www.hrc.army.mil/Enlisted
Enlisted Promotions Branch (HRC)	https://www.hrc.army.mil/TAGD/Enlisted%20Promotions
GoArmyEd	https://www.goarmyed.com
GulfLink	www.gulflink.osd.mil
Headquarters, Department of the Army	www.hqda.army.mil
Human Resources Command	www.hrc.army.mil
Installations & Facilities	www.army.mil/info/organization
iPERMS	https://iperms.hrc.army.mil
Medals and Ribbons	www.tioh.hqda.pentagon.mil
MILPER Messages	https://www.hrc.army.mil/milper
Military OneSource	www.militaryonesource.mil
Military Review Magazine	http://usacac.army.mil/CAC2/Military Review

milSuite	https://www.milsuite.mil
myArmy Benefits	http://myarmybenefits.us.army.mil
myPay	https://mypay.dfas.mil
myRecords Portal (HRC)	https://www.hrcapps.army.mil/portal
myTraining Tab (MT2)	www.train.army.mil
NCO History	www.ncohistory.com
NCO Journal	http://ncojournal.dodlive.mil
Pentagon Library	www.whs.mil/library
Per Diem rates	www.gsa.gov/perdiemrates
PS Magazine	https://www.logsa.army.mil/psmag/ pshome.html
Ready and Resilient	www.army.mil/readyandresilient
Reimer Digital Library (CAR)	https://rdl.train.army.mil
Retirement Services Office	http://soldierforlife.army.mil/retirement
Retention and Reenlistment	www.armyreenlistment.com
Sergeants Major Academy	https://usasma.bliss.army.mil
Sergeant Major of the Army	www.army.mil/leaders/sma
SHARP	www.sexualassault.army.mil
Soldier for Life	www.soldierforlife.army.mil
Soldier for Life—Transition Assistance Program (SFL-TAP)	https://www.SFL-TAP.army.mil
Soldiers Magazine Online	http://soldiers.dodlive.mil
Thrift Savings Plan	www.tsp.gov
Training and Doctrine Digital Library	www.train.army.mil
Training Support Center (ATSC)	www.atsc.army.mil
TRICARE home page	www.tricare.mil
USAJOBS (OPM)	www.usajobs.gov
Veteran's Affairs OEF/IF website	www.oefoif.va.gov
Warrior Tasks and Battle Drills (WTBD)	www.atsc.army.mil/itsd/ctt.asp

PROFESSIONAL ASSOCIATIONS

The Army is a profession. Thankfully, ours is a trusted and self-policing one where we train and develop to gain expertise to provide important services to our nation. As professionals, we have the opportunity to affiliate with people who help us maintain oversight of our chosen practice and with some of the staunchest and most trusted non-profit and private military veteran and service organizations. In the civilian sector, there are many well-known associations and societies that represent the interest of their professions, such as the American Society of Civil Engineers (ASCE) or the American Medical Association (AMA) for doctors.

Many of these military associations were created in response to perceived unmet needs of soldiers and their families. Others were conceived as the result of the challenge for military members to have a voice in a profession where civilian control of the military directly affects their ability to exercise the typical civilian rights afforded to other professions.

Not to be confused with unions, these private organizations are often filled with current and former professional practitioners who represent the Army community and can be some of the greatest advocates for soldiers to local, state, and nationally elected leaders. However, as with any volunteer off-duty activity, it is important that those who elect to participate with private organizations do so of their own free will without coercion or pressure from leaders.

The Noncommissioned Officers Association (NCOA)

The Noncommissioned Officers Association (NCOA) is a federally chartered, nonprofit, fraternal association founded in 1960. Its purpose is to accomplish the following:

- Uphold and defend the Constitution and support a strong national defense with a focus on military personnel issues.
- Promote health, prosperity, and scholarship among its members and their families through legislative and benevolent programs.
- Improve benefits for soldiers, veterans, and their families and survivors.
- Help soldiers, veterans, and their families and survivors in filing benefit claims.

Through its office near the Pentagon, NCOA actively lobbies Congress, the White House, the Department of Veterans Affairs, the military services, and other federal agencies to fulfill its goals. The association also supervises the following:

- Major nonpartisan voter registration drives in the United States and abroad.
- A nationwide network of coordinators who monitor state and local administrative and legislative activities affecting NCOA members.
- A nationwide outreach program for hospitalized veterans.
- Fellowship and intern programs for undergraduate college students.

Annual membership for NCOs is $30. The association offers many member benefits, including the Certified Merchants Program and the Buying Network, which provide substantial discounts on commercial products and services. Members may qualify for the competitive NCOA World MasterCard. Members with families may purchase TRICARE and CHAMPVA Supplemental Insurance Plans, a health insurance supplement offered through the Association and Society Insurance Corporation (ASI), or a group vision care plan with the Eye-Med Vision Care Program. Members also receive the *NCOA Journal*.

For more information, call (800) 662-2620; write to Noncommissioned Officers Association, ATTN: Membership Processing, 9330 Corporate Dr., Suite 701, Selma, TX 78154; or check their website, www.ncoausa.org.

The Association of the US Army (AUSA)

The Association of the US Army (AUSA) is a private, nonprofit organization established in 1950. It supports Active and Reserve Component members, Army civilians, retirees, and Army families. Its goals are as follows:

- Be the voice for all components of America's Army.
- Foster public support for the Army's role in national security.
- Provide professional education and information programs.

AUSA focuses on issues that affect soldiers during and after service. The association pushes for pay equity, adequate military housing, cost-of-living allowances, and standard subsistence allowances for all personnel.

Regular membership costs are stepped according to grade: $26 for E-5 through E-7 and $31 for E-8 through E-9. Among its membership benefits are opportunities to participate in chapter activities and discount product and service programs. Members in the rank of sergeant and above receive *AUSA News* and *Army* magazine. Corporals who elect to pay a discounted $21 per year for membership will receive both the newspaper and the magazine. Corporals and other soldiers whose pay grades are E-4 and below may opt to join AUSA for $14 per year, but the reduced fee does not include *Army* magazine.

For more information, check the AUSA website, www.ausa.org; write to Association of the US Army, 2425 Wilson Blvd., Arlington, VA 22201; call (800) 336-4570; or email membersupport@ausa.org.

National Guard Enlisted Association (EANGUS)

The National Guard Enlisted Association (EANGUS) exists to "promote the status, welfare, and professionalism of the enlisted members of the National Guard of the United States" and "promote adequate National Security." It handles and maintains active communications with the DoD, the National Guard Bureau, the National Guard Association, and other military support organizations in Washington, D.C.

EANGUS's home page is www.eangus.org. Users can access Thomas (the congressional database system), Senate, House, EANGUS *New Patriot* magazine and newsletter, *Congressional Quarterly*, legislative updates, and more. Email will put you in touch with the various departments at the national office that can answer your questions regarding membership, events, and legislative issues.

For more information, visit their website, www.eangus.org; write to Enlisted Association of the National Guard of the United States, 3133 Mt. Vernon Ave., Alexandria, VA 22305; call toll-free (800) 234-EANG; or email eangus @eangus.org.

11

Personal Fitness Improvement

Noncommissioned officers are expected to take part in and lead physical training sessions. Nothing improves credibility in front of troops more than setting the example during rigorous fitness training. And more importantly, the many battles in which American troops have fought and continue to fight underscore the important role physical fitness plays on the battlefield. If we fail to prepare our soldiers for their physically demanding wartime tasks, we are guilty of paying lip service to the principle of "Train as you fight." It is difficult to survive in 130-degree heat while wearing body armor when you or your soldiers aren't in shape.

During the Global War on Terrorism, the Army conducted a comprehensive review of how it trained soldiers, including the physical training program, and took a new scientific approach to physical readiness training (PRT), as compared to physical training. After testing the new program at basic training centers, the Army published a redesigned and renumbered FM 7-22, Army Physical Readiness Training, in October 2012 and redefined Army doctrine for the execution of the Army Physical Readiness Training System.

ARMY PHYSICAL READINESS TRAINING PROGRAM

The Army's Physical Readiness Training Program's objective is to enhance combat readiness by developing and sustaining a high level of physical fitness. As a component of the program, Physical Readiness Training (PRT) prepares soldiers for the physical challenges of military service under a wide range of threats, in complex operational environments, and with emerging technologies.

The Army PRT goal is to improve each soldier's physical ability to survive and win. Physical readiness takes into account all aspects of individual physical performance and emphasizes training beyond preparation for a physical fitness test. As primary trainers of their enlisted soldiers, NCOs must conduct mission- and METL-focused PRT that are based on Army or mission standards, focused, and performance oriented. To reach the end-state of PRT, NCOs must:

- Identify specific tasks that PRT enhances in support of the unit's METL on individual, crew, and small team levels.
- Prepare, rehearse, and execute PRT.
- Evaluate PRT and conduct AARs to provide feedback to the commander.

For NCOs to be successful in leading their soldiers through PRT, they must know them as individuals and be quick to recognize signs indicating their reactions to instruction. NCOs must ensure their soldiers understand the critical importance of PRT and how it will help them accomplish individual warrior tasks and battle drills, in support of the unit's MET. Noncommissioned officers will also help junior leaders to train and teach soldiers to master PRT drills, exercise activities, and assessments.

The PRT system incorporates three components of training, defined as follows:

- *Strength.* The ability to overcome resistance.
- *Endurance.* The ability to sustain activity.
- *Mobility.* The functional application of strength and endurance.

Physical Fitness and Deployment

If time permits, you should train your soldiers on the most physically demanding METL tasks, such as foot marches under combat loads, lifting and loading equipment, obstacle courses, and individual movement techniques in battle gear. Exercise your soldiers five days per week regardless of unit type, alternating aerobic activities with muscular strength and endurance exercises in accordance with FM 7-22.

Consider conducting physical training (PT) during hot periods of the day to facilitate acclimatization. It takes eight to fourteen days to acclimate to a hot, humid climate. Ensure that you adjust the exercise intensity to meet the heat index without undue risk to your soldiers. Have your soldiers drink sufficient water and maintain appropriate mineral levels in the body.

If the mission and conditions permit, conduct physical training and testing while deployed. Do anything that you can to keep your soldiers ready for any contingency.

On redeployment, resume physical training as soon as practicable. You can be assured that a long deployment will lower your unit's physical fitness level from what it was before you deployed. MOS-specific tasks such as those listed above will be easy, but returning to strength, endurance, and mobility training will be less so. Begin with lower numbers of repetitions and shorter, slower runs; increase the intensity over a period of sixty to ninety days to pre-deployment levels.

At Home Station

Soldiers in many Army units are required to take part in daily PT. AR 350-1, Army Training and Leader Development, mandates that soldiers be afforded the opportunity to exercise during duty hours at least three to five times per week. While many units exercise five times per week, many soldiers in headquarters and administrative units have to exercise on their own time.

At Service Schools

Students attending NCOES courses are required to do PT five times per week, except when in the field overnight, in compliance with Training and Doctrine Command (TRADOC). Students are required to lead fitness training on a rotational basis and are evaluated by NCO academy small-group leaders on their ability to plan and conduct the training.

As an end-of-course graduation requirement, soldiers must take and pass a standard or approved alternate Army Physical Fitness Test (APFT) administered at the schools for the following NCOES courses: WLC (Reserve Component soldiers are tested during the final resident phase—IDT, AT, or ADT—of ALC), SLC, SMC, and Sergeants Major Nonresident Course. Soldiers taking functional courses over sixty days in length may opt for an APFT. RC soldiers enrolled in NCOES courses will be tested by the end of the first week of training to allow sufficient time to retest to meet the end-of-course graduation requirement. If a soldier fails the APFT while enrolled in an NCOES course, one retest will be given.

Principles

Army PRT sessions typically follow the principles of precision, progression, and integration. These core principles ensure that soldiers perform all fitness training sessions, activities, drills, and exercises correctly, using the appropriate intensity and duration for the best conditioning and injury control.

- *Precision.* Strict adherence to optimal execution standards for PRT activities.
- *Progression.* Systematic increase in the intensity, duration, volume, and difficulty of PRT activities.
- *Integration.* Multiple training activities to achieve balance and appropriate recovery between activities.

STANDARDIZED PHYSICAL TRAINING SESSION

Physical training sessions should follow a standardized process. To get the best results, the three critical components—warm-up, activity, and cool-down—should be included, in that order.

There are three stages to a standard PT session. The initial stage occurs during early military training and is followed by improvement and maintenance. The improvement stage is when you cause a gradual increase in your overall exercise to allow for greater improvement in your fitness level. This might occur before or after a deployment or school, after a change in unit or unit MET, or after an injury or when returning to regular exercise following pregnancy. The maintenance stage goal is the long-term upkeep of cardiorespiratory, muscular strength, and endurance fitness. Maintaining progression rates throughout these three stages should be your goal for every physical training session.

The perfect push-up.

Warm-up Exercise Drills

The warm-up portion of your workout should take about fifteen minutes and be done just before the main activities of the PT session. On training days that focus mainly on strength and mobility, conduct 4 for the Core and the Hip Stability Drill, followed by Conditioning Drill 1. On training days that focus mainly on endurance and mobility, your warm-up should include Conditioning Drill 1 followed by the Military Movement Drill. After you have completed the warm-up, you are ready for more vigorous conditioning activities.

Peak musculoskeletal function needs an adequate range of motion maintained at all joints. The exercises listed in the warm-up drill below push the body to extend its range of motion by going through a variety of postures.

THE MILITARY MOVEMENT DRILL

1. Verticals	1 repetition
2. Laterals	1 repetition
3. The Shuttle Sprint	1 repetition

Standardized Physical Training Activities

Your PT sessions should continue to follow the standard regimen. Set training sessions are specified on the physical training schedule and include sustained running, speed running, Conditioning Drill 2, and Conditioning Drill 3.

Running. The body's ability to use oxygen in muscle is known as cardiorespiratory endurance. PT activities should include group runs, speed running, foot marching, obstacle and bayonet assault course negotiation, and common skills training to challenge your cardiorespiratory endurance.

Calisthenics. Muscular strength is similar to muscular endurance—they go hand-in-hand but are not the same. Muscular strength is to overcome maximum resistance in one single repetition, while muscular endurance is to overcome resistance in multiple repetitions. Equally important, mobility is the application of strength and endurance by physically capable soldiers who are able to perform their assigned duties.

You do not need a gym or expensive equipment for strength and mobility training. Calisthenics exercises are an important part of any fitness program for building muscular strength and mobility and can be done with your platoon, at home, or while away from your unit in a short time and with limited space. Resistance training benefits include an increase in bone mass and in the strength of surrounding tissue. The conditioning drills in a unit PRT program include exercises that train the major muscle groups of the arms, shoulders, chest, abdomen, back, hips, and legs. The major goal for this type of training is to develop total body strength and mobility quickly.

The following calisthenics exercises should be performed on alternate days. Additional sets and repetitions will bring about more strength gain.

Conditioning Drill 1

Conditioning Drill 1 (CD1) consists of calisthenics that develop motor skills while challenging strength, endurance, and flexibility. CD1 is always used as the warm-up activity; drill exercises should be performed in the sequence listed below.

CONDITIONING DRILL 1

1. The Bend and Reach
2. The Rear Lunge
3. The High Jumper
4. The Rower
5. The Squat Bender
6. The Windmill
7. The Forward Lunge
8. The Prone Row
9. The Bent-leg Body Twist
10. The Push-up

Conditioning Drill 2

Conditioning Drill 2 (CD2) is calisthenics intended to enhance upper-body strength, endurance, and mobility. Just like in CD1, the drill exercises are always performed in the sequence listed below. You should work with a partner when performing the pull-ups.

CONDITIONING DRILL 2

1. The Push-up
2. The Sit-up
3. The Pull-up

Conditioning Drill 3

Conditioning Drill 3 (CD3) consists of five exercises that toughen and assist in developing complex motor skills and challenge strength, endurance, and mobility. The exercises in CD3 are conducted to cadence, and the drill exercises are always performed in the sequence listed below. Exercises are done to cadence for five sets of four-count repetitions, increasing to ten sets of repetitions. Maintaining proper exercise form and properly completing the drill are more important than speed.

CONDITIONING DRILL 3

1. The Power Jump
2. The V-up
3. The Mountain Climber
4. The Leg Tuck and Twist
5. The Single-leg Push-up

Stability Training

Stability of the body's core includes more than ten repetitions of exercises 1–4 of the Hip Stability Drill (do not exceed sixty seconds for exercise 5). If you want more repetitions for any one exercise session, repeat either or both of these drills in their entirety; do not single out any one exercise.

---

4 FOR THE CORE

1. The Bent-leg Raise	Hold for 60 seconds
2. The Side Bridge	Hold for 60 seconds
3. The Back Bridge	Hold for 60 seconds
4. The Quadraplex	Hold for 60 seconds

THE HIP STABILITY DRILL

1. The Lateral Leg Raise   5 repetitions on each side
2. The Medial Leg Raise   5 repetitions on each side
3. The Lateral Bent-leg Raise   5 repetitions on each side
4. The Single-leg Tuck   5 repetitions on each side
5. The Single-leg Over   Hold for 20 seconds on each side
                                (do not exceed 60 seconds)

Standardized Cool-down

The cool-down is designed to help bring your heart rate down and to keep blood from pooling in your legs or feet. It usually starts at the end of cardiorespiratory endurance training and should last for no more than ten minutes. To begin the cool-down, reduce your rate of exercise to a walk and continue until heavy sweating subsides and your heart rate is under 100 beats per minute. Once achieved, transition to the Stretch Drill, which is designed to safely return you to your pre-exercise state after performing vigorous exercise. The Stretch Drill involves movements that slowly stretch muscles and require you to hold that position for an extended period. These exercises were designed to improve flexibility in the body's major muscle groups.

THE STRETCH DRILL

1. The Overhead Arm Pull   Hold for 20 seconds on each side
2. The Rear Lunge   Hold for 20 seconds on each side
3. The Extend and Flex   Hold for 20 seconds in each stretch position
4. The Thigh Stretch   Hold for 20 seconds on each side
5. The Single-leg Over   Hold for 20 seconds on each side

THE ARMY PHYSICAL FITNESS TEST

Soldiers taking the APFT are encouraged to make a maximum effort to pass and excel. For soldiers on active duty, the test is administered a minimum of twice a year, with at least four months separating each record test. For Guardsmen and Reservists in Troop Program Units, the test must be taken at least yearly. Soldiers returning from deployment are required to take a record APFT no earlier than three months for active components and six months for reserve component soldiers. Soldiers fifty-five years of age and older have the option of taking the three-event APFT or the alternate APFT.

Described in detail in FM 7-22, appendix A, the APFT measures upper- and lower-body muscular endurance and indicates a soldier's ability to perform physically and handle his or her own body weight. APFT standards are adjusted for age and physiological differences between the genders.

The APFT consists of push-ups, sit-ups, and a 2-mile run, done in that order on the same day. The push-ups measure the endurance of the chest, shoulder, and triceps muscles. The sit-ups measure the endurance of the abdominal and hip-flexor muscles. The 2-mile run or alternate aerobic event (800-yard swim or 6.2-mile bicycle ride) measures cardiorespiratory and leg muscle endurance. Instructions for each APFT event in FM 7-22, appendix A, must be read verbatim before each is administered.

Administering the APFT

The leader in charge ensures that the APFT is properly administered; gets all necessary equipment and supplies; arranges and lays out the test area (if necessary); trains the event supervisors, scorers, and demonstrators; ensures that events are explained, demonstrated, and scored; and reports results to superiors. Event supervisors administer test events, ensure that necessary equipment is on hand, read test instructions and have events demonstrated, supervise scoring, and rule on questions and scoring errors or disputes. Scorers supervise the testing soldier's performance, enforce test standards, count aloud the repetitions performed on the push-up and sit-up events, and record raw scores on DA Form 705, the APFT Scorecard, which as of this printing was last revised in 2010 to reflect the current standards. Support personnel handle safety and crowd control.

Test Standards

Standards for the APFT are based on extensive analysis of baseline fitness standards between genders and the need to accommodate age groups. The current standards are shown on the following charts.

Members of special populations may be unable to take some or all of the APFT events for medical or other authorized or unavoidable reasons. In order to get credit for the APFT, however, they must take and pass the 2-mile run or an alternate aerobic event, which include the 800-yard swim, 6.2-mile bicycle ride (in one gear), and 2.5-mile walk. Like the run, the alternate events must be completed unassisted in a prescribed amount of time relative to age and gender. Unlike the run, the alternates are not scored; test-takers get credit for either passing or failing the event. Soldiers who fail any or all of the events must retake the entire test. In the case of test failure, commanders may allow soldiers to retake the test as soon as the soldiers and commander feel that the soldiers are ready. Soldiers without a medical profile will be retested no later than three months following the initial APFT failure.

2-MILE RUN

Age Group	Male Min.	Male Max.	Female Min.	Female Max.
17–21	15:54	13:00	18:54	15:36
22–26	16:36	13:00	19:36	15:36
27–31	17:00	13:18	20:30	15:48
32–36	17:42	13:18	21:42	15:54
37–41	18:18	13:36	22:42	17:00
42–46	18:42	14:06	23:42	17:24
47–51	19:30	14:24	24:00	17:36
52–56	19:48	14:42	24:24	19:00
57–61	19:54	15:18	24:48	19:42
62+	20:00	15:42	25:00	20:00

PUSH-UPS

Age Group	Male Min.	Male Max.	Female Min.	Female Max.
17–21	42	71	19	42
22–26	40	75	17	46
27–31	39	77	17	50
32–36	36	75	15	45
37–41	34	73	13	40
42–46	30	66	12	37
47–51	25	59	10	34
52–56	20	56	9	31
57–61	18	53	8	28
62+	16	50	7	25

SIT-UPS

Age Group	Male/Female Min.	Male/Female Max.
17–21	53	78
22–26	50	80
27–31	45	82
32–36	42	76
37–41	38	76
42–46	32	72
47–51	30	66
52–56	28	66
57–61	27	64
62+	26	63

Soldiers in the ranks of sergeant through command sergeant major have their APFT recorded on DA Form 2166-7, the NCO Evaluation Report (NCOER). NCOER raters enter "Pass," "Fail," or "Profile" on part IVc of the NCOER. It is also used in determining promotion points for advancement to sergeant and staff sergeant. Staff sergeants can earn up to 100 points for a score of 300; sergeants can earn up to 160 points for a score of 300. According to AR 623-3, Evaluation Reporting System, these entries reflect the NCO's status on the date of the most recent APFT administered by the unit within the twelve-month period prior to the last rated day of supervision. Excellence ratings based solely on the APFT require only the bullet "Received the Physical Fitness Badge." Ratings of "Needs Improvement" must reflect the actual APFT score. Raters must explain an APFT entry of "Fail" or "Profile."

Even if not used to demonstrate excellence, annotating the APFT score on the NCOER gives DA selection boards a better picture of the soldier. For example, a soldier in the grade of E-4 or E-5 consistently scores 270 and above on the APFT. On making staff sergeant, the lowest scores drop to 15 to give higher credit to those with a high score.

In compliance with Army retention policy, soldiers who have six months or more time in service who fail two consecutive record APFTs must be processed for separation for unsatisfactory performance under Chapter 13 of AR 635-200, Enlisted Personnel. Receipt of a "Chapter 13" for fitness failure indicates that the soldier is unqualified for further service because he or she will not develop sufficiently to participate in further training or become a satisfactory soldier. It also means that failures would be likely to recur and the ability of the soldier to perform duties effectively in the future, including potential for advancement or leadership, is unlikely. Entry-level soldiers—those with less than six months' time in service—who repeatedly fail diagnostic and record APFTs may be separated under Chapter 11 of the Enlisted Personnel regulation. A "Chapter 11" covers inability, lack of reasonable effort, or failure to adapt to the military environment.

The Army Physical Fitness Badge is awarded to soldiers attaining a score of 90 points in each event for a total of 270 points. Under the current standards, soldiers must score 270 points annually to continue to wear the badge. Award of the badge also constitutes an "Excellence" block on their NCOER.

Fit soldiers also receive verbal commendations and other accolades, are retained in service and selected for advanced military schooling, and can be promoted provided they meet other service-selection criteria, including presenting a sharp military appearance—which requires weight control.

WEIGHT CONTROL

AR 600-9, The Army Body Composition Program, states that each soldier (commissioned, warrant, or enlisted) is responsible for meeting service weight control standards. To help soldiers meet their responsibility, height and weight screening tables are published in the weight control regulation. The regulation recommends that soldiers strive to remain at least 5 percent below their individual screening table weight maximum. NCO supervisors should ensure that they and their soldiers practice weight control by individually attaining and maintaining an acceptable weight and body composition through self-motivation, diet, and exercise.

For some, the Army policy is easy to follow. Others have a real problem. Whether compliance is easy or not often depends on a number of factors, including the individual's body type—ectomorph (thin), mesomorph (medium to well proportioned), or endomorph (soft and heavier). Each of the body types can meet the standards, and each can fail to comply with—and exceed—the maximum body fat allowable for gender, age, height, and weight. An ectomorph in poor shape who eats a high-fat diet may carry much excess body fat. Conversely, an endomorph on a well-balanced diet, including high fiber, and who exercises regularly may carry little body fat. AR 600-9 (as of 28 June 2013) states that the stringent Department of Defense body fat goal is 20 percent for males and 26 percent for females. Army body fat standards are as follows:

Age Group: 17–20
Male (% body fat): 20
Female (% body fat): 30

Age Group: 21–27
Male (% body fat): 22
Female (% body fat): 32

Age Group: 28–39
Male (% body fat): 24
Female (% body fat): 34

Age Group: 40+
Male (% body fat): 26
Female (% body fat): 36

Commanders and NCO supervisors must monitor soldiers under their control to ensure that the soldiers maintain proper weight, body composition (the proportion of lean body mass, including muscle, bone, and essential organ tissue, to body fat), and personal appearance. Soldiers should be coached to select their personal weight goal within or below the 5 percent zone and strive to maintain that weight through adjustment of lifestyle and fitness routines. If a soldier consistently exceeds the personal weight goal, he or she should seek the assistance of a dietitian or a master fitness trainer for advice in proper exercise and of fitness and health-care personnel for a proper dietary program. Soldiers exceeding the screening table weight or identified by the commander or supervisor for a special evaluation will have their body fat measured using the tape-test method.

When males are tape-tested, they must have their abdomen and neck measured; females have their hips, forearm, neck, and wrist measured. All measurements are taken three times and must be to within $1/4$ inch of one another to be considered valid. Valid measurements are recorded on DA Forms 5500-R (males) and 5501-R (females), Body Fat Content Worksheet. Recorded measurements are then converted to prescribed body site factors, using site factor tables in AR 600-9. If carefully measured and correctly calculated, the result will fairly accurately show a soldier's body fat percentage. The tape test is not difficult to learn to administer. The male test takes about five minutes; the female test takes a little longer because more body sites are measured and calculated.

To help soldiers fight fat, NCO supervisors must provide educational and other motivational programs to encourage personnel to attain and maintain proper weight and body fat standards. Programs include nutrition education sessions conducted by qualified health-care personnel, as well as exercise programs. Commanders must enforce body fat standards and monitor, measure, and, if necessary, place individuals into the Army Body Composition Program and flag them under the provisions of AR 600-8-2. Soldiers should be removed from the program only after they achieve their body fat standard. The screening table weight will not be used to remove soldiers from a weight control program.

Soldiers flagged will not be allowed to reenlist or extend their enlistment, will be considered nonpromotable, and will not be assigned to command positions (e.g., first sergeant and command sergeant major). Unit commanders will initiate a mandatory bar to reenlistment or administrative separation proceeding for soldiers who do not make satisfactory progress in the weight control program after a six-month period and for whom no medical reasons exist to cause the overweight condition.

Compliance with the Army Body Composition Program is considered in the selection process for promotion, professional military or civilian schooling, or assignment to command positions. All soldiers scheduled for attendance at schooling will be screened prior to departing their home station or losing command. Their height and weight will be recorded on their temporary duty orders, DD Form 1610, Request and Authorization for TDY Travel of DOD Personnel, or on their permanent-change-of-station (PCS) orders. Soldiers exceeding established screening weight will not be allowed to depart their command until the commander has determined that they meet the standards.

Noncommissioned officers who exceed the established body fat standards upon arrival at any Department of the Army (DA) board select school or those who PCS to a professional military school but do not meet body fat standards will be processed for disenrollment and, if applicable, removed from the DA board select list. Personnel arriving at professional military schools (other than DA board select or PCS schools) who do not meet body fat composition standards will be denied enrollment and reassigned in accordance with AR 600-9.

Actions to initiate mandatory bars to reenlistment, or initiation of separation proceedings for soldiers eliminated for cause from NCOES courses, will be in accordance with AR 601-280, Army Reenlistment Program, and AR 635-200, Enlisted Personnel. Additionally, soldiers considered weight control failures by the definition in AR 600-9 will be processed for separation from the Army.

Soldiers who are entered into the weight control program and then successfully meet their body fat reduction goal will be removed from the program but monitored for a year. Failure to meet the standards at any time during the monitoring period will result in initiation of separation action.

Soldiers who consider themselves too fat—or who come close to qualifying for the Army Body Composition Program—should look at modifying their lifestyles and eating habits for life. Soldiers interested in an improved diet may seek guidance in appendix C, "Weight Loss," of AR 600-9.

WEIGHT FOR HEIGHT TABLE (SCREENING TABLE WEIGHT)

Height (inches)	Minimum weight[1] (pounds)	Male weight in pounds, by age				Female weight in pounds, by age			
		17–20	21–27	28–39	40+	17–20	21–27	28–39	40+
58	91	—	—	—	—	119	121	122	124
59	94	—	—	—	—	124	125	126	128
60	97	132	136	139	141	128	129	131	133
61	100	136	140	144	146	132	134	135	137
62	104	141	144	148	150	136	138	140	142
63	107	145	149	153	155	141	143	144	146
64	110	150	154	158	160	145	147	149	151
65	114	155	159	163	165	150	152	154	156
66	117	160	163	168	170	155	156	158	161
67	121	165	169	174	176	159	161	163	166
68	125	170	174	179	181	164	166	168	171
69	128	175	179	184	186	169	171	173	176
70	132	180	185	189	192	174	176	178	181
71	136	185	189	194	197	179	181	183	186
72	140	190	195	200	203	184	186	188	191
73	144	195	200	205	208	189	191	194	197
74	148	201	206	211	214	194	197	199	202
75	152	206	212	217	220	200	202	204	208
76	156	212	217	223	226	205	207	210	213
77	160	218	223	229	232	210	213	215	219
78	164	223	229	235	238	216	218	221	225
79	168	229	235	241	244	221	224	227	230
80[2]	173	234	240	247	250	227	230	233	236

[1]Male and female soldiers who fall below the minimum weights shown in the above table will be referred by their commander for immediate medical evaluation.

[2]Add 6 pounds per inch for males over 80 inches and 5 pounds per inch for females over 80 inches.

PART III

Quick Reference

12

Administration, Logistics, and Maintenance

PERSONNEL ADMINISTRATION

No NCO can function without some knowledge of Army administration. As you rise in rank, your ability to understand and perform administrative tasks becomes more and more important. Squad leaders and platoon sergeants will have to know how to fill out leave forms (DA Form 31), turn in equipment for repair, initiate requisition actions, plan and conduct convoy operations, and conduct evaluations on subordinates, among many other tasks.

Most situations that arise in the administration of an Army unit are covered in Army regulations or other publications. Knowing where to look for guidance is almost as important as knowing the answers. The Basic References table below will help you find what you are looking for.

The Army Publishing Directorate is responsible for the Army Publishing Program and is the Army's publisher and distributor of regulations and forms. Department of the Army (DA) electronic forms are available at the Army Publishing Directorate (APD) website, www.apd.army.mil, by clicking on the eForms button. Department of Defense Forms (DD Forms) are available at www.dtic.mil/whs/directives/infomgt/forms/formsprogram.htm, and Standard Forms (SF) and Optional Forms (OF) are available on the General Services Administration (GSA) Forms Library at www.gsa.gov/portal/forms/type/ALL.

File format .XFDL requires Lotus Forms Viewer, available at no cost on the APD site. File format .PDF requires Adobe Acrobat Reader, also available on the APD site. The Army is currently in the process of transitioning its PDF forms to a fillable Adobe PDF format, which will replace both the Lotus Forms in .XFDL format and the nonfillable PDF forms that are currently available.

Soldiers should be wary of illegal forms on nongovernmental websites. Scammers are using nonapproved forms to steal personal identifying information (PII) such as birth date and Social Security numbers. Whenever you or your soldiers are filling out a form online, you should always verify that it is an official form and from an official government website.

BASIC REFERENCES

Army Regulations and Publications
Check the APD website, http://armypubs.army.mil, for online publications.

AR 25-50	Preparing and Managing Correspondence (5/17/2013)
AR 25-400-2	The Army Records Information Management System (ARIMS) (10/2/2007)
AR 27-10	Military Justice (10/03/2011)
AR 37-104-4	Military Pay and Allowances Policy (06/08/2005)
AR 135-205	Enlisted Personnel Management (3/11/2008)
AR 190-11	Physical Security of Arms, Ammunition, and Explosives (9/5/2013)
AR 220-1	Unit Status Reporting (4/15/2010)
AR 220-15	Journals and Journal Files (12/1/1983)
AR 220-45	Duty Rosters (11/27/2012)
AR 350-1	Army Training and Leader Development (12/18/2009)
AR 350-10	Management of Army Individual Training Requirements and Resources (9/3/2009)
AR 385-10	Army Safety Program (5/23/2008)
AR 600-8-1	Army Casualty Program (7/3/2007)
AR 600-8-2	Suspension of Favorable Personnel Actions (Flag) (10/23/2012)
AR 600-8-6	Personnel Accounting and Strength Reporting (9/24/1998)
AR 600-8-7	Retirement Services Program (6/6/2010)
AR 600-8-8	The Total Army Sponsorship Program (4/4/2006)
AR 600-8-10	Leaves and Passes (2/15/2006)
AR 600-8-11	Reassignment (5/1/2007)
AR 600-8-14	Identification Cards for Members of the Uniformed Services, Their Eligible Family Members, and Other Eligible Personnel (6/17/2009)
AR 600-8-19	Enlisted Promotions and Reductions (4/30/2010)
AR 600-8-22	Military Awards (12/11/2006)
AR 600-8-104	Army Military Human Resource Records Management (8/2/2012)
AR 600-9	The Army Body Composition Program (6/28/2013)
AR 600-13	Army Policy for the Assignment of Female Soldiers (3/27/1992)
AR 600-20	Army Command Policy (3/18/2008)
AR 600-25	Salutes, Honors, and Visits of Courtesy (10/24/2004)
AR 600-85	Army Substance Abuse Program (ASAP) (12/28/2012)
AR 600-100	Army Leadership (3/8/2007)

AR 601-210	Active and Reserve Components Enlistment Program (2/8/2011)
AR 601-280	Army Retention Program (1/31/2006)
AR 614-30	Overseas Service (3/30/2010)
AR 614-200	Enlisted Assignments and Utilization Management (2/26/2009)
AR 621-5	Army Continuing Education System (7/11/2006)
AR 623-3	Evaluation Reporting System (6/5/2012)
AR 635-200	Active Duty Enlisted Administrative Separations (6/6/2005)
AR 640-30	Photographs for Military Human Resources Records (9/18/2008)
AR 670-1	Wear and Appearance of Army Uniforms and Insignia (4/10/2015)
AR 710-2	Supply Policy Below the National Level (3/28/2008)
AR 750-1	Army Materiel Maintenance Policy (9/20/2007)
AR 840-10	Flags, Guidons, Streamers, Tabards, and Automobile and Aircraft Plates (11/1/1998)
CMH Pub 70-37	Time Honored Professionals: The NCO Corps Since 1775
CMH Pub 70-38	The Story of the NCO
CMH Pub 70-63	The Sergeants Major of the Army
CTA 50-900	Clothing and Individual Equipment (11/20/2008) (can be found at http://armypubs.army.mil/doctrine/CTA_1.html)
CTA 50-909	Field and Garrison Furnishings and Equipment (8/1/1993) (same website as above)
CTA 50-970	Expendable and Durable Items (1/28/2005) (same website as above)
DA Form 6	Duty Roster (July 1974)
DA Form 2166-8	Noncommissioned Officer Evaluation Report (Oct 2011)
DA Form 2166-8-1	Noncommissioned Officer Evaluation Checklist (Oct 2011)
DA Form 4187	Personnel Action Request (January 2000)
MCM 2012	Manual for Courts-Martial, United States
Pam 350-38	Standards in Training Commission (3/28/2013)
Pam 385-1	Small Unit Safety Officer/ Noncommissioned Officer Guide (5/23/2013)
Pam 600-25	U.S. Army Noncommissioned Officer Professional Development Guide (7/28/2008)
Pam 600-35	Relationships between Soldiers of Different Ranks (2/21/2000)

Pam 600-60   A Guide to Protocol and Etiquette for Official
                  Entertainment (12/11/2001)
Pam 600-69   Unit Climate Profile Commanders Handbook
                  (10/1/1986)
Pam 611-21   Military Occupational Classification and Structure
                  (1/22/2007)
Pam 710-2-1   Using Unit Supply Systems (12/31/1997)

DoD Publications
DoD Instructions   Indebtedness of Military Personnel (12/8/2008)
1344.09
DoD Instructions   Enlisted Administrative Separations (08/28/2011)
1332.14

Doctrine and Training Publications
Most Army manuals are available online at http://armypubs.army.mil/
doctrine/index.html or at the Central Army Registry, www.adtdl.army.mil.

An Army study in 2009 identified a number of Field Manuals (FM) for renaming or superseding. New manual classifications created are Army Tactics, Techniques, and Procedures (ATTP), Army Techniques Publications (ATP), Army Doctrine Publications (ADP), and Army Doctrine Reference Publications (ADRP). They also created an ATTP pilot program in which soldiers are allowed to make recommended changes to the Army's Tactics, Techniques, and Procedures publications via a wiki environment called ATTP Wiki.

This new numbering follows the principle that ADRPs augment and support principle Army Doctrine Publications (ADP). Army Tactics, Techniques, and Procedures (ATTP) manuals provide doctrinal guidance and procedures. These may be paired with Field Manuals or supersede them. ATPs provide for common understanding, foundational concepts, and methods for executing specific tasks, and describe guidance and techniques for military specialties. For example, Army Doctrine Publication 1 (ADP 1) replaced FM 1 in September 2012, and the FM is no longer in effect. Army Doctrine Reference Publication 1 (ADRP 1) was published in June 2013 to "augment" Chapter 2 of ADP 1.

Each MOS has a corresponding set of basic reference publications. The most effective NCOs will know them and what is in them, while staying up-to-date on changes. In addition, the Central Army Registry, formerly known as the Reimer Digital Library, is a valuable source for these and other publications. Additionally, if you are near a military installation they may have a Learning Resource Center (LRC) or a post library that provides you with access to MOS reference publications.

New Number	Date	Selected FM Titles	Old Number
JCS PUB 1-02	8 Nov 2010	DOD Dictionary of Military and Associated Terms	
ADP 1	17 Sep 2012	The Army	FM 1
ADP 1-02	31 Aug 2012	Operational Terms and Military Symbols	FM 1-02
FM 1-04	18 Mar 2013	Legal Support to the Operational Army	FM 27-1
FM 27-10	18 Jul 1956	The Law of Land Warfare	
ADP 3-0	10 Dec 2011	Unified Land Operations	FM 3-0
FM 3-05.70	17 May 2002	Survival	FM 21-76
TC 3-21.5	20 Jan 2012	Drill and Ceremonies	FM 3-21.5
FM 22-6	17 Sep 1971	Guard Duty	
FM 3-21.8	28 Mar 2007	The Infantry Rifle Platoon and Squad	FM 7-8
FM 3-21.9	02 Dec 2002	The SBCT Infantry Rifle Platoon and Squad	
FM 21.18	01 Jun 1990	Foot Marches	
TC 3-21.75	13 Aug 2013	The Warrior Ethos and Soldier Combat Skills	FM 21-75
FM 7-22	01 Oct 1998	Army Physical Readiness Training	TC 3-22.20
FM 23-23	30 Mar 1973	Antipersonnel Mine M18A1 and M18 (Claymore)	
FM 3-22.30	15 Oct 2009	Grenades and Pyrotechnic Signals	FM 23-30
TC 3-22.31	13 Feb 2003	40mm Grenade Launchers M203 and M79	FM 3.22.31
FM 3-22.35	25 Jun 2003	Combat Training with Pistols and Revolvers	FM 23-35
FM 3-22.68	21 Jul 2006	Crew Served Weapons	FM 23-14
FM 3-22.9	12 Aug 2009	Rifle Marksmanship M16A1, M16A2/3, M16A4, and M4 Carbine	FM 23-9
TC 3-25.150	24 Sep 2012	Combatives	FM 3-25.150
FM 3-50.1	21 Nov 2011	Army Personnel Recovery	
FM 21-10	21 Jun 2000	Field Hygiene and Sanitation	
FM 4-25.12	25 Jan 2002	Unit Field Sanitation Team	FM 21-10-1
FM 4-25.11	23 Dec 2002	First Aid	FM 21-11
ADP 5	17 May 2012	The Operations Process	FM 5-0
ATP 6-22.1	1 Jul 2014	The Counseling Process	FM 6-22
FM 6-22.5	18 Mar 2009	Combat and Operational Stress Control Manual for Leaders and Soldiers	FM 22-9
ADP 7-0	23 Aug 2012	Training Units and Developing Leaders	FM 7-0
FM 7-21.13	20 Sep 2011	The Soldier's Guide	
TC 7-27.7	17 Apr 2015	Army Noncommissioned Officers Guide	TC 22-6
FM 10-27-4	14 Apr 2000	Organizational Supply for Unit Leaders	FM 10-27-4
STP 21-1-SMCT	11 Sep 2012	Soldier's Manual of Common Tasks Warrior Skills Level 1	STP 21-1
STP 21-24-SMCT	9 Sep 2008	Soldier's Manual of Common Tasks Warrior Skills Levels 2, 3 and 4	STP 21-24 SMCT

The following websites were current as of the time this book went to print. (Keep in mind these sites can change location, URL, or be deleted for various reasons.)

Defense Link	www.defenselink.mil
Army Home Page	www.army.mil
Army Installations	www.army.mil/info/organization/installations/forts
Human Resources Command	www.hrc.army.mil
Retirement Services	www.armyg1.army.mil/rso
PCS Travel	www.dfas.mil/pcstravel.html
Military Compensation	http://militarypay.defense.gov
Military Health System	www.health.mil
Center of Military History	www.history.army.mil
Army Training Support Center	www.atsc.army.mil
Army Training and Education Network (ATN)	http://rdl.train.army.mil
HQDA WEB	www.hqda.army.mil
TRADOC	www.tradoc.army.mil
ATRRS	www.atrrs.army.mil
milSuite	https://login.milsuite.mil
Army Education	https://www.goarmyed.com

Duty Rosters

AR 220-45, Duty Rosters, clearly states the rules for preparing and maintaining DA Form 6, Duty Roster. These rules are logical and easy to understand, yet accurately putting them into practice requires meticulous attention to detail.

Duty rosters are kept to record the duty performed by each person in an organization. Commanders may establish procedures that best suit the unit, but they must comply with AR 220-45 and the rule "the longest off duty, the first on," and be impartial in assigning duties to individuals. The "From" date on the roster is always the date immediately following the "To" date on a previous roster and is entered when the new roster is filled out. The "To" date is always the date of the last detail made from the roster and is entered when the roster is closed. Intermediate dates are entered as details are made, and no date will be entered for any day that the detail was not performed.

Duty rosters contain only the names of those personnel required to perform the duty involved. When a new roster is prepared, all names are entered alphabetically by rank, beginning with the highest-ranking person and using the appropriate grade of rank. Subsequent names are added to the bottom of the roster. Frequently rosters are published in advance. When absences of personnel already assigned to duty occur, they often happen at the last moment. Many commanders allow personnel to substitute for one another on various details,

DUTY ROSTER

| GRADE | NAME | NATURE OF DUTY | ORGANIZATION | FROM (Date) | TO (Date) |

Month
Day

DA FORM 6, JUL 1974 PREVIOUS EDITIONS OF THIS FORM ARE OBSOLETE. For use of this form, see AR 220-45; the proponent agency is DCS, G-1.

APD ALD v1.02

Duty Roster

and in some units, individuals make extra money by selling their services as substitutes. In such cases, the person who maintains the duty roster must be notified of any changes, and recovery of any promised compensation is strictly up to the individuals concerned. In most cases the person scheduled for duty will be held accountable to ensure the duty is pulled, not the replacement.

Details of units are made the same way they are for individuals: in turn, according to one roster. Commanders are authorized to use other methods, however, provided that equity is maintained.

The diagonal lines in the right corner of any block indicate duty on that date. The numbers in parentheses immediately following a person's name refer to a corresponding explanatory remark on the reverse of the roster. A remark must be made to explain the reason why an individual's name is added to or deleted from a roster, but the authority responsible for the preparation and maintenance of the roster determines the necessity of using an explanatory remark each time an individual is not available.

A numbering sequence is used between duty performances for every soldier listed that increases each day they are not selected. A letter D will be used if the soldier is already on detail and a U when they are unavailable due to other circumstances such as AWOL, ill, or misconduct, and the number sequence will increase. If a soldier is on an authorized absence, like leave, pass, or temporary duty, a letter A will be used to indicate the last number charged, as shown on the accompanying duty roster.

The duty roster should be available at all times for inspection by commanders, supervisors, and personnel concerned. If you are charged with the responsibility of maintaining a duty roster, do not feel that your integrity is being impugned when a soldier subject to detail according to the roster asks to see it. Publish your rosters as far in advance as possible to give all concerned fair warning as to when they are coming up for duty. Be consistent when you publish your rosters. If you post the detail announcements on Monday, always post them on Mondays. Smart soldiers will always contact the person responsible for the duty roster when making plans, so never discourage personnel from doing this. Thinking ahead benefits everyone.

SAFETY AND RISK MANAGEMENT

The Army Safety Program

The preservation of personnel and materiel resources is critical to maintaining a unit's combat readiness, and every NCO is responsible for ensuring that unsafe acts or unsafe conditions are recognized and steps taken to correct them. By doing this, NCOs will maintain their units' ability to operate at maximum combat efficiency.

The Army Safety Program includes goals, objectives, policies, and responsibilities. Its safety goals are to reduce and keep to a minimum accidental manpower and monetary losses and provide a safe and healthful environment. Objectives include injury prevention, damage control, accident prevention, regulatory compliance, and liability reduction. Policies of the safety program support the Army mission, make accident prevention a command responsibility, and use available resources for hazards that pose the most immediate threat to safety.

Soldiers and noncommissioned officers at all levels are expected to stop unsafe acts, take responsibility for accident prevention, comply with laws and regulations, use protective gear, and report accidents and mishaps. Supervisory responsibilities are as follows:

- Maintain a safe and healthful workplace.
- Conduct inspections to ensure compliance with safety procedures.
- Train soldiers to avoid unsafe acts and conditions.
- Identify hazards before accidents occur.
- Ensure that soldiers have the ability to safely perform a stated task.
- Manage risks during planning, preparation, and execution of operations.
- Counsel and take actions to correct unsafe acts and conditions.
- Quickly report unsafe acts and conditions that cannot be corrected and protect those who identify risks and hazards.
- Conduct safety meetings.

Safety is a by-product of every successful or completed mission and must receive the highest regard. It is extremely important for you, as a supervisor, to be aware not only of potential hazards that may affect you but also of conditions that may affect those working under your authority.

Risk Management and Risk Assessment

The terms *risk management* and *risk assessment* are often used synonymously, when in fact they are different. Risk management is a process that helps leaders make sound logical decisions. When used in a positive command climate, risk management can become a mindset that governs all unit missions and activities. It enables leaders at all levels to do exactly what the term implies: manage risk. Safety risk management is a specific type of risk management and is an extension of the decision-making process already ingrained in military leaders.

Risk assessment is part of risk management. It can range from simple to complex and can be done formally, during the deliberate planning process, or informally, while conducting a hasty plan. A risk assessment allows leaders to identify hazards and threats and place them in perspective relative to the mission or task at hand. Logically, one cannot identify the risk without first determining what the hazards are.

The risk management process consists of five steps: Identify hazards, assess hazards, make risk decisions, implement controls, and supervise.

Identify Hazards. Identify the most probable hazards for the mission. Hazards are conditions with the potential of causing injury to personnel, damage to equipment, loss of materiel, or reduced ability to perform a task or mission. The most probable hazards are those created by readiness shortcomings in the operational environment that impact man and machine. The human error problem areas discussed in the previous section are generic examples of those hazards. When a list of frequently recurring hazards is applied to a specific task or mission, the most probable hazards can be identified.

Assess Hazards. Once the most probable hazards are identified, analyze each to determine the probability of its causing an accident and the probable effect of the accident. Also, identify control options to eliminate or reduce the hazard. A tool to use is the Army Standard Risk Assessment Matrix.

Make Risk Decisions. Weigh the risk against the benefits of performing the operation. Accept no unnecessary risks and make any residual risk decisions at the proper level of command.

Implement Controls. Integrate specific controls into plans, operations orders, SOPs, and rehearsals. Communicate controls down to the individual soldier.

Supervise. Determine the effectiveness of controls in reducing the probability and effect of identified hazards. Ensure that risk control measures are performing as expected. Include follow-up during and after action to ensure that all went according to plan, reevaluating or adjusting the plan as required, and developing lessons learned.

Vignette: How Can My Soldiers Get Hurt, and What Can I Do about It?
A low-risk maintenance operation was suddenly turned into a high-risk operation when an NCO parked a Mine-resistant Ambush Protected (MRAP) vehicle on a downhill slope about 15 feet from a Bradley Fighting Vehicle (BFV). It was a normal working day. The battalion had just returned from a lengthy operation, and the battalion's maintenance shops were full of equipment in need of repair. One crewmember was securing the engine compartment of the BFV so it could be inspected by a mechanic.

When the driver parked the MRAP on the slope, he set the parking brake but didn't chock the wheels. He got out to get some chow, telling a new crewmember not to move the vehicle and to come get him when mechanic was available. Ignoring the instructions he had received, the unqualified assistant entered the vehicle and started it. It lunged forward, pinning the driver of the BFV against the vehicle. The stunned assistant had to be told to back the MRAP off the BFV crewmember, who died as a result of his injuries.

The direct cause of the accident was an unlicensed, untrained driver who disobeyed his NCO's instructions. The NCO himself, however, set the scenario for this tragedy. There are always hazards associated with parking a heavy vehicle on a downhill slope. There are hazards when these vehicles are left unchocked and dependent solely on parking brakes. And there are hazards whenever untrained, unlicensed operators are involved. This leader allowed hazards to pile one on top of another because he did not enforce standards. Unchecked, these hazards were combined with a soldier's "can-do" attitude and his failure to follow instructions, which turned a seemingly low-risk operation into a high-risk operation.

RULES FOR RISK MANAGEMENT

- Integrate risk management into planning.
- Accept no unnecessary risk.
- Make risk decisions at the proper level.
- Accept risk if benefits outweigh the cost.

NCO SAFETY PROGRAM

Soldiers die in privately owned vehicle (POV) and privately owned motorcycle (POM) accidents *every week*; many of these soldiers may have survived multiple combat tours. We must ensure that the trend ceases and that soldiers and their family members survive travel on the highway. Alcohol, speed, fatigue, and failure to use seat belts and airbags are primary factors in POV fatalities. Travel planning is another critical consideration since most individuals or units will have block leave following redeployment.

Safety is an individual task, and like other individual tasks, it is an NCO responsibility. Safety should be your personal METL task. All leaders in a unit should perform the following to ensure safety:

- Make safety assessments and update them.
- Publish safety guidance and post in plain view.
- Organize units for safety.
- Develop long-, short-, and near-term safety education programs.
- Make safety a part of every quarterly training briefing (attended by the commander and first sergeant).
- Develop a safety feedback system to remain informed about real and potential hazards.
- Put safety first when executing missions.
- Include safety aspects of training in every After Action Review.
- Reward safety excellence and punish negligence.

Leaders are responsible for the protection of every soldier's life. Safety takes precedence over fairness; it is a battle-focused concept. Safety and performance complement each other, and everyone is a safety officer. Take a look at ATTP 4-33 (FM 4-30.3), Maintenance Operations, and AR 385-10, The Army Safety Program, for detailed guidance.

The Army Combat Readiness Safety Center's POV/POM Toolbox at https://safety.army.mil/povtoolbox will help you keep your soldiers informed. Prior to taking leave or using long-distance passes, units now require that soldiers fill out the online automated risk assessment tool Travel Risk Planning System (TRiPS). Based on the soldiers' input, the system notifies them of possible hazards and mitigation information based on their trip specifics. NCOs can view the activity of their subordinates up to two levels down, which allows for greater awareness and a broader view of overall travel plans.

If you or someone in your unit is in a ground accident while operating unit equipment, you will need to complete DA Form 285, Technical Report of a US Army Ground Accident. If you must complete any accident report, you can refer to the instructions in DA Pam 385-40, Army Accidents and Reporting.

SUPPLY

Everyone in the Army is accountable and responsible for government property; the amount of property for which a soldier is responsible generally increases in value as he or she advances in rank. Safeguarding government property mostly requires lots of good old-fashioned common sense.

Classes of Supply

Supplies are items necessary to equip, maintain, and operate a military command, including food, clothing, arms, ammunition, fuel, materials, and machinery of all kinds. Supplies are divided into ten major categories called classes and then into lettered subclasses known as material designators (A through T). (For a detailed discussion of supply, see *Combat Service Support Guide*, 4th Edition, by John Edwards [Stackpole Books].) For example, Class I C supplies are combat rations.

- Class I—Subsistence, including health and welfare items. Subclassifications include in-flight rations, refrigerated and nonrefrigerated subsistence, commercially bottled water, and combat rations.
- Class II—Clothing, individual equipment, tentage, organization tool sets and tool kits, hand tools, administrative and housekeeping supplies, unclassified maps, and equipment. Subclassifications include weapons, power generators, and textiles.
- Class III—Petroleum, oils, antifreeze, and lubricants.
- Class IV—Construction materials, including fortification and barrier material.
- Class V—Ammunition, including chemical, biological, radiological, and special weapons.
- Class VI—Personal demand items, including beverages ("Class VI store" items) and health and comfort packs.
- Class VII—Major end items, such as tanks and helicopters. Subclassifications include bridging and firefighting equipment, administrative and tactical vehicles, missiles, weapons, and special weapons.

- Class VIII—Medical supplies, including repair parts for medical materials.
- Class IX—Repair parts and components.
- Class X—Material to support nonmilitary programs, such as agricultural and economic development.
- Miscellaneous—Salvage, packaged water, and enemy supplies.

CLASSES OF SUPPLY

Class	Type of Supply
I	Subsistence, including health and welfare items.
II	Clothing, individual equipment, tentage, organization tools, administrative and housekeeping supplies, unclassified maps, and equipment.
III	POL—includes bulk fuels and packaged products such as antifreeze
IV	Construction items, including fortification and barrier materiel
V	Ammunition of all types
VI	Personal demand items (nonmilitary sales items) and gratuitous health and comfort pack items
VII	Major end items such as launchers, tanks, mobile maintenance shops, and vehicles
VIII	Medical supplies, including repair parts for medical equipment
IX	Repair parts and components, including kits, assemblies, and sub-assemblies—both reparable and nonreparable—required for maintenance support of all equipment
X	Materiel to support nonmilitary programs, such as agricultural and economic development, which are not included in supply classes I–IX
Miscellaneous	Salvage, packaged water, captured enemy supplies

---

Basic Principles

All persons entrusted with government property are responsible for its custody, care, and safekeeping. No commander or supervisor can assign a soldier a duty that would prevent exercising the proper care and custody of property. When you assume accountability for remotely located property, keep records to show the location of the items and the persons charged with safekeeping.

The role of the noncommissioned officer in supply accountability is to maintain supervisory responsibility over all assigned equipment; accounting for and maintaining that equipment; and reporting any lost, damaged, or destroyed property. Army property will not be used for private purpose, sold, given as a gift, lent, exchanged, or otherwise disposed of unless authorized by law. Giving or accepting an issue, document, hand receipt, or any form of receipt to cover articles that are missing—or appear to be missing—is prohibited.

Accounting for Property

Property accountability is the obligation of each individual to keep a formal and accurate record of all materials issued to them. All Army property falls into three distinct categories:

- *Nonexpendable.* Property not consumed in use that retains its original identity during the period of use. Includes all serial-numbered items, such as weapons, vehicles, office machines, and so on. Nonexpendable property requires formal accountability throughout its life. A continuous chain of receipts is required if these items pass among different persons.
- *Expendable.* Office supplies, cleaning materials, and other supplies that are consumed upon use. Expendable property does not require formal accountability except for some sensitive categories, such as drugs.
- *Durable.* Certain kinds of personal property, such as hand tools. Durable items must be issued on a hand receipt.

Responsibilities

Property responsibility is the obligation of each individual to ensure that government property issued to him or her is properly used and cared for. Responsibility for property results from possession or supervision of others who have possession of Army property. This responsibility may be assigned by appropriate authority in writing or orally.

Supervisory Responsibility. Supervisors have the responsibility to ensure the safety and care of property issued to or used by their subordinates. They are also responsible for maintaining the proper atmosphere that leads to supply discipline among subordinates.

Direct responsibility. This is a formal assignment of property responsibility to a person within the supply chain who has the property within his or her custody but not necessarily in his or her possession. Accountable officers have direct responsibility unless it has been specifically assigned to another person. They maintain formal records that show the balance, conditions, and location of all property assigned to a property account. Enlisted personnel who are sergeants or higher rank, when appointed by proper authority, may serve as accountable officers.

Personal Responsibility. All soldiers are personally responsible for the equipment (weapons, tools, field gear, etc.) issued to them for their own use.

Responsibilities of Hand-receipt Holders

Hand receipts are a listing of nonexpendable and durable items that have been issued to an individual or team. Signing a hand receipt, including signing for clothing and equipment, is probably the most familiar aspect of the supply system to most soldiers. It carries with it definite responsibilities, and you must follow these simple rules:

- Inventory equipment and supplies receipted to you.
- Have property for which you have signed on hand or accounted for by a receipt, turn-in, or some other type of authorized credit document.

- Prevent loss, damage, or destruction of property under your control.
- Get a receipt when you turn in an item.
- Report loss or theft to your superior.
- When you transfer, be sure all property is turned in or passed into the custody of your replacement or whoever succeeds you in custody of the property. You will not be allowed to clear the installation until you have accounted for all the property for which you are responsible.
- Report to your supervisor any circumstances that make the proper security of property or equipment impossible. Failure to do so can result in your being charged for any loss or damage because you knew the facts and did not report them.

Statements of Charges and Financial Liability Investigation of Property Loss

DD Form 362, Statements of Charges, and DD 200, Financial Liability Investigation of Property Loss (FLIPL), are unpleasant methods the Army has of getting its money back from soldiers who have been careless or negligent in their duty as property custodians.

A Statement of Charges is prepared in situations where:
- Liability for loss, damage, or destruction of property is admitted.
- The charge does not exceed the monthly basic pay of the person being charged.
- Individuals do not offer cash payment to make good the lost, damaged, or destroyed property. (All military personnel and civilian employees of the DA who voluntarily admit liability may offer to replace the property through cash purchase.)

If the charges levied by a Statement of Charges exceed two-thirds of an individual's monthly basic pay, the unit commander will attach a letter requesting that the charges be prorated over a two-month period or longer. If charges do not exceed two-thirds of the soldier's monthly pay, he or she may be offered the option of reimbursing the government by using DD Form 1131, Cash Collection Voucher.

A FLIPL is used to reestablish accountability for lost, damaged, or destroyed gear or property. It may be required when it is known that negligence has occurred or misconduct is suspected and liability is not admitted. In addition, a FLIPL is prepared in the following situations:
- A sensitive item is lost or destroyed.
- It is directed by higher authority.
- Property loss is discovered as a result of change of accountability inventory.
- The value of the damages or shortages in occupied government quarters exceeds the responsible person's monthly basic pay.
- A person admits liability, and the loss, damage, or destruction exceeds the individual's monthly basic pay.
- A soldier refuses to admit liability and does not offer repayment.

Senior NCOs may be appointed financial liability officers and will be required to refer to DA Pam 735-5, Financial Liability Officer's Guide. Such investigations are painstakingly thorough. The financial liability officer is charged with finding out the facts. He or she, based on the facts of the investigation, must recommend whether or not to fix liability upon the subjects.

If you are ever the subject of a FLIPL, remember these guidelines:

- Keep calm, tell the truth, and cooperate with the financial liability officer.
- The financial liability officer has a job to do—don't take it personally.
- If the financial liability officer finds you liable, he or she must show you the report and explain your right to legal counsel and to appeal the recommendation if approved.
- If you appeal, get legal counsel; consult an Army lawyer even if you don't appeal.
- You may request remission of indebtedness or an extension of the collection period if the report is approved.
- Many FLIPLs do not recommend financial liability. If you have taken every reasonable precaution to protect the property in your possession, and you can prove it, you should have nothing to fear. If responsibility is fixed on you and the report is approved, then take your medicine.

Enforcement of Supply Discipline

Various disciplinary and administrative measures are available to a commander to enforce supply discipline and reduce the incidence of lost, damaged, or destroyed government property. When property is lost, damaged, or destroyed by a subordinate, the usual reaction is to reach for AR 735-5 and initiate a FLIPL. This action may be appropriate or, in some cases, required.

Military discipline goes hand in hand with supply discipline. Commanders have the following administrative tools available in connection with the FLIPL:

- An oral reprimand. In more serious cases, a formal letter of admonition or reprimand may be used and, when appropriate, filed in the soldier's Official Military Personnel file.
- Noting a soldier's inefficiency or negligence in his or her NCOER.
- Article 15 or court-martial in cases of misconduct or neglect resulting in damaged or lost military property.

A FLIPL is not a form of punishment or a deterrent. Nonjudicial punishment, however, is both. Its use in conjunction with a FLIPL may be indicated, depending upon circumstances. Even when no liability is found, the facts may warrant command action. There is little doubt that strong measures should be taken against a supply sergeant whose stocks are found $10,000 short because of his or her misconduct or neglect. But similar action also would be appropriate against supervisors if investigation revealed inadequate supervision, such as if required inventories had never been made or verified.

MAINTENANCE AND THE NCO

The basic document covering maintenance is DA Pam 750-3, Soldiers' Guide for Field Maintenance Operations. As an NCO, you have a direct responsibility and influence on your unit's ability to maintain its equipment. Through your guidance and example, your soldiers will either maintain your unit's equipment or destroy it through neglect. Keep in mind that combat power is a combination of manpower, materiel, and readiness. One cannot survive without the others. With approximately 25 percent of the defense budget directed toward the maintenance of equipment, each leader must become fully involved in training soldiers to maintain equipment. As a member of the maintenance management team in your unit, ask yourself the following questions:

- Do we follow unit guidance on the proper ways to conduct preventative maintenance checks and services (PMCS) on all equipment assigned to our squad/section before, during, and after all periods of operation?
- Is time blocked on our training calendar, and have I reduced distractions for my operators to perform PMCS on our team equipment?
- Have I recently assessed the effectiveness of my maintenance operation?
- Am I personally involved in my unit's maintenance program?
- Do I provide training to my soldiers on maintenance techniques or in supervising PMCS?
- Do I require my soldiers to perform maintenance to the same standards as required when performing other mission tasks?

Maintenance, like training, applies to all components of the Army. Operator/crew maintenance is the most critical aspect. Noncommissioned officers must ensure their units know how to find and fix maintenance problems as early as possible. It is also important to conduct scheduled services on all assigned equipment.

13

Assignments

Soldiers who avidly read the *Army Times* or *Soldiers* magazines for any glimmer of changes to Army personnel policy while waiting for the new regulation updates to arrive in the mail will want to check out the enlisted management website, https://www.hrc.army.mil/default.aspx?id=5418. This website has everything an inquiring soldier wants to know in real time and is kept up to date.

Instead of waiting months to find out if your DA Form 4187, Personnel Action Request, for reassignment has gone through, call the iPERMS, send an email, use the fax, or—even better—sign on to the Assignment Satisfaction Key, all of which are explained below.

ENLISTED ASSIGNMENTS AND UTILIZATION MANAGEMENT

The primary goal of the enlisted personnel assignment system is to satisfy the personnel requirements of the Army. Secondary goals are:
- To professionally develop soldiers.
- To maximize dwell time.
- To meet soldiers' personal desires.

Soldiers' CONUS area of preference and overseas area of preference are considered in the assignment process, but assignments are made to fill the Army's needs at that moment in time. Consistent with Army needs, soldiers remain as long as possible at their CONUS duty stations. The Army's time-on-station (TOS) requirement for CONUS is forty-eight months; for OCONUS it is the length of the prescribed tour. Soldiers complete the forty-eight-month TOS tour requirement unless operational or training necessities are so overriding that they must be reassigned earlier. There is no statutory limitation on the amount of time soldiers may remain overseas, just as there is no statutory limit as to how long a soldier remains at a CONUS post.

COMMUNICATING WITH HUMAN RESOURCES COMMAND

The US Army Human Resources Command (HRC) continues a series of initiatives designed to increase enlisted soldiers' participation in managing their careers. What was once paper-intensive and not very responsive is now, with automation, very responsive to those soldiers who care about their assignments.

To help soldiers communicate better with their career managers, the Enlisted Personnel Management Directorate (EPMD) employs a number of online websites and digital tools. These initiatives include the Interactive Personnel Electronic Records Management System (iPERMS), expanded email capabilities, high-speed fax machines, mail-grams, and a pocket reference information card that lists telephone numbers, email addresses, and other valuable data.

EPMD encourages you to use email to contact your branch. Inquiries concerning the status of personnel actions, future schooling, or assignments are examples of typical information exchanges that can be conducted twenty-four hours a day.

Soldiers can also correspond with their career managers by using fax machines. Soldiers and personnel service centers can save time by faxing communications directly to the desired career branch within EPMD for processing.

How to Contact the Enlisted Personnel Management Directorate
Telephone:
1-888-ARMYHRC (1-888-276-9472)
DSN 983-9500
Mail:
Human Resource Service Center
US Army Human Resources Command
1600 Spearhead Div Ave., Dept. 420
Attention: (Your branch office symbol, column 3 in the following table)
Fort Knox, KY 40122-5402
Email: askhrc.army@us.army.mil
Fax:
Commercial: 502-613 + last 4 digits
DSN: 983+ last 4 digits

ENLISTED ASSIGNMENT BRANCH CONTACT INFORMATION

1 Directorate	2 Abbreviation	3 Office Symbol	4 Phone
Maneuver & Fires Division	MFD	AHRC-EPA	5726
Operations Support Division	OSD	AHRC-EPB	5910
Force Sustainment Division	FSD	AHRC-EPC	5217
Sergeants Major Branch		AHRC-EPS	5874
Command Management Branch		AHRC-EPZ-D	5455
Force Alignment Division	FAD	AHRC-EPF	5923
Readiness Division	RD	AHRC-EPD	5869
Operations Management Division	OMD	AHRC-EPO	5499

Assignment Satisfaction Key (ASK)

ASK, a Web-based application, is used with the Army Knowledge Online (AKO) user ID and password and allows soldiers to view and update assignment preferences, volunteer information, and locate other personnel information from wherever Internet access is available. The information provided via ASK is used by HRC assignment managers and professional development noncommissioned officers (PDNCO) to match soldiers' preferences and volunteer selections against Army readiness requirements worldwide. Soldiers can access ASK by selecting the ASK icon located on the HRC website or directly at https://www.ask.army.mil/ask. The ASK Portal is also available from numerous Army websites.

ASK is made up of four areas:

- *Personal contact data.* This section must be updated before the other screens can be accessed.
- *Preferences.* Soldiers update their CONUS and OCONUS locations assignment preferences and/or select a special-duty interest (i.e. drill sergeant, recruiting, or airborne).
- *Volunteer.* Soldiers may volunteer for up to three CONUS and/or three OCONUS locations; indicate interest in participating in the Assignment Incentive Pay (AIP) program; and/or volunteer for a special duty (drill sergeant, recruiting, airborne, US Army Cadet Command, US Army 3rd Infantry [The Old Guard] or explosive ordnance disposal [EOD]).
- *Volunteer for requisition.* Soldiers volunteer to fill a requisition or volunteer for training as a US Army recruiter. Final selection, in priority order, is based on the needs of the Army, the professional development requirements of the soldier, and the soldier's preference.

The Soldier Assignment Module (SAM) allows assignment managers and professional development NCOs to virtually instantly identify all open requirements inquiring soldiers may be eligible for, enables the Army to home in on the most eligible soldiers, and identifies all volunteers for a specific assignment location.

Except for CONUS requirements that will be filled from OCONUS returnees who are immediately available, the primary considerations in reassigning a soldier will be the soldier's current qualifications and ability to fill a valid requirement. Other factors such as availability, volunteer status, TOS, and other criteria will be secondary. When soldiers with the required qualifications are identified, then the other factors and criteria will be considered.

Electronic Military Personnel Office (eMILPO)

Electronic Military Personnel Office (eMILPO) is an online Army personnel database accessible twenty-four-seven. A Web-based application, eMILPO allows unit personnel, human resource managers, and commanders to see personnel actions and is a fast and easy way for performing personnel actions and managing strength accountability. All Army components as well as Army National Guard human resource personnel use eMILPO for preparation of DD Form 93 (Record of Emergency Data) and Soldier Group Life Insurance (SGLI).

Interactive Personnel Electronic Records Management System (iPERMS)
All soldiers, regardless of component, are responsible for updating their individual Official Military Personnel File (OMPF) and Army Military Human Resource Record (AMHRR). They must keep these personnel records updated at all times by routinely reviewing them online, at a minimum of once a year, to ensure they are accurate and that all of their required documents are properly filed. These records are easily viewed at the iPERMS website, https://iperms.hrc.army.mil.

Authorized personnel with a Common Access Card (CAC) can access iPERMS by going directly to the iPERMS website or through the My Records portal. To access iPERMS via the website, follow these steps:
1. Click Accept.
2. Click CAC Login.
3. Click I Accept.
4. Click Soldier (view your own record).

To access iPERMS via the My Records online portal, follow these steps:
1. Go to www.hrc.army.mil.
2. Under Soldier Services, select My Records.
3. Enter your AKO login and password, or use your CAC.
4. If you entered your AKO login and password, select Login.
5. Select the Reserve Record icon if retired or the Active Army icon if active duty.
6. On the left side you will see a menu; select Documents.

HRC My Record Portal
My Record is HRC's self-service portal for active-duty and Reserve soldiers. To view or print your records, you must log in from the Web using your CAC. After you have logged in, you must click on your service record icon. From there you will be taken to your dashboard to view your information. On the left side of the page under the Navigation heading, click on Documents to view those in your record. To print, click on the document of your choosing and click the printer icon once it's open.

MANNING STRATEGIES
As of this update the United States remains at war. At the same time, the Army is in transition and began a drawdown in 2013 that is predicted to continue until 2017. Due to uncertainty and operational requirements, soldiers are assigned to locations based on whether or not a unit is deployed or preparing to

deploy. As major combat operations wind down in Iraq to meet pull-out dead-lines, Brigade Combat Teams (BCTs) are experiencing increased unit dwell periods as compared to recent years. However, it is an uncertain environment. The primary assumption is that soldiers and units will continue operational deployments and unit rotations for the near future, but recent world events have military units returning to Iraq.

Demand for trained and ready forces has increased, and the conversion to modular unit designs required the Army to adopt an Army Force Generation (ARFORGEN) process to support unit manning requirements. ARFORGEN is the managed increase of unit capability over time to ensure unit members are appropriately trained and ready for operational deployment. Units are manned and prioritized based on three categories of readiness: Reset, Train/Ready, and Available. This process allows the Army to prioritize as well as field its forces based on national requirements.

Soldiers' assignment cycles are matched with Army priorities that group units into five categories: Directed-fill Forces, ARFORGEN Forces, Urgent Forces, Essential Forces, and Important Forces. Units are manned and equipped at various levels based on their category and deployment date. NCOES and other leader development opportunities and reenlistment options should occur during the unit's Reset and Train/Ready periods. Soldiers will depart for new assignments and military educational opportunities during the last six months of a unit's Available phase.

Hitchin' a ride.

Stabilization

Army Forces generation must be flexible enough to support the uncertainty of demand and surge, measured by mobilization, Boots on Ground (BOG), and dwell periods. In a normal, predictable period, it is expected that active-duty forces will be Available for nine months and in "dwell" (a combination of Reset and Train/Ready) for twenty-seven months. It is during the Reset period of a lifecycle manned unit that new soldiers replace soldiers scheduled for expiration of term of service (ETS), retirement, or permanent change of station (PCS). Replacement also helps to minimize Headquarters Department of the Army (HQDA) directed departures and to retain as many soldiers already assigned to the unit as possible. Some soldiers with recent operational experience, however, will be transferred to fill other high-priority assignments. Stabilizing and retaining soldiers in their recently redeployed units is the optimal solution.

Stop Loss

The Stop Loss program is authorized by statute and allows the military services to retain trained, experienced, and skilled manpower by suspending certain laws, regulations, and policies that allow separations from active duty, including retirement. Those affected by the order generally cannot voluntarily retire or leave the service as long as Reserves are called to active duty or until relieved by proper authority. There are two types of Stop Loss that apply to soldiers in the Reserve Components (RC): Unit Stop Loss and Skill-Based Stop Loss.

Assignments

Normally, the military personnel office (MILPO), in coordination with the unit, compares authorized and projected positions with current assigned strength and known or projected gains and losses to determine the requirements for assignments. Requisitions are then prepared for these requirements and submitted to HRC in Alexandria, Virginia. Upon receipt, HRC edits and validates the requisitions. It is the responsibility of the requisitioning unit to not over- or under-requisition and to resolve any discrepancy before submitting the validated requisition for processing. Soldiers become available to be assigned against these requisitions for a variety of reasons. Those who enlist in the Army are available for assignment on completion of training and award of an MOS. Others are available when they have done one of the following:

- Volunteered for reassignment.
- Completed an overseas tour of duty.
- Completed schooling or training.
- Completed a stabilized tour of duty.
- Completed normal time on station in CONUS for a given MOS ("turn-around time" varies by MOS).

Army Exceptional Family Member Program (AR 608-75)

The Exceptional Family Member Program (EFMP) is based on Public Law 94-142, which entitles handicapped children to free education and all medically related services in pursuit of education. The EFMP includes all family members with special medical and educational needs and allows the HRC to consider these factors throughout the assignment process. Soldiers enroll through their local Army medical treatment facility. The military sponsor and the attending medical or educational specialist complete the enrollment forms. When HRC nominates a soldier enrolled in the EFMP for assignment, the assignment manager coordinates with the gaining command to determine if needed medical services are available. When services are not available, HRC considers alternative assignment locations based on existing priorities or sends the soldier in an unaccompanied status.

Assignment of Female Soldiers

Currently female soldiers are authorized to serve in all types of units except those battalion-size or smaller that have a routine mission to engage in direct combat. However, in January 2013 the DoD rescinded its direct Combat Exclusion Rule for females in the military, with plans to expand integration of women to previously closed units. The Joint Chiefs of Staff recently announced their intent to integrate women into combat occupational fields to the maximum extent possible. As of this writing, the services are validating occupational performance standards, both physical and mental, for all MOSs, specifically those that remain closed to women. Additionally, they are ensuring that sufficient midgrade/senior women will be given command assignments by the time integration occurs to ensure its success.

Homebase/Advance Assignment Program (HAAP)
and Deployment Stabilization

The Homebase/Advance Assignment Program (HAAP) is governed by AR 614-200, Enlisted Assignments and Utilization Management, Chapter 9, Section I. Participation is optional. HAAP is designed to reduce permanent-change-of-station (PCS) costs and the number of PCS moves by soldiers and their families. The program has two options. Homebase assignment projects the enlisted soldier to return to the same installation upon completion of a twelve-month, dependent-restricted short tour. Advanced assignment projects the enlisted soldier to be assigned to a new duty station upon completion of a twelve-month, dependent-restricted short tour.

Only corporals and specialist (P) sergeants through master sergeants assigned to twelve-month dependent-restricted short tour areas are authorized to participate in HAAP. HAAP assignments will not be given to enlisted soldiers who voluntarily elect to serve a twelve-month "all others" tour when assigned to an accompanied tour area.

The following primary factors determine HAAP assignments:

- The needs of the Army.
- Assignment preference considerations.
- Professional development.
- Least-cost factors.

Family members who relocate to the advance assignment are not authorized placement on the waiting list for on-post government quarters. Placement begins when the soldier completes the dependent-restricted short tour and signs in at the new duty station. Additionally, after completing a tour in Korea or other dependent-restricted areas, soldiers will be exempt from operational deployment at their new duty station, which will allow soldiers time to become reacquainted with their families.

Compassionate Actions

AR 614-200 establishes specific policies governing individual requests submitted by soldiers for a PCS or deletion from assignment instructions. A soldier may submit a request for any of the following reasons:

- Extreme family problem that is temporary and can be resolved in one year.
- Extreme family problem that is not expected to be resolved in one year.
- Sole surviving son or daughter (AR 614-200, paragraphs 5–12, and DA Pamphlet 600-8 apply).

The sole surviving son or daughter of a family that has suffered the loss of the father, the mother, or one or more sons or daughters in the military service will not be required to serve in combat. Soldiers who become sole surviving sons or daughters after their enlistment may request discharge under AR 635-200. A soldier may waive entitlement to assignment limitations, whether entitlement was based on his or her own application or the request of his or her immediate family.

Soldiers pending compassionate requests are not exempt from PCS moves or temporary duty (TDY) while waiting for resolution. Soldiers whose units are ordered to combat zone or hostile fire areas will remain at the home station until reassigned.

Married Army Couples Program

AR 614-200, section 4, and AR 614-30, Overseas Tours, apply to married couples. Army requirements and readiness goals are paramount when considering personnel for assignment. Married Army couples desiring joint assignment to establish common household (joint domicile) must request such assignment. The assignment desires of soldiers married to other soldiers are fully considered. An enrollment application must be turned in within thirty days from the date of marriage, and either one servicemember or both must apply, depending on location. When one soldier is considered for reassignment, their spouse is also considered for assignment to the same location or area automatically. When published, assignment instructions for each will list whether or not a joint assignment was approved.

Exchange Assignments
DA Pam 600-8, Military Human Resources Management and Administrative Procedures, and AR 614-200, paragraphs 5–11, apply. For mutual convenience, CONUS–assigned soldiers may request an exchange assignment with a soldier within CONUS; a soldier assigned overseas may request an exchange assignment with a soldier within his or her same overseas command. DA Pam 600-8 contains detailed guidance for preparing and processing requests for an exchange assignment.

CAREER DEVELOPMENT PROGRAM ASSIGNMENTS
A career development program is a system of intensive management of selected MOSs or career management fields (CMFs). These programs are established to ensure there are enough highly trained and experienced soldiers to fill positions that require unique or highly technical skills. To develop soldiers with the necessary proficiency, career fields within each program often require the following:
- Frequent movement from one job to another to gain experience.
- An above-average frequency of advanced training.
- Lengthy or frequent training periods.

Unless otherwise stated in AR 614-200, volunteers for a career development program should submit applications on DA Form 4187, Personnel Action, using DA Pam 600-8 for detailed application procedures. In applying for career programs and related training, applicants should consider the prerequisites listed in DA Pam 351-4, US Army Formal Schools Catalog, for the appropriate course of instruction. Only the most highly qualified and career-motivated soldiers will be accepted.

Chapter 6 of AR 614-200 contains the minimum requirements (subject to change) for each career program. Attaining the prerequisites does not automatically ensure entry into a career program. The appropriate career management branch selects the best-qualified soldiers.

Waivers are not granted for remaining service requirements for formal training. Waivers for other eligibility requirements or selection standards are considered unless otherwise stated in AR 614-200. Waivers cannot be implied—each must be specifically requested. On the application for entry into the program or training requested, the applicant must include the reason for the waiver.

Career development programs include the following:
- Intelligence.
- Explosive ordnance disposal (EOD).

- Technical escort training.
- Army Bands Career Program (ABCP).

Assignment to Specific Organizations and Duty Positions

AR 614-200, Chapter 8, contains specific policies and procedures for nomination, evaluation, selection, and assignment of enlisted soldiers to the following:

- Presidential support activities.
- Observer controller at combat training centers.
- US Military Entrance Processing Command.
- Enlisted aides to general officers.
- Inspector general positions.
- Drill Sergeant Program.
- International and OCONUS joint headquarters, US military missions, military assistance advisory groups, joint US military advisory groups, and similar activities.
- The US Central Command; Headquarters, Department of the Army and HRC; The US Disciplinary Barracks; The US Army Intelligence and Security Command; Office of the Assistant Chief of Staff for Intelligence and field activities; Defense Courier Service; The US Criminal Investigation Command; The US Transportation Command; The North Atlantic Treaty Organization (NATO); The USMA, US ACOM and General Staff College, US Army War College, and US Army Officer Candidate School; The USASOC and its subordinate commands and units; and joint communications support element.
- Selection and assignment for first sergeant positions.

A question these duties generate is "Will selection make me a better leader?" The answer, of course, depends on what you have done up to the point at which you are placed on the special duty. If you have been working in your MOS, have leadership positions commensurate with your rank, and have the right balance of TO&E and TDA assignments, then my answer would be yes. These duties are not, however, a quick fix for someone who has neglected his or her career path—they are tough, demanding jobs. If you qualify and are up to the challenge, then by all means volunteer!

Enlisted Instructors

Soldiers may volunteer or be selected for an instructor or advisor position (AR 614-200, Chapter 6, Section II), as appropriate, at the following:

- Active Army to Reserve Component (AC to RC), including full-time manning (FTM) and Reserve Officers' Training Corps (ROTC).
- Uniformed service schools.
- US Army Sergeants Major Academy (USASMA).

The initial selection criteria for instructor duty are as follows:

- Be a high school graduate or possess the GED equivalent.

- Have no personal habits or character traits that are questionable from a security standpoint, such as financial irresponsibility, unusual foreign holdings or interest, heavy drinking, drug abuse, gambling, or emotional instability. This restriction does not apply to soldiers declared rehabilitation successes under the Army Substance and Abuse Program (ASAP).
- Possess mature judgment and initiative.
- Have served at least three years of active Federal service in any branch of the Armed Forces.
- Have three years' time remaining in service upon arrival at assignment or the ability to reenlist or extend to meet the requirement.
- Have a security clearance consistent with that required to attend the requisite instructor course.
- Meet minimum reading grade level (RGL) and language grade level (LGL). This is measured by the Test of Adult Basic Education (see AR 350-1) and is required for attendance to the requisite instructor course.
- Display good military bearing.
- Meet the body composition requirements in AR 600-9.
- Be able to pass the APFT.
- Be fully qualified in the MOS for which instructor duty is desired.
- Have recently held a leadership assignment.
- Have a demonstrated ability to be an instructor.
- Have no speech impediment.

Drill Sergeant Program

The Drill Sergeant (DS) Program (AR 614-200, paragraphs 8–14) is designed to allow highly motivated, well-qualified professionals to serve as cadre during the formative weeks of an enlistee's training; therefore, only the most professionally qualified soldiers will be assigned to DS duty. Candidates must meet the following minimum prerequisites:

- Be physically fit (maximum profile guide is 111221; some are waiverable), meet body composition requirements in AR 600-9, and be able to pass the APFT (no substitution of events) upon arrival at DS school.
- Have a medical clearance if over forty years old.
- Have no record of emotional instability as determined by screening of health records and clinical evaluation by competent mental health officer.
- Have no speech impediment.
- Be a high school graduate or possess the GED equivalent.
- Display good military bearing.
- Have demonstrated both leadership ability during previous tours of duty and capability to perform in positions of increasing responsibility as senior NCO in the Army, as reflected on the NCOERs.

- Have no court-martial convictions.
- Have no record of disciplinary action, to include letters of reprimand, or time lost under 10 USC 972 during current enlistment or in last five years, whichever is longer.
- Active Army soldiers may not have received enlistment or selective reenlistment bonuses for current service obligation if PMOS is not among those authorized for DS positions (Active Army only).
- Have a minimum GT score of 100. This criterion may be waived by the commander of Fort Jackson to not less than 90 on a case-by-case basis for sergeant through sergeant first class candidates. Requests for waiver will be for soldiers who have a successful record of service in leadership positions and have completed college degree requirements, or who are continuing to further their education at the collegiate academic level.
- Have qualified with M16A2 or M-4 carbine rifle within last six months.
- Be sergeant through sergeant first class (sergeant must have a minimum of one year's time in grade and be a graduate of the WLC prior to nomination). Not applicable to USAR/ARNGUS soldiers or DS school first sergeant positions.
- Have a minimum of four years total active Federal service. Sergeant candidates must also have a minimum of one year's time in grade and have two years of service remaining after the completion of DS duty.
- Have a commander's evaluation by a lieutenant colonel or higher.

Being a drill sergeant is a rewarding challenge—you teach civilians to be soldiers.

- Have a thorough background screening conducted by their component's authority prior to attendance at DS school.
- Have no reports of unfavorable information disqualifiers (Type 1—automatic rejection).

Soldiers assigned to DS duty incur a twenty-four-month obligation after successful completion of Drill Sergeant School and a stabilized tour for twenty-four months, with an option to extend an additional six to twelve months. Normally the tour of duty for a drill sergeant will not exceed thirty-six months.

Selection and Assignment of First Sergeants

> The soldier having acquired that degree of confidence of his officers as to be appointed first sergeant of the company, should consider the importance of his office; that the discipline of the company, the conduct of the men, their exactness in obeying orders, and the regularity of their manners, will in great measure depend on his vigilance.
>
> —von Steuben, *Regulations for the Order and Discipline of the Troops of the United States*, approved by Congress 29 March 1779

Only the most highly qualified and motivated senior soldiers are selected and assigned to first sergeant positions. They are the unit examples, encouraging soldiers to "Be like me." This, to many, is the best assignment, bar none, in the Army. Success as a first sergeant is a real indication of future potential.

Most DA selection boards look closely at a soldier's performance as a first sergeant when selecting for the Sergeants Major Academy and promotion to sergeant major. Sergeants first class and master sergeants are assigned as first sergeants based on outstanding qualities of leadership, dedication to duty, integrity and moral character, professionalism, MOS proficiency, appearance and military bearing, physical fitness, and proven performance or potential for the first sergeant position.

In order to be a first sergeant, a soldier must be assigned to that position. When loss of position or authorization occurs, those personnel filling first sergeant positions will revert to their former rank. Soldiers will be stabilized as first sergeant for twenty-four months, with the exception that OCONUS stabilization will not involuntarily exceed normal tour length. Immediately upon a soldier's assignment to first sergeant position, a request for stabilization must be submitted to HRC (AHRC-EPO-P). The effective start date of stabilization is the date the soldier is assigned to the position.

Selection priorities of soldiers for assignment to first sergeant positions are based on primary MOS, career field, possession of the skill qualifier "M," and rank or grade. Exceptions may be made when the commander determines it as essential to mission accomplishment. Soldiers who meet the above requirements and who complete the First Sergeants Course (FSC) are eligible for award of the "M" (first sergeant) special qualification identifier after 180 days successful first sergeant duty.

Command Sergeants Major Assignment Procedures

Command sergeants major (CSMs) are the epitome of the Noncommissioned Officer Corps and must be the best and brightest. Held responsible for the individual and small-unit training of enlisted soldiers, the command sergeant major position at battalion and brigade level must be filled with those who have the career management background relating to that unit. For example, armor battalion must be filled with command sergeants major who have career management field (CMF) 19 background. The assignment priority is as follows:

The three basic levels of command sergeant major positions are battalion level, brigade or group level, and nominative positions. Initially, command sergeants major are assigned at battalion level. They may be considered for progression to a BDE-level or nominative position based on performance and evaluation by a DA selection board. The Army uses a centralized selection list to select NCOs for appointment to command sergeant major. Tours are assigned based on requirements of the Army's force generation process; lengths are usually established by the Sergeant Major Management Office (SMMO), and all command sergeants major are expected to serve for the full tour length. The projected change of responsibility date (PCORD) will be used to determine when incumbent command sergeants major will relinquish their positions and to designate future command sergeants major requirements to be filled. After successful performance at brigade or group level, command sergeants major may be considered for nominative positions. Prerequisites for a nominative position (general officer command and Senior Executive Services directors) are established in the Command Sergeant Major and Sergeant Major Nominative Process policy, and by achieving any special qualifications specified by the nominative commander.

OVERSEAS SERVICE

Many Americans work very hard all their lives, and then in their declining years, when they at last have the leisure and money to travel, they see the world. Soldiers not only see the world when they are young, but also have the unique opportunity to live among foreign peoples for extended periods of time and learn about their cultures from firsthand experience.

There are two ways that you can approach your overseas tour. You can go kicking and screaming and spend your time isolated in the American community of some foreign country, never venturing very far outside the cocoon of familiar surroundings, counting the dreary days until you rotate. Or you can approach foreign service as a thrilling adventure to be experienced to the fullest, and you can be a goodwill ambassador for the United States of America.

Most major overseas commands operate orientation programs for newly arrived personnel in the command. These courses attempt to expose soldiers to the culture in which they will be living in order to lessen the effect of culture shock that some people experience the first time they encounter a foreign society. When you receive overseas assignment instructions, it would be a very good idea for you (and your spouse, if you have one) to study the language of the country to which you will be going. Some special assignments require extensive formal language training, but most Army installations do provide some language instruction for soldiers and their dependents who are bound overseas. Learning the rudiments of a foreign language can be fun, and speaking a foreign language is a very valuable skill to have once you arrive at your overseas duty station.

Standards of living overseas vary depending on the country. Germany's standard of living is very high, and your money will not go far there. Other countries are beset with substantial economic problems, and the standards of living in those places can sometimes be so low that only the very rich can afford luxuries that are considered common in the United States, and you won't be able to afford them at local prices. Be aware that in countries where a status of forces agreement (SOFA) exists between the US government and the foreign government, soldiers may be tried for offenses under the laws of the country concerned.

As with everything else, what you get out of your situation is what you make of it. And remember that your overseas tour will not last forever; sooner or later you must leave to come home. Emotional attachments are very hard to break off, so be warned if you establish any kind of relationship with a foreign man or woman. What usually starts as a casual, fun-filled lark, a pleasant way to pass the time, frequently develops into a serious involvement. If it is not consummated by marriage, its termination can be an emotional trauma that will be very painful for both of you.

Types of Overseas Tours

The Army has two overseas tour types, long tours and short tours, with lengths determined by the appropriate overseas command or agency. Within those tour types, soldiers may be authorized to have family members and dependents travel with them in an accompanied status, or they (or the overseas command) may desire a dependent-restricted unaccompanied tour. Some locations are designated dependent-restricted areas and family members may be unfeasible or forbidden. Accompanied tours are not a right, and soldiers must request them. Personnel joined by their dependents at government expense must have enough remaining service to serve the tour prescribed for those "with dependents."

Army personnel married to each other and serving in the same overseas area serve tours in accordance with AR 614-30, Overseas Tours. They must extend or reenlist, if necessary, to have enough time in service to serve the tour prescribed before they can comply with orders directing movement.

The short tour is served by soldiers who meet at least one of the following criteria:

- Elect to serve overseas without dependents.
- Are serving in an area where dependents are not permitted.
- Do not have dependents (this rule does not apply in areas where personnel who have dependents must serve "with dependents" tours).
- Are divorced or legally separated and pay child support.

Tours normally will be the same for all personnel at the same station. Where there are personnel of more than one service, the service with the main interest (normally, the most personnel in the area) develops a recommended tour length that is coordinated with the other services. Tour length may vary within any given country or area, depending on the specific duty station. AR 614-30 lists overseas duty tours for military personnel.

Policies

The chief consideration in selecting a soldier for service overseas is that a valid authorization exists for his or her military qualifications. Equitable distribution is made, within a given MOS and grade, of overseas duty assignments, considering both desirable and undesirable locations. All reasonable efforts are made to minimize periods of forced separations and any adverse effects of overseas service encountered by soldiers and their families.

Between overseas tours, with the exception of Alaska and Hawaii, soldiers are assigned in their sustaining base for at least twelve months on station. Consistent with Army needs, soldiers are retained as long as possible in the continental United States. Among individuals who have previous overseas service, those with the earliest date of return from overseas normally will be selected first. Subject to personnel requirements to short-tour areas, soldiers who have completed a normal overseas service tour in a short-tour area will not be assigned to another short-tour area on their next overseas assignment.

Short-tour and Long-tour Eligibility

AR 614-30, Chapters 3 and 7, apply. Personnel are assigned to short-tour overseas assignments according to the following priorities:

1. Intertheater consecutive overseas tour (COT) volunteers after completion of current OCONUS tour.
2. From CONUS:
   a.) HQDA approved volunteers.
   b.) No previous OCONUS service.
   c.) No previous short tour and last OCONUS assignment was an "accompanied" tour.

d.) Last OCONUS assignment was an accompanied tour in a long-tour area and has previously served a short tour.

e.) Last OCONUS tour was a short tour in accompanied status.

f.) No previous short tour and last assignment was an "unaccompanied" tour.

g.) Serving in a long-tour area of Alaska or Hawaii and completed the prescribed thirty-six-month tour.

h.) In CONUS and last OCONUS tour was a short tour in an unaccompanied status.

The order of long-tour selection priorities is:

1. Intertheater COT volunteers after completion of current OCONUS tour.
2. From CONUS:

a.) HQDA approved volunteers.

b.) No previous OCONUS service.

c.) Last OCONUS assignment was an accompanied tour in a short-tour area.

d.) Last OCONUS assignment was an unaccompanied tour in a long-tour area.

3. Serving in a long-tour area of Alaska and Hawaii and completed the prescribed thirty-six-month tour.

Deferments and Deletions

AR 600-8-11, Reassignment, Chapter 2, applies. Because of the possible adverse effect on command operational readiness, granting of deferments for overseas service is strictly controlled and held to an absolute minimum. The needs of the service are the major determining factor in granting deferments.

Normally, once an application has been submitted, the soldier will be retained at the home station, pending a final decision. When a soldier requests deferment and it results in his or her having less remaining time in service than the length of the prescribed tour, the individual will continue on the overseas assignment. Unless he or she voluntarily reenlists or extends to be eligible to complete the prescribed tour, the individual must sign a counseling statement, which is a bar to reenlistment.

The following conditions normally warrant compassionate deferments or deletion from overseas assignment:

- A recent severe psychotic episode involving a spouse or child after a soldier receives assignment instructions.
- The soldier's children are being made wards of the court or are being placed in an orphanage or a foster home because of family separation. This separation must be because of military service and not because of neglect or misconduct on the part of the soldier.
- Adoption cases in which the home study (deciding whether a child is to be placed) has been completed and a child is scheduled to be placed in the soldier's home within ninety days.

- Illness of a family member (see AR 614-30 for details).
- Terminal illness of a family member where death is anticipated within one year.
- The death of a soldier's spouse or child, after receipt of assignment instructions.
- Prolonged hospitalization of more than ninety days when the soldier's presence is deemed essential to resolve associated problems.
- Documented rape of the soldier's spouse or child within ninety days of the scheduled movement date, when the soldier's presence is deemed essential to resolve associated problems.
- Selection to attend the Basic or Advanced NCO Course or Officer Candidates School (OCS), where attendance will delay overseas travel more than ninety days.
- Enrollment in the Drug and Alcohol Abuse Residential Rehabilitation Treatment Program.
- Pregnancy or related complications exceeding ninety days.

Change in Overseas Tour Status

Requests to modify your tour are normally approved, provided the government has not expended funds for shipment of household goods or movement of dependents and the gaining command has concurred with the change. Additionally, you may be required to extend or reenlist to meet tour length requirements.

Requests are normally not favorably considered if the government has expended funds for shipment of household goods or movement of family members. Exceptions to policy are considered under extenuating circumstances. Army Regulation 55-46, Travel of Dependents and Accompanied Military and Civilian Personnel to, from, or between Overseas Areas; the Joint Federal Travel Regulation (JFTR); and AR 614-30 are the applicable regulations.

Consecutive Overseas Tours

Regulatory guidance pertaining to consecutive overseas tours (COTs) is found in AR 614-30, Chapter 4. Soldiers who volunteer to serve two full consecutive OCONUS tours are authorized government-paid travel for themselves and command-sponsored family members to leave locations equal to the distance to the soldier's home of record. Soldiers may travel greater distances provided they pay the additional travel costs. The leave location is not restricted to CONUS and must normally be between the two tours. The government-paid travel is the only benefit associated with a COT; any leave used is chargeable to the soldier.

To be eligible for a COT, soldiers must complete the prescribed tour plus any voluntary extensions and agree to serve another full tour plus leave and travel time between tours. COTs fall into two categories: OCONUS tours that involve a PCS, and OCONUS tours that do not involve a PCS.

Curtailment of Tours

AR 614-30, Chapter 5, applies to curtailment of tours. Overseas commanders may curtail overseas tours when military requirements so dictate. They may also disapprove curtailment requests.

When curtailments of more than sixty days are considered, commanders must recommend curtailments and request reassignment instructions from HRC as early as possible but no later than forty-five days before the departure date. Curtailing a tour must not cause an emergency requisition to fill the vacated position.

Overseas commanders may, at any time, curtail the tour of a soldier who has discredited or embarrassed or may discredit or embarrass the United States or jeopardize the commander's mission. They may also curtail tours when family members are moved to the United States because of criminal activity, a health problem, or death in the immediate family living with the sponsor. In exceptional cases, the commander may waive advance HQDA coordination and attach the soldier to the nearest personnel assistance point for issue of PCS orders. These exceptions are as follows: potential defectors, extreme personal hardship, and expeditious removal of a soldier in the best interests of the service (for example, when a soldier causes an embarrassment to the command in its relationship with a foreign government).

Unless an official evacuation is ordered, pregnant soldiers are not automatically reassigned or do not have their tours cut short. Commanders may curtail unaccompanied pregnant soldiers in long-tour areas to dates that coincide with their seventh month of pregnancy. Under certain conditions, pregnant soldiers also may be curtailed in short-tour areas. Such a curtailment does not, however, preclude the solder from being reassigned overseas again after completion of the pregnancy and discharge from inpatient status.

Concurrent and Deferred Travel

Soldiers being transferred overseas should seek command sponsorship of their family members, as well as concurrent or deferred travel for family members. Sponsorship of soldiers' families is dependent upon the availability of government or economy housing; if housing will be available within 60 days, concurrent travel is normally authorized. If housing will not be available until between 61 and 140 days, deferred travel is normally authorized.

SPONSORSHIP

Every new assignment will raise questions and concerns for soldiers and their families. The sponsorship program (AR 600-8-8, The Total Army Sponsorship Program) assists soldiers and their dependents in establishing themselves at a new duty station and guides soldiers while they adjust to their new work environment.

A "sponsor" is an individual designated by name at a gaining organization to assist incoming members and their families in making a smooth transition into the unit and community environment. Sponsors should be a grade equal to or higher than that of the incoming soldier; be the same sex, marital status, and MOS; be familiar with the surrounding area; and not have received assignment instructions.

Sponsors' duties are varied and may include:

- Forwarding a welcoming letter to the incoming soldier. It should include the sponsor's duty address and telephone number (and home address and home telephone number as well, but this is not specifically required by the regulation).
- Trying to provide information requested by incoming soldiers.
- Advising the incoming soldier that he or she will be met at the point of arrival in the area or at the aerial port of debarkation.
- Offering to assist in getting temporary housing (guesthouse or similar accommodations). The sponsor should contact the housing referral office for guidance and information. Sponsors are not required to contract for permanent or temporary housing, but if the sponsor desires to provide this service and the incoming soldier agrees, the sponsor should seek legal advice about the commitments and liabilities involved.
- Accompanying the incoming soldier after his or her arrival in the unit while he or she goes through in-processing.
- Acquainting the incoming soldier with the surrounding area and facilities.
- Introducing the incoming soldier to his or her supervisors and immediate chain of command.

Gaining commanders are required to send incoming soldiers welcoming letters. Informality and information sharing are the primary goals of these letters. This letter also responds to any request for specific information appearing in item 42 of DA Form 4787, Reassignment Processing. The welcoming letter and its enclosures should contain, at a minimum, the gaining unit's address and telephone number and the following information:

- The projected availability of government and economy housing, including when available, rent and utility costs, security deposit, and advance rent requirements.
- The location of the family housing referral office.
- Education facilities available for dependents in both the military and the civilian communities.
- The types of household goods that are essential, optional, or not required at an overseas location.
- The type of climate and recommended clothing.
- Local vehicle registration, safety, emission standards, insurance requirements, and, when available, typical insurance rates.
- The availability of military and civilian medical and dental care facilities.
- Community services and facilities that are available both on post and off post.

- The host nation's culture, customs, and lifestyle.
- Local firearms laws and restrictions.
- Problems that might be encountered when shipping pets to the overseas command.

Commanders are also responsible for ensuring that sponsors are provided enough time off from their duties to help new soldiers. In addition, commanders arrange transportation so that sponsors can meet new members and their dependents at the point of arrival and bring them back to the unit (overseas only).

The incoming soldier should answer the sponsor's letter immediately and do the following:

- Inform the sponsor of his or her time, date, and point of arrival (including flight numbers). Any changes to the itinerary should be reported to the sponsor immediately.
- Provide the sponsor a unit mailing address and telephone number (commercial or DSN).
- Inform the sponsor of the expected departure date from the losing duty station.
- If desired, provide the sponsor with leave addresses and telephone numbers.

ORIENTATION

Commanders and supervisors are responsible for conducting a thorough and timely orientation to start new arrivals off properly. These orientations should make new soldiers feel needed and wanted and instill in them the motivation to contribute to the unit's mission.

14

Evaluation and Management Systems

THE NCO EVALUATION REPORTING SYSTEM

The NCO Evaluation Reporting (NCOER) System is designed to strengthen the ability of the NCO Corps to meet its professional duties. It enables the best NCOs to serve in positions of increasing responsibility by providing information on individual performance and potential from raters and senior raters to promotion and selection boards. The NCOER System process merges major elements of counseling, assessment, and documentation, as well as other personnel functions, to manage the needs of the Army, rating officials, and rated soldiers. Its basic purpose is to compel rated soldiers to meet or exceed the standards; it is also used to evaluate soldiers for selection and development. The process assists the Army in identifying the best-qualified soldiers for promotion and assignment to positions of greater responsibility and in determining those who will be kept on active duty, retained in grade, or separated. AR 623-3, Evaluation Reporting System, provides detailed information.

As of this writing, the Army has completed an Evaluation Reporting System review and is in the process of revamping the NCO Evaluation Report, which is currently scheduled to be phased in by September 2015. As much of the change is in draft form, speculated, or not yet approved, we will only discuss the current NCOER and its policies and procedures in this guide until the latest DA Form 2166-9 and Support Form are completed and become policy. In the meantime, to stay current with the latest changes you can visit the Evaluation Entry System (EES) homepage at https://evaluations .hrc.army.mil.

Current evaluations are based on two forms: DA Form 2166-8-1, NCOER Counseling and Support Form, which is used when counseling NCOs, and DA Form 2166-8, NCO Evaluation Report (NCOER). These two forms are used to evaluate all NCOs except command sergeants major serving at three- and four-star nominative positions.

Study the NCOER carefully! It states very clearly what the Army expects of its noncommissioned officers. The current Army NCOER emphasizes Army Values, NCO responsibilities, and counseling duties, as well as soldier skills, values, attributes, and current performance and potential.

Performance Counseling/Checklist

Performance counseling is developmental counseling; it informs soldiers face-to-face about their jobs and expected performance standards. It also provides performance feedback. The goal of this part of the system is to help NCOs be successful and meet applicable standards. Although past performance must be acknowledged, the best counseling looks ahead to the future and what can be improved.

Counseling takes place within thirty days of each rating period and at least quarterly thereafter. The first session tells the rated NCO a description of his or her duties, what is expected, and major goals. The quarterly sessions (for active-duty NCOs) tell what he or she has done well and what could be done better. After initial counseling, Army National Guard (ARNG) and US Army Reserve (USAR) soldiers are counseled semiannually. This by no means precludes telling soldiers how they are doing on a daily basis!

The NCO Counseling/Checklist Record is designed to be used with the NCOER as the only counseling support document. It includes the information needed to assist you in preparing and conducting a counseling session. It also provides a section to record counseling results. After a counseling session, the rater maintains the checklist until the next session or the end of the rating period. The counseling form includes reference material related to counseling, Army Values, and NCO responsibilities.

Types of NCOERs

Only the following reports, authorized by AR 623-3, may be submitted.

Annual Reports. Annual reports are submitted twelve months after the ending month of the last report. If twelve months have elapsed since the ending month of the last report but the required three-month minimum rating period or rater qualification criteria have not been met, the annual report period is extended until the minimum requirements are satisfied. Reports can reflect a rating period greater than twelve months, including the nonevaluated time, but the rated months cannot exceed twelve months of evaluated time. There are two types of "Extended Annual" reports; one is mandatory for use during any period of nonrated time since the previous report, and the other is optional for use only in exceptional situations.

Change-of-Rater Reports. Provided that minimum rater qualifications are met and no other reports have been submitted in the preceding three months, change-of-rater reports are rendered when the rated NCO is no longer under the supervision of the rater, or if reduced to specialist rank or below.

NCO EVALUATION REPORT

For use of this form, see AR 623-3; the proponent agency is DCS, G-1.

PART I - ADMINISTRATIVE DATA

a. NAME (Last, First, Middle Initial)

b. SSN

c. RANK ( )

d. DATE OF RANK

e. PMOSC

f.1. UNIT   ORG.   STATION   ZIP CODE OR APO,   MAJOR COMMAND

f.2. STATUS CODE

g. REASON FOR SUBMISSION

h. PERIOD COVERED		i. RATED MONTHS	j. NON-RATED CODES	k. NO. OF ENCL	l. RATED NCO'S EMAIL ADDRESS (.gov or .mil)	m. UIC	n. CMD CODE	o. PSB CODE
FROM	THRU							
YEAR MONTH DAY	YEAR MONTH DAY							

PART II - AUTHENTICATION

a. NAME OF RATER (Last, First, Middle Initial)   SSN   SIGNATURE   DATE (YYYYMMDD)

RANK   PMOSC/BRANCH   ORGANIZATION   DUTY ASSIGNMENT   RATER'S AKO EMAIL ADDRESS (.gov. or .mil)

b. NAME OF SENIOR RATER (Last, First, Middle Initial)   SSN   SIGNATURE   DATE (YYYYMMDD)

RANK   PMOSC/BRANCH   ORGANIZATION   DUTY ASSIGNMENT   SENIOR RATER S AKO EMAIL ADDRESS (.gov. or .mil)

c. NAME OF REVIEWER (Last, First, Middle Initial)   SSN   SIGNATURE   DATE (YYYYMMDD)

RANK   PMOSC/BRANCH   ORGANIZATION   DUTY ASSIGNMENT   REVIEWER'S AKO EMAIL ADDRESS (.gov. or .mil)

d. ☐ CONCUR WITH RATER AND SENIOR RATER EVALUATIONS   ☐ NONCONCUR WITH RATER AND/OR SENIOR RATER EVAL (See attached comments)

e. RATED NCO: I understand my signature does not constitute agreement or disagreement with the evaluations of the rater and senior rater. I further understand my signature verifies that the administrative data in Part I, the rating officials in Part II, the duty description to include the counseling dates in Part III, and the APFT and height/weight entries in Part IVc are correct. I have seen the completed report. I am aware of the appeals process of AR 623-3.

SIGNATURE   DATE (YYYYMMDD)

PART III - DUTY DESCRIPTION (Rater)

a. PRINCIPAL DUTY TITLE

b. DUTY MOSC

c. DAILY DUTIES AND SCOPE (To include, as appropriate, people, equipment, facilities and dollars)

d. AREAS OF SPECIAL EMPHASIS

e. APPOINTED DUTIES

f. COUNSELING DATES   INITIAL   LATER   LATER   LATER

PART IV - ARMY VALUES/ATTRIBUTES/SKILLS/ACTIONS (Rater)

a. ARMY VALUES. Check either "YES" or "NO". (Bullet Comments are mandatory. Substantive bullet comments are required for "NO" entries.)

	YES	NO
1. LOYALTY: Bears true faith and allegiance to the U. S. Constitution, the Army, the unit, and other Soldiers.		
2. DUTY: Fulfills their obligations.		
3. RESPECT/EO/EEO: Treats people as they should be treated.		
4. SELFLESS-SERVICE: Puts the welfare of the nation, the Army, and subordinates before their own.		
5. HONOR: Lives up to all the Army values.		
6. INTEGRITY: Does what is right - legally and morally.		
7. PERSONAL COURAGE: Faces fear, danger, or adversity (physical and moral).		

V A L U E S

Loyalty
Duty
Respect
Selfless-Service

Honor
Integrity
Personal Courage

Bullet comments

DA FORM 2166-8, OCT 2011   PREVIOUS EDITIONS ARE OBSOLETE.   Page 1 of 2
APD PE v1.02ES

NCO Evaluation Report

RATED NCO'S NAME (Last, First, Middle Initial)		SSN	THRU DATE

PART IV (Rater) - VALUES/NCO RESPONSIBILITIES

Bullet comments are mandatory.
Substantive bullet comments are required for "EXCELLENCE" or "NEEDS IMPROVEMENT."

b. COMPETENCE
- o Duty proficiency; MOS competency
- o Technical & tactical; knowledge, skills, and abilities
- o Sound judgment
- o Seeking self-improvement; always learning
- o Accomplishing tasks to the fullest capacity; committed to excellence

EXCELLENCE (Exceeds std)	SUCCESS (Meets std)	NEEDS IMPROVEMENT (Some) (Much)

c. PHYSICAL FITNESS & MILITARY BEARING

APFT   HEIGHT/WEIGHT   /

- o Mental and physical toughness
- o Endurance and stamina to go the distance
- o Displaying confidence and enthusiasm; looks like a Soldier

EXCELLENCE (Exceeds std)	SUCCESS (Meets std)	NEEDS IMPROVEMENT (Some) (Much)

d. LEADERSHIP
- o Mission first
- o Genuine concern for Soldiers
- o Instilling the spirit to achieve and win
- o Setting the example; Be, Know, Do

EXCELLENCE (Exceeds std)	SUCCESS (Meets std)	NEEDS IMPROVEMENT (Some) (Much)

e. TRAINING
- o Individual and team
- o Mission focused; performance oriented
- o Teaching Soldiers how; common tasks, duty-related skills
- o Sharing knowledge and experience to fight, survive and win

EXCELLENCE (Exceeds std)	SUCCESS (Meets std)	NEEDS IMPROVEMENT (Some) (Much)

f. RESPONSIBILITY & ACCOUNTABILITY
- o Care and maintenance of equipment/facilities
- o Soldier and equipment safety
- o Conservation of supplies and funds
- o Encouraging Soldiers to learn and grow
- o Responsible for good, bad, right & wrong

EXCELLENCE (Exceeds std)	SUCCESS (Meets std)	NEEDS IMPROVEMENT (Some) (Much)

PART V - OVERALL PERFORMANCE AND POTENTIAL

a. RATER. Overall potential for promotion and/or service in positions of greater responsibility.

AMONG THE BEST	FULLY CAPABLE	MARGINAL

b. RATER. List 3 positions in which the rated NCO could best serve the Army at his/her current or next higher grade.

_____

_____

_____

e. SENIOR RATER BULLET COMMENTS

c. SENIOR RATER. Overall performance

1	2	3 Successful	4 Fair	5 Poor

d. SENIOR RATER. Overall potential for promotion and/or service in positions of greater responsibility.

1	2	3 Superior	4 Fair	5 Poor

DA FORM 2166-8, OCT 2011

Page 2 of 2
APD PE v1.02ES

NCO Evaluation Report *continued*

Change of Duty Report. When a soldier is reassigned to new duties while still serving under the same rater, a change of duty report is mandatory. This is also required if a soldier leaves active duty or is declared missing, but is optional for retirement.

Temporary Duty, Special Duty, or Compassionate Reassignment Reports. Provided minimum rater qualifications are met, change-of-rater-reports for both the NCO and their eligible subordinates will be submitted prior to departure when an NCO leaves for one of the following reasons:

- For temporary duty (TDY) or special duty (SD) to attend training scheduled for ninety calendar days or more at a service school.
- To attend a civilian academic or training institution on a full-time basis for a period of ninety calendar days or more.
- To perform duties not related to his or her primary functions in his or her parent unit under a different immediate supervisor for ninety days or more.

NCOs on TDY or SD who are not responsible to rating officials in their parent organization will be rated by the TDY or SD supervisor. NCOs attached to organizations pending a compassionate reassignment remain responsible to their parent unit and will not receive an evaluation report from the organization to which they are attached.

Complete-the-Record Reports. At the option of the rater, a complete-the-record report may be submitted on a soldier who is to be considered by a DA centralized board for promotion, school, or command sergeant major selection, provided the soldier is in the zone of consideration, has been in the current duty assignment under the same rater for at least ninety days, and has not had a previous report for the current duty assignment.

Senior Rater Option Reports. Provided minimum rater qualifications are met, when a change in senior rater occurs, the senior rater may direct that a report be made on any NCO for whom he or she is the senior rater if the senior rater has served in that position for at least sixty rated days and the rated NCO has not received a report in the preceding ninety rated days. The senior rater will submit a senior rater option report in instances when the senior rater's departure would result in a report submitted without a senior rater evaluation.

Sixty-day Short-tour Option Report. Provided minimum rater qualifications are met, at the rater's option the rater may prepare a sixty-day option report on a rated NCO who must be serving in an overseas designated short tour for a period of fourteen months or less. The senior rater must meet the minimum time-in-position requirements to evaluate (sixty rated days) and must approve or disapprove submission of the report. If disapproved, the rater will inform the rated NCO that the report has been disapproved and will destroy it.

Relief-for-Cause Reports. Relief for cause is the early release of a soldier from a specific duty or assignment, directed by superior authority and based on a decision that the soldier has failed in his or her duty performance through inefficiency or misconduct. The reasons for relief must be clearly explained by the rating official in his narrative portion of DA Form 2166-8, along with a statement that the soldier concerned has been informed of the reasons for the relief. When the relief is directed by someone not on the designated rating chain, that official describes the reasons for the relief in an enclosure to the report. The minimum rating period for these kinds of reports is normally thirty days, but a general officer in the chain of command (or the general court-martial convening authority) may waive this requirement and authorize the relief report to be written in clear-cut cases of misconduct. Relief-for-cause reports are signed at any time during the closing or following month of the report. Regardless of who directs the relief, the rater will enter the bullet "the rated NCO has been notified of the reason for the relief" in part IV.f of the form.

Restrictions

A number of restrictions apply to the type of material that may be included in an efficiency report:

- The zeal with which a soldier performs his or her duty as a member of a court-martial, counsel for an accused, or an Equal Opportunity NCO cannot be referred to in an efficiency report.
- No reference may be made to unproven derogatory information in a report. This prohibition prevents allegations from being included in reports and excludes information that would be unjustly prejudicial.
- Although incidents caused by alcohol or drug abuse should be taken into account by rating officials, a soldier's voluntary participation in the Army Substance Abuse Program (ASAP) is not normally mentioned. While paragraph 3-28 of AR 623-3 authorizes raters to mention a soldier's voluntary entry into the ASAP and successful rehabilitation "as a factor to the rated soldier's credit," this kind of information should not be included in a report unless previous reports cited problems arising from substance abuse.
- Soldiers who seek out mental health counseling voluntarily or enter a mental health-care program for behavioral health issues will not be penalized by mention of that treatment in an evaluation report if it was not reported by the chain of command.

Commander's Inquiry

When a commander learns that a report made by a subordinate or a member of a subordinate command may have been illegal or unjust or may have violated the provisions of AR 623-3, he or she must investigate. The commander does not have the authority to direct that an evaluation be changed and may not use command influence to alter the honest evaluation of an NCO by the rating official. However, he or she may provide results of a commander's inquiry to the rating chain.

When a report has been corrected under the circumstances mentioned above, it is forwarded with no reference to action taken by the commander.

Rater Qualifications and Responsibilities

With few exceptions, the rater must be the first-line supervisor of the rated soldier for a minimum of ninety rated days and senior to the rated soldier either by grade or by date of rank. Members of other US military services who meet these qualifications may also be raters.

Commanders may appoint an employee of a DoD or US Government agency (including nonappropriated fund rating officials). The civilian rater must be officially designated on a published rating scheme established by the local commander. Only in rare instances will members of allied armed forces be authorized to serve as raters.

Raters must counsel the rated soldier and assess his or her performance, using all reasonable means to do so, and then prepare a fair, correct report. Without a doubt, you will find NCOER counseling of good soldiers a pleasant experience. Counseling bad soldiers is a difficult experience, yet you must face up to it if you are to be a good leader. Ensure that you keep the counseling record, DA Form 2166-8-1, up to date and fulfill your rating duties by properly counseling your soldiers.

Senior Rater Qualifications and Responsibilities

The senior rater must be in the direct line of supervision of the rated soldier for a minimum period of sixty rated days and senior to the rater in grade or date of rank.

Members of other US military services who meet these qualifications may be senior raters, and civilians may be appointed as senior raters provided they are the supervisors in the best position to evaluate the soldier's performance and their appointments are published in a rating scheme established by the local commander. Members of allied forces are not authorized to be senior raters. A senior rater is not required when the rater is a general officer or equivalent.

The senior rater uses his or her position and experience to evaluate the rated NCO from a broad organizational perspective. His or her evaluation is the link between the day-to-day observation of the rated NCO's performance by the rater and the longer-term evaluation of the rated NCO's potential by DA selection boards. A senior rater fulfills his or her responsibility by using all reasonable means to become familiar with the rated NCO's duty performance throughout the rating period so that he or she can render a fair, accurate, and correct report that evaluates the rated NCO's duty performance, professionalism, and potential.

The senior rater must complete the report as follows:
- Date and sign the report in part II.b.
- Obtain the rated NCO's signature in part II of the NCOER.
- Ensure that the rated NCO is aware that his or her signature does not constitute agreement or disagreement with the evaluations of the rater and senior rater.

- Ensure that the specific bullet examples support the appropriate ratings in part IV.b–f.
- Ensure that the bullet statement "senior rater does not meet minimum qualifications" is entered in part V.e when the senior rater does not meet the minimum time requirement for evaluating the rated NCO.

Reviewer Qualifications and Responsibilities

The reviewer must be a commissioned or warrant officer, command sergeant major, or sergeant major in the direct line of supervision and senior in grade or date of rank to both the rater and the senior rater. There is no minimum time period requirement for reviewer qualification.

Commanders may appoint officers of other US Armed Forces, US Coast Guard, or DoD civilian employees in the GS-12 grade equivalent or above as reviewers when:

- Grade and chain of supervision requirements are met.
- Either the rater or senior rater is a US Army rating official.

In cases where both the rater and senior rater are other than US Army rating officials and no Army reviewer is available, then either of the following will happen:

1. The report will be reviewed by a US Army officer in the rated NCO's unit administrative office. As an exception, this officer is not required to be senior to the rater or senior rater.
2. General officers and senior executive service (SES) members or the equivalent serving with any branch of the US Armed Forces may be appointed as reviewers.

In cases where the rater or senior rater is a general officer or a civilian employee of the SES or equivalent rank and precedence, that official will also act as reviewer.

The reviewer ensures that the proper rater and senior rater complete the report, examines the evaluations, and resolves discrepancies and inconsistencies. The reviewer also ensures compliance with the provisions for change-of-rater and relief-for-cause reports. They also ensure that required comments have been made to explain low ratings on the NCOER and that allegations of injustice or illegality are resolved or brought to the commander's attention. The reviewer is responsible for ensuring that the rated soldier's, rater's, and senior rater's army.mil email addresses are placed on the NCOER, and also for forwarding the report to the military personnel office.

Responsibilities of the Rating Chain

Commanders, commandants, and organization leaders are responsible for establishing rating chains and publishing the rating schemes, either on paper or electronically, within their units for all soldiers to see.

Commanders are responsible for ensuring the following:

- Each rating official is fully qualified and knows whom he or she is responsible to rate.

- Reports are prepared by the designated individuals.
- Rating officials give timely counseling.
- Each rated soldier is provided a copy of his or her completed evaluation report.
- Soldiers receive assistance in preparing and submitting appeals.
- Rating chains match the chain of command or chain of supervision when practical.
- Rating officials provide direct and honest assessments of the soldiers they rate.
- Local procedures assist senior raters in their responsibility to ensure that completed NCOERs are properly submitted to Army Soldier Records Branch systems no later than ninety days after the "THRU" date of the report.

The Army evaluation system processes are the responsibility of the rating officials, rated soldiers, the battalion adjutant or unit personnel administration office, and HQDA. The system involves maintaining the fine art of leadership, creating a rating relationship through personal interaction, following through with the requirement for developmental counseling and reviews, and performing the final critical assessment.

EVALUATION REPORT REDRESS PROGRAM (APPEALS)

The Redress Program protects the Army's interests and ensures fairness to the NCO. At the same time, it avoids impugning the integrity or judgment of the rating officials without sufficient cause. Commander's inquiries and appeals for redress are separate actions. Rated NCOs may seek an initial means of redress through a commander's inquiry; however, a commander's inquiry is not a prerequisite for submission of an appeal.

The burden of proof rests with the soldier making an appeal. Once NCO-ERs are filed in the soldier's Official Military Personnel File (OMPF), they are presumed to be administratively correct, to have been prepared by the proper officials, and to represent the considered opinions and impartial judgments of rating officials.

The allegation of error or injustice does not constitute proof. Clear and convincing evidence must be submitted to cause alteration, replacement, or withdrawal of a report in the OMPF. The decision to appeal should not be made lightly. Frequently, sound evidence may be difficult to obtain, and in most cases, the appellant may be unable to analyze his or her own case objectively.

Normally, appeals are originated by the rated soldier, but in cases in which an appeal is originated by someone other than the rated soldier, it is not processed unless the rated soldier has been notified in person or in writing (by certified mail) and given the opportunity to submit statements pertaining to the case. Rating officials who claim "second thoughts" about ratings previously made have no grounds for submitting an appeal on behalf of the rated soldier.

Appeals alleging bias, prejudice, unjust ratings, or any matter other than administrative error will be adjudicated by the Army Special Review Board. The board's determination is final.

To be considered, substantive appeals must be received within three years of the NCOER "THRU" date. Appeals that do not meet this time restriction may be submitted to the Army Board for Correction of Military Records, in accordance with AR 15-185, Army Board for Correction of Military Records. Once the decision has been made to appeal an evaluation report, take the following steps:

- Begin reading Chapter 4, AR 623-3, "Evaluation Redress Program."
- Write down clearly and specifically what will be appealed and why it should be.
- Identify what evidence should be obtained to substantiate the appeal.
- Determine what evidence can be obtained.
- Obtain the evidence. If statements from persons are necessary, make sure the statements clearly identify their roles at the time of the contested report and ensure that the statements make specific, not general, comments. Seek statements from senior personnel who have specific knowledge of the facts and avoid statements from subordinates or persons whose knowledge of the facts may be limited. Obtain sworn statements, if possible.
- Documentary evidence, if not original, should be in certified true copies.
- Prepare the appeal in military letter format.

THE QUALITATIVE SERVICE PROGRAM
The Qualitative Service Program (QSP) was established in 1971 as the Qualitative Management Program with the intended purpose of barring nonproductive NCOs from further service in the Army. The QSP now consists of a series of centralized enlisted selection board processes designed to balance staffing levels and to allow only the highest-quality NCOs to continue service. The QSP consists of three subprograms: Qualitative Management Program (QMP), the Over-Strength Qualitative Service Program (OS-QSP), and the Promotion Stagnation Qualitative Service Program (PS-QSP)

Qualitative Management Program (QMP) Board
The QMP board applies to senior NCOs (E-7–E-9) and can deny continued service for those who do not meet Army standards in terms of performance, potential for advancement, or conduct. The QMP does *not* apply to soldiers who:

- Are in the grade of SSG (P) and below.
- Have an approved retirement.
- Are eligible for promotion to the next higher grade.

The board reviews the performance portion of the soldier's OMPF, Personnel Qualification Record, official photograph, and other authorized documents. Based upon its evaluation of past performance and potential for continued service, the board will then decide whether or not to retain the soldier. Soldiers may be referred to the QMP board if they meet any of the following selection criteria:

- Moral or ethical conduct unsuited to the values of the NCO Corps and the Army Ethic.
- Lack of potential to perform assigned duties in the current grade.
- Decline in efficiency and performance over a continuing period, as reflected by evaluation reports or failure of NCOES courses.
- Recent or continuing disciplinary problems, displayed by conviction by court-martial, nonjudicial punishment, or administrative reprimand.
- Other discriminators, such as receiving a bar to reenlistment, inability to meet physical fitness standards, or failure to comply with the Army body composition program.

Soldiers denied continued service under the QMP may appeal and request to stay on active duty based on improved performance or errors in their records when reviewed by the selection board. They may submit only one appeal and cannot submit requests for reconsideration of denied appeals. Soldiers must submit their appeals to their commanders within sixty days of formal notification of QMP selection.

Over-Strength Qualitative Service Program (OS-QSP) Board

The OS-QSP board considers staff sergeants through sergeants major and command sergeants major for denial of continued service in select MOSs when the Army exceeds its annual strength projections. When otherwise qualified, staff sergeants may request voluntary reclassification into an understrength MOS. Reclassification must be initiated and approved within thirty days from beginning retraining or separation orders will be issued.

Promotion Stagnation Qualitative Service Program (PS-QSP) Board

The PS-QSP board will consider staff sergeants through sergeants major or command sergeants major for denial of continued service who are in select MOSs with promotion stagnation—when an MOS's promotion pin-on rates, measured in years of service, are greater than the Army average. When otherwise qualified, staff sergeants selected by the PS-QSP board may seek voluntary reclassification into an understrength MOS. Reclassification must be initiated and approved within thirty days from beginning retraining or separation orders will be issued.

RETENTION CONTROL POINTS

The Retention Control Points (RCP) system consists of the use of reenlistment ineligibility points for each grade. Based on years of service, the reenlistment ineligibility point is the maximum number of years of active federal service authorized for a soldier in a specific grade.

As of March 2014 the retention control points are:

Rank	Total Active Service
PVT–PFC	5 years
CPL/SPC	8 years
SGT	14 years
SSG	20 years
SSG (promotable)	26 years
SFC	26 years
SFC (promotable)	29 years
1SG/MSG	29 years
1SG/MSG (promotable)	32 years
CSM/SGM	32 years
CSM/SGM (serving in nominative positions)	35 years

Notes:

1. Active service is defined as service on active duty, not including Title 10 of the US Code.
2. Master sergeants selected to attend the SMC for the purpose of promotion to sergeant major are authorized to serve up to thirty-two years.
3. Command sergeants major and sergeants major (HQDA and ACOM) serving in nominative positions where the officer is a general officer or SES equivalent (or serving as the commandant at the US Sergeants Major Academy or executive officer to the Sergeant Major of the Army) are authorized to serve up to thirty-five years.

BARS TO REENLISTMENT

The bar to reenlistment was designed as a rehabilitative tool, not as a form of punishment. Imposing a bar does not prevent future administrative separation. Each bar to reenlistment must be initiated separately and before the situation requires separation or judicial/nonjudicial action. The bar notifies the soldier that he or she is not qualified for reenlistment and is likely a candidate for separation if the circumstances do not change.

Advise soldiers on exactly what is expected to remove the bar to reenlistment and give specific timeline to overcome the reasons for the bar.

Mandatory Bar to Reenlistment

Commanders must initiate a bar to reenlistment or separation proceedings against soldiers who meet the following criteria:

- Do not make satisfactory progress in the Army Body Composition Program.
- Fail two consecutive APFTs.
- Are removed from NCOES courses for cause.

- Have lost PMOS qualification IAW DA Pam 611-21, Military Occupational Classification and Structure, due to fault of the soldier.
- Are denied by the commander for automatic integration onto the sergeant or staff sergeant promotion standing list IAW AR 600-8-19, Promotions and Reductions, paragraphs 3–17.
- Are involved in the use of illegal drugs or alcohol within the current enlistment/reenlistment period, resulting in an official letter of reprimand, a finding of guilty under Article 15 of the Uniform Code of Military Justice, a civilian criminal conviction, or a conviction by court-martial.
- Have two or more proceedings under Article 15 of the Uniform Code of Military Justice, resulting in a finding of guilty by a field grade commander during their current enlistment.
- Are AWOL for more than ninety-six hours during the current enlistment.

Commanders are not required to bar soldiers who are promoted or are selected for promotion for sergeant first class through master sergeant rank, or who reenlisted after the their barring incident(s) occurred.

INDEFINITE ENLISTMENT PROGRAM

Indefinite enlistment status is mandatory for all Regular Army soldiers in the rank of staff sergeant to command sergeant major who are eligible for reenlistment and have at least ten or more years of active federal service (AFS) on the date of reenlistment. From that point on, whenever the soldier is promoted, the expiration of term of service will be updated to reflect the retention control point for the new rank. After reenlisting for the indefinite program, a soldier may request voluntary separation or retirement at any time, provided he or she has fulfilled all remaining service requirements.

15

Promotion and Reduction

THE ENLISTED PROMOTION SYSTEM

The Enlisted Promotion System (EPS) has undergone extensive changes, many of which have already been implemented, while others are still pending changes or modifications. Even with rapid action revisions published to Army Regulation 600-8-19, Enlisted Promotions and Reductions, it is important that promotion-eligible soldiers talk with their chain of command and their battalion S-1 and stay aware of the latest military personnel messages relating to EPS.

All soldiers hope to get promoted, but not all are. Many times this is through neglect on their part; sometimes it's through their leaders' neglect. One of our responsibilities as noncommissioned leaders is to take care of our soldiers. A large measure of the success we achieve is through the success of our subordinates. We know we have done well when we watch a young specialist whom we have raised from private get the stripes of sergeant pinned on.

Soldiers should be counseled on their opportunities for advancement just as we expect to be counseled. Understand what it takes to be competitive in your field—for troop unit soldiers, it is leading troops at the crew, squad, or platoon levels; for someone working in an office, it may be additional civilian credentialing.

Soldiers are recommended for promotion only after they develop the skills, knowledge, and behavior to perform the duties and assume the responsibility of the next higher grade. Generally, if soldiers do well in their present grades, they will work well in the next higher grade.

The Army promotion system has the following objectives:

- Fill authorized enlisted spaces with qualified soldiers.
- Provide for career progression and rank that is in line with potential.
- Recognize the best-qualified soldier to attract and retain the highest-caliber soldier for a career in the Army.
- Preclude promoting the soldier who is not productive or not best qualified.
- Provide an equitable system for all soldiers.

233

There are three component levels for enlisted promotions: decentralized for promotions up through grade E-4; semicentralized for promotions to sergeant and staff sergeant; and centralized for promotions to sergeant first class through command sergeant major.

By using an automated promotion point worksheet (PPW) with predetermined promotion point factors, corporals, specialists, and sergeants can measure how well they qualify for promotion and can set goals to increase their promotion potential. Staff sergeants, sergeants first class, first sergeants, and master sergeants can judge their qualifications when compared with other soldiers in their MOS. The Army promotes soldiers who are qualified and who will accept Army-wide assignments.

Commanders at the grades indicated may promote soldiers, subject to authority and delegation of responsibility by higher commanders.

- *Specialist and below*. Decentralized. Unit commanders may advance or promote assigned soldiers to private, private first class, and specialist. When soldiers are fully eligible, promotions to these ranks are automatic unless the commander submits a DA Form 4187, Personnel Action, blocking the promotion no later than the twentieth of the preceding month.
- *Sergeant and staff sergeant*. Semicentralized. Lieutenant colonels or higher-ranking commanders may promote soldiers attached, assigned, or on temporary duty (TDY) to their command or installation.
- *Sergeant first class and above*. Centralized. Headquarters, Department of the Army.
- *Hospitalized soldiers*. Provided otherwise eligible, soldiers on a recommended list for promotion prior to hospitalization or assignment to a Warrior Transition Battalion (WTB) may be promoted when they have enough promotion points. If eligible, soldiers who are not on a recommended list at the time of hospitalization or assignment to a WTB may be recommended for and considered for promotion by the local medical holding facility selection board.
- *Students*. Soldiers in service schools at Army training centers may be promoted using normal promotion criteria. Soldiers assigned on TDY en route to a new duty station who are being trained or retrained may be considered for promotion by their school commander.
- *Posthumous promotion*. Human Resources Command.

With the introduction of a fully implemented Structured Self-development (SSD) training program, the Army linked SSD completion to promotion eligibility in January 2014. SSD is required learning that continues throughout a career and is closely synchronized with the NCOES and experiences in units (see Chapter 10).

Promotion of Private to Private First Class

Active Army personnel are advanced to the rank of private E-2 when they have completed six months of active federal service, unless it is stopped by the commander. ARNG and USAR personnel on initial active-duty training are advanced to private E-2 when they complete six months of service from the day of entry, unless it is stopped by the commander. To recognize outstanding performance, local commanders may advance a limited number of soldiers to private E-2 who have at least four but less than six months' active service.

Unit commanders may advance a soldier to private first class with twelve months' time in service and four months' time in grade. To recognize outstanding performance, unit commanders may advance a soldier to private first class if he or she has a minimum of six months' time in service and two months' time in grade.

Promotion to Specialist or Corporal

Normally, commanders may advance to specialist or corporal those soldiers who meet the following qualifications:

- Twenty-four months in service.
- Six months' time in grade.
- Security clearance appropriate for the MOS in which promoted; advancement may be based on granting an interim security clearance.

To recognize outstanding performance, commanders may advance soldiers on an accelerated basis, providing advancements do not cause more than 20 percent of the total number of assigned specialists and corporals to have less than twenty-four months' time in service, and providing that soldiers meet the following qualifications:

- Eighteen months in service.
- Three months' time in grade.
- Security clearance required for the MOS in which advanced (may be based on an interim clearance).

Unused waivers that are computed at unit level (not consolidated) may be returned to higher command for redistribution, providing that computation of the higher command's strength will allow additional promotions. For example, suppose that four companies in a battalion have ten promotion authorizations but use only eight. Computation of battalion strength indicates that twelve promotions would have been authorized if consolidated. Thus the two unused authorizations may be redistributed.

Promotion to Sergeant and Staff Sergeant

Field commanders and the Department of the Army both have a hand in promotions to sergeant and staff sergeant. The process begins with a recommendation by the soldier's noncommissioned officers through the chain of command to the unit commander, who then submits it to the O-5 promotion authority who conducts the local promotion board. The unit commander's recommendation states that the soldier meets the promotion criteria established for promotion to the specific grade for which the soldier is competing. To recommend or not recommend a soldier for promotion is the sole prerogative of the unit commander.

The normal sequence from recommendation to promotion to sergeant and staff sergeant follows.

1. The Soldier Meets Requirements. The time-in-service requirement for attaining eligibility for promotion to sergeant is three years' active federal service (AFS) for the primary zone and eighteen months for the secondary zone. The time-in-grade requirement for attaining eligibility for promotion to sergeant is eight months as a corporal or specialist, waiverable to four months for those recommended in the secondary zone. Soldiers in the secondary zone may be boarded with eighteen months' time in service and four months' time in grade as of the first day of the board month.

The time-in-service requirement for attaining eligibility for promotion to staff sergeant is seven years' active federal service for the primary zone and four years for the secondary zone. The time-in-grade requirement for attaining eligibility for promotion to staff sergeant is ten months as a sergeant, waiverable to five months for those recommended in the secondary zone. Soldiers in the secondary zone may be boarded with four years' time in service and five months' time in grade as of the first day of the board month.

Once a soldier reaches primary zone eligibility, commanders either must recommend that she or he appear before a promotion board or, if a soldier is fully eligible but not recommended, must complete DA Form 3355, Army Promotion Point Worksheet, and counseling documents and forward them to the promotion authority for a final decision. From that point until the soldier is recommended for promotion or is no longer eligible, unit commanders must provide copies of the soldier's counseling (at least quarterly) to the promotion authority. After forty-eight months of service and twelve months in the grade of E-4, soldiers are automatically put on the promotion list unless denied by the commander (see Command List Integration, page 246).

Soldiers competing for promotion to sergeant or staff sergeant must possess either a high school diploma, GED equivalency, or an associate's or higher degree and have completed SSD-1. Soldiers competing for promotion to staff sergeant must be graduates of the Warrior Leaders Course (WLC) before being recommended for promotion. WLC waiver policy was terminated 1 January 2014; soldiers with existing waivers who were promoted to staff sergeant had until 30 September 2014 to complete WLC or be reduced to sergeant.

2. Soldier's Chain of Command Recommends Promotion. Soldiers may only compete for promotion in their career progression military occupational specialty (CPMOS) as outlined in AR 611-201, Military Operations Specialty Code. Eligible corporals, specialists, and sergeants compete Army-wide by a three-character MOS, and their relative standing is determined by the points attained on an 800-point system. The company commander's role is to recommend soldiers for promotion to sergeant or staff sergeant and to deny, when appropriate, specified soldiers promotion list integration when an individual shows no potential for promotion. Commanders also ensure appropriate counseling for non-list integrated soldiers.

3. Administrative Points are Computed. There are 460 points for sergeant and 545 points for staff sergeant available. See the table on the next page.

4. Battalion Commander Convenes Promotion Board. Although AR 600-8-19, Enlisted Promotions, states that officers may serve as members of the promotion board with an officer as president, in most cases the board is composed of senior noncommissioned officers, with the battalion command sergeant major sitting as president. If a command sergeant major is not available, then a serving sergeant major may sit as president. Rules for conduct of the promotion board are found in AR 600-8-19.

5. Board Recommends Soldier for Promotion (Go/No Go). Based on the soldier's personal appearance, self-confidence, bearing, oral expression and conversational skill, knowledge of world affairs, awareness of military programs, knowledge of basic soldiering, and attitude, a battalion-level promotion board will convene monthly to validate a company commander's recommendation with a Go/No Go vote.

6. Total Promotion Points Computed. There are 800 total points available. The minimum promotion point score for attaining recommended list status for promotion to sergeant is 200. The minimum score for attaining recommended list status for promotion to staff sergeant is 450.

7. Education Requirements Met. Soldiers must be a graduate of the ALC in order to be unconditionally promoted to staff sergeant. Soldiers competing for promotion to this rank must be WLC graduates prior to recommendation for promotion. Soldiers competing for promotion to sergeant must be graduates of WLC before being promoted. Soldiers who are deployed and who are otherwise eligible for recommendation may be recommended and promoted to staff sergeant without the WLC with a waiver. The waiver approval authorities are the commander of HRC, the commander of USARC, or the DARNG, as appropriate. Soldiers subsequently integrated onto the staff sergeant list or selected and promoted to this rank with a waiver must complete the WLC within 270 days of their redeployment (date of return to home station). Failure to successfully complete the WLC within 270 days of redeployment will result in administrative reduction to sergeant.

8. DA Sets Monthly Promotion Points. Each month the Department of the Army establishes the total number of soldiers to be promoted based on budgetary and strength constraints. The number of promotions is allocated by primary military occupational specialty (PMOS) within these constraints. Department of the Army promotion cutoff scores are announced monthly (see the section on cutoff scores in this chapter).

9. Soldiers' Points Meet or Exceed DA Established Points. Soldiers are eligible for promotion on the first day of the second month, following approval by the promotion authority. Soldiers who meet or exceed the announced cutoff score are promoted if otherwise eligible. Each soldier promoted to staff sergeant must have a minimum of twelve months' active federal service remaining at the time of promotion. For sergeant, there is no service obligation.

Congratulations!

YOUR KEY TO SUCCESS

Become familiar with AR 600-8-19, Chapters 1 and 3, the monthly cutoff score, and applicable military personnel (MILPER) messages, available at the BNS1, Military Personnel Division (MPD) promotion section, and on HRC online at https://www.hrc.army.mil.

All AC soldiers will have real-time promotion scores based on the content of their records. The US Army HRC will capture promotion scores on a monthly basis (at a prescribed time) to establish order of merit lists (by MOS) for use in determining promotion selects.

WHERE THE POINTS COME FROM
(CHAPTER 3, AR 600-8-19)

Performance Evaluation and Military Training Points	Maximum Allowable	How Achieved	Individual Points
Duty Performance	150	Unit Commander	
a. Competence			30
b. Military Bearing			30
c. Leadership			30
d. Training			30
e. Responsibility and Accountability			30
Weapons Qualification	50	Score ranges from 50 to 14, dependent upon number of targets hit.	
Physical Readiness Test	50	Score ranges from 50 to 5, dependent upon APFT Score.	

Administrative Points

Awards:	100	
Soldier's Medal or higher award		35
Bronze Star Medal (BSM); Purple Heart		30
Defense Meritorious Service Medal; Meritorious Service Medal (MSM)		25

(continued)

WHERE THE POINTS COME FROM *continued*
(CHAPTER 3, AR 600-8-19)

Administrative Points	Maximum Allowable	How Achieved	Individual Points
Air Medal; Joint Service Commendation Medal; Army Commendation Medal (ARCOM)			20
Joint Service Achievement Medal; Army Achievement Medal (AAM)			15
Good Conduct Medal; Army Reserve Component Achievement Medal			10
Combat Infantry Badge; Combat Field Medical Badge, Combat Action Badge			15
Expert Infantry Badge; Expert Field Medical Badge; Basic U.S. Army Recruiter Badge (additional badges 5 each); Ranger Tab; Special Forces Tab; Drill Sergeant Identification Badge			10
Parachutist Badge; Air Assault Badge; Parachute Rigger Badge; Divers Badge; Explosive Ordnance Disposal Badge; Pathfinder Badge; Aircraft Crewman Badge; Nuclear Reactor Operator Badge; Awards of higher skill badge count as subsequent awards and will receive points (senior parachutist, master diver, additional recruiting badges); Driver and Mechanic Badge (maximum 5 points); Tomb Guard Identification Badge			5
Soldiers receiving incentive pay for parachute duty. Parachutist			20
		Senior	25
		Master	30
Campaign Service Star			5
Southwest Asia Medal (maximum 12 points)			3
Soldier/NCO of the Quarter—BDE Level			10
Soldier/NCO of the Quarter—Installation/Division			15
Soldier/NCO of the Year—Major Army Command (MACOM)			25
Distinguished Honor Graduate			15
Distinguished Leadership Award			10
Commandants List			5
Certificate of Achievement awarded by commanders/deputy commanders serving in positions authorized the grade of lieutenant colonel (LTC) or higher, or any general officer or CSM at the brigade or higher level (maximum 20)			5

Military Education	200		
Active Component Primary Leadership Development Course (AC WLC)			16
WLC Equivalency (as approved by Human Resources Command-Alexandria [HRC-A])			TBD
AC BNCOC			40

(*continued*)

WHERE THE POINTS COME FROM *continued*
(CHAPTER 3, AR 600-8-19)

Administrative Points	Maximum Allowable	How Achieved	Individual Points
Additional completed ALC (per week)			4
Ranger School			32
Special Forces Qualification Course			60
Battalion level or higher training certified by a DA Form 87, Certificate of Training, signed by an LTC or above (per week)			4
Completion of military correspondence, extension, or nonresident sub courses (per five hours)			1
Other courses of at least one week duration (forty hours)			4
Civilian education	100		
For each semester hour earned of business/trade school/college			1.5
Any soldier completing a degree while on active duty			10
CLEP Tests (for each semester hour earned)			1.5
Promotion Board	150		
Personal Appearance			25
Oral Expression			25
Awareness World Affairs			25
Knowledge of Military Programs			25
Basic Soldiering			25
Soldier's Attitude			25
Total Possible Points	**800**		

APFT FOR PROMOTION TO SERGEANT
(APFT SCORE/PROMOTION POINTS)

Score = Points	Score = Points	Score = Points	Score = Points
300 = 160	270 = 130	240 = 100	210 = 70
299 = 159	269 = 129	239 = 99	209 = 69
298 = 158	268 = 128	238 = 98	208 = 68
297 = 157	267 = 127	237 = 97	207 = 67
296 = 156	266 = 126	236 = 96	206 = 66
295 = 155	265 = 125	235 = 95	205 = 65
294 = 154	264 = 124	234 = 94	204 = 64
293 = 153	263 = 123	233 = 93	203 = 63
292 = 152	262 = 122	232 = 92	202 = 62
291 = 151	261 = 121	231 = 91	201 = 61
290 = 150	260 = 120	230 = 90	200 = 60
289 = 149	259 = 119	229 = 89	199 = 59
288 = 148	258 = 118	228 = 88	198 = 58
287 = 147	257 = 117	227 = 87	197 = 57
286 = 146	256 = 116	226 = 86	196 = 56
285 = 145	255 = 115	225 = 85	195 = 55
284 = 144	254 = 114	224 = 84	194 = 54
283 = 143	253 = 113	223 = 83	193 = 53
282 = 142	252 = 112	222 = 82	192 = 52
281 = 141	251 = 111	221 = 81	191 = 51
280 = 140	250 = 110	220 = 80	190 = 50
279 = 139	249 = 109	219 = 79	189 = 49
278 = 138	248 = 108	218 = 78	188 = 48
277 = 137	247 = 107	217 = 77	187 = 47
276 = 136	246 = 106	216 = 76	186 = 46
275 = 135	245 = 105	215 = 75	185 = 45
274 = 134	244 = 104	214 = 74	184 = 44
273 = 133	243 = 103	213 = 73	183 = 43
272 = 132	242 = 102	212 = 72	182 = 42
271 = 131	241 = 101	211 = 71	181 = 41
			180 = 40

APFT FOR PROMOTION TO STAFF SERGEANT
(APFT SCORE/PROMOTION POINTS)

Score = Points	Score = Points	Score = Points	Score = Points
300 = 100	270 = 75	240 = 45	210 = 28
299 = 99	269 = 74	239 = 44	209 = 28
298 = 99	268 = 73	238 = 43	208 = 27
297 = 98	267 = 72	237 = 42	207 = 27
296 = 98	266 = 71	236 = 41	206 = 26
295 = 97	265 = 70	235 = 41	205 = 26
294 = 97	264 = 69	234 = 40	204 = 25
293 = 96	263 = 68	233 = 40	203 = 25
292 = 96	262 = 67	232 = 39	202 = 24
291 = 95	261 = 66	231 = 39	201 = 24
290 = 95	260 = 65	230 = 38	200 = 23
289 = 94	259 = 64	229 = 38	199 = 23
288 = 93	258 = 63	228 = 37	198 = 22
287 = 92	257 = 62	227 = 37	197 = 22
286 = 91	256 = 61	226 = 36	196 = 21
285 = 90	255 = 60	225 = 36	195 = 21
284 = 89	254 = 59	224 = 35	194 = 20
283 = 88	253 = 58	223 = 35	193 = 20
282 = 87	252 = 57	222 = 34	192 = 19
281 = 86	251 = 56	221 = 34	191 = 19
280 = 85	250 = 55	220 = 33	190 = 18
279 = 84	249 = 54	219 = 33	189 = 18
278 = 83	248 = 53	218 = 32	188 = 17
277 = 82	247 = 52	217 = 32	187 = 17
276 = 81	246 = 51	216 = 31	186 = 16
275 = 80	245 = 50	215 = 31	185 = 16
274 = 79	244 = 49	214 = 30	184 = 16
273 = 78	243 = 48	213 = 30	183 = 15
272 = 77	242 = 47	212 = 29	182 = 15
271 = 76	241 = 46	211 = 29	181 = 15
			180 = 15

PROMOTION POINTS FOR AWARDS AND DECORATIONS

AWARD OR DECORATION	PROMOTION POINTS
Soldier's Medal or higher award/decoration	40
Bronze Star Medal with V Device	35
Bronze Star Medal	30
Purple Heart	30
Defense Meritorious Service Medal	25
Meritorious Service Medal	25
Air Medal with V Device	25
Army Commendation Medal with V Device	25
Air Medal	20
Joint Service Commendation Medal	20
Army Commendation Medal	20
Joint Service Achievement Medal	10
Army Achievement Medal	10
Good Conduct Medal	10
Army Reserve Component Achievement Medal	10
Armed Forces Reserve Medal (with or without M Device)	10
Military Outstanding Volunteer Service Medal	10

PROMOTION POINTS FOR BADGES

BADGE	PROMOTION POINTS
Combat Infantry Badge	30
Combat Medical Badge	30
Combat Action Badge	30
Expert Infantry Badge	30
Expert Field Medical Badge	30
Master Parachute Badge	20
Master Explosive Ordnance Disposal Badge	20
Senior Parachute Badge	15
Senior Explosive Ordnance Disposal Badge	15
Presidential Service Badge	15
Vice Presidential Service Badge	15
Drill Sergeant Badge	15
Basic US Army Recruiter Badge	15
Parachute Badge	10
Parachute Rigger Badge	10
Divers Badge	10
Basic Explosive Ordnance Disposal Badge	10
Pathfinder Badge	10
Air Assault Badge	10
Aircraft Crewman Badge	10
Secretary of Defense Service Badge	10
Joint Chiefs of Staff Identification Badge	10
Army Staff Identification Badge	10
Tomb Guard Identification Badge	10
Driver and Mechanic Badge	10

Certificates of Achievement

Certificates of Achievement (DA Form 2442) are awarded by commanders or deputy commanders serving in lieutenant colonel positions or higher. Command sergeants major at the brigade level and higher may also award certificates of achievement valued at 5 points per award, for a maximum of 20 points.

PROMOTION POINTS FOR AIRBORNE ADVANTAGE

SCENARIO	ADDITIONAL POINTS
Parachutist serving in TO&E/TDA position	20
Senior Parachutist serving in TO&E/TDA position	25
Master Parachutist serving in TO&E/TDA position	30

PROMOTION POINTS FOR MILITARY EDUCATION

Total Maximum Points

Promotion to Sergeant	260
Promotion to Staff Sergeant	280

PROMOTION POINTS FOR CIVILIAN EDUCATION

Total Maximum Points

Promotion to Sergeant	75
Promotion to Staff Sergeant	100

Recommended List

After completion of all promotion actions during the month, a recommended list is published. It lists all soldiers of the organization who have been selected but not yet promoted. Names are listed by grade and zone in ascending MOS and descending promotion point score order.

Soldiers are promoted from the current recommended list by MOS. Promotions are made on the first calendar day of the month in which they are authorized. Promotion orders may be published with future effective dates.

Soldiers are eligible for promotion on the first day of the second month following approval by the promotion authority and input into the automated system; for example, a soldier recommended in January 2015 became eligible for promotion on 1 March 2015.

A soldier's name on the secondary zone list for promotion to sergeant is transferred to the primary zone list on the first day of the month in which he or she completes three years of active service. He or she becomes eligible for promotion in the primary zone on the first day of the month in which he or she completes three years and three months active service.

A soldier's name on the secondary zone list for promotion to staff sergeant is transferred to the primary zone on the first day of the month in which he or she completes seven years of active service. He or she becomes eligible for promotion in the primary zone on the first day of the month in which he or she completes seven years and three months of active service.

Cutoff Scores

When a soldier's number of promotion points is known, many wonder why he or she cannot be promoted immediately if the cutoff is low enough. In the first place, soldiers may be selected for promotion three months before they have the required time in service. Junior NCO cutoff scores and the Sergeant/Staff Sergeant By-Name List are posted during the last week of every month on the HRC website, https://www.hrc.army.mil.

Second, reports from the field reflecting the number of soldiers on promotion lists, their number of points, and their zones and MOSs arrive at HQDA about the middle of the month following the month in which the soldier appeared before the promotion board.

At this point, MOS and grade vacancies are computed. The total number of promotions for a particular grade (regardless of MOS) is determined by comparing the number of personnel projected to be in that grade against the number allowed in the Army budget for the month in which promotions are to be made. This projection includes losses, those promoted in and out of the grade, and reductions. Available promotions are distributed to MOSs based on the percentage of fill.

Soldiers may add additional promotion points to the automated promotion point worksheet for the next month's promotion selection list. The eighth of each month is the last day points may be added in order for them to be considered for the next month's promotion selections. After eMILPO and ATRRS updates, soldiers should verify their worksheet for correct promotion points by comparing their copy with their ERB and training records.

Promotions go to the MOSs with the greatest need first. Secondary zone (waiver) promotions are limited, so they go to MOSs with the greatest need after the primary zone (no waiver) promotions are distributed. At this time— one to two months after the soldier appears before the promotion board—the soldier's number of promotion points comes into the process. For example, if vacancies and budget permit the promotion of a hundred soldiers from the primary zone of a particular MOS, a promotion cutoff score is established by going down the scores until the hundred limit is reached. For example, if the top hundred sergeants in an MOS have 716 or more points, the cutoff score would be 716. If the top hundred have 796 or more, the cutoff would be 796.

Command List Integration (CLI)

This policy is designed to assist the Army in filling vacant sergeant and staff sergeant authorizations. Each month, soldiers meeting the established criteria for list integration will be added to the recommended list with a minimum of 39 or 14 promotion points, dependent upon grade, unless previously denied. Commanders may block automatic integration by telling their supporting personnel which soldiers not to integrate.

Soldiers in the rank of corporal or specialist not recommended for promotion earlier will be automatically integrated onto the sergeant recommended list when they reach forty-six months of service and ten months' time-in-grade.

Soldiers in the rank of sergeant not recommended for promotion earlier will be automatically integrated onto the staff sergeant recommended list when they reach eighty-two months' time-in-service, ten months' time-in-grade, and have graduated from the Warrior Leader Course.

These rules provide for specialists and sergeants to be fully eligible for promotion recommendation one year past the fully eligible point to recommend a soldier under the existing means—that is, by board appearance.

The only avenue for soldiers automatically integrated onto the list to increase their promotion points is to appear before the promotion board. Soldiers are only promoted from CLI to sergeant when their scores meet the announced cutoff score and they have seniority over others within their PMOS listed on the CLI.

REMOVAL FROM RECOMMENDED LIST

Soldiers must be informed of removal action in writing. Once the soldier is removed, the action is final. Soldiers may be removed from promotions lists for the following reasons:

- Failure to qualify, for cause, for the security clearance required for the MOS in which the soldier is recommended. Those who fail to qualify for a security clearance through no adverse reason are reclassified and remain on the list in the new MOS.
- Failure to reenlist or extend to meet a service-remaining obligation.
- Being barred to reenlist.
- Reclassification from an MOS because of inefficiency or misconduct.
- Erroneous listing due to not meeting the criteria for promotion. ·
- Enrollment in the weight-control program.
- Failure to pass reclassification training.
- Reduction in grade after being placed on the recommended list.
- Nonjudicial punishment imposed under provision of Article 15, UCMJ (not including summarized proceedings), regardless of whether or not the punishment is suspended.

A removal board is convened when required to determine whether a soldier should be removed from a recommended list. The board will be constituted as for promotion boards. The soldier being considered for removal has certain rights. The soldier may choose to do the following:

- Appear, or decline to appear, before the board.
- Challenge any member of the board for cause.
- Request an available witness whose testimony is pertinent to the case.
- Elect to remain silent, to make a sworn or unsworn statement, or to be verbally examined by the board.
- Question any witness appearing before the board.
- Present written affidavits and depositions of witnesses.

Failure on the part of a soldier to exercise these rights is not a bar to the board proceedings or its findings and recommendations. The promotion authority is the final approval or disapproval authority on the board's recommendations. This action is final.

A soldier removed from a list and later exonerated is reinstated to the current local recommended list as soon as possible but no more than ten days after being completely exonerated.

SENIOR NCO/DA SELECTION BOARDS

The centralized promotion system was designed to accomplish the following:
1. Fill the Army's requirement for senior NCOs with qualified soldiers who have demonstrated potential for increased responsibility.
2. Provide for career progression and rank, commensurate with ability and potential.
3. Attract and retain the high-caliber individual for a career in the Army.
4. Maintain the integrity of the promotion system by providing fair and equitable advancement opportunity to the proven soldier, and preclude from promoting the individual who is not productive or progressive.

Much of the following information comes from the Human Resources Command Enlisted Personnel Management Directorate (EPMD) webpage at https://www.hrc.army.mil. No one could better define the centralized promotion system and how to prepare for the board than the proponent. The DA centralized promotion system described here is used for promotion to grades E-7, E-8, and E-9.

Board Operation

The Department of the Army Secretariat for DA selection boards convenes Enlisted Centralized Selection Boards based on guidance from HQDA at the Human Resources Command, Fort Knox, Kentucky. About four months before the convening date of each selection board, HQDA establishes and announces the zones of consideration for each board. These zones define the date of rank (DOR) requirements for consideration by the board for both primary zone (PZ) and secondary zone (SZ) selection.

The PZ consists of all soldiers of a specified grade whose DOR falls within the announced zone of consideration and who meet the requirements of AR 600-8-19, Chapter 4. The SZ provides outstanding soldiers with a later DOR an opportunity to compete for advancement ahead of their contemporaries.

The following general criteria must be met before the board convenes to qualify a soldier for inclusion in a zone of consideration:

- Meet the announced date of rank requirements and other criteria prescribed by HQDA.
- Have the required cumulative enlisted service creditable in computing basic pay for promotion to master sergeant or above.
- Be on active duty on the convening date of the board.
- Have a high school diploma or GED equivalent or an associate's or higher degree.
- Not be barred from or denied reenlistment.
- For promotion to sergeant first class, a soldier must have the security clearance required for the MOS in which promoted. For master sergeant and above, the soldier must have a favorable National Agency Check (NAC) completed or have a final secret security clearance or higher.
- Staff sergeants must have completed ALC and SSD-III before they are eligible for consideration for sergeant first class.
- Sergeants first class must complete Senior Leader Course (SLC) and SSD-IV before they are eligible for consideration for master sergeant.
- During transition, attendance to the SMC requires SSD-IV completion as well.

Soldiers compete for promotion and school selection against all other eligible soldiers in their primary MOS and zone. The number of NCOs selected for promotion in both zones is based on the Army's projected requirements in each MOS and grade. These requirements are determined by HRC and approved by the Office of the Deputy Chief of Staff for Personnel (G1), HQDA.

The My Board File is a Web application for soldiers in the zone of consideration for a DA centralized selection board and allows them to review and certify their board file. My Board File pulls data from the iPERMS OMPF/AMHRR performance folder, Department of the Army photo management system, eMILPO, and other record databases. Soldiers should review their iPERMS OMPF/AMHRR performance folder at https://iperms.hrc.army.mil. If there is an error, they must first correct those items in the appropriate database.

The HRC nominates—and the G1 approves—the individuals who sit on the board. Each board consists of officers and noncommissioned officers, with a general officer serving as board president. Nine to eleven panels compose each board, with at least four members on each panel. Panels are organized by the career management field (CMF), and the panel size varies in proportion to the number of records it must consider. Each panel has a nonvoting administrative NCO who controls the flow of records.

Prior to looking at or reviewing any file, HRC provides board members with a comprehensive orientation on the board process, evaluations reports, and detailed written guidance from the Army Deputy Chief of Staff, G-1, and the various branch proponents. The G-1's Memorandum of Instruction (MOI) gives them specific guidance on how to conduct themselves during the board process. The proponents provide specific guidance on the unique qualifications soldiers should possess to be the most competitive for selection. NCOs may wish to review a previously published MOI to better prepare themselves for an upcoming board.

During the selection board proceedings, each board member considers the soldier's entire career. This process ensures that no one success or failure, by itself, will be an overriding factor in determining the soldier's standing in relation to his or her peers. The primary areas that boards consider are:

1. Scope and variety of assignments.
2. Estimate of potential (as reflected on evaluation) expected of an NCO at the next higher grade.
3. Trends in efficiency.
4. Length of service and maturity.
5. Awards, decorations, and commendations.
6. Education—both military and civilian.
7. Moral standards.
8. Integrity and character.
9. General physical condition.

The most important document in the promotion file is the OMPF, which is stored online in the HRC My Records Portal. The OMPF is transitioning to the Army Military Human Resources Record (AMHRR). Within the OMPF, board members look primarily at each evaluation report, i.e., enlisted evaluation reports (EERs), academic evaluation reports (AERs), and NCOERs. They generally review all reports and place emphasis on the current grade or the last five years. The board also has access to the official photo, the Promotion Enlisted

Teaching, mentoring, listening, learning. SGT. RYAN HALLOCK, US ARMY

Record Brief (ERB), a synopsis of previous assignments, and whatever correspondence the soldier forwards to the board president.

Three board members vote on each file using a numerical score. Scores range from 1 to 6, with "+" or "-" used to further rank the files. The scoring system with a typical interpretation appears below:

Score	Performance	Result
6+/-	Exceptional Performer	Select Now
5+/-	Excellent	Definitely Select
4+/-	Strong	Should Select
3+/-	Successful	Select if Room
2+/-	Acceptable	Retain in Grade
1+1	Substandard	QMP Referral

Each voter places his or her score on a separate vote sheet. The other two voting members do not see that vote score. Board members may request additional information pertaining to the individual soldier before casting their independent vote. Also, board members are not told how many NCOs are authorized to be promoted until all records are voted and the scores are entered into the computer.

After all records are voted, the board identifies all primary zone soldiers whom they believe are "fully qualified"—those who meet the basic prerequisites for possible promotion to the next higher grade or attendance to a particular school. The fully qualified soldiers in each MOS are rank ordered based on the numerical scores given by the voting members. The panel selects those receiving the highest scores as "best qualified" based on specific select objectives for each MOS, which are determined by the projected needs of the Army. The same procedure is followed for selecting soldiers from the secondary zone. There are separate select objectives for the primary and secondary zones.

The board also performs a qualitative screening of soldiers whose overall records are unsatisfactory and warrant a bar to reenlistment. Soldiers identified and selected as unsatisfactory performers under the provisions of the Qualitative Service Program (QSP) receive an HQDA "Bar to Reenlistment."

PREPARING FOR DA SELECTION BOARDS

Assume that you are eligible for consideration by a DA Selection Board. How can you best present yourself to the board?

The centralized selection system relies on information contained in your OMPF/AMHRR, your official photograph, and your Enlisted Record Brief (ERB). These documents must portray an accurate profile of your ability and potential. Although the OMPF/AMHRR is used for other personnel management actions throughout your career, you must realize that the accuracy of the information on the OMPF/AMHRR may determine whether or not a board selects you for promotion.

The results of any selection board can be no more valid than the information upon which the board bases its judgment. For that reason, it is important to personally ensure that your file is current and accurate before a selection board reviews it. If you prepare your records with the same attention to detail as you would if you were preparing to appear in person, you will greatly enhance your chances of selection. Board members review your OMPF/AMHRR, Promotion ERB, correspondence to the president of the board, and official photograph, as well as a data summary of all of your evaluations.

Records Review

If you are in a zone of consideration for an upcoming board, you should review your Promotion ERB online at the HRC website. Your Promotion ERB contains your data from eMILPO. With the ERB, board members can see, at a glance, your history of assignments, military schooling, promotion dates, and other information. You must ensure all information on this document is accurate to avoid confusing anyone who reviews your file. Your attention to detail will eliminate any confusion.

After reviewing your ERB, you must certify its accuracy by validating it. Remember, your servicing S1/PSB/MPD maintains your ERB, so see them for any changes. For active-duty NCOs, all you need is an AKO account and password to access the HRC website. Go to https://www.hrc.army.mil/site/index.asp and click on View your Records, then Active Enlisted Promotion File. Look at it and compare it to your personal paper files. If it is incomplete, then get the missing documents to HRC through either iPERMS at https://iperms.army.mil/rms, your PSB, or the most expeditious means possible. HRC posts the documents that they receive to the OMPF/AMHRR within twenty-four to forty-eight hours of receipt.

Review Your Evaluation Reports. Check to see if they are all there. The NCOER is without question the most important document in your file. Missing reports reduce critical information available to selection board members. If an evaluation report is missing from your OMPF/AMHRR but you have a copy in your personal file, submit it to HRC as above. If you do not have a copy in your personal records, try to locate your rater for that time period or get your personnel service branch (PSB) or current commander to contact the rater, asking him or her to prepare a report for you. You should have the dates that you served under the commander, and you should remind him or her of your significant accomplishments during that rating period. The same steps can be taken with the senior rater and reviewer. If only one rater is located, that is better than a nonrated period. Remember, the purpose of an evaluation report is to provide information on the types of jobs you have held, your duty performance, and your demonstrated potential.

Review Commendatory and Disciplinary Data Included in Your OMPF/ AMHRR. These include certificates of achievement, awards and decorations, and Articles 15. If you have any commendatory items that are not in your file, you may send documentation directly to HRC, or your PSB will do it for you.

If you want to keep the original, most can be scanned and sent in digital form. Memorandums of appreciation or commendation are no longer authorized for file in the OMPF/AMHRR, except in exceptional cases. Make sure that any document sent to HRC contains your Social Security number.

Correct Erroneous Records. During the review of your OMPF/AMHRR, if you find an evaluation report that you successfully appealed, an Article 15 that was wholly set aside, or any erroneous/misfiled document(s), then you must contact your PSB. They will advise you on the steps to take to correct your record.

Enlisted Record Brief (ERB)

The Enlisted Record Brief (ERB) is the data information counterpart to the OMPF/AMHRR. Once you are in a zone of consideration for an upcoming board, you should review your Promotion ERB at the HRC tool MyERB, located online at: https://myerb.ahrs.army.mil. Review and authenticate your promotion ERB prior to every board.

Your promotion ERB contains your data from eMILPO and enables board members to see at a glance your history of assignments, military schooling, promotion dates, and other performance data. You should ensure all information on this document is accurate to avoid confusing anyone who reviews your file. Remember, attention to detail will eliminate any confusion and may increase your chances for selection.

Place special emphasis on the accuracy of the following information: name, Social Security number, grade, DOR, PMOS, SMOS, military and civilian education, date of birth, and basic active service date (BASD). Your servicing S1/MPD maintains your ERB, so see him or her for any changes.

Jobs also matter; boards look for NCOs who are successful in hard assignments such as serving as a platoon sergeant, a first sergeant in a combat theater, a drill sergeant, or a recruiter. These NCOs are generally rewarded. Muddy boots time also counts. Make sure your assignment history accurately reflects the job you held, as well as your current duty title.

Correspondence to the President of the Board

Memorandums to the president of the selection board are seen by voting members of the board. You may write to the board president to call attention to any matter that you feel is important to your consideration. The memorandum should not include information already in your file. The memorandum should be very brief, well written, and carefully proofread.

Official Photograph

All Army, Army Reserve, and Army National Guard Soldiers authorized DA official photos (staff sergeant and above) will be loaded into the Department of the Army Photograph Management Information System (DAPMIS). The official photo is not part of the OMPF/AMHRR; however, it can be viewed at the MyERB website, https://myerb.ahrs.army.mil/reports/soldierLogin.do. The photograph represents the soldier appearing before the board and is used in the decision-making process of the board members. Many board members have said that the photograph is the soldier's personal statement of professionalism to the board.

Although the regulation (AR 640-30, Photographs for Military Personnel Files) requires a photograph every five years, there is no prohibition against having one made sooner. If you have lost weight, been promoted, have new awards and/or decorations, or have a better-fitting uniform since your last photograph, you may want to have a new one taken. Ensure that the photograph is current and sharp, that your image does not blend with the background, and that you assemble the menu board accurately. A sloppy appearance, unauthorized awards and decorations, not wearing the chevrons of your current grade, or appearing to be overweight could affect your opportunity for selection. A missing photograph may also mislead board members to believe that you are apathetic or are trying to hide something (such as being overweight).

Discrepancies

The following are some common discrepancies found by DA Enlisted Selection Boards in the OMPF/AMHRRs of soldiers. These are not inclusive of every discrepancy; they are offered simply as a tool to use when reviewing your files.

1. Missing or outdated photographs.
2. Missing or incomplete ERB data.
3. Missing NCOER.
4. Height and weight differences—getting taller as you gain weight.
5. Blank or incorrect PMOS/SMOS/BASD/DOR.
6. P3 profile with no MOS/Medical Retention Board (MMRB).
7. Blank or incorrect military/civilian education entries.
8. Wearing of unauthorized badges, tabs, awards, and decorations.

The bottom line: Review your OMPF/AMHRR online often to ensure that all authorized documents are filed, your official photograph is on hand, and your ERB is correct.

Summary

At least six months before your records are to appear before a DA selection board, you should begin getting your records in order. Your file is appearing before the board in your place; take your time and make sure it is complete and accurate. Three parts of your file—your photograph, your OMPF/AMHRR, and your Promotion ERB—contain over 95 percent of the information that the selection board members will use to decide whether or not to select you for promotion, school attendance, or QSP. You must not ignore the importance of that fact. *Review your file!*

ADDITIONAL INFORMATION

Acceptance

Unless a soldier declines promotion, it is accepted as of the effective date of the announcing order. Letters of declination must be sent through command channels to the MPD office no later than thirty days after the effective date of the promotion given in the orders. Soldiers who decline promotion will be considered by the next regularly constituted board, provided they are otherwise eligible.

Soldiers promoted to sergeant first class and above incur a two-year service obligation; the obligation begins from the effective date of the promotion.

Lateral Appointments

Lateral appointments of specialists to the rank of corporal are an option available to battalion commanders to fill vacant NCO positions; these appointments can be completed through an informal memorandum process and without a board action. As long as a specialist is in a valid MTOE/TDA NCO position by MOS, the commander may authorize a lateral appointment to corporal. Soldiers appointed to corporal will keep that rank when reassigned from the NCO position, even if it involves a permanent station move. AR 614-200, paragraph 3-15, is the authorization; the regulation applies to all three components, including Active Guard and Reserve positions.

Battalion commanders laterally appoint master sergeants to first sergeant once the NCO is assigned to a valid first sergeant position and any required training from AR 614-200, paragraph 7-5, is completed. Once the NCO is released from first sergeant duties, the unit initiates lateral appointment action back to master sergeant.

Once assigned to a command sergeant major position, a sergeant major will be laterally appointed, or reappointed, to the rank of command sergeant major. Lateral appointments between command sergeants major and sergeants major are made by the Human Resources Command (HRC), and the effective date is the date on which the soldier assumes command sergeant major duties. Date of rank remains unchanged. When reappointed to sergeant major, the effective date for lateral appointment is the day after the soldier completes the command sergeant major assignment, and the date of rank remains unchanged (AR 614-200, paragraph 7-5).

Frocking

Soldiers on promotion lists who are assigned to first sergeant, sergeant major, or command sergeant major positions before they can be promoted may be frocked. When a soldier is frocked, he or she assumes the insignia of a higher grade so that his or her title is commensurate with the duty position, although no pay or allowances are authorized in the higher grade. Sergeants first class (promotable) to first sergeants, master sergeants (promotable) to sergeants major in certain assignments, graduates of the SMC, and command sergeants major (designate) may be frocked.

Enlisted Standby Advisory Board (STAB)

The Enlisted Standby Advisory Board (STAB) considers the following records:

- Those from a primary or secondary zone not reviewed by a regular board.
- Those from a primary zone that were not properly constituted due to a material error when reviewed by the regular board. The deputy chief of staff for personnel or a designee will approve cases for referral to a STAB upon declaring invalid, in whole or in part, an adverse NCOER or academic evaluation report that was reviewed by a promotion board, providing that with the absence of this report, or portions thereof, there is a reasonable chance that the soldier would have been recommended for promotion. An error is major when, had it not existed, the soldier would clearly have been more competitive and when his or her qualifications would appear to have been scored to equal those of others who were selected.
- Those of recommended soldiers on whom derogatory information has developed that may warrant removal from a recommended list.

Only those soldiers who were not selected from a primary zone of consideration will be reconsidered for promotion. Soldiers who were considered in a secondary zone are not reconsidered.

Removal from a Recommended List

Commanders may recommend that a soldier's name be removed from a DA-recommended list at any time. The recommendation for the removal must be fully documented and justified. HQDA makes the final decision on the removal based on the results and recommendation of the DA Enlisted STAB.

Removal may be recommended for a number of reasons, including the following:
- Failure to make progress in the weight-control program.
- Reprimand, admonition, censure, and other nonpunitive measures, including for substandard duty performance over a period of time.
- Misconduct.

Before forwarding a recommendation for removal, the initiator must send it in writing to the soldier. All documents must be included. The soldier must be allowed to respond to the proposed action and may submit a rebuttal within fifteen days after receipt of the written notice. The commander initiating the removal may extend this time only for unusual circumstances beyond the soldier's control. A soldier who elects not to rebut must send a signed statement saying that he or she has reviewed the proposed action and elects not to submit a rebuttal.

Removal from a DA promotion recommended list has far-reaching, long-lasting effects on the soldier. The probability of subsequent selection for promotion is extremely low.

REDUCTIONS IN GRADE

Commanders at the grades indicated may administratively reduce the grade of assigned soldiers:

- Specialist or corporal and below—company, troop, battery, and separate detachment commanders.
- Sergeant and staff sergeant—field-grade commanders of any organization that is authorized a lieutenant colonel or higher-grade commander. For separate detachments, companies, or battalions, the reduction authority is the next senior headquarters within the chain of command authorized a lieutenant colonel or higher-grade commander.
- Sergeant first class and above—commanders of organizations that are authorized a colonel or higher-grade commander. For separate detachments, companies, or battalions, reduction authority is the next senior headquarters within the chain of command authorized a colonel or higher-grade commander.

Erroneous Enlistment Grades
Soldiers in higher grades than authorized upon enlistment or reenlistment in the Regular Army or Army Reserve will be reduced to the one to which they are entitled. Authorized grades are prescribed in AR 601-210, AR 140-11, and AR 140-158.

Misconduct
For reductions imposed by court-martial, see the Manual for Courts-Martial. Sergeants first class and above cannot be reduced under the provision of Article 15, Uniform Code of Military Justice (UCMJ).

Inefficiency
Inefficiency is defined as "demonstration of characteristics which show that the person cannot perform the duties and responsibilities of the grade and MOS" (AR 600-8-19, Chapter 7). It may include any act or conduct that shows a lack of abilities and qualities required and expected of a person of that grade and experience. Commanders may consider misconduct, including conviction by civil court, as bearing on efficiency.

A soldier may be reduced under the authority of AR 600-8-19, Chapter 7, for long-standing unpaid personal debts that he or she has not made a reasonable attempt to pay.

An assigned soldier who has served in the same unit for at least ninety days may be reduced one grade for inefficiency. The commander starting the reduction action will document the soldier's inefficiency. The documents should establish a pattern of inefficiency rather than identify a specific incident.

The commander reducing a soldier will inform him or her, in writing, of the action contemplated and the reasons. The soldier must acknowledge receipt of the letter by endorsement and may submit any pertinent matters in rebuttal. Sergeants and above may request to appear before a reduction board. If appearance is declined, it must be done in writing and will be considered as acceptance of the reduction action. A reduction board, when required, must be convened within thirty days after the individual is notified in writing.

Reduction Boards

When required, reduction boards are convened to determine whether an enlisted soldier's grade should be reduced. This convening authority must ensure that the following conditions exist:

- The board consists of officers and enlisted personnel of mature judgment and senior in grade to the person being considered for reduction.
- For inefficiency cases, at least one member must be thoroughly familiar with the soldier's specialty.
- The board must consist of at least three voting members and will comprise both officer and enlisted voting members.
- The board has an officer or senior enlisted member (or both) of the same sex as the soldier being considered for reduction.
- The composition of the board represents the ethnic population of soldiers under its jurisdiction.
- No soldier with direct knowledge of the case is appointed to the board.
- A soldier who is to appear before the board will be given at least fifteen working days' written notice before the date of the hearing so that the soldier or his or her counsel has time to prepare the case.

The convening authority may approve or disapprove any portion of the recommendation of the board, but his or her action cannot increase the severity of the board's recommendation. If he or she approves a recommended reduction, he or she may direct it. When the board recommends a reduction and the convening authority approves it, the soldier will be reduced without regard to any action taken to appeal the reduction.

The soldier has the right to the following:

- Decline, in writing, to appear before the board.
- Have a military counsel of his or her own choosing, if reasonably available, or employ a civilian counsel at own expense, or both.
- Appear in person, with or without counsel, at all open proceedings of the board.
- If the soldier appears before the board without counsel, have the president counsel him or her on the action being contemplated, the effect of such action on his or her future in the Army, and the right to request counsel.
- Challenge (dismiss) any member of the board for cause.
- Request any reasonably available witness whose testimony the soldier believes to be pertinent to the case. When requested, the soldier must tell the nature of the information the witness will provide.
- Submit to the board written affidavits and depositions of witnesses who are unable to appear before the board.

- Employ the provisions of Article 31, UCMJ (prohibition against compulsory self-incrimination), or submit to an examination by the board.
- Have his or her counsel question any witness appearing before the board.

Failure of the soldier to exercise his or her rights is not a bar to the board proceedings or its findings and recommendations.

Appeals

Appeals of reduction for misconduct are governed by Article 15, UCMJ; paragraph 135, MC; and AR 27-10.

Appeals of reduction for failure to complete training will not be accepted. Appeals from staff sergeants and below of reduction for inefficiency or conviction by civil court are allowed. They must be submitted in writing within thirty workdays from the date of reduction. The officer having general court-martial jurisdiction, or the next higher authority, may approve, disapprove, or change the reduction if he or she determines that the reduction was proper, was without sufficient basis, or should be changed. His or her action is final.

Written appeals from sergeants first class and above of reduction for inefficiency or conviction by civil court must also be submitted within thirty days of the date of reduction. A copy of all correspondence and the appeal are furnished to the next authority above the officer who reduced the soldier. This officer, if a general, will take final action on the appeal. If not reviewed at the appellate level by a general officer, the file is then sent to the first general officer next in the chain of command above the officer who acted on the appeal for final review and action. This authority personally reviews the file, including action taken on the appeal, and makes final corrections where indicated.

Other Reasons for Reductions

When a separation authority determines that a soldier is to be discharged from the service under other than honorable conditions, the soldier will be reduced to the lowest enlisted grade. Board action is not required for such actions. Also, soldiers appointed to a higher grade on entering or while attending a service or civilian school and who fail to complete the course successfully may be reduced.

Restoration to Former Grades

Grade restoration may result from the setting aside, mitigation, or suspension of nonjudicial punishment; when a court-martial sentence is set aside or disapproved; when a conviction by a civil court is reversed; upon voluntary reduction; or when officers—taking final appeal or review action after reduction—direct that the soldier be restored to his or her former grade or any intermediate grade, on determining that the reduction was without sufficient basis.

16

Pay and Entitlements

This chapter explains the basic facts about Army pay and benefits and provides a quick reference for questions that may come up during day-to-day duties. The soldier who enlists in the Army for the money is in the wrong business. Relatively substantial paychecks do not begin until a soldier reaches the senior noncommissioned ranks with twenty to twenty-six years of service, although service overseas in a combat zone does increase take-home pay substantially. That said, if pay and benefits were the only inducement to a military career, then we would have no Army. Unlike first-term soldiers, soldiers who reenlist understand the "score" and accept the challenges and rewards of being a soldier.

PAY AND ALLOWANCES
Military pay consists of basic pay, special and incentive pay, and allowances. Pay is computed on the basis of a thirty-day month, and you may elect to be paid once a month (at the end of the month) or twice a month (on the fifteenth and the thirtieth of each month).

In order to change your pay option, contact your local finance and accounting office to execute DFAS Form 705, Defense Finance and Accounting Service Military Leave and Earnings Statement. Which option you select depends upon how you budget your money. Some soldiers find that they can get along quite well with one lump-sum payment at the end of the month; others prefer to get paid twice a month. Read the pay elections form carefully before filling it out. Submit your options to the finance officer as early in the month as possible to give the finance center enough time to process your request so that your new option will be reflected during the next pay period.

Your pay is your responsibility; report discrepancies immediately. To do so, you must know what you are authorized.

Online Finance
The Defense Finance and Accounting Service (DFAS) MyPay website, https://mypay.dfas.mil/mypay.aspx, allows you to access your pay record and update certain payroll information directly without having to fill out any paper

DEFENSE FINANCE AND ACCOUNTING SERVICE MILITARY LEAVE AND EARNINGS STATEMENT

ID	NAME (LAST, FIRST, MI) 1	SOC. SEC. NO. 2	GRADE 3	PAY DATE 4	YRS SVC 5	ETS 6	BRANCH 7	ADSN/DSSN 8	PERIOD COVERED 9

ENTITLEMENTS | DEDUCTIONS | ALLOTMENTS | SUMMARY

ENTITLEMENTS		DEDUCTIONS		ALLOTMENTS		SUMMARY	
TYPE	AMOUNT	TYPE	AMOUNT	TYPE	AMOUNT	+ AMT FWD	13
						+ TOT ENT	14
10		11		12		- TOT DED	15
						- TOT ALMT	16
						= NET AMT	17
						- CR FWD	18
						= EOM PAY	19

			DIEMS 23	RET PLAN 24
TOTAL 20	21	22		

LEAVE

BF BAL 25	ERND 26	USED 27	CR BAL 28	ETS BAL 29	LV LOST 30	LV PAID 31	USE/LOSE 32

FICA TAXES

WAGE PERIOD 39	SOC WAGE YTD 40	SOC TAX YTD 41	MED WAGE YTD 42	MED TAX YTD 43	WAGE PERIOD 33	WAGE YTD 34	M/S 35	EX 36	ADD'L TAX 37	TAX YTD 38

FED TAXES

STATE TAXES 44	WAGE PERIOD 45	WAGE YTD 46	M/S 47	EX 48	TAX YTD 49

PAY DATA

BAQ TYPE 50	BAQ DEPN 51	VHA ZIP 52	RENT AMT 53	SHARE 54	STAT 55	JFTR 56	DEPNS 57	2D JFTR 58	BAS TYPE 59	CHARITY YTD 60	TPC 61	PACIDN 62

BASE PAY RATE 63	BASE PAY CURRENT 64	SPEC PAY RATE 65	SPEC PAY CURRENT 66	INC PAY RATE 67	INC PAY CURRENT 68	BONUS PAY RATE 69	BONUS PAY CURRENT 70

Thrift Savings Plan (TSP)

CURRENTLY NOT USED 71	TSP YTD DEDUCTIONS 72	DEFERRED 73	EXEMPT 74	CURRENTLY NOT USED 75

REMARKS

YTD ENTITLE 77	YTD DEDUCT 78

76

www.dfas.mil

DFAS Form 702, Jan 02

Defense Finance and Accounting Service Military Leave and Earnings Statement

forms. MyPay also enables you to review or make changes to your federal and state tax information, financial allotments, home or correspondence address, savings bonds, and direct deposit or electronic funds transfer (EFT) information without the problems involved with paperwork. When you make a change, the system saves the transaction and sends it to the payroll system the next day for update. This system also allows you to view and print your Leave and Earnings Statement (LES) online.

MyPay accounts are established on the third and thirteenth of each month. By using your DoD Common Access Card (CAC), you can access myPay after you receive your first paycheck. You access the system by selecting SmartCard Login on the myPay home page. If you have login troubles, contact the DMDC Help Desk at (800) 538-9552.

The LES
Study your LES very carefully. Should you discover any item you believe to be in error or should there be an entry recorded there that you do not understand, consult with your local finance office immediately. If, during a routine audit of your pay record, it should be discovered that you have been overpaid at some time in the past, the government will collect what is due.

Basic Pay
Basic pay is established by law and is what a soldier receives based on grade and length of service, exclusive of any special or incentive pay or allowances.

Reserve Drill Pay
Reserve drill pay, like basic pay, is established by law and, like basic pay, is what a soldier receives based on grade and length of service. Unlike monthly basic pay, however, reserve drill pay is computed and paid for the number of days' service rendered. It is comparable to basic pay.

Collections of Erroneous Payments
Overpayments for two months in a row are collected from the next month's pay. If these payments are two or more months old, collection is delayed to allow time for unit commanders to arrange for prorated collection, if necessary, before computer collection action is initiated.

Normally, the amount deducted for any period will not exceed an amount equal to two-thirds of a soldier's pay. Monthly installments may be increased or decreased to reflect changes in pay.

Soldiers may appeal the validity of a debt, the amount, or the rate of payment. If an enlisted soldier's appeal is denied, the chief of personnel operations, Department of the Army, may consider his or her case for remission or cancellation of the indebtedness.

Advance Payments

An advance of pay is authorized upon permanent change of station to provide a soldier funds for expenses, such as transportation, temporary storage of household goods, packing and shipping costs, and securing new living quarters. Advance payments are limited to no more than one month's advance pay of basic pay less deductions or, if warranted, not more than three months' basic pay less deductions at the old station, en route, or within sixty days after reporting to a new station.

Requests for advance pay from enlisted personnel in pay grades E-1–E-4 must be approved by their commander. This approval must be indicated in DA Form 2142, Pay Inquiry Form, together with a statement that the circumstances in the individual's case warrant advancing the amount requested and that advancing a lesser amount would result in hardship to the soldier or his or her family.

The commander's approval for an advance of pay is not required for enlisted personnel in pay grades E-5–E-9, but advances are not made to senior-grade personnel when it is apparent that the tour of duty (obligated service) will terminate before completion of the scheduled repayment of the advance.

Lump-sum Payments

A lump-sum payment is made to pay bonuses and accrued leave paid on immediate reenlistments. These payments are made by cash or check using a local payment. Lump-sum payments are always made in even dollar amounts. The maximum amount that may be paid is the gross amount of the enlistment minus the estimate of federal and, when applicable, state taxes. When the computation results in a new amount due in dollars and cents, the amount to be paid may be either the lesser full dollar amount or rounded to the next higher dollar.

OTHER PAY

Combat Zone Tax Exclusion (CZTE)

Soldiers who serve in a combat zone can exclude some types of pay from their taxable income. The Combat Zone Tax Exclusion (CZTE) is unlimited for enlisted members and warrant officers; for officers, it is limited to the maximum enlisted pay amount, plus the amount of Hostile Fire Pay/Imminent Danger Pay payable for the qualifying month. This benefit can reduce tax liability and may result in lower taxes or a higher tax refund.

BASIC PAY (Effective January 1, 2015)

Years of Service

Grade	<2	2	3	4	6	8	10	12	14	16	18	20	22	24	26	28	30	32	34
Commissioned officers																			
O-10[1]	0.00	0.00	0.00	0.00	0.00	0.00	0.00	0.00	0.00	0.00	0.00	16,072.20	16,150.50	16,486.80	17,071.50	17,071.50	17,925.30	17,925.30	18,821.10
O-9[1]	0.00	0.00	0.00	0.00	0.00	0.00	0.00	0.00	0.00	0.00	0.00	14,056.80	14,259.90	14,552.10	15,062.40	15,062.40	15,816.00	15,816.00	16,606.80
O-8[1]	9,946.20	10,272.00	10,488.30	10,548.60	10,818.60	11,269.20	11,373.90	11,802.00	11,924.70	12,293.40	12,827.10	13,319.10	13,647.30	13,647.30	13,647.30	13,647.30	13,989.00	13,989.00	14,338.50
O-7[1]	8,264.40	8,648.40	8,826.00	8,967.30	9,222.90	9,475.80	9,767.70	10,059.00	10,351.20	11,269.20	12,043.80	12,043.80	12,043.80	12,043.80	12,105.60	12,105.60	12,347.70	12,347.70	12,347.70
O-6[2]	6,186.60	6,796.80	7,242.90	7,242.90	7,270.50	7,582.20	7,623.30	7,623.30	8,056.50	8,822.40	9,272.10	9,721.50	9,977.10	10,236.00	10,738.20	10,738.20	10,952.40	10,952.40	10,952.40
O-5	5,157.60	5,810.10	6,212.10	6,288.00	6,539.10	6,689.10	7,019.10	7,261.50	7,574.70	8,053.80	8,281.20	8,506.50	8,762.40	8,762.40	8,762.40	8,762.40	8,762.40	8,762.40	8,762.40
O-4	4,449.90	5,151.30	5,495.10	5,571.60	5,890.50	6,232.80	6,659.10	6,990.60	7,221.00	7,353.60	7,430.10	7,430.10	7,430.10	7,430.10	7,430.10	7,430.10	7,430.10	7,430.10	7,430.10
O-3	3,912.60	4,435.20	4,787.10	5,219.40	5,469.60	5,744.10	5,921.10	6,213.00	6,365.40	6,365.40	6,365.40	6,365.40	6,365.40	6,365.40	6,365.40	6,365.40	6,365.40	6,365.40	6,365.40
O-2	3,380.70	3,850.20	4,434.30	4,584.00	4,678.50	4,678.50	4,678.50	4,678.50	4,678.50	4,678.50	4,678.50	4,678.50	4,678.50	4,678.50	4,678.50	4,678.50	4,678.50	4,678.50	4,678.50
O-1	2,934.30	3,054.30	3,692.10	3,692.10	3,692.10	3,692.10	3,692.10	3,692.10	3,692.10	3,692.10	3,692.10	3,692.10	3,692.10	3,692.10	3,692.10	3,692.10	3,692.10	3,692.10	3,692.10
Officers with more than 4 years' active duty as enlisted or warrant officer																			
O-3[3]	0.00	0.00	0.00	0.00	5,469.60	5,744.10	5,921.10	6,213.00	6,459.30	6,600.90	6,793.20	6,793.20	6,793.20	6,793.20	6,793.20	6,793.20	6,793.20	6,793.20	6,793.20
O-2[3]	0.00	0.00	0.00	0.00	4,678.50	4,827.60	5,079.00	5,273.10	5,418.00	5,418.00	5,418.00	5,418.00	5,418.00	5,418.00	5,418.00	5,418.00	5,418.00	5,418.00	5,418.00
O-1[3]	0.00	0.00	0.00	3,692.10	3,942.30	4,088.40	4,237.20	4,383.60	4,584.00	4,584.00	4,584.00	4,584.00	4,584.00	4,584.00	4,584.00	4,584.00	4,584.00	4,584.00	4,584.00
Warrant officers																			
W-5	0.00	0.00	0.00	0.00	0.00	0.00	0.00	0.00	0.00	0.00	0.00	7,189.50	7,554.30	7,825.80	8,126.70	8,126.70	8,533.50	8,533.50	8,959.80
W-4	4,043.40	4,349.70	4,474.20	4,597.20	4,808.70	5,018.10	5,229.90	5,548.80	5,828.10	6,094.20	6,311.70	6,523.80	6,835.80	7,092.00	7,384.20	7,384.20	7,531.80	7,531.80	7,531.80
W-3	3,692.40	3,846.30	4,004.10	4,056.00	4,221.30	4,546.80	4,885.50	5,045.10	5,229.60	5,419.80	5,761.50	5,992.50	6,130.50	6,277.50	6,477.30	6,477.30	6,477.30	6,477.30	6,477.30
W-2	3,267.30	3,576.30	3,671.70	3,736.80	3,948.90	4,278.30	4,441.50	4,602.00	4,798.50	4,951.80	5,091.00	5,257.50	5,366.70	5,453.70	5,453.70	5,453.70	5,453.70	5,453.70	5,453.70
W-1	2,868.30	3,176.70	3,259.80	3,435.00	3,642.60	3,948.30	4,091.10	4,290.30	4,486.80	4,641.30	4,783.20	4,956.00	4,956.00	4,956.00	4,956.00	4,956.00	4,956.00	4,956.00	4,956.00
Enlisted members																			
E-9[4]	0.00	0.00	0.00	0.00	0.00	0.00	4,885.20	4,995.90	5,135.40	5,299.20	5,465.10	5,730.30	5,954.70	6,190.50	6,551.70	6,551.70	6,879.00	6,879.00	7,223.10
E-8	0.00	0.00	0.00	0.00	0.00	3,999.00	4,175.70	4,285.20	4,416.60	4,558.80	4,815.30	4,945.20	5,166.60	5,289.30	5,591.40	5,591.40	5,703.60	5,703.60	5,703.60
E-7	2,780.10	3,034.20	3,150.30	3,304.20	3,424.50	3,630.90	3,747.00	3,953.40	4,125.00	4,242.30	4,367.10	4,415.40	4,577.70	4,664.70	4,996.20	4,996.20	4,996.20	4,996.20	4,996.20
E-6	2,404.50	2,645.70	2,762.40	2,876.10	2,994.60	3,261.00	3,364.80	3,565.80	3,627.90	3,672.00	3,724.20	3,724.20	3,724.20	3,724.20	3,724.20	3,724.20	3,724.20	3,724.20	3,724.20
E-5	2,202.90	2,350.80	2,464.50	2,580.60	2,761.80	2,951.40	3,107.10	3,125.70	3,125.70	3,125.70	3,125.70	3,125.70	3,125.70	3,125.70	3,125.70	3,125.70	3,125.70	3,125.70	3,125.70
E-4	2,019.60	2,122.80	2,238.00	2,351.40	2,451.60	2,451.60	2,451.60	2,451.60	2,451.60	2,451.60	2,451.60	2,451.60	2,451.60	2,451.60	2,451.60	2,451.60	2,451.60	2,451.60	2,451.60
E-3	1,823.40	1,938.00	2,055.30	2,055.30	2,055.30	2,055.30	2,055.30	2,055.30	2,055.30	2,055.30	2,055.30	2,055.30	2,055.30	2,055.30	2,055.30	2,055.30	2,055.30	2,055.30	2,055.30
E-2	1,734.00	1,734.00	1,734.00	1,734.00	1,734.00	1,734.00	1,734.00	1,734.00	1,734.00	1,734.00	1,734.00	1,734.00	1,734.00	1,734.00	1,734.00	1,734.00	1,734.00	1,734.00	1,734.00
E-1	1,546.80	1,734.00	1,734.00	1,734.00	1,734.00	1,734.00	0.00	0.00	0.00	0.00	0.00	0.00	0.00	0.00	0.00	0.00	0.00	0.00	0.00

Notes:

1. Basic pay for an O-7 to O-10 is limited by Level II of the Executive Schedule which is $15,125.10. Basic pay for O-6 and below is limited by Level V of the Executive Schedule which is $12,391.80.

2. While serving as Chairman, Joint Chief of Staff/Vice Chairman, Joint Chief of Staff, Chief of Staff, Chief of Navy Operations, Commandant of the Marine Corps, Army/Air Force Chief of Staff, Chief of the National Guard Bureau, or Commander of a unified or specified combatant command, basic pay is $21,147.30. (See note 1 above).

3. Applicable to O-1 to O-3 with at least 4 years and 1 day of active duty or more than 1460 points as a warrant and/or enlisted member. See Department of Defense Financial Management Regulations for more detailed explanation on who is eligible for this special basic pay rate.

4. For the Master Chief Petty Officer of the Navy, Chief Master Sergeant of the AF, Sergeant Major of the Army or Marine Corps, Senior Enlisted Advisor to the Chief of the National Guard Bureau, or Senior Enlisted Advisor of the JCS, basic pay is $7,894.50. Combat Zone Tax Exclusion for O-1 and above is based on this basic pay rate plus Hostile Fire Pay/Imminent Danger Pay which is $225.00.

5. Applicable to E-1 with 4 months or more of active duty. Basic pay for an E-1 with less than 4 months of active duty is $1,430.40.

6. Basic pay rate for Academy Cadets/Midshipmen and ROTC members/applicants is $1,027.20.

DRILL PAY (Effective January 1, 2015)

Grade	<2	2	3	4	6	8	10	12	14	16	18	20	22	24	26	28	30
Commissioned officers																	
O-7	8,264.40	8,648.40	8,826.00	8,967.30	9,222.90	9,475.80	9,767.70	10,059.00	10,351.20	11,269.20	12,043.80	12,043.80	12,043.80	12,043.80	12,105.60	12,105.60	12,347.70
O-6	6,186.60	6,796.80	7,242.90	7,242.90	7,270.50	7,582.20	7,623.30	7,623.30	8,056.50	8,822.40	9,272.10	9,721.50	9,977.10	10,236.00	10,738.20	10,738.20	10,952.40
O-5	5,157.60	5,810.10	6,212.10	6,288.00	6,539.10	6,689.10	7,019.10	7,261.50	7,574.70	8,053.80	8,281.20	8,506.50	8,762.40	8,762.40	8,762.40	8,762.40	8,762.40
O-4	4,449.90	5,151.30	5,495.10	5,571.60	5,890.50	6,232.80	6,659.10	6,990.60	7,221.00	7,353.60	7,430.10	7,430.10	7,430.10	7,430.10	7,430.10	7,430.10	7,430.10
O-3	3,912.60	4,435.20	4,787.10	5,219.40	5,469.60	5,744.10	5,921.10	6,213.00	6,365.40	6,365.40	6,365.40	6,365.40	6,365.40	6,365.40	6,365.40	6,365.40	6,365.40
O-2	3,380.70	3,850.20	4,434.30	4,584.00	4,678.50	4,678.50	4,678.50	4,678.50	4,678.50	4,678.50	4,678.50	4,678.50	4,678.50	4,678.50	4,678.50	4,678.50	4,678.50
O-1	2,934.30	3,054.30	3,692.10	3,692.10	3,692.10	3,692.10	3,692.10	3,692.10	3,692.10	3,692.10	3,692.10	3,692.10	3,692.10	3,692.10	3,692.10	3,692.10	3,692.10
Officers with more than 4 years' active duty as enlisted or warrant officer																	
O-3E	0.00	0.00	0.00	0.00	5,469.60	5,744.10	5,921.00	6,213.00	6,459.30	6,600.90	6,793.20	6,793.20	6,793.20	6,793.20	6,793.20	6,793.20	6,793.20
O-2E	0.00	0.00	0.00	4,584.00	4,678.50	4,827.60	5,079.00	5,273.10	5,418.00	5,418.00	5,418.00	5,418.00	5,418.00	5,418.00	5,418.00	5,418.00	5,418.00
O-1E	0.00	0.00	0.00	3,692.10	3,942.30	4,088.40	4,237.20	4,383.60	4,584.00	4,584.00	4,584.00	4,584.00	4,584.00	4,584.00	4,584.00	4,584.00	4,584.00
Warrant officers																	
W-5	0.00	0.00	0.00	0.00	0.00	0.00	0.00	0.00	0.00	0.00	0.00	7,189.50	7,554.30	7,825.80	8,126.70	8,126.70	8,533.50
W-4	0.00	4,349.70	4,474.20	4,597.00	4,808.70	5,018.10	5,229.90	5,548.80	5,828.10	6,094.20	6,311.70	6,523.80	6,835.80	7,092.00	7,384.20	7,384.20	7,531.80
W-3	0.00	3,846.30	4,004.10	4,056.00	4,221.30	4,546.80	4,885.50	5,045.10	5,229.60	5,419.80	5,761.50	5,992.50	6,130.50	6,277.50	6,477.30	6,477.30	6,477.30
W-2	0.00	3,576.30	3,671.70	3,736.80	3,948.90	4,278.30	4,441.50	4,602.00	4,798.50	4,951.80	5,091.00	5,257.50	5,366.70	5,453.70	5,453.70	5,453.70	5,453.70
W-1	0.00	3,176.70	3,259.80	3,435.00	3,642.60	3,948.30	4,091.10	4,290.30	4,486.80	4,641.30	4,783.20	4,956.00	4,956.00	4,956.00	4,956.00	4,956.00	4,956.00
Enlisted members																	
E-9	0.00	0.00	0.00	0.00	0.00	0.00	0.00	4,995.90	5,135.40	5,299.20	5,465.10	5,730.30	5,954.70	6,190.50	6,551.70	6,551.70	6,879.00
E-8	0.00	0.00	0.00	0.00	0.00	3,999.00	4,175.70	4,285.20	4,416.60	4,558.80	4,815.30	4,945.20	5,166.60	5,289.30	5,591.40	5,591.40	5,703.60
E-7	2,780.10	3,034.20	3,150.30	3,304.20	3,424.50	3,630.90	3,747.00	3,953.40	4,125.00	4,242.30	4,367.10	4,415.40	4,577.70	4,664.70	4,996.20	4,996.20	4,996.20
E-6	2,404.50	2,645.70	2,762.40	2,876.10	2,994.60	3,261.00	3,364.80	3,565.80	3,627.30	3,672.00	3,724.20	3,724.20	3,724.20	3,724.20	3,724.20	3,724.20	3,724.20
E-5	2,202.90	2,350.80	2,464.50	2,580.60	2,761.80	2,951.40	3,107.10	3,125.70	3,125.70	3,125.70	3,125.70	3,125.70	3,125.70	3,125.70	3,125.70	3,125.70	3,125.70
E-4	2,019.60	2,122.80	2,238.00	2,351.40	2,451.60	2,451.60	2,451.60	2,451.60	2,451.60	2,451.60	2,451.60	2,451.60	2,451.60	2,451.60	2,451.60	2,451.60	2,451.60
E-3	1,823.40	1,938.00	2,055.30	2,055.30	2,055.30	2,055.30	2,055.30	2,055.30	2,055.30	2,055.30	2,055.30	2,055.30	2,055.30	2,055.30	2,055.30	2,055.30	2,055.30
E-2	1,734.00	1,734.00	1,734.00	1,734.00	1,734.00	1,734.00	1,734.00	1,734.00	1,734.00	1,734.00	1,734.00	1,734.00	1,734.00	1,734.00	1,734.00	1,734.00	1,734.00

E-1 > 4 months: 1,546.80

E-1 < 4 months: 1,430.40

Assignment Incentive Pay (AIP)

Assignment Incentive Pay (AIP) is used to voluntarily fill hard-to-fill assignments and is taxable unless in a combat zone. In Afghanistan, soldiers can receive $300 per month for a three-month extension, $600 per month for a six-month extension, and $900 per month for a twelve-month extension. In South Korea, soldiers extending their twelve-month tours for an additional year receive $300 in assignment incentive pay.

Reserve Component soldiers assigned in Afghanistan who have completed twenty-two months of mobilization and volunteer (for ARNG with the consent of the governor) to extend on active duty beyond twenty-four months of cumulative mobilization time will be offered the opportunity to contract for AIP. Soldiers will be offered $1,000 per month for extended duty beyond completion of their twenty-second month of mobilization. The AIP terminates when the soldier leaves the Central Command area of operations.

Experimental Stress Duty Pay

Experimental stress duty pay is authorized for all Army personnel who, on or after 1 July 1965, participate as human experimental subjects in duties using acceleration or deceleration experimental devices, in thermal stress experiments, and in low-pressure or high-pressure chamber duty.

Foreign Duty Pay

All enlisted personnel assigned to an area outside the contiguous forty-eight states and the District of Columbia where an "accompanied by dependents" tour of duty is not authorized have entitlement to foreign duty or "overseas pay." Chapter 6, part 1, of the DoD Pay Manual lists the places where foreign duty pay is authorized.

Hardship Duty Pay (HDP)

Hardship duty pay (HDP) is extra money paid to servicemembers assigned where living conditions are substantially below those conditions in CONUS. Hardship duty pay is payable to members entitled to basic pay, at a monthly rate not to exceed $300, while they are performing specified hardship duty. HDP is paid to members for performing specific missions or when assigned to designated locations. Except for certain restrictions, HDP is payable in addition to all other pay and allowances. Hardship duty pay for mission assignment (HDP-M) is payable to members, both officer and enlisted, for performing designated hardship missions. HDP-M is payable at the full monthly rate, without prorating or reduction, for each month during any part of which the member performs a specified mission. Hardship duty pay for location assignment (HDP-L) is payable only to enlisted members when they are assigned to duty in designated locations.

Hostile Fire Pay/Imminent Danger Pay (HFP/IDP)

Hostile fire pay or imminent danger pay (HFP/IDP) is paid to soldiers permanently assigned to units performing duties in designated hostile fire areas or to soldiers assigned to temporary duty in such areas. Hostile fire pay is authorized on a prorated basis. While drawing hostile fire pay, soldiers are exempt from federal and state taxes (see CZTE above). The 2012 National Defense Authorization Act modified HFP/IDP payments, limiting eligibility to only the actual days served in a qualifying area. Soldiers can receive IDP or HFP but not both.

Soldiers such as these in Afghanistan earn hostile fire pay while on duty in regions designated by the Secretary of Defense.

Pay Allowances Continuation (PAC)

Pay allowances continuation (PAC) is special pay for soldiers while they recover from wounds, injuries, and illness that occurred in combat. Under the PAC program, soldiers who were initially admitted as inpatients are entitled to this pay even if they later receive outpatient rehabilitation or care in other treatment facilities. The PAC program is not limited only to soldiers evacuated from a combat operation or combat zone for hospitalization; those hospitalized for traumatic brain injury (TBI) or post-traumatic stress disorder (PTSD) after leaving a combat zone may also qualify.

Diving Pay

To qualify for special pay for diving duty, a soldier must be a rated diver in accordance with AR 611-75, Management of Army Divers, and be assigned to a table of organization and equipment (TO&E) or a table of distribution and allowances (TDA) position of MOS 00B, or to a position that has been designated as diving duty by the assistant chief of staff for force development, Department of the Army.

Demolition Duty Pay

Demolition duty pay is a form of hazardous duty pay and is an entitlement for qualified Explosive Ordnance Disposal specialists and select combat engineers. These specialties are required to perform actions involving the demolition of explosives as their primary duty, and include the requisite training.

Flight Pay

Crewmember pay is typically paid to aircraft crew chiefs, flight engineers, flight stewards, crewmember flight instructors, and standardization flight instructors. Each aircraft type has a specific allotment of associated nonrated crewmembers, whose pay is similar to that of crewmembers. It covers soldiers who are required to perform frequent and regular aerial flight in the discharge of their primary duties, including maintenance personnel, physician assistants, aviation platoon NCO leaders, avionics technicians, aerial photographers, and aeromedical psychological investigators.

Parachute Pay

Soldiers who have received a designation as a parachutist or parachute rigger—or who are undergoing training for such designations and are required to engage in parachute jumping from an aircraft in aerial flight and to perform the specified minimum jump of once per three months—are authorized parachute duty pay. In imminent danger areas, however, the commanding officer may determine a soldier cannot meet the minimum requirements due to the absence of jump equipment, aircraft, or military operations. In this situation, the soldier may perform the required four jumps anytime in the twelve-month period. An additional amount is authorized for parachutists who are assigned to positions requiring high-altitude, low-opening (HALO) jump status. In an effort to attract soldiers to volunteer for and to continue performing parachute duty and to compensate soldiers performing hazardous duty involving jumping, the Army offers extra pay incentives of $165 per month (HALO jumpers receive $225 per month).

Special Duty Assignment Pay

Special duty pay is authorized on a graduated scale for enlisted members in designated specialties who are required to perform extremely demanding duties or duties with an unusual degree of responsibility. Qualifying jobs include career counselors, recruiters, and drill sergeants.

ALLOWANCES

Basic Allowance for Subsistence (BAS)
Basic Allowance for Subsistence (BAS) is a pay rate for rations and meals factored for a servicemember and is not intended to cover spouses and/or family members' food/subsistence costs. Changes in food prices as measured by the US Department of Agriculture influence modifications to BAS. Effective 1 January 2014, all enlisted military members in a proper status draw a full BAS monthly rate of $357.55. Servicemembers who draw BAS are required to pay for their own meals, even if provided by the government.

Entitlement to BAS terminates automatically upon permanent change of station (PCS). Soldiers should take care during in-processing at a new duty station that their entitlement is revalidated for personnel authorized separate rations.

The Family Subsistence Supplemental Allowance
The Family Subsistence Supplemental Allowance (FSSA) is a nontaxable supplemental subsistence allowance and increases a soldier's BAS by the amount equal to the total dollars required to bring his or her household income to 130 percent of the federal poverty line. FSSA does not exceed more than $500 per month. The program is voluntary; soldiers must apply and be certified to receive FSSA.

Basic Allowance for Housing
Basic Allowance for Housing (BAH) is based on pay grade, geographic assignment, and dependency status. BAH is an extra allowance for soldiers based on housing costs in their local civilian housing markets and is payable when government quarters are not provided.

BAH terminates for married personnel when they occupy government quarters or when dependency terminates. Dependency is verified by the local finance and accounting officer. The documentary evidence that must be submitted to substantiate dependence includes the original or certified copy of a marriage certificate, the individual's signed statement (when called to active duty or active duty for training for ninety days or less), birth certificate, a public church record of marriage issued over the signature of the custodian of the church or public records, or, if applicable, a divorce decree. Entitlements must be recertified upon PCS.

Reserve Component (RC) mobilized soldiers are entitled to BAH based on their primary residence; however, they are not authorized *to change* the BAH when they are ordered to active duty, regardless of whether or not their primary residence changes.

Family Separation Allowance (FSA)

The Family Separation Allowance (FSA) is paid to a soldier who has dependents and is serving in an overseas location where dependents are not permitted. It is in the amount of $250.00 per month.

Soldiers in a temporary-change-of-station (TCS) status may be authorized FSA Type II (T) at the rate of $250 per month when they are away from their permanent duty station (for mobilized RC personnel this is their home of residence) continuously for a period of thirty days) and when the soldiers' dependents are not residing at or near the TCS. Army/service married couples who were living together prior to and immediately before the deployment and single soldiers with authorized primary dependents may be paid Family Separation Allowance for Temporary Duty (FSA-T). Relocation of dependents at government expense is not authorized.

Station Allowances

The Overseas Housing Allowance (OHA) is authorized to assist a member in defraying the housing costs incurred incident to assignment to a PDS outside the United States. Every member authorized to live in private sector leased/owned housing is authorized OHA, if they complete an approved DD form 2367, Individual Overseas Housing Allowance Report. OHA is calculated by comparing the member's monthly rent to the prescribed locality rental allowance, selecting the lesser of the two, and then adding the appropriate utility/recurring maintenance allowance. To calculate OHA, visit the DFAS OHA calculator at www.defensetravel.dod.mil/site/ohaCalc.cfm. The housing must be the actual residence that the soldier occupies and from which the member commutes to and from work on a daily basis. A list of areas where station allowances are authorized is in the DoD Pay Manual, Chapter 4, part 3, and in Joint Travel Regulations, Volume 1, Chapter 4, part G.

In addition to the OHA, the Cost-of-Living Allowance (COLA) is paid to servicemembers to partially offset high costs when stationed overseas (including Alaska and Hawaii). COLA helps maintain purchasing power so that soldiers can purchase about the same goods and services overseas as in the United States. It does not reimburse expenses, but rather is designed to offset higher overseas prices of goods and services. It does not compensate for remoteness, hardship, or nonavailability of goods and services.

COLA and OHA are separate allowances—COLA partially offsets non-housing expenses, and OHA partially reimburses for housing expenses when housing is not provided by the government. A COLA rate query tool listed by location is available online at www.defensetravel.dod.mil/colaCalc.cfm. A Temporary Lodging Allowance (TLA) and) Temporary Lodging Expense (TLE) may also be paid in certain cases.

RC mobilized soldiers may receive COLA based on the location of their residence when ordered to active duty. CONUS COLA is normally determined by the zip code of the soldier's residence. Regular active-duty soldiers located in CONUS or OCONUS areas who are authorized COLA will continue to draw COLA as determined by the area to which they are assigned.

Temporary Lodging Allowance (TLA)

Temporary Lodging Allowance (TLA) is the allowance received when arriving at an overseas base to offset some of the expense of temporary housing and meals. The amount of TLA depends on variables including family size, cost, and cooking/dining facilities of quarters, as well as other allowances the family is receiving.

Temporary Lodging Expense (TLE)

Temporary Lodging Expense (TLE) is the allowance received when arriving at a CONUS base to offset some of the expense of temporary housing and meals. The TLE is up to $110 per day, and can last up to ten days. It applies to Stateside base arrivals from both CONUS and OCONUS bases.

Clothing Maintenance Allowance

A clothing allowance is currently authorized for soldiers and noncommissioned officers to help pay for the upkeep and maintenance and replacement of the initial issue of uniforms. There are four main types of clothing allowance: Initial, Replacement, Maintenance, and Extra. Clothing maintenance allowance is paid at two different rates:

- *Initial*. Covers replacement of unique military items that would normally require replacement during the first three years of service.
- *Replacement*. Covers the replacement of unique military items after the first three years of service.

Female personnel are also authorized an initial cash allowance established by AR 700-84, Issue and Sale of Personal Clothing, for the purchase of undergarments, dress shoes, and stockings.

A soldier receives the clothing maintenance allowance annually, on the last day of the month in which the soldier's anniversary date of enlistment falls. When duty assignments require soldiers to wear civilian clothing, soldiers receive lump-sum extra clothing allowance payments under the following circumstances:

- Permanent duty requiring civilian clothing.
- Temporary duty in graduations of fifteen to thirty days and over thirty days.

BONUSES

Enlistment Bonus

The enlistment bonus is an incentive offered to those enlisting in the Regular Army for duty in a specific MOS. The objective of the bonus is to increase the number of enlistments in MOSs that are critical and have inadequate first-term manning levels. Section A, Chapter 9, part 1, of the DoD Pay Manual gives basic conditions of entitlement, amount of the bonus, time of payment, and reduction and termination of the award.

Selective Reenlistment Bonus (SRB)

The Selective Reenlistment Bonus (SRB) is a retention incentive paid to soldiers in certain selected MOSs who reenlist or voluntarily extend their enlistment for a minimum of three years. The objective of the SRB is to increase the number of reenlistments or extensions in critical MOSs that do not have adequate retention levels to man the career force.

The SRB is established in three zones. Zone A consists of reenlistments falling between twenty-one months and six years of active service; zone B consists of reenlistments or extensions falling between six and ten years of service; and zone C consists of reenlistments between ten and fourteen years of active federal service.

Payments are based on multiples, not to exceed six, of a soldier's monthly basic pay at the time of discharge or release from active duty or the day before the beginning of extension, multiplied by years of additional obligated service. The SRB is paid by installments. Up to 50 percent of the total bonus may be paid as the first installment, with the remaining portion paid in equal annual amounts over the remainder of the enlistment period.

A list of the MOSs designated for award of SRB and enlistment bonuses are released by message from the HRC.

BENEFITS AND ENTITLEMENTS

MyArmyBenefits

MyArmyBenefits is the official Army Benefits website with fact sheets about the many benefits soldiers, Active, Guard, Reserve, retired, and their families are entitled to. The site is an archive of over 150 information papers that explain benefit eligibility and it highlights the details. Also, they have a Benefit Library so members can review what each state offers veterans as well. For updates and all the latest information, visit http://myarmybenefits.us.army.mil.

Allotments

An allotment is a specified amount of money withheld from military pay, normally upon the soldier's authorization, for a specific purpose. There are two types of allotments: discretionary and non-discretionary. Payment is made by government check and mailed to the payee.

Allotments are made either by filling out DD Form 2558, Authorization to Start, Stop, or Change an Allotment for Active Duty or Retired Personnel, or via the Defense Accounting Service's website, MyPay, https://mypay.dfas.mil. These forms are prepared by the individual's military personnel office, unit personnel office, or finance office, and by Army Emergency Relief and the American Red Cross. Preparation of allotment documents in the finance office, rather than in the personnel office, is intended to eliminate delays of one or more days. When there is a delay near the end of the processing month, the effective date of an allotment may be delayed a full month. Commanders may have DD Form 2558 prepared in the unit personnel office if it will save time and assure that there will be no delays in transmission to the finance office.

Soldiers are allowed up to six discretionary allotments and need to correctly identify the individual, institution, or business to receive the allotment. For specifically dedicated agencies or for a specific purpose, the non-discretionary allotment is used without limitations on the number.

Allotments can be used for the following purposes:

Repayment of Army Emergency Relief (AER) Loans. These allotments are authorized in multiples and are established for a definite term of no less than three months (although this provision may be waived in certain cases).

Combined Federal Campaign (CFC) Contributions. This allotment is authorized to be in effect one at a time only. CFC allotments are made for a period of twelve months, beginning in January and ending in December. Military personnel who execute the Payroll Withholding Authorization for Voluntary Charitable Contributions (a Civil Service form) may do so in lieu of DD Form 2558.

Payment to a Dependent (SPT-V). This kind of allotment is authorized in multiples and is paid to a soldier's dependent without regard to whether the soldier is already receiving BAH. In addition, involuntary SPT-V allotments can be administratively established. Normally, the amount of these allotments is not permitted to exceed 80 percent of a soldier's pay. Only one SPT-V allotment may be made to the same person.

Payment to a Financial Institution for Credit to a Member's Account (FININ). Only two of these allotments are authorized to be in effect at any one time. FININ allotments are for payment to a financial organization for credit to the allotter's savings, checking, or trust accounts. The FININ allotment may be established for an indefinite term and for any amount the soldier designates, provided he or she has sufficient pay to satisfy the deduction of the allotment.

Payment for Indebtedness to the United States (FED). FED allotments are for the purpose of payment of delinquent federal, state, and local taxes and/or indebtedness to the United States. A separate allotment is required for each debt or overpayment to be repaid.

Payment of Home Loans (HOME). Only one HOME allotment is authorized to be in effect at any one time. This allotment is for repayment of loans for the purchase of a house, mobile home, or house trailer. A HOME allotment is established for an indefinite term and for any amount designated, provided the soldier's pay credit is sufficient to satisfy the deduction of the allotment.

Payment of Commercial Life Insurance Premiums (INS). These allotments are authorized in multiples and must be made payable to a commercial life insurance firm. INS allotments are not authorized for payment of insurance on the life of a soldier's spouse or children except under a family group contract or for health, accident, or hospitalization insurance. INS allotments are established for an indefinite period and in the amount of the monthly premium, as indicated by the number on DA Form 1341.

Repayment of American Red Cross Loans (REDCR). REDCR allotments are authorized in multiples to repay Red Cross loans.

Educational Savings Allotment (EDSAV). This allotment is authorized to allow soldiers entering service after 13 December 1976 (except those who enlisted under the Delayed Entry Program before 1 January 1977) to participate in the Veterans Educational Assistance Program (VEAP). Only one such allotment is authorized. The EDSAV allotment is established with no discontinuance date. The soldier may stop it at any time after one year of participation.

Class X Allotments. A Class X allotment is paid locally and is authorized in emergency circumstances when other classes of allotments are impracticable. This instance applies overseas only. Class X allotments may be ordered by a commander as a standby allotment when adequate provision for the financial support of a soldier's dependents has not been made.

Thrift Savings Plan (TSP)

The purpose of the Thrift Savings Plan (TSP) is to provide retirement income. It offers soldiers the same type of savings and tax benefits that many private corporations offer their employees under so-called 401(k) plans. Under the plan, soldiers save a portion of their pay in a special retirement account administered by the Federal Retirement Thrift Investment Board. Each year, the IRS determines the maximum amount contributable to tax-deferred savings plans like the TSP and limits the amount of income soldiers may elect to defer during a tax year. As an example, the elective deferral limit for the 2014 tax year was $17,500.

Participation in the TSP is neither optional nor automatic. Soldiers must sign up through their finance office to participate. They contribute to the TSP from their own pay on a pretax basis, and the amount they contribute and the earnings attributable to their contributions belong to them. Soldiers keep the earnings, even if they do not serve the twenty years ordinarily necessary to receive military retired pay.

While a soldier is a member of the uniformed services, any tax-deferred money withdrawn before the age of fifty-nine-and-a-half as a result of financial hardship is subject to the IRS 10 percent early withdrawal penalty, as well as regular income tax. With respect to post-separation withdrawals, if the soldier separates from the service during or after the year in which he or she turns age fifty-five, the withdrawals are not subject to the early withdrawal penalty. If a soldier separates before the year he or she reaches age fifty-five, the soldier can transfer the TSP account to an IRA or other eligible retirement plan (e.g., 401(k) plan or a civilian TSP account) or begin receiving annuity payments without penalty.

Savings Deposit Program (SDP)

Formerly known as the Uniformed Services Deposit Program (USSDP), the Department of Defense Savings Deposit Program was created as a savings opportunity specifically for servicemembers in a combat zone. Soldiers may deposit up to $10,000 per deployment and earn 10 percent interest annually. To be eligible, they must serve at least thirty days in a qualified hazardous duty area and be receiving Hostile Fire Pay. The interest earned is compounded quarterly, and even though income earned in combat is not taxable, the interest earned on SDP is taxable.

Transportation of Household Goods

Transportation of household goods at government expense is authorized for soldiers in accordance with the following table. For information on authorized weight limitations for other grades, see the Joint Federal Travel Regulations (JFTR).

PCS WEIGHT ALLOWANCE (POUNDS)

Pay Grade	With Dependents	Without Dependents
E-9	14,500	12,000
E-8	13,500	11,000
E-7	12,500	10,500
E-6	11,000	8,000
E-5	9,000	7,000
E-4 (over 2 years' service)	8,000	7,000
E-4 (2 years' service or less)	7,000	3,500
E-3	5,000	2,000
E-2, E-1	5,000	1,500

HOUSING

Your home is one the most important influences on how you embrace Army life. Whether you choose to live on the installation in military housing or off post, the Army tries to provide you with military housing to make you as comfortable as possible.

Unaccompanied Housing

Bachelor accommodations for enlisted personnel range from the fairly austere communal living conditions offered to junior enlisted personnel in troop units to the small but private and well-appointed quarters offered senior NCOs in bachelor enlisted quarters (BEQ). During the course of an Army career, and based on assignment and location, a servicemember may be assigned to these types of housing units.

Soldiers in the ranks of private through specialist (except for initial-entry trainees) are allowed at least 90 square feet of living space. Noncommissioned officers authorized barracks space are allowed 135 square feet per living area with a private room and a bath shared with no more than one other. Living space is calculated on the building specification. If you live in an older barracks, you are authorized the minimum of 90 square feet; however, if you live in the newer design you may have more living space.

The First Sergeants Barracks Program (FSBP) is the Army's current effort to increase the quality of life for single soldiers and to better manage barracks across the entire Army. The FSBP allows Army garrisons to supervise property and equipment more like a realtor does with apartments. This reduces overcrowding in the barracks and allows for improved distribution of unused and excess space, especially in times of deployment. The FSBP helps to improve the time to repair facilities and to decrease or account for building damages, extending the life of the facilities. Although the FSBP takes the burden of property management off the unit, it does not mean that noncommissioned officers should not check on their soldiers and their living conditions in either unaccompanied or family housing.

Family Housing

Family housing—where available—ranges in style from detached single-family housing to high-rise apartment-style buildings accommodating scores of families. In some cases, the quarters you are assigned will be in excellent condition and will require little maintenance to keep them that way; others will cause you constant maintenance headaches.

When reporting to some new duty stations, you will find pleasant family housing waiting for you; at other stations, you will have to wait weeks or even months to get any kind of quarters. In some areas, the waiting list for government housing is so long that you might find it necessary to buy or rent off post. Your family housing officer will be of great assistance to you if you should decide to occupy off-post quarters. Each installation and each major overseas command has a different family housing situation.

Because of your rank, you may very well find yourself either the senior occupant of a multiple dwelling or responsible for a number of families in such a dwelling. These assignments are necessary, and you should consider them part of your obligation as an NCO to the military community in which you live. You should perform them with the same dedication and enthusiasm that you devote to your primary duties, but be prepared for many headaches, and expect that from time to time your patience will be tested.

Occupancy of family quarters carries the responsibility for doing "handyman work." The facilities engineer performs all maintenance and repairs other than those that are within the capabilities of the occupants. Emergency work or work beyond your individual capabilities can be obtained by making a service call or submitting a job order request to the installation repair and utilities office. Do not, however, expect the engineers to drop everything and run to your quarters, no matter how severe the emergency.

If you are fortunate enough to be assigned to a single-family dwelling, you will be expected to perform that type of self-help maintenance that is done by any prudent homeowner to conserve funds and preserve the premises. This may include minor carpentry, maintenance of hardware (door hinges and so forth), touch-up and partial interior painting, caulking around doors and windows, repair of screens, repair of simple plumbing malfunctions (minor leaking, defective washers, simple drainage stoppages), and so forth. Accumulate a set of tools that you can use around the house or apartment for this minor maintenance work.

No matter where you live—family quarters or the barracks—you are expected to conserve energy and utilities. Soldiers are among the most flagrant violators of good energy conservation, wasting water and electricity and fuel as if there were no tomorrow. Remind yourself and others to be conservation conscious.

Your quarters will be inspected by someone from the housing office before you are cleared to vacate your quarters. This inspection can be very rigorous. The specific details will be furnished to you by the housing officer. Some people prefer to hire a civilian contractor to do the work for them. You can avoid this unnecessary expense if you and your family take proper care of your quarters while you are living in them. For example, use rugs on the floors, keep the walls clean and in good repair, and keep your appliances clean.

Residential Communities Initiative (RCI)
The Army's Residential Communities Initiative (RCI) program comprises 45 installations where private sector housing experts have assumed responsibility to manage 88,000 military homes. RCI equates to 98 percent of the Army's family housing inventory in the United States.

Commissary and Post Exchange Services
Commissaries and post exchanges particularly benefit young service families that live in areas where the cost of living is high. Without the commissary and post exchange, some families of military servicemembers could not make ends meet. The price a servicemember pays for a grocery item in the

commissary is the same price the government pays for it: If an item is sold to the government for 85 cents, then that is its cost to you. Even the 5 percent commissary surcharge instituted by Congress and tipping do not add as much to the cost of an item as do the standard markups found on similar items in civilian retail outlets.

The commissary surcharge pays for operating supplies, equipment, utilities, facility alterations, and new construction. Civilian payroll of commissary stores is taxpayer funded to keep the costs separate from the goods and services offered.

The post exchange service was designated the Army and Air Force Exchange Service (AAFES) in 1948. What originally began as an outlet "to supply troops at reasonable prices with articles of ordinary use . . . not supplied by the Government . . . to afford them the means of rational recreation and amusement" has since become a multibillion-dollar enterprise that spans the globe. Many post exchange stores are actually department stores designed for family shoppers, although single soldiers can buy all the necessities of barracks life. Some stores even permit personnel in uniform to be waited on first during certain hours of the day, such as the lunch hour.

Several hundred military exchanges are operated throughout the world by the DoD. (AAFES, headquartered in Dallas and headed by a general officer, operates outlets worldwide.) At a minimum, AAFES customers are not charged state sales tax

IDENTIFICATION CARDS

The Common Access Card (CAC) is an official DoD identification card that has an integrated circuit chip embedded in the credit card-sized document. This "smart card" is the Armed Forces of the United States Geneva Conventions Identification Card and is used as the standard identification for active-duty uniformed service personnel, Selected Reserve, DoD civilian employees, and eligible contractor personnel. It is also the principal card used to enable physical access to buildings and controlled spaces, and it provides access to DoD computer networks and systems. There are four different types of CAC cards; however, the standard card for active-duty personnel is also used in accordance with Geneva Convention requirements

Your CAC is possibly the most important military document you possess. DD Form 1173, Uniformed Services Identification and Privilege Card, is equally important to military family members. These cards identify the bearers as persons who are entitled to the wide range of privileges and benefits authorized for military personnel and their dependents.

The CAC is issued to active-duty Armed Forces, Selected Reserves, and National Guard servicemembers. If you are a military retiree or military family member, you must have a Uniformed Services ID Card to access military service benefits or privileges.

DD Form 2 (Reserve), Armed Forces of the United States Geneva Conventions Identification Card, is a green card issued to members of the Individual Ready Reserves and Inactive National Guard.

DD Form 2 (Retired) is a blue card issued to retired personnel of the uniformed services who are entitled to retirement pay. The blue card is also issued to persons who retired from ARNG or USAR at age sixty after completing federal service under Section 1331, Title 10, US Code, and for personnel permanently retired for physical disability.

The DD Form 2 (Retired Reserve) is a pink card issued to persons who have retired from ARNG or USAR and are under the age sixty and not yet entitled to retirement pay.

All ID cards are the property of the US government. They are not transferable. The individual (or sponsor) to whom the card is issued must turn in cards in the following circumstances:

- Expiration of the card.
- Change in eligibility status (changes in grade or rank and changes caused by disciplinary action, discharge, death, retirement, reenlistment, age, marriage, or release to inactive duty).
- Replacement by another card.
- Request from competent authority.
- Demand of the installation commander, verifying activity, or issuing activity.
- Recovery of a lost card after a replacement has been issued.
- Request by the installation commander for temporary safekeeping while an individual is taking part in recreation and gymnastic activities.
- Official placement of a sponsor in a deserter status.
- Change in the status of a sponsor if it terminates or modifies the right to any benefit for which the card may be used.

If you lose your identification card, you will be required to present documentation from the local security office confirming that it has been reported lost or stolen. That document is required to be scanned and stored in the Defense Enrollment Eligibility Reporting System (DEERS).

Any NCO performing his or her official duties may confiscate an ID card that is expired, mutilated, used fraudulently, or presented by a person not entitled to use it. Managers and employees of benefit and privilege activities may confiscate any expired or obviously altered ID card or document.

Dependent ID Cards

DD Form 1173, United States Uniformed Services Identification and Privilege Card, is used throughout the DoD to identify persons, other than active-duty or retired military personnel, who are eligible for benefits and privileges offered by the Armed Forces.

Dependent ID cards are authorized for issue to lawful spouses; unremarried former spouses married to the member or former member for a period of at least twenty years (during which period the member or former member performed at least twenty years of service); children (adopted, legitimized, stepchildren, and wards); parents (in special cases); and surviving spouses of active-duty or retired members. See AR 640-3, Identification Cards, Tags and Badges, for specific details.

Generally, DD Forms 1173 are replaced for the same reasons that govern replacement of military ID cards. To verify initial eligibility for issue of a dependent ID card and entry into DEERS, sponsors must be prepared to show marriage certificates, birth certificates, death certificates (in the case of unremarried widows or widowers), or any other documentation prescribed by AR 600-8-14 required to establish dependency. DEERS can be updated online at https://www.dmdc.osd.mil/milconnect or by calling (800) 538-9552.

Abuse of Privileges

All CACs, DD Forms 2, DD Forms 1173, and other authorized identification documents issued to Army members and their dependents may be confiscated and overstamped for abuse of privileges in Army facilities. (Medical benefits, however, cannot be suspended for these reasons.) Abuse of privileges includes the following:

- Unauthorized resale of commodities bought in Army activities to unauthorized persons, whether or not to make a profit (customary personal gifts are permissible).
- Shoplifting.
- Unauthorized access to activities.
- Misuse of a privilege (such as allowing an unauthorized person to use an otherwise valid ID card to gain access to a facility).
- Issuing dishonored checks in Army facilities.

Penalties for abuse of privileges in an appropriated or nonappropriated fund facility are a warning letter, temporary suspension of privileges, and indefinite suspension of privileges.

milConnect

MilConnect is a Web application that offers soldiers, spouses, and their children (eighteen years and older) a way to access their personal information, view health-care eligibility, and review personnel records and other information from a centralized dashboard. This tool is available at https://www.dmdc.osd.mil/milconnect.

The following services can be completed on milConnect:
- Update contact information in DEERS.
- View current health-care enrollments.

- Manage TRICARE enrollments.
- Locate the nearest Military ID card issuing facility.
- View personnel information.
- Transfer education benefits to eligible family members under the Post-9/11 GI Bill.
- View ID cards.
- View Servicemembers Group Life Insurance information (except Marines and Coast Guard).
- Obtain proof of insurance if currently in a TRICARE managed program.
- Find answers to frequently asked questions about health-care eligibility and more.

LEAVES AND PASSES

Leave
AR 600-8-10, Leaves and Passes, governs leaves and passes and is designed to allow soldiers to use their authorized leave to the maximum extent possible. All members of the Army serving on active duty are entitled to leave with pay and allowances at the rate of two-and-a-half calendar days each month of active duty or active duty for training, including the following:

- Members of the Army serving in active military service, including members of the Army National Guard and the Army Reserve serving on active duty for a period of thirty days or more.
- Members of the Army National Guard and Reserve serving on initial active duty for training or active duty for training for a period of thirty days or more and for which they are entitled to receive pay.
- Members of the Army National Guard who are serving on full-time training duty for a period of thirty days or more and for which they are entitled to receive pay.

The following circumstances do not qualify as periods of earned leave:

- AWOL.
- Confinement as a result of a court-martial sentence (providing the court-martial results in a conviction) or for more than one day while awaiting court-martial.
- When in excess leave.
- Unauthorized absence as a result of detention by civil authorities.
- Absence due to misconduct.
- Absence because in custody of civil authorities.
- Absence of over one duty day due to use of drugs or alcohol or because of disease or injury resulting from misconduct.

The total accumulation of accrued leave (earned leave) at the end of a fiscal year (September 30) cannot exceed 60 days. Leave accumulated after that date is forfeited. The single exception to this policy applies to personnel who were prohibited from taking leave during the latter part of the fiscal year due to assignment or deployment to hostile fire or imminent danger pay areas. Eligible members can accumulate up to 30 additional days in excess of 60 but cannot carry over more than 120 days into the next fiscal year. Leave that begins in one fiscal year and is completed in another is apportioned to the fiscal year in which each portion falls. Upon discharge and immediate reenlistment, separation at expiration of term of service (ETS), or retirement, soldiers are authorized to settle their leave accounts for a lump-sum cash payment at the rate of one day of basic pay for each day of earned leave, up to 60 days. Public Law 94-212, 9 February 1976, limited settlement for accrued leave during a military career to a maximum of 60 days.

The following types of leave are authorized:

- *Advance leave.* Leave granted before its actual accrual, based on a reasonable expectation that it will be earned by the soldier during the remaining period of active duty.
- *Annual leave.* Leave granted in execution of a command's leave program, chargeable to the soldier's leave account; also called "ordinary leave," as distinguished from emergency leave and special leave.
- *Convalescent leave.* A period of authorized absence granted to soldiers under medical treatment that is prescribed for recuperation and convalescence for sickness or wounds. Also called "sick leave," (sick-in-quarters, sick-in-hospital) convalescent leave is not chargeable. Soldiers who sustain illness or injury while eligible for hostile fire pay are entitled to funded transportation per Joint Federal Travel Regulation (JFTR), paragraph U7210. Reference AR 600-8-10, paragraph 5-5.
- *Emergency leave.* Leave granted for a bona fide personal or family emergency requiring the soldier's presence. Emergency leave is chargeable.
- *Environmental and morale leave.* Leave granted in conjunction with an environmental and morale leave (EML) program established at overseas installations where adverse environmental conditions exist that offset the full benefit of annual leave programs. This leave is chargeable.
- *Excess leave.* This leave is in excess of accrued and/or advance leave, granted without pay and allowances.
- *Graduation leave.* A period of authorized absence granted, as a delay in reporting to the first permanent duty station, to graduates of the US Military Academy who are appointed as commissioned officers. Not chargeable, provided it is taken within three months of graduation.
- *Leave awaiting orders.* This is an authorized absence, chargeable to accrued leave and in excess of maximum leave accrual, taken while awaiting further orders and disposition in connection with disability separation proceedings under the provisions of AR 635-40, Physical Evaluation for Retention, Retirement, or Separation.

- *Reenlistment leave.* This leave is granted to enlisted personnel as a result of reenlistment. May be either advance leave, leave accrued, or a combination thereof, and is chargeable against the soldier's leave account.
- *Rest and recuperation (R&R) leave.* This leave is granted in conjunction with rest and recuperation programs established in those areas designated for hostile fire pay, when operational military considerations preclude the full execution of ordinary annual leave programs. R&R leave is chargeable to the normal leave account; however, the Army pays for transportation to and from the leave destination. The US Central Command (CENTCOM) R&R Leave Program was created for deployed members of all services who are serving within the CENTCOM region as an opportunity for rest and recuperation as well as to prepare for family reintegration. Soldiers are eligible for up to 15 days of uncharged leave after spending 270 days in a CENTCOM-designated area. The commander determines priority for personnel who are eligible for R&R leave based on the criteria above, as well as operational, safety, and security requirements.
- *R&R leave—extensions of overseas tours.* This is a nonchargeable increment of R&R leave authorized for enlisted soldiers in certain specialties who voluntarily extend their overseas tours. It is authorized in lieu of the $50-per-month special pay. The tour extension must be for a period of at least twelve months. Options under this program include nonchargeable leaves of fifteen or thirty days.
- *Special leave.* This is leave accrual authorized in excess of sixty days at the end of a fiscal year for soldiers assigned to hostile fire/imminent danger areas or certain deployable ships, mobile units, or other duty.
- *Transition leave.* This leave is granted in connection with separation, including retirement, upon the request of the individual.

When possible, soldiers should be encouraged to take at least one annual leave period of about fourteen consecutive days or longer (AR 600-8-10, Leaves and Passes, paragraph 203b). Personnel who refuse to take leave when the opportunity is afforded them should be counseled and informed that such refusal may result in the loss of earned leave at a later date.

Leave is requested on DA Form 31, Request and Authority for Leave, part I. Requests for leave must be processed through the individual's immediate supervisor, although this step may be waived where supervisory approval or disapproval is inappropriate. This approval authority (generally the soldier's commanding officer) ascertains that the individual has sufficient leave accrued to cover the entire period of absence requested.

Personnel should be physically present when DA Form 31 is authenticated and when commencing and terminating leave. Commanders may, at their discretion, authorize telephonic confirmation of departure and return.

Pass

A pass is an authorized absence not chargeable as leave granted for short periods to provide respite from the working environment or for other specific reasons, at the end of which the soldier is actually at his or her place of duty or in the location from which he or she regularly commutes to work. This provision includes both regular and special passes.

Regular Passes. These are granted to deserving military personnel for those periods when they are not required to be physically present with their unit for the performance of assigned duties. Normally, regular passes are valid only during specified off-duty hours and for no more than seventy-two hours, except for public holiday weekends and holiday periods which, by discretion of the president, are extended to the commencement of working hours on the next working day.

Special Passes. These are granted for periods of three or four days (seventy-two to ninety-six hours) to deserving personnel on special occasions or in special circumstances for the following reasons: as special recognition for exceptional performance of duty, such as soldier of the month or year; to attend spiritual retreats or to observe other major religious events; to alleviate personal problems incident to military service; to vote; or as compensatory time off for long or arduous duty away from the home station or for duty in an isolated location where a normal pass is inadequate.

Passes may not be issued to soldiers so that two or more are effective in succession or used in a series through reissue immediately after return to duty.

Extension of a pass is authorized provided the total absence does not exceed seventy-two hours for a regular pass, seventy-two hours for a special three-day pass, and ninety-six hours for a special four-day pass. Special passes will not be extended in combination with public holiday periods or other off-duty hours in cases in which the combined total will exceed the maximum limits of a three-day or four-day pass. Passes cannot be taken in conjunction with leave, and extensions beyond the authorized maximum are chargeable to leave (see AR 600-8-10).

17

Uniforms, Insignia,
and Personal Appearance

Discipline in an Army is often judged by the manner of the soldier's individual personal appearance and how he or she wears the prescribed uniform. Since its creation the Army has changed, improved, and updated its uniforms to meet changing requirements. Today's soldiers are part of that legacy.

WEARING THE UNIFORM

Your Army uniform is the outward evidence of your profession, your standing in that profession, and a prime indicator of the degree of respect with which you regard your service to the United States of America and the Army. The condition of your uniform and the way you wear it are also a reflection of your own self-respect.

One of the basic responsibilities of every NCO is to know the composition of the Army uniforms and how to wear them properly. Remember that when you pass by a deficiency without comment, you have set a new standard.

Occasions When the Uniform Is Required to Be Worn

The Army uniform is worn by all personnel when on duty unless Headquarters, Department of the Army (HQDA) has authorized the wearing of civilian clothes. The following general rules apply:

- Installation commanders may prescribe the uniforms to be worn in formations; duty uniforms are generally prescribed by local commanders or heads of agencies, activities, or installations.
- The wearing of combinations of uniform items not prescribed in AR 670-1, Wear and Appearance of Army Uniforms and Insignia, is prohibited.
- Uniform items changed in design or material may continue to be worn until wear-out date unless specifically prohibited by HQDA.

Occasions When the Uniform May Not Be Worn

The wearing of the Army uniform is prohibited for all Army personnel under the following circumstances:

- In connection with the promotion of any political interests or when engaged in off-duty civilian employment.
- When participating in public speeches, interviews, picket lines, marches, rallies, or public demonstrations, except as authorized by competent authority.
- When wearing the uniform would bring discredit upon the Army.
- When specifically prohibited by Army regulations.

WEARING OF HEADGEAR

The Army uniform is not complete unless the proper form of hat, cap, or beret is worn with it. Headgear is worn when outdoors and when indoors under arms.

Soldiers are exempt from wearing headgear to evening social events (after retreat); however, the appropriate headgear is worn when wearing these uniforms on all other occasions. Headgear is not required to be worn when it would interfere with the safe operation of military vehicles. Military headgear also is not required to be worn in privately owned or commercial vehicles.

Patrol Cap

The patrol cap is the Army standard headgear for the Army Combat Uniform (ACU) in garrison, or in a field environment when a helmet is removed.

Berets

The black beret is the Army standard headgear for the Army Service Uniform (ASU) and is worn by those soldiers not currently wearing the green, maroon, or tan beret. Soldiers are authorized to wear the beret with the utility uniform in garrison environments when authorized by their commander. Commanders may authorize the wear of the patrol cap on work details or in other situations when wear of the beret is impractical. The beret is not worn on deployments unless authorized by the commander.

For enlisted soldiers, the crest of the assigned unit is worn centered on the blue Army flash on the black beret. Soldiers wear the beret so that the headband is straight on the head, 1 inch above the eyebrows, with the flash over the left eye and the excess material draped over to the right, down to at least the top of the ear but no lower than the middle of the ear. A dip is formed in the wool, just behind the flash stiffener, and a slight fold is formed to the right front of the beret, next to the flash. Soldiers will tie off the adjusting ribbon into a nonslip knot, cut off the excess adjusting ribbon as close to the knot as possible, and tuck the knot into the edge binding at the back of the beret. The beret is formfitting to the head when worn properly; therefore, soldiers may not wear hairstyles that distort the beret.

The blue service cap is optional headgear for the ASU and mess dress uniforms, and the white service cap is optional for the white mess dress uniforms.

UNIFORM APPEARANCE

The word "uniform" as used in this context means "conforming to the same standard or rule." Although absolute uniformity of appearance by all soldiers at all times cannot reasonably be expected as long as armies are composed of so many various individuals, uniformed soldiers should project a military image that leaves no doubt that they live by a common standard.

One important rule of uniformity is that, when worn, items of the uniform should be kept buttoned, zippered, and snapped; metallic devices (such as collar brass insignia) should be kept in proper luster; and shoes should be cleaned and shined. In instances where boots are worn with uniforms, soldiers will not blouse boots any lower than the third eyelet from the top.

Lapels and sleeves of coats and jackets for both male and female personnel should be roll pressed (without creasing). Trousers, slacks, and sleeves of shirts and blouses should be creased.

Care and Maintenance of the Uniform

All solid brass items (belt buckles, belt-buckle tips, collar brass insignia) should be maintained in a high state of luster at all times. These items come coated with a lacquer, and if their surfaces are kept protected and gently rubbed clean with a soft clean cloth, they will keep their shine for a long time. When the lacquer coating becomes scratched, the item can be kept shined only by completely removing the lacquer surface. The safest and most reliable method for removing the coating from brass items is to use Brasso polish applied with thumb and forefinger or a cloth.

Spit-shining does make shoes, boots, and equipment look sharp, but it dries out the leather. Replace heels on shoes and boots after wear of $7/16$ inch or more. To check your soldiers' footgear, attempt to roll a pencil under the heel.

Pay attention to the removal of stains from your clothing. Never press dirty clothing, and be careful when you do press clothing that the iron is not too hot. Use a damp cloth between the iron and the fabric when pressing wool items, dampen the surface of cotton clothing before applying the iron, and observe the various fabric settings on the iron when pressing synthetic fabric.

Frequent cleaning of uniform items will increase their longevity and maintain the neat soldierly appearance that the uniform is designed to project. Rotating items of clothing, such as shoes and boots, will contribute to their longer life.

Fitting of Uniforms

Uniform items purchased in the clothing sales store are fitted (or should be fitted) before they are taken off the premises. Personnel who purchase uniform items through the military clothing store (post exchange) or from commercial sources should pay close attention to the proper fit of the items before wearing them. An NCO should be able to tell at a glance whether a soldier (male or female) is wearing a properly fitted uniform. Fitting instructions and alterations of uniforms are made in accordance with AR 700-84, Issue and Sale of Personal Clothing, and TM 10-227, Fitting of Army Uniforms and Footwear.

The Clothing Allowance System

Clothing allowances are provided so that each soldier may maintain the initial clothing issue. Monthly clothing allowances provide for the cost of replacement and purchase of new items or the purchase of additional clothing items, but not for cleaning, laundering, and pressing. The basic allowance begins on the soldier's 181st day of active duty and is paid each month for the remainder of the first 3-year period. The standard allowance begins the day after the soldier completes 36 months on active duty. The clothing allowance accrues monthly and is paid annually during the month of the soldier's basic active service date.

CLASSIFICATION OF SERVICE AND UTILITY FIELD UNIFORMS

Class A Army Service Uniform (ASU). To streamline the number of uniforms soldiers purchase and maintain throughout their careers, the Army is phasing out the green and white service uniforms and the blue service uniform is the approved Army Service Uniform (Class A).

For men, the ASU consists of the Army blue coat and trousers, a short- or long-sleeved white shirt with pleated pockets, a black four-in-hand tie (tied in a slip knot with the ends left hanging), and other accessories. For women, it consists of the Army blue coat and skirt or slacks, a short-sleeved or long-sleeved white shirt, a black neck tab, and authorized accessories. The Army maternity uniform (slacks or skirt) is also a Class A service uniform when the tunic is worn.

Class B Service Uniform. For men, the Class B service uniform is the same as the Class A, except the service coat is not worn. The black tie is required when wearing the long-sleeved white shirt and is optional with the short-sleeved shirt. For women, it is the same as the Class A, except the service coat and the maternity tunic are not worn. The black neck tab is required when wearing the long-sleeved white shirt and the long-sleeved maternity shirt. It is optional with the short-sleeved version of both shirts.

Soldiers who wear green, tan, or maroon berets; soldiers assigned to air assault coded positions; and military police on duty are permitted to blouse their trousers with the black leather combat boot while wearing the blue ASU. The Army black beret, organizational berets, and drill sergeant hats are authorized for wear with the Class A and Class B uniforms.

The Army Class A and Class B variations may be worn by male personnel when on duty, off duty, or during travel. These uniforms are also acceptable for informal social functions after retreat, unless other uniforms are prescribed by the host.

Class C Uniforms. These are utility, field, and other organizational uniforms, such as the Army combat uniform (ACU), hospital duty, and food service uniforms.

Optional Dress Uniforms. The Army blue mess uniform and white mess uniform are available for optional purchase by enlisted soldiers.

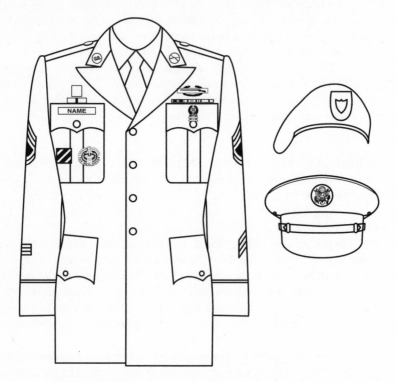

Class A Army Service Uniform (Blue) for Men

MEN'S ARMY SERVICE UNIFORM

The Army Class A ASU consists of the blue coat and trousers, worn with either the wrinkle-resistant short- or long-sleeved white shirt with permanent military creases and shoulder loops with a black four-in-hand necktie. The new blue coat has a tailored, athletic cut to improve uniform fit and appearance. The coat should fit with a slight drape in both the front and the back. The length of the coat will extend to below the crotch. No pronounced tightness at the waist or flare below the waist is authorized.

Blue uniform trousers are straight-legged with belt loops and will reach the top of the instep. They are cut on a diagonal line to reach a point approximately midway between the top of the heel and the top of the standard shoe in the back. The trousers may have a slight break in the front.

Noncommissioned officers wear trousers with a gold braid sewn on the outside of the seam of each trouser leg of the new blue ASU. Rank insignia is sewn on the sleeve halfway between the elbow and the shoulder seam of the coat. When awarded, sew-on service stripes (hash marks) are placed 4 inches above the bottom of the left sleeve and centered on the sleeve; overseas bars are placed 4 inches above the bottom of the right sleeve. Both service and overseas bars are gold, trimmed in blue.

The beret is the primary headgear worn with the ASU by all soldiers; however, the commander has the option to direct the wear of service cap for corporals and above.

Accessories Applicable to the Class A ASU

The US insignia disk is worn on the right lapel collar approximately 1 inch above the notch. The branch insignia disk is worn on the left lapel collar approximately 1 inch above the notch. Both are centered on the lapel collar to be parallel with the inside of the lapel.

Distinctive unit insignia (unit crests) of the currently assigned unit are worn centered on both shoulder loops (epaulets) of the coat between the outside edge of the shoulder loop button and the seam of the loop.

The nameplate is worn on the right breast pocket of the coat, centered between the top of the button and the top of the pocket. Unit awards, such as the Presidential Unit Citation, Joint Meritorious Unit Award, and so forth, are worn $1/8$ inch above the right breast pocket.

Individual decorations and service ribbons are worn $1/8$ inch above the left breast pocket of the coat. When combat and special skill badges are worn, they are centered $1/4$ inch above the ribbons. When more than one badge is worn above the ribbons, badges will be stacked $1/2$ inch apart and may be aligned to the left to present a better appearance.

Marksmanship badges are worn on the left breast pocket flap $1/8$ inch below the top seam of the pocket. If more than one badge is worn, they are spaced 1 inch apart and centered in relation to the bottom edge of the ribbons and the pocket button. When special skill badges, such as a driver's badge, are worn on the pocket flap, they are placed to the right of the marksmanship badges.

The Combat Service Identification badge (CSIB) is worn centered on the wearer's right (or optionally, left) breast pocket of the ASU coat for male soldiers.

The Leader Identification Insignia is not worn on the blue ASU.

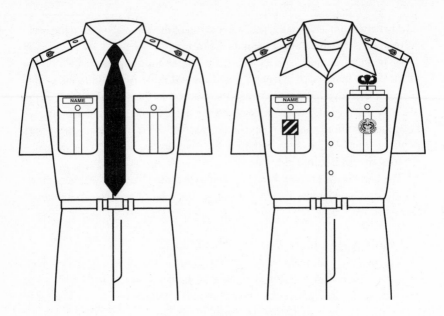

Class B Uniforms for Men

Men's Class B ASU

The men's Class B ASU omits the coat. It consists of the long-sleeved or short-sleeved white shirt worn with blue trousers. The black four-in-hand necktie must be worn with the long-sleeved shirt and is optional for the short-sleeved shirt.

The Combat Service Identification badge (CSIB) is worn centered on the wearer's right (or optionally, left) breast pocket of the ASU coat for male soldiers.

Individual awards and decorations are authorized to be worn on the Class B uniform shirts. Their placement is as on the coat. Check AR 670-1 for additional details. Rank insignia is worn on the Class B uniform shirt on shoulder marks for NCOs and on the shirt collars for non-NCO enlisted grades.

WOMEN'S ARMY SERVICE UNIFORM

The Army Blue ASU for females includes the Army blue coat, skirt or slacks, and a long- or short-sleeved white shirt with black neck tab.

Like the men's uniform, the new blue coat has a tailored, athletic cut to improve uniform fit and appearance. The coat should fit with a slight drape in both the front and the back. The length of the coat will extend to below the crotch.

Noncommissioned officers wear trousers with a gold braid sewn on the outside of the seam of each trouser leg of the new blue ASU. Rank insignia is sewn on the sleeve halfway between the elbow and the shoulder seam of the coat. When awarded, sew-on service stripes (hash marks) are placed 4 inches above the bottom of the left sleeve and centered on the sleeve; overseas bars are placed 4 inches above the bottom of the right sleeve. Both service and overseas bars are gold, trimmed in blue.

The beret is the primary headgear worn with the ASU by all soldiers; however, the commander has the option to direct the wear of service cap for CPLs and above.

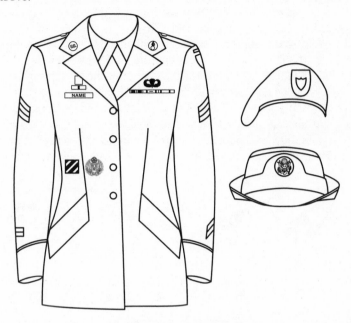

Class A Army Service Uniform for Women

Accessories Applicable to the Class A ASU

Specifications for wear of the organizational shoulder sleeve insignia (patch), unit crests, rank insignia, service stripes, overseas bars, and regimental crests are generally the same for the women's Class A uniform as they are for the men's Class A uniform and are described above. There are, however, some differences.

The US insignia disk is centered on the right collar of the coat approximately ⅝ inch up from the notch, with the center line of the insignia parallel to the inside edge of the lapel. The branch insignia disk is centered in the same manner on the left collar.

The key to the alignment of accessories on the women's Class A uniform is the placement of the plastic nameplate. The nameplate can be adjusted to conform to individual figure differences.

The nameplate is centered horizontally on the right side between 1 and 2 inches above the top button of the coat. Individual and service ribbons are aligned on the left side parallel to the bottom edge of the nameplate. Other badges are aligned with the nameplate or the ribbons in the same manner as on the men's Class A uniform. Female soldiers wear the Combat Service Identification Badge (CSIB) on the right (or optionally, left) side parallel to the waistline on the ASU coat.

Women's Class B Uniforms

The women's Class B uniform consists of the long-sleeved or short-sleeved white shirt worn with blue slacks or skirt. The black neck tab must be worn with the long-sleeved shirt and is optional for the short-sleeved shirt. Soldiers are required to have one long-sleeved and two short-sleeved white shirts.

Individual awards and decorations are authorized to be worn on the Class B uniform shirts. Their placement is as on the coat. Check AR 670-1 for additional details. Shoulder mark rank insignia is worn on the Class B uniform shirt for all NCOs and on the shirt collars for non-NCO enlisted grades.

The Army black beret, the service cap, organizational berets, and drill sergeant hats are authorized for wear with the Class A and Class B uniforms. No hair should show on the forehead below the front bottom edge of the beret or hat, which should be situated approximately 1 inch above the eyebrows.

Class B Uniforms for Women

Maternity Uniform

The pregnant soldier is provided with a special uniform with considerable flex-ibility. The ensemble of components can be combined to form both a Class A and a Class B uniform. The Class A uniform is composed of a blue maternity tunic, matching maternity slacks or skirt, a long- or short-sleeved white mater-nity shirt, and a black neck tab.

Accessories, insignia, awards, badges, and accoutrements for the maternity uniforms follow the same regulations as those for the servicewomen's Class A, Class B, and dress blue uniforms.

ARMY DRESS BLUE ARMY SERVICE UNIFORM

The Army dress blue ASU is authorized for wear by enlisted personnel, both men and women. Although primarily a uniform for social functions of a gen-eral or official nature before or after retreat, it may be worn on duty if pre-scribed by the commander. The dress blue ASU includes the Army blue ASU coat and trousers, a long-sleeved white shirt, and a black bow tie for males. The Army dress blue ASU for females include the Army blue coat, skirt, and a long-sleeved white shirt with black neck tab. Currently, females in Army bands, honor guards, and female chaplains are authorized to wear Army blue slacks in the performance of their duties.

The black beret and service cap are authorized for wear with this uniform when the dress blue ASU is worn for evening social occasions (after retreat). Commanders can direct no headgear required.

Combat boots and organizational items, such as brassards, military police accessories, and distinctive unit insignia, are not authorized for wear with the dress blue ACU. All other accessories and insignia authorized for wear on the Class A Service Uniform are authorized for wear on the dress blue ASU.

SERVICE DRESS TROPICAL UNIFORM

The newly prescribed service dress tropical (Class B with ribbons) uniform is an alternate Class A uniform for hot weather. If directed for wear by local com-manders in hot weather climates, it is a seasonal uniform worn for parades, cer-emonies, or official functions. The service dress tropical uniform consists of the white short-sleeved shirt (standard issue or lay-flat collar) with accou-trements as worn on the ASU jacket and without a necktie or necktab; the ASU trousers, low waist with belt loops, for male soldiers; and the ASU slacks, low waist, or skirt for female soldiers.

WORK AND DUTY UNIFORMS

Because they are issued as utility, field, training, or combat uniforms, these uni-forms are not normally considered appropriate for social or official functions off post for events like memorial services and funerals. Work and duty uniforms are not intended for all-purpose wear when other uniforms are more appropriate.

Army Combat Uniform (ACU)

The Army Combat Uniform (ACU) is used as a combat uniform designed to be worn under body armor. It replaces both the temperate and enhanced hot weather Battle Dress Uniform in the clothing bag, and the clothing bag and the Desert Camouflage Uniform as an organizational clothing and individual (OCIE) item. The ACU consists of a jacket, trousers, moisture-wicking T-shirt, and the brown combat boots. The patrol cap is normal garrison headgear for the ACU; the beret can be worn if authorized by the commander. There is a matching sun (boonie) hat for use during field or combat operations. Nonsubdued sleeve insignia are not authorized on utility uniforms.

The patrol cap is the standard Army headgear and is worn with the ACU in field environments when the Kevlar helmet is not worn. Soldiers wear the ACU patrol cap straight on the head so that the cap band creates a straight line around the head, parallel to the ground. The patrol cap will fit snugly and comfortably around the largest part of the head without distortion or excessive gaps. The cap is worn so that no hair is visible on the forehead beneath the cap. Sewn- or pin-on rank is worn on the ACU patrol cap. The last-name tape will be worn centered on the hook and loop pads on the back of the ACU patrol cap.

The Army will begin issuing an ACU in a new pattern called Operational Camouflage (OCP) to new soldiers in the fall of 2015. As of this writing,

Army Combat Uniform (ACU)

soldiers should be able to purchase this new pattern at military clothing sales stores. The Army uniforms will undergo a complete transition. There has not been a wear-out date set for the current camouflage digital pattern, but it is expected to be completed in 2018.

Maternity Work Uniform

This uniform is authorized for year-round on-duty wear by pregnant soldiers. It is not intended as a travel uniform, but it may be worn in transit between the individual's quarters and duty station.

Cold Weather Uniform

The Generation II, extended cold weather clothing system (ECWCS) is authorized for wear in accordance with CTA 50-900, Clothing and Individual Equipment. All personnel will wear the last-name tape centered on the bottom of the left sleeve pocket flap, and are not authorized to wear the nametape in any other location on the parka. The nametape is a strip of universal camouflage pattern, $5^{1}/_{4}$ inches long and 1 inch wide with $^{3}/_{4}$-inch block lettering. No other size nametape is authorized to be worn on the ACU Gortex Parka (Generation II).

The Generation III ECWCS is a seven-layered ensemble designed to provide soldiers with advanced wet and cold weather protection. It consists of two kits. The top kit is composed of seven components: light- and medium-weight cold weather undershirts, foliage green fleece jacket, wind jacket, soft shell mid-weight jacket, hard shell extreme cold weather/wet weather jacket, and the extreme cold weather parka. The bottom kit is composed of five pieces: light- and medium-weight cold weather drawers, soft shell mid-weight trousers, hard shell extreme cold weather/wet weather trousers, and extreme cold weather trousers. Nametapes are worn on the right chest and US Army on the left.

Soldiers issued the Generation III ECWCS top kit components with the rank tab on the soldier's left side (above the US Army insignia) are authorized to wear those items as designed. Generation III ECWCS may be issued with the rank insignia on either the left or right side until the inventory is exhausted and both versions are authorized to be worn.

Hospital Duty Uniform (Male)

This year-round duty uniform for all male soldiers in the Army Medical Specialist Corps and those in medical, dental, or veterinary MOSs is worn in medical healthcare facilities as prescribed by the medical commander. The commander may authorize the wear of this uniform in a civilian community when in support of civilian activities.

Hospital Duty and Maternity Uniform (Female)

This authorized year-round uniform is worn by Army Medical Specialist Corps personnel and enlisted women with medical, dental, or veterinary MOSs.

Hospital Duty Uniforms

Flight Uniform

This uniform is authorized for year-round wear when on duty in a flying or standby-awaiting-flight status. Commanders may direct exceptions to the wear policy.

Combat Vehicle Crewman (CVC) Uniform

The Combat Vehicle Crewman (CVC) is a year-round duty uniform for combat vehicle crewmen when on duty or as directed by the commander. This uniform is not for travel and is not intended for wear as an all-purpose uniform when other uniforms are more appropriate.

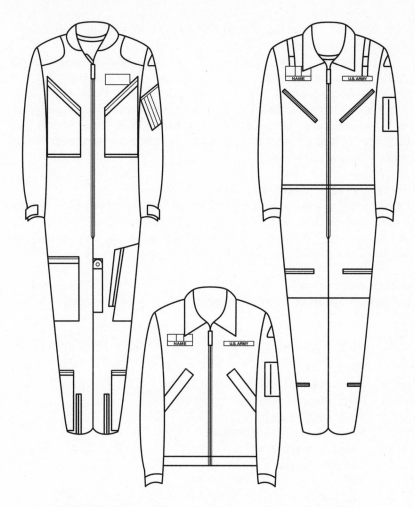

Flight Uniform and Combat Vehicle Crewman Uniform

OPTIONAL UNIFORMS

Optional uniforms are the Army blue mess uniform and the Army white mess uniform. These are traditionally worn for more formal events or during social functions. The more senior an NCO, the higher the likelihood of invitations to attend formal events.

PHYSICAL FITNESS UNIFORM

The Improved Physical Fitness Uniform (IPFU) is currently being phased out but is authorized to be worn until 30 September 2017. It consists of a gray and black running jacket, black running pants, black moisture-wicking shorts, either the gray long-sleeved or short-sleeved moisture-wicking T-shirt, and a black knit or microfleece cap.

The Army has begun phasing in the Army Physical Fitness Uniform (APFU), which has a mandatory possession date of 1 October 2017. It is a moisture-wicking ensemble of lightweight, quick-dry material and consists of a black and gold jacket, black pants, short- or long-sleeved T-shirt, and black trunks. An optional APFU made of different material with improved pant liner and unisex and female sizes is also available (optional uniforms must be purchased with personal funds).

DISTINCTIVE UNIFORM ITEMS

The following uniform items are distinctive and should not be sold to or worn by unauthorized personnel: all Army headgear, badges, decorations, service medals, awards, tabs, service ribbons, appurtenances, and insignia of any design or color that have been adopted by the Department of the Army.

Headgear

The following items of headgear are authorized for Army personnel:

Item	Female Version*
Beret, black	
Beret, green (Special Forces)	
Beret, maroon (Airborne)	
Beret, tan (Ranger)	
Cap, cold weather (AG 489)	
Cap, cold weather, utility	
Cap, food handler's, white, paper	
Cap, hot weather (Boonie)	
Cap, patrol (ACU)	
Cap, service, blue	Hat, service, blue
Cap, service, white	Hat, service, white
Hat, drill sergeant	Hat, drill sergeant

*These are distinctively female items. Other items of headgear listed may be worn by female soldiers, as prescribed in AR 670-1.

Leader Identification Insignia

The Leader Identification Insignia is a green cloth loop, $1^5/8$ inches wide, worn in the middle of both shoulder loops of the Army green and cold weather coats by commanders, deputy commanders, platoon leaders, command sergeants major, first sergeants, platoon sergeants, section leaders (when designated in

TO&E), squad leaders and tank commanders, and rifle squad fire team leaders. The Leader Identification Insignia is not worn on the blue ASU.

Unit Insignia and Heraldic Items

Distinctive unit insignia (DUI) are made of metal or of metal and enamel and are usually based on elements of the design of the coat of arms or historic badge approved for a specific unit. Sometimes erroneously referred to as "unit crests," distinctive unit insignia are subject to the approval of the Institute of Heraldry, US Army, and, like shoulder sleeve insignia, are authorized for wear on the uniform as a means of promoting esprit de corps.

When authorized, these insignia are worn by all assigned personnel of an organization, except general officers. A complete set of insignia consists of three pieces: one for each shoulder loop and one for headgear (garrison, utility, cold weather caps, or berets).

Regimental Insignia

Regimental DUI are worn by all personnel affiliated with a regiment. The "crest" of the affiliated regiment is worn centered and $1/8$ inch above the pocket seam or $1/2$ inch above unit and foreign awards, if worn, on the Army Service and mess uniforms. The DUI worn on the shoulder loops of the Army service (enlisted men only) coats and jackets are always the unit of assignment. If assigned and affiliated to the same regiment, then all three crests are the same.

Combat Service Identification Badge

The Combat Service Identification Badge is a silver or gold metal and enamel device 2 inches (5.08 centimeters) in height consisting of a design similar to the unit Shoulder Sleeve Insignia (SSI). It designates the shoulder patch worn by the soldier while in a combat theater.

Distinctive Items—Infantry

Infantry personnel are authorized to wear the following distinctive items:
- A shoulder cord of infantry blue formed by a series of interlocking square knots around a center cord. The cord is worn on the right shoulder of the Army Class A and mess dress coat and shirt when in Class B uniform, passed under the arm and through the shoulder loop and secured to the button on the shoulder loop.
- A plastic infantry blue disk, $1^{1}/4$ inches in diameter, is worn by enlisted personnel of the infantry, secured beneath the branch of the service and the US insignia, with a $1/8$-inch border around it. It is authorized to be worn on the Army Service and mess dress uniforms.
- An insignia disk, service cap, of infantry blue plastic, $1^{3}/4$ inches in diameter. This disk is worn secured beneath the insignia on the service cap. Criteria for wear are the same as those for the infantry blue insignia disk.

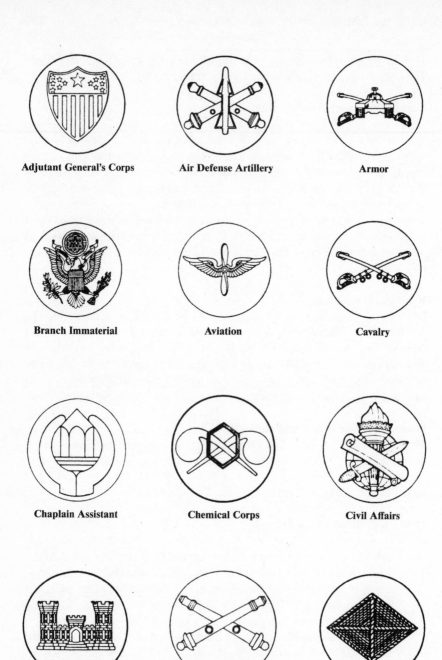

Adjutant General's Corps

Air Defense Artillery

Armor

Branch Immaterial

Aviation

Cavalry

Chaplain Assistant

Chemical Corps

Civil Affairs

Corps of Engineers

Field Artillery

Finance

Enlisted branch insignia

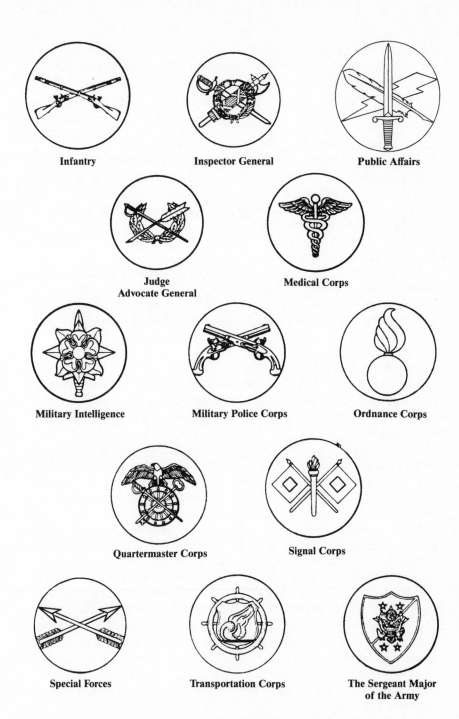

Infantry

Inspector General

Public Affairs

Judge
Advocate General

Medical Corps

Military Intelligence

Military Police Corps

Ordnance Corps

Quartermaster Corps

Signal Corps

Special Forces

Transportation Corps

The Sergeant Major
of the Army

Enlisted branch insignia *continued*

Organizational Flash

This shield-shaped embroidered patch with a semicircular bottom approximately $2^1/4$ inches long and $1^7/8$ inches wide is worn centered on the stiffener of the beret by personnel authorized to wear one of the organizational berets (Ranger, Special Forces, and Airborne).

Airborne Background Trimming

Background trimming is authorized for wear with the Parachutist or Air Assault Badge. When authorized, such background will be worn by all personnel of an airborne-designated organization who have been awarded one of the Parachute badges or by personnel in an organization designated air assault who have been awarded the Air Assault Badge.

PERSONAL APPEARANCE

A vital ingredient of the Army's strength and military effectiveness is the pride and discipline that soldiers bring to their service. It is the responsibility of noncommissioned officers to assure that the military personnel under their supervision present a neat and soldierly appearance. It is the duty of each individual soldier to always take pride in his or her appearance.

Standards for All

The principle that soldiers should always maintain a neat and well-groomed personal appearance applies equally to men and to women, though the specific grooming standard for each reflects the traditional differences in appearance between the sexes.

Dreadlocks are prohibited; however, recent changes permit cornrows, twists, and larger braids for female hairstyles. Many hairstyles are acceptable; hair color must look natural on the soldier. No tinted or color contact lenses may be worn. Fingernails must be neatly trimmed—males to the tip of the finger, females $1/4$ inch from the tip. Recent changes state any tattoo or brand anywhere on the head, face, neck, wrists, hands, or fingers is prohibited, except for permanent makeup. Tattoos and brands are permanent and can be extremely difficult to reverse. Before you get one, you may want to talk it over with your chain of command to make sure you fully understand the changing policies relating to tattoos. Be sure to read paragraph 3-3 (tattoo, branding, and body mutilation policy) of AR 670-1 for the latest updates. As of this writing, tattoos that are otherwise authorized may be applied on the body as long as they cannot be seen in the Class A uniform or above the T-shirt neckline, minus a few exceptions (permanent makeup and one ring tattoos). Tattoos—regardless of location on the body, including the hands and neck—that are extremist, indecent, sexist, or racist are prohibited as they are prejudicial to good order and discipline within units.

Soldiers who have lost a spouse, mother, father, child, or stepchild to combat are authorized to wear the Gold Star lapel button (see page 332) on their

Class A uniforms, with the pin for enlisted soldiers centered vertically and horizontally on the left lapel of the Class A uniform.

Wearing of Civilian Jewelry

The wearing of a personal wristwatch, identification wrist bracelet, and not more than two rings (a wedding set is considered one ring) is authorized with the Army uniform as long as they are not prohibited for safety reasons and the style is conservative and in good taste. Bracelets are limited to the following types: medical alert, MIA, POW, and KIA (black or silver only) bracelets. Soldiers are only authorized to wear one item on each wrist (for example, a watch on the left wrist and a KIA bracelet on the right, or a POW bracelet on one wrist and an MIA bracelet on the other). The wearing of a purely religious medal on a chain around the neck is authorized, provided that neither the medal nor the chain is exposed.

No jewelry, watch chains, or similar civilian items, including pens or pencils, should be allowed to appear exposed on the uniform. Exceptions are that a conservative tie tack or tie clasp may be worn with the black four-in-hand necktie, and a pen or pencil of any color may appear exposed in the pen/pencil slots on the ACU coat, and on the hospital duty and food service uniforms.

Attaching jewelry or ornamentation to, through, or under your skin, tongue, or other body part is prohibited—except for females with pierced ears. Female soldiers may wear screw-on or post-type earrings with the service, dress, or mess uniforms. Earrings may not be worn with Class C utility uniforms (utility, field, or organization, including hospital duty and food service uniforms). Earrings should be small (6 millimeters or $1/4$ inch in diameter) in gold, silver, or white pearl, unadorned and spherical. When worn, they must fit snugly against the ear and must be worn as a matched pair with only one in each earlobe.

The use of gold caps or dental ornamentation is prohibited. Teeth, whether natural or veneered, will not be decorated with jewels or ornamentation.

One electronic device is authorized for wear on the uniform in official duties. It must be black in color and measure no larger than 4 by 2 by 1 inches. Items that do not comply must be carried elsewhere. Soldiers are prohibited from wearing wireless Bluetooth devices and non-wireless earpieces while wearing Army uniforms, except while operating a commercial or military vehicle (including a motorcycle or bicycle).

Sunglasses are not authorized to be hung on uniforms or from restraints down the front of uniforms, or attached to chains, bands, or ribbons, while in a garrison environment.

Standards for Men

Many hairstyles are acceptable in the Army. The hair must be neatly groomed, and the length and bulk of the hair must not be excessive or present a ragged, unkempt, or extreme appearance. Hair must present a tapered appearance and, when combed, must not fall over the ears or eyebrows or touch the collar.

Block cuts are permitted in moderate degree, but in all cases the bulk and length of hair may not interfere with the normal wear of headgear or protective mask. Men may shave their heads bald.

A soldier's face should be clean-shaven. Army regulations do permit mustaches, but no portion of a mustache is permitted to cover the upper lip line or extend beyond the crease of the upper and lower lips. Handlebar mustaches, goatees, and beards are not authorized. Where beard growth is prescribed by appropriate medical authority, as is sometimes necessary in the treatment of different types of skin disorders, the length required for medical treatment should be specified: for example, "A neatly trimmed beard is authorized. The length will not exceed one-quarter inch." If you should have such a soldier under your authority, follow his medical progress closely and be sure he keeps his exemption slip handy at all times when in uniform.

Men are not authorized to wear nail polish.

Standards for Women

Hair must be neatly groomed. The length or bulk of the hair should not be excessive or present a ragged, unkempt, or extreme appearance. Females may wear braids, twists, and cornrows. Hair may not fall over the eyebrows or extend below the bottom edge of the collar. Hairstyles may not interfere with the proper wearing of military headgear or protective masks.

Cosmetics should be applied conservatively and in good taste. Females may only wear clear polish while in any uniform; two-tone or multitone manicures and nail designs are prohibited.

Wearing of Civilian Clothing

Civilian clothing is authorized for wear off duty unless prohibited by the installation commander within CONUS or the major command overseas. When on duty in civilian clothes, soldiers will conform to the appearance standards of AR 670-1, unless specifically authorized for mission requirements.

Security Badges

Security identification badges are worn in restricted areas as prescribed by local commanders. They are usually laminated plastic identification badges worn suspended from clips. They should never be worn outside the secure area for which they authorize an individual access. To prevent the possibility of losing them, some personnel suspend them from a chain worn around the neck and, when in public, under their outer garments.

SOURCES

AR 600-8-22, Military Awards
AR 670-1, Wear and Appearance of Army Uniforms and Insignia
AR 700-84, Issue and Sale of Personal Clothing
FM 21-15 (3-21-15), Care and Use of Individual Clothing and Equipment

18

Awards and Decorations

The Army's awards and decorations program provides tangible recognition for acts of combat valor, noncombat exceptional service or achievement, special skills or qualifications, and acts of heroism not involving actual combat.

RECOMMENDATIONS

It is the responsibility of any soldier having personal knowledge of an act, an achievement, or a service believed to warrant the award of a decoration to submit a formal recommendation for consideration. And yes, it is possible that a private may recommend a captain for a decoration, but usually the system works the other way. As an NCO, you must be alert for service or acts that warrant special recognition. The only consideration that you should use is this one: Does the person's act or service warrant an award?

CRITERIA

Award recommendations must be factual and specific, and they must clearly demonstrate that the person being recommended deserves recognition. If your narrative does not support award of a decoration—if you use clichés in place of straightforward and factual prose narrative writing—your recommendation likely will be disapproved.

Time Limitation

Awards for meritorious service should be anticipated, and your recommendation should be submitted far enough in advance to ensure that the award is ready in time to be presented to the individual before his or her departure.

Another reason for acting quickly is that the closer you are to the act or service for which an individual is being recommended, the fresher the details will be in your memory. In any event, each recommendation for an award of a military decoration must be entered into military channels within two years of the act, achievement, or service to be honored. No recommendation except the Purple Heart is awarded more than three years after the act or period of service to be honored (with the exception of lost recommendations or those circumstances covered in AR 600-8-22, Military Awards, paragraph 1-14c). If a soldier under your supervision deserves an award, let him or her know that you've submitted a recommendation. If the recommendation is not approved, at least the soldier will know you tried and will respect you for it.

PRECEDENCE

Decorations, the Good Conduct Medal, and service medals are ranked in the following order of precedence when worn or displayed:

US military decorations
US unit awards
US nonmilitary decorations
US service (campaign) medals, and service and training ribbons
US Merchant Marine awards
US nonmilitary unit awards
Foreign military decorations
Foreign unit awards
Non-US service awards
State awards for ARNG soldiers

US military decorations are ranked in the following order of precedence when worn or displayed:

Medal of Honor (Army, Navy, Air Force)
Distinguished Service Cross
Navy Cross
Air Force Cross
Defense Distinguished Service Medal
Distinguished Service Medal (Army, Navy, Air Force, Coast Guard)
Silver Star
Defense Superior Service Medal
Legion of Merit
Distinguished Flying Cross
Soldier's Medal
Navy and Marine Corps Medal
Airman's Medal
Coast Guard Medal
Bronze Star Medal
Purple Heart
Defense Meritorious Service Medal
Meritorious Service Medal
Air Medal
Aerial Achievement Medal
Joint Service Commendation Medal
Army Commendation Medal
Navy Commendation Medal

Air Force Commendation Medal
Coast Guard Commendation Medal
Joint Service Achievement Medal
Army Achievement Medal
Navy Achievement Medal
Air Force Achievement Medal
Coast Guard Achievement Medal
Combat Action Ribbon

US service (campaign) medals, and service and training ribbons authorized for wear on the uniform are listed below, in their order of precedence:

1. Prisoner of War Medal
2. Good Conduct Medal—Good Conduct Medals from the other services follow the Army Good Conduct Medal in order of precedence. The Army Reserve Components' Achievement Medal and equivalents awarded by other service Reserve components follow the Army Good Conduct Medal and Good Conduct Medals from the other US services, in order of precedence.
3. American Defense Service Medal
4. Women's Army Corps Service Medal
5. American Campaign Medal
6. Asiatic-Pacific Campaign Medal
7. European-African-Middle Eastern Campaign Medal
8. World War II Victory Medal
9. Army of Occupation Medal
10. Medal for Humane Action
11. National Defense Service Medal
12. Korean Service Medal
13. Antarctica Service Medal
14. Armed Forces Expeditionary Medal
15. Vietnam Service Medal
16. Southwest Asia Service Medal
17. Kosovo Campaign Medal
18. Afghanistan Campaign Medal
19. Iraq Campaign Medal
20. Global War on Terrorism-Expeditionary Medal
21. Global War on Terrorism-Service Medal
22. Korean Defense Service Medal
23. Armed Forces Service Medal
24. Humanitarian Service Medal
25. Military Outstanding Volunteer Service Medal
26. Army Sea Service Ribbon
27. Navy Sea Service Deployment Ribbon

28. Armed Forces Reserve Medal
29. NCO Professional Development Ribbon
30. Army Service Ribbon
31. Overseas Service Ribbon
32. Army Reserve Components Overseas Training Ribbon
33. Coast Guard Special Operations Service Ribbon
34. Air Force Combat Readiness Medal

Personnel may wear service medals and service and training ribbons awarded by other US services on the Army uniform, except for the Air Force Longevity Service Award ribbon and Air Force, Navy, and Coast Guard marksmanship medals and ribbons. Personnel will wear service and training medals and ribbons awarded by other US services after US Army service and training ribbons, and before foreign awards.

US unit awards are given to an operating unit and are worn by members of that unit who participated in the cited action. Personnel who did not participate in the cited action, but who are assigned in the cited unit, are authorized temporary wear of some unit awards. US unit awards authorized for wear on Army uniforms are listed below in their order of precedence:

Presidential Unit Citation (Army, Air Force)
Presidential Unit Citation (Navy)
Joint Meritorious Unit Award
Valorous Unit Award
Meritorious Unit Commendation (Army)
Navy Unit Commendation
Air Force Outstanding Unit Award
Coast Guard Unit Commendation
Army Superior Unit Award
Meritorious Unit Commendation (Navy)
Navy "E" Ribbon
Air Force Organizational Excellence Award
Coast Guard Meritorious Unit Commendation

WEARING OF MEDALS AND RIBBONS

All individual US decorations and service medals (full-size medals, miniature medals, and ribbons) are worn above the left breast pocket or centered on the left side of the coat or jacket of the prescribed uniform (with the exception of the Medal of Honor, which may be worn suspended around the neck). Decorations are worn with the highest displayed above and to the wearer's right of the others.

Full-size decorations and service medals may be worn on the Army Service Uniforms when worn for social functions or when directed. They are worn in order of precedence from the wearer's right to left, in one or more lines, without overlapping within a line, with $^1/_8$-inch space between lines. No line will contain fewer medals than the one above it. The Medal of Honor is worn with the neckband ribbon around the neck, outside the shirt collar and inside the coat collar, with the medal hanging over the necktie.

Miniature decorations and service medals are authorized for wear on the mess and evening mess uniforms only. They may be worn side by side or overlapped, but the overlap will not exceed 50 percent and will be equal for all. There are no miniature medals authorized for the Medal of Honor.

Service ribbons are worn in the order of precedence from the wearer's right to left in one or more lines either without a space between rows or with a $^1/_8$-inch space. No row should contain more than four service ribbons. Male and female personnel are authorized to wear them on the Army green, white, and blue uniforms.

Retired personnel and former soldiers may wear either full-size or miniature medals on appropriate civilian clothing on Veterans Day, Memorial Day, and Armed Forces Day, and at formal occasions of ceremony and social functions of a military nature.

Unauthorized Wearing of Decorations and Badges

Federal law prescribes stiff penalties for the unauthorized wearing of US decorations, badges, appurtenances, and unit awards:

> Whoever knowingly wears . . . any decoration or medal authorized by Congress for the Armed Forces of the United States or any of the service medals or badges awarded to the members of such forces, or the ribbon, button, or rosette of any such badge, decoration or medal, or any colorable imitation thereof, except when authorized under regulations made pursuant to law, shall be fined not more than $250 or imprisoned not more than six months, or both.
>
> —62 Stat. 732, June 25, 1948, as amended 18 U.S.C. 704

The US Code (18 U.S.C. 703) further prescribes:

> Whoever, within the jurisdiction of the United States, with intent to deceive or mislead, wears any naval, military, police, or other official uniform, decoration, or regalia of any foreign state, nation, or government with which the United States is at peace, or anything so nearly resembling the same as to be calculated to deceive, shall be fined not more than $250 or imprisoned not more than six months or both.

1			
2	3	4	5
6	7	8	9
10	11	12	13
14	15	16	17
18	19	20	21
22	23	24	25
26	27	28	29
30	31	32	33
34	35	36	37
38	39	40	41

1. Medal of Honor
2. Distinguished Service Cross
3. Defense Distinguished Service Medal
4. Distinguished Service Medal
5. Silver Star
6. Defense Superior Service Medal
7. Legion of Merit
8. Distinguished Flying Cross
9. Soldier's Medal
10. Bronze Star Medal
11. Purple Heart
12. Defense Meritorious Service Medal
13. Meritorious Service Medal
14. Air Medal
15. Aerial Achievement Medal
16. Joint Service Commendation Medal
17. Army Commendation Medal
18. Army Achievement Medal
19. Prisoner of War Medal
20. Good Conduct Medal
21. Army of Occupation Medal
22. Medal for Humane Action
23. National Defense Service Medal
24. Antarctica Service Medal
25. Armed Forces Expeditionary Medal
26. Vietnam Service Medal
27. Southwest Asia Service Medal
28. Kosovo Campaign Medal
29. Afghanistan Campaign Medal
30. Iraq Campaign Medal
31. Global War on Terrorism-Expeditionary Medal
32. Global War on Terrorism-Service Medal
33. Korean Defense Service Medal
34. Armed Forces Service Medal
35. Humanitarian Service Medal
36. Military Outstanding Volunteer Service Medal
37. Armed Forces Reserve Medal
38. NCO Professional Development Ribbon
39. Army Service Ribbon
40. Overseas Service Ribbon
41. Army Reserve Components Overseas Training Ribbon

Order of Precedence of Most Commonly Worn Decorations, Service Medals, and Ribbons

The Medal of Honor

The Army and Air Force version of the Medal of Honor is the highest award for the risk of life "above and beyond the call of duty" involving actual conflict with an enemy; the Navy version can and has been awarded to noncombatants in peacetime, and Congress has similarly awarded special medals to honor individual exploits during peacetime.

The Medal of Honor is designed in the form of a five-pointed star, made of silver and heavily electroplated in gold. In the center of the star appears the head of Minerva—the Roman goddess whose name is associated with wisdom and righteousness in war—surrounded by the words "United States of America." An open laurel wreath, enameled in green, encircles the star, and the oak leaves at the bases of the prongs of the star are likewise enameled. The medal is suspended by a blue silk ribbon, spangled with thirteen white stars (representing the thirteen original states), and attached to an eagle supported by a horizontal bar upon which is engraved the word "Valor."

The reverse of the medal is plain so that the name of the recipient may be engraved thereon; the reverse of the bar is stamped "The Congress to . . ."

On 21 December 1861, President Lincoln approved the Medal of Honor for enlisted men of the Navy and Marine Corps; a similar medal was established for the Army on 12 July 1862, further amended by legislation enacted on 3 March 1863 to include officers and making the provisions retroactive to the beginning of the Civil War. The first Army Medals were awarded on 25 March 1863. The Medal of Honor is awarded only to US citizens. The Army Medal may be awarded only to military personnel on active federal service (paragraph 3.6, AR 600-8-22).

Distinguished Service Cross

Established by legislation on 9 July 1918 (as amended 25 July 1963), the Distinguished Service Cross (DSC) evolved from the Certificate of Merit of 1847. The DSC is the second highest decoration for valor in war and is bestowed to recognize extraordinary heroism in connection with military operations in time of war. Unlike the Medal of Honor, however, the DSC may be awarded for heroism involving several acts over a short period of time that need not have been performed in actual conflict with an enemy but must have involved extraordinary risk of life. Successive awards are denoted by oak-leaf clusters (paragraph 3.7, AR 600-8-22).

Defense Distinguished Service Medal

Established by Executive Order 11545, 9 July 1970, the Defense Distinguished Service Medal (DDSM) is awarded to any military officer who, while assigned to joint staffs and other joint activities of the Department of Defense, distinguishes himself or herself by exceptionally meritorious service in a position of unique and great responsibility. It is not awarded for a period of service for which a Distinguished Service Medal or similar decoration is awarded. Subsequent awards are denoted by oak-leaf clusters (paragraph 2.3, AR 600-8-22).

Distinguished Service Medal

Established by an act of Congress of 9 July 1918, the Distinguished Service Medal (DSM) is awarded to any person who, while serving in any capacity with the US Army, has distinguished himself or herself by exceptionally meritorious service in a duty of great responsibility. Awards may be made to persons other than members of the armed forces of the United States for wartime services only, and then only under exceptional circumstances with the approval of the President. Successive awards are denoted by oak-leaf clusters (paragraph 3.8, AR 600-8-22).

Silver Star
Established by an act of Congress of 9 July 1918 (as amended by an act of 25 July 1963), the Silver Star (SS) is the third-ranking US decoration for heroism in wartime.

When first established, the SS was worn in the form of a small silver star, $3/16$ inch in diameter, upon the respective service medal and ribbon to indicate each separate citation for gallantry in action earned during the campaign for which the service medal was authorized. These stars were known as "citation stars."

The current version of the SS is gilt bronze in the shape of a star $1^1/4$ inches across. On the obverse is a laurel wreath, within which is a silver star $3/16$ inch in diameter; on the reverse are inscribed the words "For Gallantry in Action." The SS may be awarded by any commander who has the authority to award the DSC and, like the DSC, may be awarded for acts of heroism that take place over a period of time. Successive awards are denoted by oak-leaf clusters (paragraph 3.9, AR 600-8-22).

Defense Superior Service Medal
Established by Executive Order 11904, 6 February 1976, the Defense Superior Service Medal (DSSM) may be awarded to US personnel who give superior meritorious service in a position of significant responsibility. It is not awarded to any individual for a period of service for which a Legion of Merit or similar decoration is awarded. Successive awards are denoted by oak-leaf clusters (paragraph 2.4, AR 600-8-22).

Legion of Merit
Established by an act of Congress of 20 July 1942, the Legion of Merit (LM) is awarded to any member of the armed forces of the United States or a friendly foreign country who distinguishes himself or herself by outstanding meritorious conduct in the performance of outstanding services. Successive awards are denoted by oak-leaf clusters (paragraph 3.10, AR 600-8-22).

Distinguished Flying Cross
Established by an act of Congress of 2 July 1926, the Distinguished Flying Cross (DFC) may be awarded, in war or peace, to US military personnel who distinguish themselves by heroism or extraordinary achievement while participating in aerial flight. Such awards are made only to recognize single acts of

heroism or extraordinary achievement that are not sustained operational activities against an armed enemy. An act of heroism must be evidenced by voluntary action above and beyond the call of duty. Achievement awards must have resulted in an accomplishment so exceptional and outstanding as to clearly set the individual apart from other persons in similar circumstances. Awards to foreign personnel serving with the US Armed Forces may be made only in connection with actual wartime operations. Successive awards are denoted by oak-leaf clusters (paragraph 3.11, AR 600-8-22).

Soldier's Medal
Established by an act of Congress of 2 July 1926, the Soldier's Medal (SM) is awarded to US and foreign military personnel in recognition of heroism not involving actual conflict with an enemy. The performance must have involved personal hazard or danger and voluntary risk of life of approximately the same degree as that required for award of the Distinguished Flying Cross, but awards of the SM are not made solely on the basis of having saved a life. Subsequent awards of this decoration are denoted by oak-leaf clusters (paragraph 3.12, AR 600-8-22).

Bronze Star Medal
Originally established by Executive Order 9419 of 4 February1944 (superseded by Executive Order 11046 of 26 August 1962), the Bronze Star Medal (BSM) can be awarded to US and foreign personnel, both military and civilian, for acts that display heroism, meritorious achievement, or service performed in connection with military operations against an armed force. A bronze V device is worn to denote awards for heroism, and successive awards are denoted by oak-leaf clusters (paragraph 3.13, AR 600-8-22).

Purple Heart
Originally established by Gen. George Washington on 7 August 1782, the Purple Heart (PH) is the oldest US military decoration. The PH is awarded in the name of the president to any member of the Armed Forces or any civilian of the United States who, while serving under competent authority in any capacity with one of the US armed services after 5 April 1917, has been wounded or killed or who has died or may die after being wounded.

A "wound" is defined as any injury (not necessarily one that breaks the skin) caused by an outside force or agent. Multiple injuries suffered at the same moment from the same agent are considered as one wound. Specific examples of injuries that would be authorized the award of the PH are those incurred while making a parachute landing from an aircraft that had been brought down by enemy fire, or injuries received as the result of a vehicle accident caused by enemy fire. Subsequent awards of the Purple Heart are denoted by oak-leaf clusters (paragraph 2-8, AR 600-8-22).

Defense Meritorious Service Medal
Established by Executive Order 12019 of 3 November 1977, the Defense Meritorious Service Medal (DMSM) is awarded in the name of the Secretary of Defense to any member of the armed forces who, while serving in any joint activity of the Department of Defense on or after 3 November 1977, for a period of sixty days or more, demonstrates incontestably exceptional service or achievement of a magnitude that clearly places him or her above his or her peers. Subsequent awards of the DMSM are denoted by oak-leaf clusters (paragraph 2-5, AR 600-8-22).

Meritorious Service Medal
Established by Executive Order 1144.8 on 16 January 1969, the Meritorious Service Medal (MSM) is awarded to any member of the armed forces of the United States who, while serving in a noncombat area after 16 January 1969, has distinguished himself or herself by outstanding meritorious achievement or service. The achievement or service must have been comparable to that required for the Legion of Merit but in a position of lesser, though considerable, responsibility. This decoration is the equivalent of the Bronze Star Medal for recognition of outstanding meritorious noncombat achievement or service and takes precedence with, but after, the BSM when both are worn on the uniform. This decoration is not awarded to foreign personnel. Subsequent awards are denoted by oak-leaf clusters (paragraph 3-14, AR 600-8-22).

Air Medal
Established by Executive Order 9242-A, 11 September 1942, the Air Medal (AM) is awarded to any person who, while serving in any capacity in or with the Army, shall have distinguished himself or herself by meritorious achievement while participating in aerial flight. Awards may be made in recognition of single acts of merit or heroism or for meritorious service. A system of denoting successive awards of the medal was devised using bronze Arabic numerals instead of oak-leaf clusters. Therefore, an individual holding fifteen awards of the AM wears the numeral 14 on the suspension ribbon and service ribbon (paragraph 3-15, AR 600-8-22).

Joint Service Commendation Medal
The Joint Service Commendation Medal (JSCM) is awarded to any member of the Armed Forces who distinguishes himself or herself by meritorious achievement or service while serving in any joint assignment. Awards made for acts or services involving direct participation in combat operations on or after 25 June 1963, may be denoted by the bronze V device. Subsequent awards of the JSCM are denoted by oak-leaf clusters (paragraph 2-6, AR 600-8-22).

Army Commendation Medal

The Army Commendation Medal (ARCOM) is awarded to any member of the Armed Forces who distinguishes himself or herself by heroism, meritorious achievement, or meritorious service. The ARCOM may also be awarded to a member of the armed forces of a friendly foreign nation who distinguishes himself or herself by an act of heroism, extraordinary achievement, or meritorious service that has been of mutual benefit to a friendly nation and the United States. Awards of the ARCOM may be made for acts of valor performed under circumstances described above that are of lesser degree than those required for award of the Bronze Star Medal and may include acts that involve aerial flight. Awards may also be made for noncombat acts of heroism that do not meet the requirements for award of the Soldier's Medal. This decoration is primarily awarded to company-grade officers, warrant officers, and enlisted personnel (paragraph 3.16, AR 600-8-22).

Joint Service Achievement Medal

The Joint Service Achievement Medal (JSAM) is awarded to any member of the Armed Forces of the United States, below the grade of full colonel, who distinguishes himself or herself by meritorious achievement or service while serving in any joint activity after 3 August 1983. Military personnel on temporary duty to a joint activity for at least sixty days are also eligible.

The required achievement or service, while of lesser degree than that required for award of the Joint Service Commendation Medal, must have been accomplished with distinction. Subsequent awards are designated by oak-leaf clusters (paragraph 2.7, AR 600-8-22).

Army Achievement Medal

The Army Achievement Medal (AAM) is awarded to any member of the Armed Forces of the United States, or to any member of the armed forces of a friendly foreign nation, who, while serving in any capacity with the Army in a noncombat area on or after 1 August 1981, distinguishes himself or herself by meritorious service or achievement of a lesser degree than that required for award of the Army Commendation Medal. Subsequent awards are designated by oak-leaf clusters (paragraph 3.7, AR 600-8-22).

Prisoner of War Medal

The Prisoner of War Medal (POWM) is authorized for all US military personnel who were taken prisoner of war after 6 April 1917 during an armed conflict and who served honorably during the period of captivity (paragraph 2.9, AR 600-8-22).

Good Conduct Medal

The Good Conduct Medal (GCM) is awarded to enlisted personnel for exemplary behavior, efficiency, and fidelity to active federal military service. Generally, the qualifying period is three years of continuous active service completed on or after 26 August 1940. Exceptions are for those who are separated from the service by reason of physical disability incurred in the line of duty, who died or were killed before completing one year of service, or who separated after more than one year but less than three years (draftees). Those exceptions apply only to the first award.

Isolated examples of nonjudicial punishment are not necessarily automatically disqualifying but must be considered on the basis of the soldier's whole record; consideration as to the nature of the infraction, the circumstances under which it occurred, and when it occurred must be duly weighed by the individual's commander. Conviction by court-martial terminates a period of qualifying service; a new period begins following the completion of the sentence imposed by court-martial.

Successive awards of the GCM are identified by clasps, or bars $^1/_8$ inch by $1^3/_8$ inches, of bronze, silver, or gold, with loops (also called knots) that indicate each period of service for which the medal is authorized. The first award is the actual medal itself. Successive awards are indicated by clasps with loops (Chapter 4-1, AR 600-8-22).

Army Reserve Components Achievement Medal

The Army Reserve Components Achievement Medal (ARCAM) may be awarded upon recommendation of the unit commander for three years of honest and faithful service on or after 28 March 1995 or four years before that date. Service must have been consecutive, in the grade of colonel or below, and in accordance with the standards of conduct, courage, and duty required by law and customs of the service of an active-duty member of the same grade. The reverse of this medal is struck in two designs for award to personnel whose service has been primarily in the Army Reserve or in the National Guard (Chapter 4-14, AR 600-8-22).

US ARMY AND DEPARTMENT OF DEFENSE UNIT AWARDS

Unit awards are authorized in recognition of group heroism or meritorious service, usually during a war, as a means of promoting esprit de corps. They are of the following categories: unit decorations, infantry and medical streamers, campaign streamers, war service streamers, and campaign silver bands.

US unit decorations, in order of precedence listed in this section, have been established to recognize outstanding heroism or exceptionally meritorious conduct in the performance of outstanding services. These awards may be worn permanently by those who served with the unit during the cited period. The Presidential Unit Citation (Army), the Valorous Unit Award, the Meritorious

Unit Commendation, and the Army Superior Unit Award may be worn temporarily by those serving with the unit subsequent to the cited period.

Presidential Unit Citation

The Presidential Unit Citation is awarded to units of the Armed Forces of the United States and cobelligerent nations for extraordinary heroism in action against an armed enemy occurring on or after 7 December 1941. The unit must display such gallantry, determination, and esprit de corps in accomplishing its mission under extremely difficult and hazardous conditions as to set it apart from and above other units participating in the same campaign. The degree of heroism required is the same as that which would warrant award of a Distinguished Service Cross to an individual. The Presidential Unit Emblem (Army) is a blue ribbon set in a gold-colored metal frame of laurel leaves (paragraph 7-13, AR 600-8-22).

Joint Meritorious Unit Award

The Joint Meritorious Unit Award is awarded to joint activities of the Department of Defense for meritorious achievement or service, superior to that normally expected, during combat with an armed enemy of the United States, during a declared national emergency, or under extraordinary circumstances that involve the national interest (paragraph 7-15, AR 600-8-22).

Valorous Unit Award

Criteria for the Valorous Unit Award are the same as those for the Presidential Unit Citation except that the degree of valor required is that which would merit award of the Silver Star to an individual. The emblem is a scarlet ribbon with the Silver Star color design superimposed in the center, set in a gold-colored metal frame with laurel leaves (paragraph 7-14, AR 600-8-22).

Meritorious Unit Commendation

The Meritorious Unit Commendation is awarded for at least six months of exceptionally meritorious conduct, in support of military operations, to service and support units of the Armed Forces of the United States and cobelligerent nations. The degree of achievement is that which would merit the award of the Legion of Merit to an individual. The emblem is a scarlet ribbon set in a gold-colored metal frame with laurel leaves (paragraph 7-15, AR 600-8-22).

Army Superior Unit Award

The Army Superior Unit Award is given for outstanding meritorious performance of a difficult and challenging mission under extraordinary circumstances by a unit during peacetime. The emblem is a scarlet ribbon with a vertical green stripe in the center, on each side of which is a narrow yellow stripe, set in a gold-colored metal frame with laurel leaves (paragraph 7-16, AR 600-8-22).

US SERVICE MEDALS

Service or campaign medals denote honorable performance of military duty within specified limited dates in specified geographical areas. With the exception of the Humanitarian Service Medal, the Armed Forces Reserve Medal, the Army Reserve Component Achievement Medal, the Army Service Ribbon, and the NCO Professional Development Ribbon, they are awarded only for active federal military service.

Service medals are worn in order by the date when the person became eligible for the award, not by the date of entry in the records or the date upon which the award was established. Foreign military service medals are worn following authorized US decorations. Not more than one service medal is awarded for service involving identical or overlapping periods of time, except that each of the following groups of service medals may be awarded to an individual provided he or she meets the criteria prescribed by Chapter 5, AR 600-8-22. For information concerning the criteria for the award of any service medal not listed below, see Chapter 5, AR 600-8-22.

Army of Occupation Medal

Established by the War Department General Orders 32, 1946, this medal is awarded for service for thirty consecutive days at a normal post of duty with the Army of Occupation of Berlin during the period 1945–1990. This medal was previously authorized for post–World War II occupation duty in Germany, Austria, Italy, Japan, and Korea (see paragraph 1, AR 600-8-21, Soldier Applications Program). Berlin service does not authorize the wearing of a clasp on either the service medal or the service ribbon (paragraph 5-11, AR 600-8-22).

National Defense Service Medal

The National Defense Service Medal (NDSM) is awarded for honorable active service for any period between the periods 27 June 1950 to 27 July 1954; 1 January 1961 to 14 August 1974; 2 August 1990 to 30 November 1995; and 11 September 2001 to a date to be later determined. Subsequent award of the NDSM is denoted by a bronze service star (paragraph 2-10, AR 600-8-22).

Antarctica Service Medal

Any member of the Armed Forces of the United States who participates in or has participated in scientific, direct support, or exploratory operations in Antarctica under sponsorship and approval of the US government is eligible for this medal. This includes flights as a member of the crew of an aircraft flying to or from the Antarctic Continent or as a member of a US ship operating south of latitude 60 degrees south in support of US programs in Antarctica (paragraph 2-11, AR 600-8-22).

Armed Forces Expeditionary Medal

The Armed Forces Expeditionary Medal is authorized for US military operations, US operations in direct support of the United Nations, and US operations of assistance for friendly foreign nations. Operations are defined as military actions or the carrying out of strategic, tactical, service, training, or administrative military missions and the process of carrying on combat, including movement, supply, attack, defense, and maneuvers needed to gain the objectives of any battle or campaign.

Designated areas and dates of service for eligibility are in AR 600-8-22. Subsequent awards of this medal are denoted by bronze service stars (paragraph 2-12, AR 600-8-22).

Vietnam Service Medal

The Vietnam Service Medal is awarded to all members of the armed forces who served in Vietnam and contiguous waters or airspace there after 3 July 1965 and through 28 March 1973. Members of the armed forces in Thailand, Laos, or Cambodia or the airspace thereover who during the same period served in direct support of operations in Vietnam are also eligible. See AR 600-8-22, appendix B, for authorized campaigns and dates. One bronze service star (or a combination of bronze and silver stars, as applicable) may be worn on the suspension ribbon and bar representing this medal (paragraph 2-13, AR 600-8-22).

Southwest Asia Service Medal

The Southwest Asia Service Medal (SWASM) is awarded to US military personnel who have served in the Persian Gulf area since 2 August 1990 through 30 November 1995. Subsequent awards of the SWASM are denoted by service stars affixed to the medal (paragraph 2-14, AR 600-8-22).

Kosovo Campaign Medal

The Kosovo Campaign Medal is to recognize the accomplishments of military servicemembers who participated in, or were in direct support of, the conflict in Kosovo. Members authorized the Kosovo Campaign Medal must have participated in or served in direct support of the Kosovo operation after 24 March 1999. Servicemembers must be bona fide members of a unit participating in, or engaged in direct support of, the operation for thirty consecutive days in the area of eligibility, or for sixty nonconsecutive days provided this support involves entering the area of eligibility. One bronze service star is worn on the suspension and service ribbon of the Kosovo Campaign Medal for qualified participation during the campaign period. Meeting the qualification in each of the two campaigns would warrant the medal and two bronze service stars (paragraph 2-15, AR 600-8-22).

Afghanistan Campaign Medal

The Afghanistan Campaign Medal is awarded to soldiers who deploy to Afghanistan in direct support of Operation Enduring Freedom (OEF) on or after 24 October 2001 to a date to be determined or the cessation of OEF. The area of eligibility encompasses all land area of the country of Afghanistan and all air spaces above the land. One bronze service star shall be worn on the suspension and campaign ribbon of the ACM for one or more days of participation in each designated campaign phase. Approved designated ACM Campaign Phases and inclusive periods are listed below (paragraph 2-16, AR 600-8-22).

Liberation of Afghanistan: 11 September 2001–30 November 2001
Consolidation I: 1 December 2001–30 September 2006
Consolidation II: 1 October 2006–30 November 2009
Consolidation III: 1December 2009–30 June 2011
Transition I: 1 July 2011–to a date to be determined

Iraq Campaign Medal

The Iraq medal was awarded to soldiers who deploy to Iraq in direct support of Operation Iraqi Freedom (OIF) on or after 19 March 2003, or on or after 1 September 2010 for Operation New Dawn (OND), to 31 December 2011. The area of eligibility encompasses all land area of the country of Iraq and the contiguous water area out to 12 nautical miles, and all air spaces above the land area of Iraq and above the contiguous water area out to 12 nautical miles. Under no condition will personnel receive more than one of the following for the same action, time period, or service: the Iraq Campaign Medal, the Global War on Terrorism Expeditionary Medal, the Global War on Terrorism Service Medal, or the Armed Forces Expeditionary Medal. Approved designated ICM Campaign Phases and inclusive periods are listed below (paragraph 2-17, AR 600-8-22).

Liberation of Iraq: 19 March 2003–1 May 2003
Transition of Iraq: 2 May 2003–28 June 2004
Iraqi Governance: 29 June 2004–15 December 2005
National Resolution: 16 December 2005–9 January 2007
Iraqi Surge: 10 January 2007–31 December 2008
Iraqi Sovereignty: 1 January 2009–31 August 2010
New Dawn: 1 September 2010–31 December 2011

Global War on Terrorism Expeditionary Medal

The Global War on Terrorism Expeditionary Medal (GWOTEM) is awarded to servicemembers who serve in military expeditions to combat terrorism on or after 11 September 2001. After 30 April 2005, the GWOTEM was no longer authorized to be awarded for service in Afghanistan and/or Iraq. It is still authorized for service in the other geographical areas of eligibility (paragraph 2-18, AR 600-8-22).

The Global War on Terrorism Service Medal

The Global War on Terrorism Service Medal (GWOTSM) is awarded to servicemembers who have participated in or served in support of Global War on Terrorism Operations outside the designated areas of eligibility (AOE) for the Global War on Terrorism Expeditionary Medal, on or after 11 September 2001 to a date to be determined. All soldiers serving on active duty between 11 September 2001, and March 2004 are authorized the GWOTSM. After March 2004, battalion commanders, the award approval authority, must determine if a soldier serving on active duty has qualified for the GWOTSM. Soldiers are not awarded more than one of the following medals for the same act, time period, or service: Afghanistan Campaign Medal, Iraq Campaign Medal, Global War on Terrorism Expeditionary Medal, or Armed Forces Expeditionary Medal (paragraph 2-19, AR 600-8-22).

Korea Defense Service Medal

The Korea Defense Service Medal (KDSM) is authorized to members of the Armed Forces who have served on active duty in support of the defense of the Republic of Korea from 28 July 1954 to a date to be determined. The area of eligibility encompasses all land area of the Republic of Korea, and the contiguous water out to 12 nautical miles, and all air spaces above the land and water areas. Effective 3 February 2004, the Overseas Service Ribbon (OSR) was no longer authorized for overseas tours in the Republic of Korea (paragraph 2-20, AR 600-8-22).

Armed Forces Service Medal

Awarded to members of the Armed Forces who, as of 1 June 1992, are participating, or have participated, as members of US military units in a US military operation that is deemed to be a significant activity, and are encountering, or have encountered, no foreign armed opposition or imminent threat of hostile action. Servicemembers must be bona fide members of a unit participating for one or more days in the operation or engaged in direct support in the area of eligibility, or for sixty nonconsecutive days provided this support involves entering the area of eligibility or participating as a regularly assigned aircrew member of an aircraft flying into, out of, within, or over the area of eligibility in support of the operation. Second and subsequent awards will be denoted by bronze service stars (paragraph 2-21, AR 600-8-22).

Humanitarian Service Medal

The Humanitarian Service Medal is authorized to be awarded to any Armed Forces personnel who directly participated in a Department of Defense–approved humanitarian act or operation, except when a by-name eligibility list is published. No more than one award of this medal may be made for the same act or operation. Subsequent awards are designated by bronze numerals (paragraph 2.22, AR 600-8-22).

Military Outstanding Volunteer Service Medal

Received by members of the Armed Forces of the United States who, subsequent to 31 December 1992, perform outstanding volunteer community service of a sustained, direct, and consequential nature. To be eligible, an individual's service must (1) be to the civilian community, including the military family community; (2) be significant in nature and produce tangible results; (3) reflect favorably on the military service and the Department of Defense; and (4) be of a sustained and direct nature.

The Military Outstanding Volunteer Service Medal (MOVSM) is intended to recognize exceptional community support over time and not a single act or achievement. Further, it is intended to honor direct support of community activities (paragraph 2-23, AR 600-8-72).

Armed Forces Reserve Medal

Awarded for honorable and satisfactory service as a member of one or more of the Reserve Components of the Armed Forces of the United States for a period of ten years within a twelve-year period. Subsequent ten-year awards are denoted by a bronze hourglass. A gold hourglass is awarded on completion of the fourth ten-year period.

Awarded for mobilization on or after 1 August 1990, to members called to active duty in support of US military operations or contingencies designated by the Secretary of Defense, the "M" device is worn to indicate mobilization. Subsequent mobilizations are denoted by the wearing of a number to indicate the number of times mobilized. No hourglass is worn unless authorized as explained above (paragraph 5-8, AR 600-8-22).

NCO Professional Development Ribbon

Established by the Secretary of the Army on 10 April 1981, and effective 1 August 1981, the NCO Professional Development Ribbon is awarded to members of the US Army, Army National Guard, and Army Reserve for successful completion of designated NCO professional development courses. The ribbon is awarded for four levels of professional development: (1) Primary; (2) Basic; (3) Advanced; and (4) the Sergeants Major Academy (paragraph 5-6, AR 600-8-22).

Army Sea Duty Ribbon

Established by the Principal Deputy Assistant Secretary of the Army (Manpower and Reserve Affairs) on 17 April 2006, the Army Sea Duty Ribbon (ASDR) is awarded to members of the Active Army, Army National Guard, and United States Army Reserve for completion of designated periods of sea duty aboard Class A and Class B United States Army Vessels (USAV), as defined in AR 56-9, Watercraft, table 1-1. The ASDR is also authorized to be awarded for duty aboard other qualifying vessels when the vessels meet the requirements of AR 600-88, Sea Duty, paragraph 1-7 (paragraph 5.7, AR 600-8-22).

DECORATIONS, AWARDS, AND SERVICE MEDALS

U.S. ARMY AND DEPARTMENT OF DEFENSE MILITARY DECORATIONS

Medal of Honor
(Army)

**Southwest Asia Service
Medal**

**Kosovo Campaign
Medal**

**Afghanistan Campaign
Medal**

**Iraq Campaign
Medal**

**Global War on Terrorism
Expeditionary**

**Global War on Terrorism
Service Medal**

Korean Defense Service Medal

Armed Forces Service Medal

Humanitarian Service Medal

Military Outstanding Volunteer Service Medal

Armed Forces Reserve Medal

Air Medal

**Joint Service
Commendation
Medal**

**Army
Commendation
Medal**

**Joint Service
Achievement
Medal**

**Army
Achievement
Medal**

**Prisoner of War
Medal**

**Good Conduct Medal
(Army)**

**Army Reserve
Components
Achievement Medal**

**National Defense Service
Medal**

**Antarctica Service
Medal**

**Armed Forces
Expeditionary Medal**

**Vietnam Service
Medal**

**Distinguished Service
Cross (Army)**

**Defense
Distinguished Service
Medal**

**Distinguished Service
Medal (Army)**

Silver Star

**Defense
Superior Service
Medal**

Legion of Merit

Distinguished Flying Cross

Soldier's Medal (Army)

Bronze Star Medal

Purple Heart

Defense

Meritorious Service Medal

U.S. ARMY SERVICE AND TRAINING RIBBONS

NCO Professional Development Ribbon **Army Service Ribbon** **Overseas Service Ribbon (Army)** **Army Reserve Components Overseas Training Ribbon**

U.S. ARMY AND DEPARTMENT OF DEFENSE UNIT AWARDS

Presidential Unit Citation (Army) **Joint Meritorious Unit Award** **Valorous Unit Award**

Meritorious Unit Commendation (Army) **Army Superior Unit Award**

ARMY SERVICE UNIFORM

Class A Uniform **Class B Uniform**

NON-U.S. SERVICE MEDALS

United Nations Medal

NATO Medal

Multinational Force and Observers Medal

Republic of Vietnam Campaign Medal

Kuwait Liberation Medal (Kingdom of *Saudi Arabia*)

Kuwait Liberation Medal (Government of *Kuwait*)

**Nuclear Reactor
Operator Badge
(Basic)**

**Nuclear Reactor
Operator Badge
(Second Class)**

**Nuclear Reactor
Operator Badge
(First Class)**

**Nuclear Reactor
Operator Badge
(Shift Supervisor)**

**Parachute Rigger
Badge**

**Driver and Mechanic
Badge**

Marksmanship Badges

Marksman

Sharpshooter

Expert

Identification Badges

Presidential Service

Vice-Presidential Service

Secretary of Defense

Joint Chiefs of Staff

Army Staff

**Basic
Military Free Fall
Parachutist Badge**

**Jumpmaster
Military Free Fall
Parachutist Badge**

**Basic Parachutist
Badge**

**Senior Parachutist
Badge**

**Master Parachutist
Badge**

**Combat Parachutist
Badge (1 Jump)**

**Combat Parachutist
Badge (2 Jumps)**

**Combat Parachutist
Badge (3 Jumps)**

**Combat Parachutist
Badge (4 Jumps)**

**Combat Parachutist
Badge (5 Jumps)**

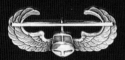

Air Assault Badge

Glider Badge

**Special Forces Tab
(Metal Replica)**

**Ranger Tab
(Metal Replica)**

Sapper Tab

**Presidents Hundred
Tab**

**Pathfinder
Badge**

**Salvage Diver
Badge**

**Second Class Diver
Badge**

**First Class Diver
Badge**

**Master Diver
Badge**

**Scuba Diver
Badge**

**Special Operations
Diver Badge**

**Special Operations
Diving Supervisor
Badge**

**Basic Explosive
Ordnance Disposal
Badge**

**Master Explosive
Ordnance Disposal
Badge**

**Senior Explosive
Ordnance Disposal
Badge**

U.S. ARMY BADGES AND TABS

Combat and Special Skill Badges

**Combat Infantryman Badge
1st Award**

**Combat Medical Badge
1st Award**

**Combat Infantryman Badge
2nd Award**

**Combat Medical Badge
2nd Award**

**Combat Infantryman Badge
3rd Award**

**Combat Medical Badge
3rd Award**

Expert Infantryman Badge

Expert Field Medical Badge

Combat Action Badge

**Master Aviator
Badge**

**Basic Aviator
Badge**

**Senior Aviator
Badge**

**Master
Flight Surgeon
Badge**

**Basic
Flight Surgeon
Badge**

**Senior
Flight Surgeon
Badge**

**Master
Aircraft Crewman
Badge**

**Basic
Aircraft Crewman
Badge**

**Senior
Aircraft Crewman
Badge**

Guard,
Tomb of the Unknown Soldier

Drill Sergeant

U.S. Army Recruiter, Basic
(Active Army)

U.S. Army Recruiter, Basic
(Army National Guard)

U.S. Army Recruiter
(U.S. Army Reserve)

U.S. Army Instructor, Basic

Army Service Ribbon

Established by the Secretary of the Army on 10 April 1981, and effective 1 August 1981, the Army Service Ribbon is awarded to members of the US Army, Army National Guard, and Army Reserve who have successfully completed initial entry training. Enlisted persons are eligible upon completion of initial MOS–producing courses. For those enlisted persons assigned an MOS based on civilian or other-service acquired skills, it is awarded after four months of honorable active service (paragraph 5.5, AR 600-8-22).

Overseas Service Ribbon

Established by the secretary of the Army on 10 April 1981 and effective 1 August 1981, the Overseas Service Ribbon is awarded to all members of the US Army, Army National Guard, and Army Reserve credited with a normal overseas tour completed in accordance with AR 614-30, Overseas Service. A soldier who has overseas service credited by another armed service is also eligible for this ribbon. The ribbon is not authorized for completion of an overseas tour of duty for which a service medal has been authorized (paragraph 5-4, AR 600-8-22).

Army Reserve Components Overseas Training Ribbon

Established by the Secretary of the Army on 11 July 1984, the ribbon is awarded to members of the US Army Reserve components for successful completion of annual training or active-duty training for a period of not less than ten days on foreign soil (paragraph 5-3, AR 600-8-22).

NON-US SERVICE MEDALS

United Nations Medal

This medal may be awarded to personnel who have been in the service of the United Nations for a period of not less than six months with one of the units designated in paragraph 9.10, AR 600-8-22. The United Nations has, to date, cast medals for eleven different operations. Effective 13 October 1995, soldiers awarded any of these medals may wear the first medal and ribbon for which they qualify. Not more than one UN Medal may be worn. Award of a medal in a different UN mission is denoted by a bronze service star on the one UN Medal (paragraph 9-10, AR 600-8-22).

NATO Medal

Qualifying periods of service for the NATO medal are either thirty days (continuous or accumulated) in the territory and airspace of the former Republic of Yugoslavia and the Adriatic Sea, or ninety days (continuous or accumulated) in the area of operations outside the former Republic of Yugoslavia and the Adriatic Sea between 1 July 1992 and a date to be determined (paragraph 9-11, AR 600-8-22).

Multinational Force and Observers Medal
To qualify for this medal, a soldier must have served with the Multinational
Force and Observers at least ninety days after 3 August 1981. Subsequent
awards for each completed six-month tour are indicated by an appropriate
numeral, starting with numeral "1" (paragraph 9.12, AR 600-8-22).

Republic of Vietnam Campaign Medal
Authorized for acceptance by Department of Defense instructions 1348.17,
31 January 1974, by members of the Armed Forces who meet the following
criteria:
  • Have served in the Republic of Vietnam for six months during the
    period 1 March 1961 to 28 March 1973, inclusive.
  • Have served outside the geographical limits of the Republic of Vietnam
    and contributed direct combat support to the Republic of Vietnam
    Armed Forces for six months. Such persons must meet the criteria
    established for the Armed Forces Expeditionary Medal (Vietnam) or the
    Vietnam Service Medal during the period of service required to qualify
    for the Republic of Vietnam Campaign Medal.
  • Have served under the above conditions for less than six months but
    have been wounded by hostile forces, captured, or killed in action or
    otherwise in the line of duty (paragraph 9.13, AR 600-8-22).

Kuwait Liberation Medal (Kingdom of Saudi Arabia)
Awarded by the kingdom of Saudi Arabia to members of the Armed Forces of
the United States who served within the designated war zone of Operation
Desert Storm during the period 17 January 1991 through 28 February 1991
(paragraph 9-14, AR 600-8-22).

Kuwait Liberation Medal (Government of Kuwait)
Awarded by the government of Kuwait to US military personnel who were
assigned to one of several designated areas in and around Kuwait from 2
August 1990 to 31 August 1993. To be eligible, personnel must have been
attached to, or regularly served for one day or more, with an organization participating in ground and/or shore operations; with a naval vessel directly supporting military operations; or as a crewmember in one or more aerial flights
that directly supported military operations in the designated areas. Temporary
duty for thirty or sixty nonconsecutive days supporting such operations during
the designated period also qualifies for award of the medal. The time requirement may be waived for temporary duty soldiers who actually participated in
combat operations (paragraph 9.15, AR 600-8-22).

FOREIGN INDIVIDUAL AWARDS
Decorations received from a foreign government in recognition of active field
service in connection with combat operations or for outstanding or unusually

meritorious performance may be accepted and worn upon approval of the Department of the Army. Without this approval, they become the property of the United States and must be deposited with the Department of the Army for use or disposal.

Qualification and special skill badges may be accepted if awarded in recognition of meeting the criteria, as established by the awarding foreign government, for the specific award.

Foreign badges are authorized for wear only on service and dress uniforms. The German marksmanship award (Schützenschnur) may be worn only by enlisted personnel, on the right side of the uniform with the upper portion attached under the center of the shoulder loop and the bottom portion attached under the lapel.

US ARMY BADGES AND TABS
Badges and tabs are appurtenances of the uniform. In the eyes of their wearers, several badges have significance equal to or greater than all but the highest decorations. There is no established precedence with badges as there is with decorations and service medals or ribbons. The badges are of three types: combat and special skill, marksmanship and tabs, and identification. Badges are awarded in recognition of attaining a high standard of proficiency in certain military skills. Subdued combat and special skill badges and Ranger, Sapper, and Special Forces tabs are authorized on field uniforms.

COMBAT AND SPECIAL SKILL BADGES
The following badges are awarded to denote excellence in performance of duties under hazardous conditions and circumstances of extraordinary hardship as well as for special qualifications and successful completion of prescribed courses of training (see Chapter 8, AR 600-8-22, for details).

Combat Infantryman Badge (CIB). Awarded to infantry personnel in the grade of colonel or below who, after 6 December 1941, satisfactorily perform duty while assigned or attached as a member of an infantry Stryker, Ranger, or Special Forces brigade, regiment, or unit of smaller size, or an advisor in an equivalent coalition unit, during any period that such unit is engaged in active ground combat (paragraph 8.6, AR 600-8-22). A soldier must be personally present and under fire while serving in an assigned infantry or Special Forces primary duty position, in a unit engaged in active ground combat to close with and destroy the enemy with direct fires.

Combat Medical Badge (CMB). Awarded to medical personnel assigned, attached to, or under operational control of any combat arms units of brigade or smaller size, who satisfactorily perform medical duties while the unit is engaged in active ground combat, provided they are personally present and under fire. For the Global War on Terror, requirements are for medical personnel assigned, attached to, or under operational control of any ground combat arms units of brigade or smaller size, who satisfactorily perform medical duties while the unit is engaged in active ground combat, provided they are personally present and under fire. Retroactive awards are not authorized for service prior to 18 September 2001 (paragraph 8.7, AR 600-8-22).

Combat Action Badge. Awarded to any soldier performing assigned duties in an area where hostile fire pay or imminent danger pay is authorized, who is personally present and actively engaging or being engaged by the enemy, and performing satisfactorily in accordance with the prescribed rules of engagement, according to its authorizing language. Lastly, the soldier must not be assigned or attached to a unit that would qualify him or her for the CIB or CMB.

Stars for Combat Infantryman Badge, Combat Medical Badge, and Combat Action Badge. The second and succeeding awards of the Combat Infantryman, the Combat Medical, and the Combat Action Badges, made to recognize participation and qualification in additional declared wars, are indicated by the addition of stars to the basic badges.

Expert Infantryman Badge. Awarded to infantry personnel of the Active Army, ARNG, and USAR who satisfactorily complete prescribed proficiency tests (paragraph 8.8, AR 600-8-22).

Expert Field Medical Badge. Awarded to Army Medical Service personnel who satisfactorily complete prescribed proficiency tests (paragraph 8.9, AR 600-8-22).

Army Astronaut Badge. The Army Astronaut Badge has been added to the authorized special skill badges, but the requirements for award of this badge are not stated in the regulations. These badges are awarded in three degrees: basic, senior, and master.

Army Aviation Badges. There are nine badges relating to Army aviation—three each for Army aviators, flight surgeons, and aircraft crewmen—in the degrees of basic, senior, and master.

The *Master Army Aviator Badge*, the *Senior Army Aviator Badge*, and the *Army Aviator Badge* are awarded upon satisfactory completion of prescribed training and proficiency tests as outlined in AR 600-105, Aviation Service of Rated Army Officers.

The *Master Aircraft Crewman Badge*, the *Senior Aircraft Crewman Badge*, and the *Aircraft Crewman Badge* are authorized for award to enlisted personnel who meet the prescribed requirements (paragraph 8.24, AR 600-8-22).

Glider Badge. This badge is no longer awarded but is still authorized for wear by individuals who were previously awarded the badge (paragraph 8.29, AR 600-8-22).

Parachutist Badges. To be awarded the *Master Parachutist Badge*, an individual must meet the following criteria: have participated in sixty-five jumps, twenty-five with combat equipment, four at night, and five mass tactical jumps; have graduated as jumpmaster or served as jumpmaster on one or more combat jumps or on thirty-three noncombat jumps; have been rated excellent in character and efficiency; and have served on jump status for not less than thirty-six months (paragraph 8.13, AR 600-8-22).

For the *Senior Parachutist Badge*, an individual must meet the following criteria: have been rated excellent in character and efficiency with participation in thirty jumps, including fifteen jumps made with combat equipment, two night jumps, and two mass tactical jumps; have graduated from a jumpmaster course or served as jumpmaster on one or more combat jumps or fifteen non-combat jumps; and have served on jump status for not less than twenty-four months (paragraph 8.12, AR 600-8-22).

The *Parachutist Badge* is awarded for satisfactory completion of the course given by the Airborne Department of the Infantry School or while assigned or attached to an airborne unit or for participation in at least one combat jump (paragraph 8.11, AR 600-8-22).

Combat Parachutist Badge. Participation in a combat parachute jump entitles the individual to wear a bronze star, or stars, affixed to the Parachutist Badge.

Pathfinder Badge. Awarded upon successful completion of the Pathfinder course conducted at the Infantry School (paragraph 8.22, AR 600-8-22).

Air Assault Badge. Awarded to personnel who have satisfactorily completed either the Training and Doctrine Command (TRADOC) prescribed training course or the standard air assault course while assigned or attached to the 101st Air Assault Division since 1 April 1974 (paragraph 8.23, AR 600-8-23).

Diver Badge. Awarded after satisfactory completion of prescribed proficiency tests (AR 611-75, Management of Army Divers). Five badges are authorized for enlisted personnel (paragraph 8.17, AR 600-8-22).

Driver and Mechanic Badge. Awarded only to enlisted personnel to denote a high degree of skill in the operation and maintenance of motor vehicles (paragraph 8.28, AR 600-8-22).

Explosive Ordnance Disposal Badges. There are three badges under this heading, any of which may be awarded to soldiers: *Master Explosive Ordnance Disposal Badge*, *Senior Explosive Ordnance Disposal Badge*, and *Explosive Ordnance Disposal Badge*. They are awarded to individuals assigned to duties involving the removal and disposition of explosive ammunition under hazardous conditions (paragraph 8.18, AR 600-8-22). This is now a Group 3 badge.

Military Freefall Parachutist Badge. Awarded to qualified US Army personnel who have qualified as high-altitude parachute specialists. There are two badges under this heading, either of which may be awarded: the *Military Free Fall Parachutist Badge* and the *Military Master Free Fall Parachutist Badge*.

Nuclear Reactor Operator Badges. The *Shift Supervisor Badge*, the *Operator First Class Badge*, and the *Operator Basic Badge* were awarded upon completing the Nuclear Power Plant Operators Course or equivalent training and after operating nuclear power plants for specific periods. These badges are no longer awarded but are still authorized for wear by individuals to whom they were previously awarded (paragraph 8.30, AR 600-8-22).

Parachute Rigger Badge. Awarded to any individual who successfully completes the Parachute Rigger Course conducted by the US Army Quartermaster School and who holds a Parachute Rigger MOS or skill identifier (paragraph 8.14, AR 600-8-22).

Physical Fitness Training Badge. This badge is awarded to soldiers who obtain a minimum score of 270 on the Army Physical Fitness Test (APFT) and who meet the weight-control requirements of AR 600-9 (paragraph 8.48, AR 600-8-22).

Ranger Tab. Awarded to any person who successfully completes a Ranger course conducted by the Infantry School or who was awarded the CIB while serving during WWII as a member of the 1st through 6th Ranger Battalions or the 5307th Composite Group (paragraph 8.46, AR 600-8-22).

Sapper Tab. Awarded after successful completion on or after 14 June 1985 of a Sapper Leaders Course conducted by the US Army Engineer School or retroactively.

Space Badge. There are three levels of the Space Badge: Basic, Senior and Master. The Space Badge is awarded to active Army, Army Reserve, and National Guard soldiers who successfully finish space-related training and attain the required Army space experience.

Special Forces Tab. The Commander, US Army John F. Kennedy Special Warfare Center, Fort Bragg, North Carolina, may award the Special Forces Tab to any individual who has successfully completed the Special Forces Qualification Course or the Special Forces Officer Course. The Special Forces Tab may be awarded to any person on active duty or on active status in the Reserve Components, in retired status, or honorably discharged who meets the appropriate criteria listed in paragraph 8.47, AR 600-8-22.

MARKSMANSHIP BADGES AND TABS

These badges and tabs include basic marksmanship qualification badges, excellence in competition badges, distinguished designation badges, the US Distinguished International Shooter Badge, and the President's Hundred Tab.

Only members of the Armed Forces of the United States and civilian citizens of the United States are eligible for these qualification badges. Qualification badges for marksmanship are of three types: basic qualification, excellence in competition, and distinguished designation. **Basic Qualification Badges** (including *Expert*, *Sharpshooter*, and *Marksman Badges*) are awarded to those individuals who attain the qualification score prescribed in the appropriate field manual for the weapon concerned. **Excellence in Competition Badges** are awarded to individuals in recognition of an eminent degree of achievement in firing the rifle or pistol. **Distinguished Designation Badges** are awarded to individuals in recognition of a preeminent degree of achievement in target practice firing with the military service rifle or pistol (paragraph 8.44, AR 600-8-22).

The **Distinguished International Shooter Badge** is awarded to military or civilian personnel in recognition of an outstanding degree of achievement in international competition (paragraph 8.50, AR 600-8-22).

A **President's Hundred Tab** is awarded to each person who qualifies among the top one hundred contestants in the President's Match held annually at the National Rifle Matches (paragraph 8.51, AR 600-8-22).

IDENTIFICATION BADGES
Identification badges are worn to signify special duties.

Presidential Service Identification Badge. The Presidential Service Certificate and the Presidential Service Badge were established by Executive Order 11174, 1 September 1964. The Presidential Service Certificate is awarded in the name of the President of the United States as public evidence of deserved honor and distinction to members of the Armed Forces who have been assigned duty in the White House for at least one year after 20 January 1961. It is awarded to Army members by the Secretary of the Army upon recommendation of the military aide to the president. The Presidential Service Badge is issued to members of the Armed Forces who have been awarded the Presidential Service Certificate. Once this badge is awarded, it may be worn as a permanent part of the uniform (paragraph 8.35, AR 600-8-22).

Vice Presidential Service Identification Badge. The Vice Presidential Service Badge was established by Executive Order 11544, 8 July 1970. It may be awarded upon recommendation of the military assistant to the vice president and may be worn as a permanent part of the uniform (paragraph 8.36, AR 600-8-22).

Secretary of Defense Identification Badge. Military personnel who have been assigned to duty and have served not less than one year after 13 January 1961 in the office of the Secretary of Defense are eligible for this badge. Once awarded, it may be worn as a permanent part of the uniform. It also is authorized for temporary wear by personnel assigned to specified offices of the Secretary of Defense (paragraph 8.37, AR 600-8-22).

Joint Chiefs of Staff Identification Badge. This badge may be awarded to military personnel who have been assigned to duty and who have served not less than one year after 16 January 1961, in a position of responsibility under the direct cognizance of the Joint Chiefs of Staff. Once awarded, the badge may be worn as a permanent part of the uniform (paragraph 8.8, AR 600-8-22).

Army Staff Identification Badge. This badge has been awarded by the Army since 1920 and is the oldest of the five types of identification badges now authorized for officers. It was instituted to give a permanent means of identification to those commissioned officers who had been selected for duty on the War Department General Staff, with recommendation for award based upon performance of duty. It has been continued under the present departmental organization.

Between 30 September 1979 and 28 May 1985, the badge could be awarded to the Sergeant Major of the Army and to other senior NCOs (SGM E-9) assigned to duty with the same staff units. Effective 28 May 1985, qualifying service must be of at least one year while assigned to permanent duty on the Army General Staff or assigned to the Office of the Secretary of the Army. Once awarded, this badge may be worn as a permanent part of the uniform (paragraph 8.39, AR 600-8-22).

Guard, Tomb of the Unknown Soldier Identification Badge (paragraph 8.40, AR 600-8-22).

Army ROTC Nurse Cadet Program Identification Badge (paragraph 8.41, AR 600-8-22).

Drill Sergeant Identification Badge (paragraph 8.42, AR 600-8-22).

US Army Recruiter Identification Badge (paragraph 8.43, AR 600-8-22).

Army National Guard Recruiter Identification Badge (paragraph 8.44, AR 600-8-22).

US Army Reserve Recruiter Identification Badge (paragraph 8.45, AR 600-8-22).

Career Counselor Badge (paragraph 8.46, AR 600-8-22).

Army Instructor Badge (TRADOC Reg 600-21).

APPURTENANCES

Appurtenances are devices affixed to service or suspension ribbons or worn in place of medals or ribbons. They are worn to denote additional awards, participation in a specific event, or other distinguished characteristics of the award.

Oak-leaf Cluster

A bronze or silver twig of four oak leaves with three acorns on the stem, $^{13}/_{32}$ inch in length for the suspension ribbon and $^{5}/_{16}$ inch in length for the service ribbon, is issued in lieu of a decoration for second or succeeding awards of decorations (other than the Air Medal) and service medals. A silver oak-leaf cluster is issued to be worn in lieu of five bronze clusters. Oak-leaf clusters of $5^{1}/_{16}$ inches, joined together in series of two, three, and four clusters, are authorized for optional purchase and wear on service ribbons.

Numerals
Arabic numerals $3/13$-inch high are issued in lieu of a medal or ribbon for second and succeeding awards of the Air Medal, the Humanitarian Service Medal, the Multinational Force and Observers Medal, the Army Reserve Components Overseas Training Ribbon, and the Overseas Service Ribbon. The numeral worn on the NCO Professional Development Ribbon denotes the highest completed level of NCO development. The numerals are worn centered on the suspension ribbon of the medal or the ribbon bar.

V Device
The V Device is a bronze letter V, $1/4$-inch high with serifs at the top of the members (the little strokes at the tops of the arms of the V that look like little rectangles). The V Device denotes awards of a medal for heroism and may be awarded with the Bronze Star Medal, the Air Medal, the Joint Service Commendation Medal (when the award is for acts or services involving direct participation in combat operations), and the Army Commendation Medal.

Clasps
Clasps are authorized to be worn on the Good Conduct Medal, the Army of Occupation Medal, and the Antarctic Service Medal.

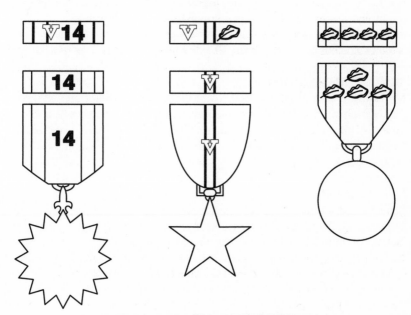

Appurtenances of Medals and Ribbons

Service Stars
The service star is a bronze or silver five-pointed star $^3/_{16}$ inch in diameter. Service stars joined together in a series of two, three, and four stars are authorized for optional purchase and wear on service ribbons. Service stars, signifying participation in a combat campaign, are authorized for wear on the Armed Forces Expeditionary Medal and the Vietnam Service Medal. (Note: Bronze and silver stars are worn on US Navy decorations in the same manner as oakleaf clusters are worn on Army and Air Force decorations.)

Arrowhead
The arrowhead is a bronze replica of an Indian arrowhead, $^1/_4$-inch high. It denotes participation in a combat parachute jump, combat glider landing, or amphibious assault landing while assigned or attached as a member of an organized force carrying out an assigned tactical mission. It is worn on the service and suspension ribbons of the Asiatic-Pacific Campaign, European-African-Middle Eastern Campaign, Korean Service Medal, Vietnam Service Medal, Armed Forces Expeditionary Medal, and Global War on Terrorism Expeditionary Medal.

SERVICE RIBBONS
Service ribbons are identical to the suspension ribbons of the medals they represent and are mounted on bars equipped with attaching devices; they are issued for wear in place of medals. The service ribbon for the Medal of Honor is the same color as the neck band, showing five stars in the form of a letter M.

MINIATURE MEDALS
Miniature replicas of all medals except the Medal of Honor are authorized for wear on specified uniforms, such as the blue and white mess uniforms, in lieu of the issued medals. Miniatures of decorations are issued only to foreign nationals. Awards issued by the Secretary of Defense include miniature medals.

LAPEL BUTTONS
Lapel buttons are authorized for wear on the left lapel of civilian clothing only. They are available for service ribbons and other decorations and badges. Included in this category are the Army Lapel Button, which is awarded to any soldier (except retirees) who completed nine months' honorable active federal service after 1 April 1984, and the US Army Retired Lapel Button.

Gold Star Lapel Button
This button is authorized for wear on the ASU of soldiers who have lost a spouse, mother, father, child, or stepchild to combat. Enlisted soldiers wear the pin centered vertically and horizontally on the left lapel of the green uniform.

Next of Kin Button
This button is authorized for wear on the ASU of soldiers who have lost a spouse or child, or soldiers who are the primary next of kin of a soldier who lost his or her life while serving on active duty or while assigned in the USAR or ARNG.

CERTIFICATES AND LETTERS
As a senior NCO, you may write and sign letters of appreciation and commendation for other enlisted personnel. Frequently, soldiers will ask for these accolades, but you should be constantly alert to any circumstances that may authorize a letter of appreciation or commendation for a deserving individual. When writing these letters, you should give them your best effort and put as much into composing them as you would into the writing of a recommendation for a decoration. Remember that a letter or certificate from an overseas commander or brigade or higher command sergeant major is worth five promotion points.

An important responsibility is to see that your commander is aware of those deeds that deserve special recognition, and you should not be hesitant to recommend personnel for consideration. But do the commander a favor: Prepare a draft citation or letter and offer it along with your verbal recommendations. The commanding officer may sign the final product, but if the person being recommended is one of your soldiers, you should write the original draft—you know your soldiers better than the commander does.

Certificates and letters may be nothing more than pats on the back. Nevertheless, they go a long way toward boosting the morale of most recipients, and their judicious use is a good way to recognize faithful and competent service.

Certificate of Achievement
Commanders may recognize periods of faithful service, acts, or achievements that do meet the standards required for decorations by issuing to individual military personnel a DA Form 2442, Certificate of Achievement. Certificates of achievement are awarded under local criteria and may be used for awarding the Good Conduct Medal, for participation in the Department of the Army Suggestion Program, or to recognize meritorious acts or service.

Letters of Commendation and Appreciation
Acts or services that do not meet the criteria for decorations or a certificate of achievement may be recognized by written expressions of commendation or appreciation. These letters are typed on letterhead stationery and do not contain formalized printing, seals, or other distinguishing features that depart from normal letter form.

19

Military and Social Customs

The customs of the service make up the unwritten "common law" of the Army. Customs are rich in tradition and knowing what they are and observing them should be second nature.

Of course, times are changing. Today, hardly anyone remembers the ancient taboos against soldiers carrying packages or pushing baby carriages while in uniform. But customs that are still accepted should be observed, and the soldier who flouts them should be made to understand just how important it is to maintain customs and tradition.

Following are some customs observed today:

- AR 670-1, Wear and Appearance of Army Uniforms and Insignia, authorizes an umbrella as an optional purchase item for male and female soldiers. It must be of a plain black design with no logos and only used during inclement weather. Umbrellas are not authorized in formations or while wearing field uniforms.
- Never sit on another soldier's bed or bunk in the barracks without permission.
- Never criticize a subordinate NCO in front of his or her troops.
- Never criticize the Army in front of civilians.
- Never accept gifts from subordinates.
- Never go over the heads of superiors.
- Never offer excuses.
- Act upon the commander's "desires" or "suggestions" as if they were orders (which they are, really, but politely phrased).
- Never "wear" a superior's rank by saying something like, "The commander wants this done right away." Phrase the request as your own.
- Never turn and walk the other way to avoid giving the hand salute.
- Never run indoors to avoid standing reveille or retreat.
- With the exception of on-the-spot corrections of military courtesy and discipline breaches, give orders to another NCO's troops only when absolutely necessary for mission accomplishment.

- Never appear in uniform while under the influence of alcohol.
- Treat others with the same dignity and respect with which you expect to be treated.

Remember these two responses to questions or orders from your superiors, and you will never go wrong: "I don't know, sir, but I'll find out," and "I'll do it or have it done."

ETIQUETTE

Etiquette is the set of rules or forms for manners and ceremonies established as acceptable or required in professional or official life. As a professional NCO, you must know these rules as they pertain to official social events. Guidance set forth in this section goes hand in hand with courtesy, and if you take courtesy to others as your guiding principle, no matter what the situation, you can never go wrong. Your soldiers look to you to set the example both on duty and off and will follow your lead, whether you realize it or not.

Proper Speech

You should make every effort to develop and maintain good speech habits. Speech begins with a good vocabulary and an understanding of grammar and pronunciation. Constantly misusing and mispronouncing words in front of your soldiers will undermine your authority and cause you to lose their respect. Lighten up on the profanity. A few well-chosen words are much more effective than a daily dose of four-letter words. A good speaker is listened to and understood.

Being able to converse in an interesting, intelligent, and entertaining manner is a social asset that will reflect favorably upon you. Never discuss your personal or business affairs at social gatherings. Never gossip, criticize others, boast, or engage in arguments.

Telephone Etiquette

Observe proper telephone courtesy at all times. When answering the phone, identify your unit or office first and then give your rank and name in a clear and normal tone of voice. If you are the first sergeant of Alpha Company, do not simply bellow your rank into the telephone, but give the caller the same courtesy you demand of your troops when they answer the telephone.

Pay attention to the caller's rank, title, and name and use them, wherever appropriate, during the conversation. If the person being called is not in, offer to take a message or refer the caller to another party who may be able to help. Listen patiently and politely. Speak distinctly and with confidence.

When calling someone else, give your rank and name first. If you should reach discourteous or bewildered people on the other end of the line, bear with them. It does no good for you to lose your patience. Should you dial a wrong number, it is impolite to hang up without saying anything. The proper procedure is to excuse yourself for the interruption and then check the number you have dialed. Never ask, "What number is this?" but say, "Have I reached 979-9383?"

Never let a telephone ring endlessly because you happen to be talking to someone on another line. Ensure that all calls are answered within four rings. If a phone near you is not answered by then, pick it up yourself.

Etiquette in the Workplace

Good manners are never out of place. Never sit with your feet on your desk. Never sit at your desk reading non-job-related materials. The worst impression you can give a visitor is to be seen reading a novel with your feet propped up on the desk.

When a superior who is not your immediate supervisor enters your work area, you are obliged to stand. And when someone comes to see you, on business or just calling, you should stand and greet that person. If you cannot stand—for example, if you are on the telephone—indicate by a nod of the head or a gesture with a free hand that the visitor should be seated. Never keep a person standing unless he or she is to be disciplined.

If coffee or tea is available, offer it to your visitor. This may not always be appropriate, as when an NCO from another staff section drops by to deliver a report, but if the person is a friend or well known to you, make the offer a standard part of your greeting. Never lean or sit on another person's desk. If the person you are visiting is thoughtless enough not to offer you a seat, remain standing.

You should consider that a visit in person takes precedence over a telephone call. If you happen to be on the telephone when a visitor arrives, finish your conversation quickly and call the other party back later.

It is best not to eat where you work. Give yourself a break. Find a few minutes to step outside your work area, find a quiet spot, and eat your lunch there.

Be tolerant. At work, certain people just do not get along, generally for the most frivolous reasons. Over a period of time, minor problems can turn into animosity. Set the example. If you encounter someone you dislike, suppress your intolerance. Allowing other people to annoy you is evidence of your own lack of self-discipline.

Netiquette

Besides operational security concerns while online, you should consider some informal rules and behaviors when using digital information systems such as professional forums, portals, Army Knowledge Online discussion groups, social media sites, blogs, and email. In the civilian sector, network etiquette, or "Netiquette," is usually enforced by fellow users who are quick to point out infractions of these rules. For soldiers, poor online conduct can take on serious ramifications. You are personally responsible for all content you publish, and even family member activity can come under scrutiny. Some tried-and-true Internet Netiquette tips worth considering are:

- Always identify yourself.
- Include a subject line.
- Avoid sarcasm.
- Respect others' privacy.
- Acknowledge and return messages promptly; let people know their message has been received.
- No spam (junk mail).
- Be concise. If you include a signature, keep it short.
- Use appropriate language.
- Copy with caution. Watch the CC: line when replying and know to whom you are talking.
- Do not overly use the Reply All button.
- Clean up emails before forwarding them.
- Don't forward hoaxes.
- Talk about only one main subject per email.
- Remember that punctuation matters.
- Avoid embarrassing emails.
- Do not use shorthand lingo of text messaging in official or formal communications.

Consider setting digital boundaries in your professional and personal life. Make it your policy to not email or text about work-related topics after hours; instead, call if it is really important. Set up an out-of-office response on your email system to announce times you are unavailable, and be sure to include when you will be available upon return.

SALUTING

The hand salute is a formal sign of courtesy between soldiers. It is both recognition of rank and authority and a greeting exchanged between members of a unique professional organization with special rules and codes of conduct. Precisely whom to salute is defined in AR 600-25, Salutes, Honors, and Visits of Courtesy. But the best rule to follow when saluting is "When in doubt, whip it out." The salute is a recognized form of greeting, and no soldier should feel embarrassment because he or she may have saluted someone who is not strictly entitled to it by AR 600-25.

All soldiers in uniform are required to salute when they meet and recognize persons entitled to the salute. Salutes are exchanged between officers (commissioned and warrant) and enlisted personnel. Salutes are exchanged with personnel of the Army, Navy, Air Force, Marine Corps, and Coast Guard entitled to the salute. It is customary to salute officers of friendly foreign nations as well. Civilians may be saluted by persons in uniform when appropriate, but the uniform hat or cap should not be raised as a form of salutation. Salutes are not required if the senior or subordinate or both are in civilian attire.

Soldiers under arms give the salute prescribed for the weapon with which they are armed. The practice of saluting others in official vehicles is appropriate and should be observed. Salutes are not required to be given by or to personnel who are driving or riding in privately owned vehicles except by gate guards.

Don't salute when driving any type of vehicle. Salutes are not required in public areas, such as theaters, outdoor athletic facilities, or other situations when the act would be inappropriate or impractical.

Accompanying the hand salute with an appropriate greeting, such as "Good morning, sir," or "Good morning, ma'am," is proper. Personnel do not salute indoors except when reporting to a superior officer.

The salute is given when the person approaching or being approached is recognized as being authorized a salute, usually at six paces. The officer is obliged to return the salute.

If a superior remains in your area but does not engage in conversation, he or she is saluted only once, upon the initial greeting; should a superior engage you in conversation, however, then you must salute when he or she finishes talking to you and departs.

Always salute with precision and enthusiasm. Never salute with anything in your hands or mouth. Never duck your head when you salute, but always keep your chin up and your back straight. Give a greeting clearly, in a normal tone of voice. You should not greet people in the same tone of voice you use when shouting out commands on the drill field.

Do not salute when in the following situations:

• A prisoner.
• Marching—the officer or NCO in charge salutes for everyone.
• Indoors, except when reporting or on guard duty.
• Carrying articles or occupied so that saluting would be awkward.
• When it is inappropriate to do so, such as when assisting a superior who is injured.
• In ranks—the officer or NCO in charge will salute for the whole formation.
• Engaged in athletics or sports.
• In places of public assembly or conveyance.
• Maneuvering against a hostile force or participating in field training.

"Outdoors" may actually be indoors, such as in gymnasium buildings used for drill halls and other roofed structures commonly used for drilling and exercising. Theater marquees and covered walkways open on both sides are considered outdoors, and it is appropriate to salute when underneath them.

Saluting in Groups

Individuals in formations never salute except at the command *Present arms*. The officer or NCO in charge does the saluting for the entire group. If the troops are not at attention when it becomes necessary to salute a senior, the person in charge calls them to attention before saluting.

A soldier in formation, not standing at attention, comes to the position of attention when spoken to by a senior.

When a group not in formation is approached by a superior, the first person to see him or her calls *Attention*, and all come to attention and salute, unless they are at work or engaged in organized athletics.

Saluting on Guard

In garrison, guards armed with a rifle halt and face toward the music when the national anthem or "To the Color" is played, or face toward the person or the colors to be saluted, and present arms. When challenging, the first salute is given when the officer has been recognized and advanced.

A sentinel armed with a pistol gives the hand salute, except when challenging, in which case the weapon is held at the *Raise pistol* position and kept there until the challenged party departs.

If the officer to whom a sentinel may be talking salutes a senior, the sentinel also salutes. Wherever he is posted, indoors or outdoors, a guard or a sentinel salutes all officers, except when saluting would endanger the officers or interfere with duty performance.

Reporting

If you are reporting to your commander, salute and formally report. If you are told to report to a senior officer to discuss an ongoing project, whether you salute depends on the protocol considered acceptable based on the particular staff and the frequency with which you visit.

When reporting to a commander, a salute is always given at the report and again when dismissed. When reporting indoors and without arms, first remove your hat and then knock on the commander's door. When given permission to enter, advance to within two paces from the commander's desk, halt, salute, and make your report: "Sir [or Ma'am], Sergeant Smith reporting as directed." Hold the salute until it is returned. After stating your business, salute again, and exit the room.

When reporting while under arms, never remove your hat. If carrying a rifle, enter with the weapon at the trail and give the rifle salute at *Order arms*. Otherwise, give the hand salute. Outdoors, a soldier may approach an officer with the weapon at either trail or right shoulder arms and execute the rifle salute at order or right shoulder arms.

FORMS OF ADDRESS

Either the rank or title "sir" or "ma'am" should be used when addressing an officer or a civilian.

Privates and privates first class are addressed as "private." Corporals and specialists are called "corporal" and "specialist," respectively. Sergeants through the rank of master sergeant are referred to as "sergeant," except first sergeants, who are called "first sergeant." Likewise, sergeants major and command sergeants major (including the Sergeant Major of the Army) are called "sergeant major."

BUGLE CALLS

These signals to the troops are transmitted on the bugle. Traditionally, Army bugle calls have been divided into four major categories:

- Alarm ("Fire," "To Horse").
- Formation ("Adjutant's Call," "Assembly").
- Service ("Church Call," "Fatigue," "First Sergeant's Call," "Mess Call," "Officer's Call," "Recall," "Retreat," "Reveille," "School Call," "Sick Call," "Taps," "Tattoo," "To the Color").
- Warning ("Boots and Saddles," "Drill Call," "First Call," "Guard Call," "Stable Call," "To Quarters").

Bugle calls help order the activities of soldiers throughout the day. At most installations, the few calls that are used are played from recordings on a public address system, although a live bugler is sometimes used to sound retreat and reveille.

Following are brief explanations of some of the more common calls in the normal order they are sounded.

First Call

This call is actually the first of the day. It is given as a warning that reveille is to take place within a few minutes.

Reveille

The word "reveille" is originally from the Latin *evigilare*, to watch or to wake. The custom of sounding some sort of call to signify the beginning of the day is very ancient. The British adopted the practice from the French and were calling it "revelly" as early as 1644. Although "First Call" is actually the initial bugle call of the Army day, reveille has come into our vocabulary as the word for the bugle call that signifies to awake.

Mess Call

In former days, this call was affectionately dubbed "Soupy."

Retreat

The term "retreat" is taken from the French word *retraite* and refers to the evening ceremony in which the unit honors the US flag when it is lowered for the night. The bugle call sounded at retreat was first used in the French army and dates back to the Crusades. Retreat was sounded at sunset to notify sentries to start challenging until sunrise and to tell the rank and file to go to their quarters.

To the Color
This call is the bugle call played immediately after retreat. The first note of "To the Color" signals that the flag is to be lowered. While this call is being sounded, military personnel in uniform give the appropriate salute. On many posts, the interval between the end of retreat and the beginning of "To the Color" is used to fire a salute cannon. This call was adopted by the US Army in 1835, replacing the cavalry "To the Standard."

Tattoo
This call is usually played at or very near 2100 hours and signifies that lights should be off within fifteen minutes. It is the longest bugle call in the US Army—twenty-eight bars. The first eight bars are from the French "*L'extinction des feux*" ("Lights Out") and the following twenty bars are a British army infantry tattoo.

The commonly accepted origin of the tattoo is from the practice in seventeenth-century armies of provost marshals visiting the civilian inns and taverns at night, informing the proprietors when it was time for the troops to return to garrison. Eventually, that custom gave way to a party of drummers parading around a garrison at the same time each night, beating a signal to inform soldiers it was time for them to return to quarters. The first beat of the drum as the musicians fell in was known as "first post" and the final beat as "last post." "Last post" is sometimes used today as another name for a military obituary.

Taps
This call is the last bugle call of the military day. "Taps" is also traditionally played at military funerals. Originally, the US Army used the French "*L'extinction des feux*" to end the day. The music for "Taps" was written by Maj. Gen. Daniel Butterfield in July 1862 at Harrison's Landing, Virginia, when he was a member of the Army of the Potomac during the Peninsular Campaign of the Civil War.

SOCIAL FUNCTIONS
Entertaining is part of military life, and over your career you will attend a variety of social functions, from the very casual to the very formal. Protocol is designed to let us know what to expect in a given situation. For most of us, it is a combination of military traditions, etiquette, and common sense. Knowing some of these guidelines will help you feel more comfortable in any given situation. When in doubt, take your cue from what someone senior is doing. They might not always be right, but at least you will be in good company.

In the course of your military life, and especially as you become more senior, you will receive many invitations to social events, both military and civilian. Keeping a few main points in mind will help you avoid misunderstandings and hurt feelings. At times, you will find that an invitation will conflict with another obligation or interest. When it comes to deciding which function to attend, put your family first. Hail and farewells are usually held monthly and probably will be your next priority. These get-togethers are opportunities for you to get to know other people in the company or battalion.

If you are invited to dinner at the sergeant major's house, remember that he and his wife have been entertaining for many more years than you have. Over their years in the military, they have developed a style that is comfortable for them. Do not be afraid to reciprocate with an invitation because your "picnic in the backyard with the kids" might fall short. Your leadership will be happy for the chance to get to know you better in any setting.

R.S.V.P.

"R.S.V.P." means "please respond and let us know if you are coming." If you receive an invitation to an event, answer yes or no within forty-eight hours after receiving an invitation. If you are having trouble giving a response within this timeframe, call the host to regret and explain your situation. Do not wait for your host to call you to see if you received an invitation or to ask if you are coming.

A small gift is always appreciated when visiting someone's home. This does not have to be expensive. A batch of muffins, homemade cookies, jellies, a bottle of wine, and flowers are all appropriate. It sends the message that you appreciate the invitation. A phone call or short "thank you" note afterwards thanking the hosts is always appropriate and sure to be appreciated.

TYPES OF FUNCTIONS

Cocktail Parties
Cocktails are usually served from 5:00 PM or 6:00 PM until 7:00 PM or 8:00 PM They are usually about two hours long. Hors d'oeuvres or appetizers are served. Plan for dressy attire for women and coat and tie for men unless special dress is requested on the invitation (Texas casual, aloha, beach, etc.).

Open House
This literally means the home is open to guests between set hours. Guests are free to arrive and depart between those hours. Check the invitation for dress.

Buffet
A buffet supper is a dinner party served buffet style. It is a convenient way to serve guests, especially a number of guests in a limited space. At a buffet supper, the plates, silverware, napkins, and platters of food are arranged on the

dining room table or buffet table, and guests serve themselves. You also might be invited to someone's home for "heavy hors d'oeuvres," which is very similar to the buffet dinner. There is no need to eat before you go. At these functions, a variety of hors d'oeuvres will be served—from dips, to meats on small rolls, to desserts. Again, dress should be indicated on your invitation and could range from casual to informal.

Seated Dinner
These dinners may range from the very casual family style to the very formal, with place cards and many courses. Check your invitation for dress.

Hail and Farewell
Unit members and guests share the cost and planning of these get-togethers. They range from dinners at local restaurants, to picnics and barbecues, to treasure hunts. This is a time to welcome incoming members and say farewell to members who are leaving the unit. These get-togethers build unit spirit and camaraderie, and are successful only if everyone supports them and participates in them.

Promotion Party
A time-honored tradition is the promotion party, which is given shortly after the promotion by an officer or NCO or a group of people with similar dates of rank. It does not have to be a fancy affair, but it provides a chance to invite friends and their spouses to share the good fortune.

Dining-in
The dining-in is an old military tradition that has been passed down from the British. As the most formal of events, a dining-in allows officers and NCOs of a unit to celebrate unit successes and to enjoy its traditions and heritage. It is strictly an officer and NCO affair. Dress for soldiers is usually ASU with a bow tie.

Dining-out
When spouses are invited to a dining-in, it becomes a dining-out. Dress for spouses is formal gowns or tuxedos; for soldiers, it is ASU with a bow tie. All stand for the posting and retiring of the colors and for the invocation and toasts. Men and women stand and drink for all toasts, except that women sit for the toast "to the ladies." If you do not drink alcoholic beverages, toast with the beverage of your choice or simply lift your glass as a token. You may also stand if the guest speaker receives a standing ovation.

Receptions
A reception is usually held in honor of a special guest or guests, or after a change of command. There may or may not be a receiving line. Guests should

mingle and visit with other guests. Before departing, be sure to thank the hostess and host and bid good-bye to the guest of honor.

Receiving Line

At official functions ranging from a change of command to a unit social, you may be invited to greet the host, hostess, or guest of honor in a receiving line. A receiving line is a formal way for the host and/or hostess to greet guests and to introduce other dignitaries in the line. It is especially important to be punctual, as sometimes units go through the line together. Keep these few pointers in mind. Set your drink and/or cigarette aside before going through the line. Except for receiving lines at the White House, diplomatic corps, and Air Force functions, the lady goes before the gentleman. The unit adjutant will look to you to give them your name. Do not shake this person's hand. Simply state your name. This person will turn to the guest of honor and pass your name along. You will shake hands with the rest of the people in the receiving line. You can greet them, welcome them, and wish them well in their new assignment. Do not talk long, even if you know the guest(s) of honor.

FLAGS, FLAG CUSTOMS, AND FLAG CEREMONIES

A "flag" is a general descriptive term for a cloth device with a distinguishing color or design that has a special meaning or serves as a signal. The flag of the United States, the white flag of truce, and weather flags are examples.

In the military service, the *color* is a flag of a dismounted unit; an *ensign* is a national flag; a *pennant* is a small triangular flag, usually flown for identification of a unit; a *standard* is a flag of a mounted unit; and a *guidon* is a swallow-tailed flag carried by Army units for identification, especially in drills and ceremonies.

The United States Flag

The flag of the United States is displayed at all Army installations. It represents the Union—the fifty stars on a field of blue. The field is always to the left of the observer because it is the "field of honor."

The flag should never be used as part of a costume or dress, or on a vehicle or float unless it is attached to a staff, nor should it be displayed as drapery. Bunting—strips of cloth in the colors of the flag—is used for draping and decoration. No lettering or any other kind of object should ever be placed on the flag, and its use in advertising is discouraged.

Soiled, torn, or weathered flags should be burned, privately.

Three different sizes of US flags are flown on Army installations:

- *Post flag.* Flown in fair weather, except on those occasions when the garrison flag is prescribed. Its dimensions are 19 feet fly by 10 feet hoist.

- *Garrison flag*. Flown on holidays and important occasions. Its dimensions are 38 feet fly by 20 feet hoist.
- *Storm flag*. Flown in lieu of the post flag in inclement weather. It is also used to drape caskets at a military funeral. Its dimensions are $9^{1}/4$ feet fly by 5 feet hoist.

Flag Displays

Officers look to NCOs for flag protocol, as they should; the more senior an NCO becomes, the more AR 840-10, Flags, Guidons, Streamers, Tabards, and Automobile and Aircraft Plates, becomes a part of daily life. Although the regulation covers in depth the use and etiquette for flags, some common-sense rules need to be emphasized.

When displayed in a line, flags may be set up in one of two ways: from the flag's right to left (the most common method) or with the highest precedence flag in the center if no foreign national colors are present. When set up from right to left, the highest precedence flag always goes on the right of all other flags, but if you look at the flag display from the audience, the highest precedence flag (normally the US flag) is on your far left; other flags extend to your right in descending precedence. When set up with the highest precedence flag in the center, other flags are placed, in descending precedence, first to the right, then to the left, alternating back and forth (see AR 840-10, figure 2-3).

Remember the following when displaying flags:

1. When the US flag is displayed with foreign national flags, all flags will be comparable in size. The flagstaffs or flagpoles on which they are flown will be of equal height. The tops of all flags should be of equal distance from the ground (AR 840-10, paragraph 2-4b).
2. The flagstaff head (finial) is the decorative ornament at the top of a flagstaff. The only finials authorized on the flag by Army organizations are the following:
   a. Eagle (presidential flagstaffs)
   b. Spearhead (the only device used with Army flags)
   c. Acorn (markers and marking pennants flagstaffs)
   d. Ball (outdoor wall mounted for advertising or recruiting)
3. When displaying the Army flag, the Army's first and last streamers (Lexington 1775 is first) are always positioned at the center facing forward (AR 840-10, paragraph 6). Remember that the Army flag and all other organizational colors are not complete without their streamers.
4. Ensure all finials are positioned in the same direction. For most Army flags, this means that the flat portion of the finial is facing forward.
5. Ensure that general officer personal flags are hung on the staff right side up. When properly hung, the point of the star(s) will point to the right as the flag is viewed. Flags are displayed by seniority and then by service.

6. When using spreaders (horizontal devices that allow the flag to flare slightly, thereby giving it a better appearance) to display flags, ensure that the flag is draped across the spreader from the flag's left to right.

Display of National Flag and Colors

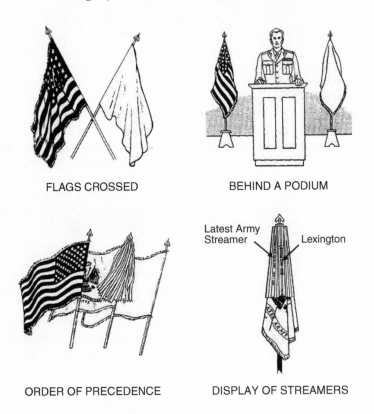

FLAGS CROSSED   BEHIND A PODIUM

ORDER OF PRECEDENCE   DISPLAY OF STREAMERS

Flag displays

Also remember the following when rendering honors:
- The flag of the United States, the national color, and the national standard are not dipped by way of salute or compliment. An exception to this is the rule followed by naval vessels when, upon receiving a salute of this type from a vessel registered by a nation formally recognized by the United States, the compliment must be returned.

- The organizational color or standard may be dipped in salute in all military ceremonies while the US national anthem, "To the Color," or a foreign national anthem is being played, and when giving honors to the organizational commander or an individual of higher grade, including a foreign dignitary of higher grade, but not otherwise.
- The US Army flag is considered an organizational color and is dipped when the US national anthem, "To the Color," or a foreign national anthem is played. It is also dipped when giving honors to the chief of staff of the US Army, his direct representative, or an individual of higher grade, including a foreign dignitary of equivalent or higher grade, but in no other case.

Flag Detail

Generally, a flag detail responsible for raising and lowering the national colors consists of one noncommissioned officer in charge (NCOIC), two halyard pullers, and two to eight flag handlers. The purpose of the handlers is to ensure correct folding and unfolding of the flag and to ensure that it does not touch the ground. Two handlers are needed when raising or lowering the storm flag, six handlers for the post flag, and eight handlers for the garrison flag.

Members of the flag detail are equipped according to local standing operating procedure and letter of instructions.

During the ceremony, the NCOIC subtly gives necessary commands or directives to ensure proper performance by the flag detail. On windy days, the NCOIC may assist the flag handlers in securing or folding the flag.

SURVIVOR ASSISTANCE AND HONORING THE DEAD

Chances are that at some point in your military career you will be detailed to act as a casualty notification officer (CNO), casualty assistance officer (CAO), or body escort. You will find the experience one of the most difficult and trying duties you will ever face. Performing these duties well brings great satisfaction to you and comfort to the bereaved family.

Notification of Next of Kin

As a CNO, you represent the Secretary of the Army. You are expected to be courteous, helpful, and compassionate. Your presence should soften the blow, if possible, and demonstrate the Army's concern.

Department of the Army policy is to make personal notification of the next of kin of all deceased and missing soldiers. The deceased soldier's desires for notification of next of kin listed on DD Form 93, Record of Emergency Data, will be followed.

Paragraph 6-3, AR 600-8-1, Army Casualty Program, prescribes that enlisted personnel in the senior grades may be used as notifiers providing that an officer is not available and the grade of the enlisted person used is equal to or higher than that of the deceased.

If the person to be notified is not fluent in English, a qualified interpreter should accompany you. The linguist should interpret only what is spoken between you and the next of kin. Contact your installation personnel officer in cases that require a linguist.

Be prepared for an adverse reaction on the part of the person being notified. If you know beforehand that the next of kin has a medical problem, consult the family doctor. If one cannot be identified, consult any physician in the area where notification is to be made. If you feel it is best, get the doctor to go with you when you make notification. You might find it helpful to have with you the telephone numbers for a local hospital, ambulance service, and fire department rescue squad.

If the person being notified suffers medically as a result of the news, you must keep your casualty commander notified. Additionally, all personal notifications must be confirmed promptly by commercial telegram. These details are set forth in Army Regulation 600-8-1.

Be careful to observe the following basic guidelines:

- Present the best possible military appearance. Be in a Class A uniform.
- Make your visit promptly after receiving casualty information, but only during the hours from 0600 to 2200, unless otherwise directed.
- Be natural in speech, manner, and method of delivery. What you say is of the utmost importance.
- If the next of kin is alone at the time of your visit, offer to call someone or ask a neighbor to step in.
- You may inform the next of kin that casualty assistance will be rendered, but do not specify a date or time on which such a visit will be made.
- If the next of kin are not at home when you visit, make an effort to locate them, using neighbors or local authorities, as necessary. Be most discreet so as not to compromise the purpose of your visit, especially if you deal with friends or neighbors. Should the next of kin be on vacation and too far away for you to carry out your visit, redirect action at once by telephone through the casualty reporting chain of command.
- Once you begin notification action, you must continue to completion.
- You may inform the primary next of kin that personal notification will be made to the secondary next of kin if required. When notifying the secondary kin, you may inform them that the primary kin have already been notified.
- Inform the next of kin that a letter from the soldier's commander will give more complete details (see Chapter 6, AR 600-8-1).

Be careful to observe the following prohibitions:

- DO NOT notify by telephone, unless there are indications the family will receive the information through unofficial sources.
- DO NOT call for an appointment before making the visit.

- DO NOT hold notes or a prepared speech in your hand when approaching the residence of the next of kin.
- DO NOT disclose the purpose of your visit or the contents of your message except to the next of kin.
- DO NOT leave word with neighbors or others to have the next of kin contact you, should you find them away from home.
- DO NOT speak hurriedly.
- DO NOT pass on any gory or embarrassing details.
- DO NOT use military jargon when speaking with the next of kin.
- DO NOT touch the next of kin unless there is extreme shock or fainting.
- DO NOT discuss entitlements. Advise that the survivor assistance officer (SAO) will be in touch.
- DO NOT discuss disposition of remains or personal effects.
- DO NOT inform the secondary kin that they will receive an SAO visit.
- DO NOT commit either your organization or the Department of the Army to carrying out any action or obtaining any information by a given time.
- DO NOT, under ANY circumstances, "fortify" yourself with alcohol or any other substance before making the visit.

Casualty Assistance

As a casualty assistance officer (CAO), you are charged by the Secretary of the Army to render assistance necessary to settle the personal affairs of a deceased soldier. Keep the thoughts and feelings of the next of kin uppermost in your mind at all times. Above all, be prepared. Nothing can reflect more adversely upon you than to demonstrate ignorance or indecision when dealing with the next of kin. Should you be asked questions for which you do not know the answers, remain cool and assure the next of kin that you will get the answers. A thorough study of the references given to you by your local casualty office should ensure that you are not caught unprepared for any contingency.

Your point of contact as a CAO is the local Casualty Assistance Center (CAC). You may receive assistance from the staff judge advocate, surgeon, provost marshal, public affairs officer, and finance, housing, and transportation officers. You are expected to make contacts with these officers, as required, without referral by the casualty section.

The casualty branch of your local adjutant general office should furnish you a complete packet relating to your duties as notifier/CAO at the time you receive a case for action. This packet should contain details pertaining to the services available to you locally to assist you in the completion of your duties. The details should include a telephone directory of those services, as well as most of the information sources listed below:

AR 27-1, Judge Advocate Legal Services
AR 37-104-3, Military Pay and Allowances Policy

AR 600-8-1, Army Casualty Program
AR 600-8-14, Identification Cards For Members of the Uniformed Services, their Eligible Family Members, and other Eligible Personnel
AR 600-8-22, Military Awards
AR 600-25, Salutes, Honors, and Visits of Courtesy
DA Pam 55-2, Transportation and Travel: It's Your Move
DoD Military Pay and Allowances Entitlements Manual
DoD A Survivor's Guide to Benefits

BODY ESCORT DETAIL

Body escort detail is an extremely important duty. Soldiers selected to act as escort represent the Army and the United States. The escort's mission is to see that the remains of the deceased reach the final destination chosen by the next of kin and that they are treated with honor, respect, and dignity during transport.

Maintaining a correct state of personal appearance is of primary importance. The uniform for this duty is the ASU. Neatness and cleanliness of your person are a part of the respect shown for the dead.

You will receive a package containing papers necessary to your assignment, including VA Form 40-1330, Claim for Standard Government Headstone or Marker, and DD Form 1375, Request for Payment of Funeral and/or Interment Expenses. You will also receive a statement of condition of remains (a locally reproduced form) and the deceased's death certificate, which you should give to the funeral director when you arrive at your destination.

You are responsible for the remains from the time you sign for them to the time you obtain a receipt for them from the funeral director at your destination. The statement of the condition of the remains serves as your receipt.

When remains are to be transported in a casket, they may be sent by air or by rail, although the latter is used less often than air transportation. Regardless of how the remains are being shipped, you should be at the terminal well before the time of departure. Determine at that time where you should go to make sure that the casket has arrived. Examine the casket and check the label at the head of the casket that shows the deceased's name and Social Security number. Sign your name on the label to show that you have checked it. Be sure that no cargo is placed on the casket.

When the casket is placed in the cargo compartment of the airplane, it is moved in a feet-first position. On the aircraft, the body should be placed in a head-first position, with the head toward the nose of the aircraft. The airline employees should be reminded of this. In a railcar, the remains are placed feet-first.

Salute the casket while it is being loaded on the carrier.

When traveling by airplane, tell the flight attendant that you are escorting a deceased person and wish to be the first to leave after landing. When the casket is being moved, you should accompany it to ensure proper handling and to make sure that the remains do not become separated from you.

If any emergency or unavoidable delay occurs, notify the receiving funeral home by telephone. Also call the mortuary officer at the shipping installation. You may call this officer collect. Be sure to include the new arrival time and flight number of the airplane.

When you reach your destination, go immediately to watch the casket being unloaded. As soon as the remains arrive in the terminal, drape the flag over the casket with the blue-starred field above the left shoulder of the deceased. The remainder of the flag should be draped evenly over the casket. Secure the flag on the shipping case with the elastic flag band. If the casket was shipped by rail, remove the baggage tag and turn it in at the baggage room.

The funeral director will meet you at the terminal. The remains will be loaded into a hearse for transfer to the funeral home. The casket should be moved feet-first.

Salute the remains before the door of the hearse is closed.

Draping the Flag over a Closed Casket or Shipping Case

Cremated remains are shipped in an urn placed inside a shipping box that you hand-carry and keep in your possession at all times. You will also carry along the flag, folded and in a plastic case; you do not place or drape the flag on the shipping box.

When you arrive at your destination, remove the urn from the shipping box. During the interment service, the flag may be taken out of its case, folded to resemble a cocked hat, and placed in front of the urn. At the end of the service, it is put back into its case and presented to the next of kin.

When escorting cremated remains, you will obtain from the funeral director a receipt for the remains instead of a statement on the condition of the remains. In all other aspects, the details of escort duty for cremated remains are the same as for escorting a body in a casket.

Ordinarily, the family of the deceased will not be present at the terminal when you arrive, and your first contact with them will not occur until you have reached the funeral home. Should they be present at the terminal, be sure to introduce yourself to them at that time. If there is a CAO present, be sure to make yourself known. He or she may be of great help to you if you should need assistance.

You should accompany the funeral director in the hearse. Use this opportunity to find out all you can about the next of kin and the other relatives of the deceased whom you will meet at the funeral home. Try to find out their attitude and any other facts that will help to make your assignment easier.

When you arrive at the funeral home, salute the casket as it is being unloaded.

Once at the funeral home, you and the funeral director will fold the flag that has been draped over the casket. The funeral director will inspect the casket to see that it has not been damaged during shipment. If the remains are to be viewed, he or she also opens the casket for inspection. You are responsible for inspecting the uniform and decorations of the deceased. If the casket is to be closed, arrange the flag as you did at the terminal (see previous illustration).

When you and the funeral director have completed these steps, he or she will prepare the statement of the condition of the remains and sign it. You are responsible for returning the statement to the supervisor of mortuary operations at the installation that prepared the remains. You will also give the funeral director the certificate of death, which will have been included in your packet.

Honoring our fallen comrades.

If there is a CAO present, he or she will handle all matters pertaining to insurance, back pay, casualty information, awards, military funeral arrangements, and such. If a CAO or SAO is not present, offer the family your assistance and sympathy but remain quiet, tactful, and dignified. Offer to remain for the funeral services. If the family wants you to stay, you are required to do so.

If burial is to be made in a private cemetery, show the family VA Form 40-1330 and DD Form 1375. If the remains are consigned to a funeral director before interment in a government or national cemetery, show the family DD Form 1375. Explain to the next of kin that the forms should be filled in as soon as possible and mailed to the military activity listed on the form.

When you have completed your assignment, you are to return to your duty station. After your return, you are required to submit a short report in letter-form concerning your escort duty. Be sure to include any problems you encountered during your escort duty and how they were resolved.

20

Military Justice

A fact of military life is that, despite the availability of information on the subject and the effort of commanders to keep their soldiers informed, many individuals simply do not know very much about the military justice system. Specific provisions pertaining to administration of the military justice system are in the *Manual for Courts-Martial* and AR 27-10, Military Justice. It is the noncommissioned officer's business to know nonjudicial punishment thoroughly—as thoroughly as any commander—and, since noncommissioned officers are normally the first to know an offense was committed, it would be very good to consider that "prevention is the best cure."

TRIAL DEFENSE SERVICES

Trial Defense Services (TDS) are a separate part of the Judge Advocate General (JAG) Corps and are like civilian defense attorneys. They are independent of local commands and local staff judge advocate offices to protect the rule of impartiality, and as such, they are shielded from possible undue command influence. TDS are the "soldier's lawyer" who will represent you if you are facing court-martial, Article 15, or civilian criminal charges. TDS also assists soldiers facing involuntary separation proceedings under AR 635-200, Enlisted Personnel, Chapters 5–13, 15, and 18.

NONJUDICIAL PUNISHMENT

Article 15 of the UCMJ provides commanding officers with the authority and procedures to impose disciplinary punishments for minor offenses without a court-martial. Such punishments may be in addition to or in lieu of admonition or reprimand. Unless the accused is embarked on a vessel, Article 15 punishment may not be imposed if the accused demands trial by court-martial.

Punishments authorized under Article 15 are less severe than court-martial punishments. Unlike a special or general court-martial, Article 15 is not considered a federal conviction for a criminal offense. Article 15 is intended to provide a swift, efficient, and relatively easy method for punishing those committing minor offenses, for maintaining discipline, and for deterring future offenses. Under Article 15, commanders have wide latitude in punishments that may be imposed, ranging from oral reprimand to reduction in pay grades, fines, restriction, extra duty, or a combination of these. Article 15 is the most likely contact that NCOs will have with the military justice system.

It is a mistake to disregard the effect of an Article 15 on a soldier's career. For a noncommissioned officer, an Article 15 usually means that the soldier's career will be limited to the lower NCO grades, whether that was the intent or not. The original copy of DA Form 2627, Record of Proceedings under Article 15, UCMJ, may be filed in either the Official Military Personnel File performance portion or the restricted portion of the permanent record. Records of Article 15 punishments can be used in a wide variety of personnel decisions and can lead to an involuntary administrative discharge.

Article 15 is not a legal process. Legal rules of evidence do not apply, and providing defense counsel at the hearing is not mandatory. Nevertheless, the accused does have protection against arbitrary use of Article 15. In addition to the right to demand trial in lieu of Article 15 punishment, the accused has the right to consult with counsel to decide whether to accept the punishment; if the accused accepts Article 15 and considers the punishment too harsh, he or she may appeal it. Other rights include the right to remain silent, to fully present his or her case in the presence of the imposing commander, to call witnesses, to present evidence, to be accompanied by a spokesperson, to request an open hearing, and to examine available evidence.

In order to find the soldier guilty, the commander must be convinced beyond a reasonable doubt that the soldier committed the offense. The maximum punishment depends on the rank of the commander imposing punishment and the rank of the soldier being punished.

Persons Subject to Nonjudicial Punishment

Punishment may be imposed under Article 15 by a commanding officer upon commissioned and warrant officers and enlisted military personnel, with the exception of US Military Academy cadets.

Nonjudicial punishment may not be imposed on an individual by a commanding officer after the person ceases to be in his or her command. The commander who has instituted the proceedings may, in the case of such a change in status, forward the record of proceedings to the gaining commander for appropriate disposition.

Purposes of Nonjudicial Punishment

Nonjudicial punishment may be imposed in appropriate cases for the following purposes:

- To correct, educate, and reform offenders who have shown that they cannot benefit by less stringent measures.
- To preserve, in appropriate cases, an offender's record of service from unnecessary stigmatization by record of court-martial conviction.

- To further military efficiency by disposing of minor offenses in a manner requiring less time and personnel than trial by court-martial.

Generally, the term *minor offenses* includes misconduct not involving any greater degree of criminality than is involved in the average offense tried by summary court-martial.

Nonpunitive measures usually deal with misconduct resulting from simple neglect, forgetfulness, laziness, inattention to instructions, sloppy habits, immaturity, difficulty in adjusting to disciplined military life, and similar deficiencies. These measures are primarily tools for teaching proper standards of conduct and performance and do not constitute punishment. They can include denial of pass or other privileges, counseling, administrative reduction in grade, extra training, bar to reenlistment, and MOS reclassification. Certain commanders have the authority, apart from any under Article 15, to reduce enlisted persons administratively for inefficiency or other reasons. *Nonpunitive measures and nonjudicial punishment should not be confused.*

A written admonition or reprimand should contain a statement indicating that it has been imposed merely as an administrative measure and not as punishment under Article 15. On the other hand, admonitions and reprimands that are imposed as punishment under Article 15 should be clearly stated to have been imposed as punishment under that article.

Commanding officers also have the authority to impose restraints or restrictions upon a soldier for administrative purposes, such as to ensure the soldier's presence within the command. This authority exists apart from the authority to impose restriction as nonjudicial punishment. These nonpunitive measures may also include, subject to any applicable regulation, administrative withholding of privileges.

Extra training or instruction is one of the most effective nonpunitive measures available to a commander. It is used when a soldier's duty performance has been substandard or deficient. For example, a soldier who fails to maintain proper attire may be required to attend classes on the wearing of the uniform and stand inspection until the deficiency is corrected.

Summarized Proceedings

Summarized Proceedings under Article 15 may be used if, after a preliminary inquiry, a commander determines that the punishment for an offense should not exceed extra duty or restriction for fourteen days; oral reprimand or admonition; or any combination of these punishments. The record of these proceedings is made on DA Form 2627-1, Summarized Record of Proceedings under Article 15, UCMJ. Generally, Summarized Proceedings are conducted as they are for more serious cases prosecuted under nonjudicial punishment, except the individual normally is allowed twenty-four hours to decide whether or not to demand trial by court-martial and to gather matters in defense, extenuation, or mitigation. Because of the limited nature of the punishments imposed under these proceedings, the soldier has neither the right to consult with legally qualified counsel nor the right to a spokesperson.

MAXIMUM PUNISHMENTS FOR
ENLISTED MEMBERS UNDER ARTICLE 15

	Summarized	Company Grade	Field Grade
Extra Duty	14 days	14 days	45 days
Restriction	14 days	14 days	60 days (45 days if combined with extra duty)
Correctional Custody		7 days (E-1–E-3)	30 days (E-1–E-3)
Reduction		1 Grade (E-1–E-4)	1 or more grade (E-1–E-4) 1 grade (E-5–E-6)
Forfeitures		7 days	$^1/_2$ of 1 month's pay for 2 months
Reprimand/Admonition	Oral	Oral/written	Oral/written

Note: The maximum punishment imposable by any commander under Summarized Proceedings cannot exceed extra duty for fourteen days, restriction for fourteen days, oral reprimand, or any combination thereof.

1. Combinations of extra duties and restriction cannot exceed the maximum allowed for extra duty.
2. Subject to limitations imposed by superior authority and presence of adequate facilities. If punishment includes reduction to private first class or below, reduction must be unsuspended.
3. Only if imposed by a field-grade commander of a unit authorized to have a commander who is a lieutenant colonel or higher.
4. Amount of forfeiture is computed at the reduced grade, even if suspended, if reduction is part of punishment.

Nature of Punishments
Nonjudicial punishments include the following actions:
- *Admonition and Reprimand.* An admonition or reprimand may be imposed in lieu of or combined with Article 15 punishments.
- *Restriction.* The severity of this type of restraint is dependent upon its duration and geographical limits specified when punishment is imposed. A soldier undergoing restriction may be required to report to a designated place at specified times if it is considered reasonably necessary to ensure that the punishment is being properly executed.
- *Extra Duties.* This form involves the performance of duties in addition to those normally assigned to the person undergoing the punishment. These may include fatigue duties. In general, extra duties that would demean his or her position as a noncommissioned officer may not be assigned to a corporal or above.

A Reduction in grade involves these considerations:
- *Promotion authority.* The grade from which the soldier is reduced must be within the promotion authority of the imposing commander or the officer to whom authority to punish under Article 15 has been delegated.
- *Date of rank.* When a soldier is reduced in grade as a result of unsuspended reduction, the date of rank in the grade to which reduced is the date the punishment of reduction was imposed.
- *Entitlement to pay.* When a soldier is restored to a higher pay grade because of a suspension or when a reduction is mitigated to a forfeiture, entitlement to pay at the higher grade is effective on the date of the suspension or mitigation.
- *Senior NCOs.* Sergeants first class and above may not be reduced under the authority of Article 15.
- *Forfeiture of pay.* Pay refers to basic pay of the individual plus any foreign duty pay. Forfeitures imposed by a company-grade commander may not be applied for more than one month, while those imposed by a field-grade commander may not be applied for more than two months. The maximum forfeiture of pay to which a soldier is subject during a given month, because of one or more actions under Article 15, is one-half his or her pay per month. Article 15 forfeitures cannot deprive a soldier of more than two-thirds of his or her pay per month.

Lateral appointments or reductions of corporal to specialist are not authorized. An NCO may be reduced to a lower pay grade provided the lower grade is authorized in his or her primary MOS.

Combination and Apportionment

No two or more punishments involving deprivation of liberty may be combined in the same nonjudicial punishment to run either consecutively or concurrently, but other punishments may be combined. Restriction and extra duty may be combined in any manner to run for a period not in excess of the maximum duration imposable for extra duty by the imposing commander.

Suspension, Mitigation, Remission, and Setting Aside

Suspension. The purpose of suspending nonjudicial punishment is to grant a deserving soldier a probational period during which the individual may show that he or she deserves a remission of the suspended portion of his or her nonjudicial punishment. If, because of further misconduct within this period, it is determined that remission of the suspended punishment is not warranted, the suspension may be vacated and the suspended portion of the punishment executed.

Mitigation. Often there are factors other than the facts and circumstances of the offense that show that the accused should receive a light punishment.

FORFEITURES OF PAY AUTHORIZED UNDER ARTICLE 15

Maximum monthly authorized forfeitures of pay under Article 15, UCMJ, may be computed using the applicable formula below:

1. Upon enlisted persons:

$$\frac{(\text{monthly basic pay}^{1,2} + \text{foreign pay}^{1,3})}{2} = \text{maximum forfeiture per month if imposed by major or above}$$

$$\frac{(\text{monthly basic pay}^{1,2} + \text{foreign pay}^{1,3}) \times 7}{30} = \text{maximum forfeiture if imposed by captain or below}$$

2. Upon commissioned and warrant officers when imposed by an officer with general court-martial jurisdiction or by a general officer in command:

$$\frac{(\text{monthly basic pay}^{2})}{2} = \text{maximum authorized forfeiture per month}$$

---

[1] Amount of forfeiture is computed at the reduced grade, even if suspended, if reduction is part of the punishment imposed.
[2] At the time punishment is imposed.
[3] If applicable.

Examples include lack of past criminal record, good duty performance, and family hardship.

Remission. Remission can cancel any portion of the unexecuted punishment. Remission is appropriate under the same circumstances as mitigation.

Setting Aside and Restoration. Under this action, the punishment or any part or amount thereof, whether executed or unexecuted, is set aside, and any property, privileges, or rights affected by the portion of the punishment set aside are restored. The basis for this action is ordinarily a determination that, under all the circumstances of the case, the punishment has resulted in a clear injustice.

Notification and Explanation of Rights

The imposing commander must ensure that the soldier is notified of the intention to dispose of the matter under Article 15. The imposing commander may delegate notification authority to another officer, warrant officer, or NCO (sergeant first class and above), providing that person outranks the person being notified. If an NCO is selected, that person should normally be the unit first sergeant or another NCO who is the senior enlisted person in the command in which the accused is serving.

The soldier must be given a "reasonable time" to consult with counsel, including time off from duty, if necessary, to decide whether to demand trial. The amount of time granted is normally forty-eight hours.

Before deciding to demand trial, the accused is not entitled to be informed of the type or amount of punishment he or she will receive if nonjudicial punishment is imposed. The imposing commander will inform the soldier of the maximum punishment allowable under Article 15 and the maximum allowable for the offense if the case proceeds to a trial by court-martial and conviction for the offense.

Right to Demand Trial

The demand for trial may be made at any time before imposition of punishment. The soldier will be told that if trial is demanded, it could be by summary, special, or general court-martial. The soldier will also be told that he or she may object to trial by summary court-martial and that at a special or general court-martial he or she would be entitled to be represented by qualified military counsel or by civilian counsel obtained at the soldier's expense.

Appeals

Only one appeal is permitted under Article 15 proceedings. An appeal not made within a "reasonable time" may be rejected as untimely by the superior authority. The definition of what constitutes a "reasonable time" varies according to the situation. Generally, an appeal, including all documentary matters, submitted more than five calendar days (including weekends and holidays) after punishment is imposed will be presumed to be untimely. If, at the time of imposition of punishment, the soldier indicates a desire not to appeal, the superior authority may reject a subsequent election to appeal, even if it is made within the five-day period.

Appeals are made on DA Form 2627, Record of Proceedings under Court-Martial, UCMJ, or DA Form 2627-1 and forwarded through the imposing commander or successor-in-command to the superior authority. The superior must act on the appeal unless otherwise directed by competent authority. A soldier is not required to state the reasons for the appeal, but he or she may present evidence or arguments proving innocence or why the sentence should be mitigated or suspended. Unless an appeal is voluntarily withdrawn, it must be forwarded to the appropriate superior authority. A timely appeal does not terminate because a soldier is discharged from the service but will be processed to completion.

Announcement of Punishment

The punishment may be announced at the next unit formation after punishment is imposed or, if appealed, after the decision. It also may be posted on the unit bulletin board. The purpose of announcing the results is to avert the perception of unfairness of punishment and to deter similar misconduct by others.

Records of Punishment

DA Forms 2627 are prepared in an original and six copies. What happens to those copies, especially the original, is of the utmost importance to soldiers who receive punishment under nonjudicial proceedings.

Original. For enlisted soldiers, the original copy is forwarded to the US Army Enlisted Records and Evaluation Center, Fort Knox, Kentucky. The decision on where in the punished soldier's Official Military Personnel File (OMPF) this copy will be placed is determined by the imposing commander at the time punishment is imposed and is final. The imposing commander will decide if it is to be filed in the performance section or the restricted section of the individual's OMPF.

Copy One. For those Articles 15 filed in the performance section of the OMPF, copy one is placed in the unit nonjudicial punishment files. This copy will be maintained permanently and will be forwarded to the gaining unit upon the soldier's transfer unless the original is transferred from the performance to the restricted section, at which time it is destroyed. Otherwise, it is kept in the unit personnel files and destroyed two years from the date of punishment or on the soldier's transfer, whichever occurs first.

Other Copies. Copies two through four are used variously as prescribed by AR 27-10, Military Justice, depending on whether forfeiture of pay is involved and whether the punished soldier appeals. Copy five is given to the individual.

Transfer or Removal of Records

Sergeants and above and commissioned and warrant officers may request the transfer of a record of nonjudicial punishment from the performance to the restricted section of their OMPF. To support such a request, the individual must submit substantive evidence that the purpose of the Article 15 has been served and that transfer of the record is in the best interests of the Army. The request must be made in writing to the Department of the Army Suitability Evaluation Board: President, Army Review Boards Agency (ARBA), 251 18th Street South, Suite 385, Arlington, VA 22202-3531.

Soldiers may also apply to the Army Board for Correction of Military Records (ABCMR) for the correction of military records by the secretary of the Army. AR 15-185, Army Board for Correction of Military Records, contains policies and procedures for making such applications.

COURTS-MARTIAL

Courts-martial are the agencies through which Army magistrates try personnel accused of violations of the punitive articles of the UCMJ. These are Articles 77 through 134 of the UCMJ and are designed to provide punishment of three broad groups of crimes and offenses:

- Crimes common to both military and civilian law, such as murder, rape, sodomy, arson, burglary, larceny, and frauds against the United States.
- Crimes and offenses peculiar to the military services, such as desertion, disobedience, misbehavior before the enemy, and sleeping on post.
- General offenses that are prosecuted under Article 134, the General Article, which covers "all disorders and neglects to the prejudice of good order and discipline in the armed forces, all conduct of a nature to bring discredit upon the armed forces, and crimes and offenses not capital."

During peacetime, courts-martial may impose sentences ranging from simple forfeiture of pay to confinement and forfeiture of all pay and allowances to death. (See *Manual for Courts-Martial*, Appendix 12, for the Maximum Punishment Chart.) During time of war, a general court-martial may impose any penalty authorized by law, including death.

Who May Initiate Charges

Charges are initiated by anyone bringing to the attention of the military authorities information concerning an offense suspected to have been committed by a person subject to the UCMJ. This information may be received from anyone, whether subject to the UCMJ or not.

Action by Immediate Commander

Upon receipt of information that an offense has been committed, the commander exercising immediate jurisdiction over the accused under Article 15, UCMJ, must make a preliminary inquiry into the charges in order to permit an intelligent disposition of them.

Based on the outcome of the preliminary inquiry, a commander may decide that all or some of the charges do not warrant further action, and those charges may be dismissed. The commander may also decide, based on the preliminary investigation, that the offenses committed warrant punishment under Article 15, UCMJ, or he or she may refer more serious charges to higher authority for trial by courts-martial.

Preparation of Charge Sheets

Rule 307 and *Manual for Courts-Martial*, Appendix 4, contain specific instructions on the preparation of charge sheets, together with specimen forms for charges and specifications under the punitive articles of the UCMJ. If you're not a legal clerk, it's important to get help from your Trial Defense Services (TDS) officer.

Composition of Courts-martial

General courts-martial consist of a military judge and no fewer than five members, or of a military judge alone. *Special courts-martial* consist of no fewer than three members or, if so detailed, a military judge and no fewer than three members, or a military judge alone. *Summary courts-martial* consist of one commissioned officer.

Any commissioned officer on active duty with the Armed Forces is eligible to serve on courts-martial. Any warrant officer on active duty with the Armed Forces is eligible to serve on general and special courts-martial for the trial of any person other than a commissioned officer. Any enlisted person on active duty with the Armed Forces who is not a member of the same unit as the accused is eligible to serve on general and special courts-martial for the trial of any enlisted person who has personally requested in writing before assembly that enlisted members serve on the court.

Convening Authorities

General courts-martial may be convened by the president of the United States; the Secretary of the Army; the commander of a territorial department, Army group, Army, Army corps, division, separate brigade, or corresponding unit; or any other commander designated by the Secretary of the Army or empowered by the president to convene such courts-martial. It is unlawful for any commander who is an accuser to convene a general court-martial for the trial of the person so accused.

Special courts-martial may be convened by any person who has the authority to convene a general court-martial or by the commanding officer of a district, garrison, fort, camp, station, or other place where members of the Army are on duty.

Summary courts-martial may be convened by any person who also has the authority to convene a general or special court-martial; the commander of a detached company or other detachment of the Army, as well as any other officer empowered by the Secretary of the Army, may also convene such a court-martial. When only one commissioned officer is present with a command or detachment, that officer is the summary court-martial authority of that command or detachment and hears and determines all summary court cases.

Challenges

The military judge and members of a general or special court-martial may be challenged by the accused or the trial counsel for cause stated to the court. The military judge, or, if none, the court, determines the relevancy and validity of challenges for cause. Challenges by the trial counsel are ordinarily presented and decided before those by the accused are offered.

Each accused and the trial counsel is entitled to one peremptory challenge, meaning the accused may challenge any member of the court to sit on his or her trial without offering any reasons for the challenge.

Appeals

At the close of a trial or soon thereafter, if the accused is found guilty, the defense counsel should prepare a recommendation for clemency setting forth any matters as to clemency he or she desires to have considered by the members of the court of the reviewing authority. If the accused is convicted, the defense counsel advises him or her of appellate rights.

The Court of Military Review. In every case of trial by court-martial in which the sentence, as approved, extends to death, dishonorable or bad conduct discharge, or confinement for one year or more, the Judge Advocate General (JAG) will refer the record to a court of military review.

For each case referred, the court of military review may act only with respect to the findings and sentence as approved by the convening authority. If the court sets aside the findings and sentence, it may—except when the setting aside is based on lack of sufficient evidence—order a rehearing. If it sets aside the findings and sentence and does not order a rehearing, it orders that the charges be dismissed.

The Court of Military Appeals. The US Court of Military Appeals, established under Article I of the Constitution, reviews the record in all of the following cases:

- Those in which the sentence, as affirmed by a court of military review, extends to death.
- Those reviewed by a court of military review that the JAG orders sent to the Court of Military Appeals for review.
- Those reviewed by a court of military review in which the Court of Military Appeals has granted a review. Reviewed cases may be forwarded to the US Supreme Court.

Remission and Suspension of Sentences

The Secretary of the Army or designated representative may remit or suspend any amount of the unexecuted part of any sentence other than a sentence approved by the president, including all uncollected forfeitures. The Secretary of the Army may, for cause, substitute an administrative form of discharge for a discharge or dismissal executed in accordance with the sentence of a court-martial. The convening authority may suspend the execution of any sentence except a death sentence.

Effective Dates of Sentences

Whenever a sentence includes a forfeiture of pay or allowances in addition to confinement, the forfeiture applies to pay or allowances becoming due on or after the date the sentence is approved by the convening authority.

Confinement included in a sentence begins to run from the date of sentencing by the court-martial. Reductions are effective on the date the sentence is approved. All other sentences of courts-martial are effective on the date ordered executed.

NCO Responsibilities

If you should be appointed to serve on a general or special court-martial as a member of the court, your duties and responsibilities will be very carefully explained to you before the court convenes and as the trial proceeds. If a soldier should seek your advice regarding what he or she should do in the event that charges are brought against the individual, advise the person concerned to seek assistance from an officer of the JAG Corps.

Unless you are a legal clerk, your acquaintance with the military justice system will probably be only a superficial one. Your closest contact with it will come through your commander's exercise of judicial authority under Article 15 of the UCMJ, and you should be intimately familiar with every aspect of that part of the system. But you are neither an expert in military law nor a lawyer, and you should never take upon yourself the duties of counsel.

The *Manual for Courts-Martial* is an important text. Every soldier should know what it contains and how to use it to answer questions on the military justice system. Do not, however, use that acquaintance to practice law.

SOURCES

FM 7-21.13, The Soldier's Guide
AR 27-10, Military Justice, 2005
Commander's Legal Handbook
The Judge Advocate General's Legal Center and School
Manual for Courts-Martial, 2012
Servicemember's Legal Guide, 5th Edition, by Lt. Col. Jonathan P. Tomes,
    USA (Ret.) (Stackpole Books)

21

Personal Affairs

Busy NCOs often allow their personal needs to pile up under more pressing professional matters. Doing so can be costly to you and to your loved ones.

Consider, for example, that neglecting to get life insurance and a last will and testament can cause surviving family members to be left out in the cold, financially and otherwise. Consider, too, that medical bills for unforeseen illnesses and injuries can devastate your financial future. What can you do about portions of major bills disallowed by TRICARE or the Dependent Dental Plan? Do you really understand your family's medical and dental benefits and how and under what circumstances TRICARE supplements are strongly recommended?

Suppose you're the kind of NCO who takes pride in hitting the ground running when assigned to a new job. What happens, for example, when you deploy overseas and your spouse and children remain behind in local quarters? Do your family members have what they need to achieve a decent quality of life and standard of living in their new environment? Where can they turn for help when associated problems arise?

What if, for some reason beyond your control, your end-of-month Leave and Earnings Statement (LES) reads "No pay due" and you must pay rent and meet other living expenses? Who can help to fully or partially defray necessary payments to landlords, banks, and other creditors until your pay is sorted out?

Are your personal affairs in order? To what extent? Do you keep records? Where are they? Who else knows where your vital records are kept? Does your spouse or other next of kin know important account numbers and first and supplemental points of contact?

You must make the effort to consider and take charge of your personal affairs. It is your responsibility to plan for your personal needs and those of your family. Commanders, sergeants major, first sergeants, and other leaders frown on NCOs who are unable or unwilling to ensure that they are fully deployable. Deployability includes personal readiness.

IMPORTANT PERSONAL RECORDS

The simplest way to keep your survivors informed about arrangements you have made for them is to prepare a record of your personal affairs. At the minimum, be sure that they know the location of the following:

- Your birth certificate and those of all members of your immediate family.
- Your marriage certificate.
- Divorce papers or previous spouse's death certificate, if applicable.
- Your life insurance policies.

If you put the original of your will and other key documents in a safe deposit box, be sure that your spouse or executor has access to it. If you die and no one has access to the box, a court order must be obtained to open it.

A personal affairs record is a necessity for the married soldier because it serves as a vital source of information for his or her family. It can be detailed, but make sure it includes at least the following:

- Insurance policy numbers and their amounts. Include automobile and homeowner's policies.
- Previous years' tax records.
- Copies of titles and bills of sale.
- Information on bank accounts.
- A list of all pay allotments.
- Information regarding any veterans' benefits to which you may be entitled.

If you are married, be sure someone in your family knows how to pay your household bills, when they are due, and where to find them.

Military Records

Keep a file of all records about your military service. Keep copies of or digitize orders, your discharge certificate, awards, citations, letters of appreciation and commendation, medical and dental records, Leave and Earnings Statements, and other information about your military history, even old NCOERs. Information is frequently needed throughout your active service career and afterward when you apply for certain benefits.

Emergency Data

Your DD Form 93, Record of Emergency Data, must be accurate and up-to-date at all times. This record tells your military personnel office (MILPO) where your next of kin can be located immediately. It also gives the name of the person you want to receive your pay if you are missing in action as well as other information of benefit to your dependents.

Family Care Plan

The wrong time for you, either as dual military parents or a single parent, to begin planning who will take care of your children is when you find yourself on a short-notice deployment. AR 600-20, Army Command Policy, stipulates that every single-parent soldier, dual military parents, and single and dual military pregnant soldiers must develop a family care plan. The plan, DA Form 5305, as a minimum includes proof that a guardian has agreed to care for dependent children under the age of eighteen. Powers of attorney for medical care, guardianship, and the authorization to start or stop financial support should be in the packet, and the children should have military ID cards. Lastly, the regulation requires a letter of instruction to the guardian/escort. This letter should contain specific instructions needed for the guardian to ensure the care of the dependents.

Although not required for the packet, birth certificates, Social Security cards, shot records, other medical or insurance cards, medication dosages (if necessary), and lists of family member addresses and phone numbers in case of emergency should be kept in a central location (an accordion-style organizer or file cabinet special drawer is suitable) and labeled to make it easy for the guardian to find documents fast. You might also want to contact financial institutions, children's doctors, schools, and daycare providers prior to deployment, so there will not be questions when your guardian comes to sign your child out of school or takes him or her to the doctor.

Power of Attorney

A power of attorney is a legal document by which you give another person the power to act as your agent, either for some particular purpose or for the transaction of your business in general. In the wrong hands, a power of attorney can ruin you because the agent who holds such a power has, within the limits granted by it, full authority to deal with your property without consulting you. Grant it only to someone you can trust and then only when you must.

You may never need a power of attorney, or if you do need one, it may only be required to perform certain acts and no others—a limited or special power of attorney. Always consult a legal assistance officer or a lawyer before assigning a power of attorney, and cancel it as soon as it is no longer required.

Bank Accounts

If you are married, you and your spouse should decide who manages the accounts. Make them joint accounts so that if anything happens to you, your family will have ready access to funds.

Current regulations require soldiers to have guaranteed direct deposit to a financial institution. With a guaranteed direct deposit from the US Army Finance Center, you do not have to bother with anything but picking up your Leave and Earnings Statement on payday.

Your Will

The importance of having a will cannot be overemphasized. You may not consider that you "own" very much, but not having a will could cause many legal complications after your death. If you were to die without a will—intestate—your estate would be distributed according to the descent and distribution laws of your state of legal residence, or in the case of real property located in another state, the laws of that state.

If you are married, both you and your spouse should have wills, even if each will makes the same distribution of property and assets. It is particularly important to have a will if you have minor children so that their interests can be protected through a guardianship of your choice in the event both you and your spouse die.

Once you have made your will, review it periodically to keep it up-to-date. As circumstances change, you may want to update it to be sure that it still expresses your desires about the distribution of your property and assets.

Keep your will in a safe place. The safest place to keep it (and other important papers) is in a safe deposit box at your bank. It is not a bad idea to send a copy of your will together with a statement as to the location of the original to the principal beneficiary or the person named in the will as the executor.

Commercial Life Insurance

It is beyond the scope of this book to discuss everything to look for when you are shopping for life insurance. What kind of policy to get and how much insurance you may need depends strictly upon your individual or family situation. You are particularly insurable if you are still relatively young and have school-age children who depend upon you. Shop around. There are numerous good individual and group insurance plans available; there are some pretty bad ones available as well (and plenty of unscrupulous insurance agents willing to take your money from you).

Servicemembers Group Life Insurance (SGLI)

The military automatically provides the maximum coverage of $400,000 under Servicemembers Group Life Insurance (SGLI); you may decline this coverage or request a reduced amount. The DoD currently pays the premiums to servicemembers who are deployed in a designated combat zone for $150,000 of SGLI coverage. When you leave the service, your SGLI is convertible to Veterans Group Life Insurance (VGLI).

Family SGLI

Family Servicemen's Group Life Insurance (FSGLI) automatically provides life insurance coverage for the spouses and dependent children of all soldiers who have full-time SGLI coverage. Spousal coverage is a maximum of $100,000 and can be in lesser amounts in increments of $10,000. Dependent child coverage is set at $10,000 per each dependent child and is provided at no cost to the soldier.

Servicemembers Group Life Insurance Traumatic Injury Protection Program (TSGLI)

Every member who has SGLI also has TSGLI. This coverage applies to active-duty members, Reservists, National Guard members, funeral honors duty, and one-day muster duty. This is a traumatic injury protection rider under Service-members Group Life Insurance (SGLI) and provides for payment to any member of the uniformed services covered by SGLI who sustains a traumatic injury that results in certain severe losses. TSGLI will pay benefits of between $25,000 and $100,000 depending on the loss directly resulting from the traumatic injury. This benefit is also provided retroactively for members who incurred severe losses as a result of traumatic injuries between 7 October 2001 and 1 December 2005, regardless of the geographic location where the injury occurred and whether coverage was in effect at the time of injury.

The Servicemembers Civil Relief Act (SCRA)

The Servicemembers Civil Relief Act (SCRA) of 2003 provides protection of rights, privileges, immunities, and benefits to servicemembers serving on active duty. These benefits include protection against paying taxes in both the home state and the state in which servicemembers are stationed, exemption from personal property taxes when stationed in a state that is not their domicile, the privilege to have civil court cases delayed, and special treatment of certain financial obligations. Servicemembers may also qualify for lowering their interest rates to 6 percent for obligations incurred prior to entering active service. For more information, go to www.defense.gov/specials/relief_act_ revision or see a legal assistance attorney. All mobilized Reserve Component (RC) soldiers can receive finance support and information from the local servicing finance office or defense military pay office (DMPO).

Reemployment Rights

RC soldiers who are mobilized are exempt from the Uniformed Services Employment and Reemployment Rights Act (USERRA) five-year limit for retaining reemployment rights. If you have questions about employment or reemployment rights, check the Employer Support of the Guard and Reserve (ESGR) website, www.ESGR.org.

HOUSING

Renting

Military families often must rent local housing while waiting for government quarters to become available. If you find yourself in that situation, you might want to consider renting an apartment on a month-by-month basis. Should you sign a lease for a specified period of time and then have to break it because a set of quarters unexpectedly becomes available, you have to forfeit your deposit (usually an amount equal to a month's rent).

Renting an apartment gives single soldiers a degree of independence and privacy not available in the barracks, and for this reason, many soldiers want to move off post.

Whether you can move off post depends on the following:

- Your post commander's policy. It is also up to the commanding officer of your unit. Some commanders are liberal in granting this privilege; it depends upon your unit's mission. Commanders of headquarters units can be more liberal than those of tactical or combat support units.
- The amount and quality of troop housing available. Some small, specialized units have trouble finding adequate troop housing, especially at overcrowded installations in metropolitan areas. Where sufficient troop housing is available, however, commanders normally fill up the billets first before allowing lower-ranking single personnel to move off post.
- Nonabuse of the privilege. Your commander will revoke permission to live off post as soon as you start coming to work late, running up debts, or causing disturbances among the local population.

Be sure that you can afford to live off post. Your military pay combined with your housing and subsistence allowances may be enough, depending on the geographical area, but just enough and no more. If supporting yourself in an apartment leaves you flat broke at the end of the month, you are better off living in the barracks.

Some soldiers find it a good idea to team up with two or three friends and rent a place by splitting all the costs. This is an excellent idea if your companions can be trusted to pay their share, take care of the communal areas, and respect your privacy and personal property.

OWNERSHIP OF PROPERTY

Joint ownership of property can have certain advantages in establishing an automatic and known passage of ownership upon the death of one owner but it can also have certain disadvantages. Inquire into federal and state laws regarding ownership of family property and take actions that put your estate in the most favorable ownership positions.

In the event of your death, your immediate personal effects will be forwarded at government expense to the person entitled to their custody. This does not give the recipient legal title to them, but they should be retained for disposition under the law.

If you own real estate in your name and it is not paid for, show on your personal affairs record whether there is a mortgage or a deed of trust against it, along with the name of the person or organization to whom you are indebted. Also include information about property taxes and insurance.

Transfer of automobile ownership is sometimes complicated because of varying state laws. Remember that joint titling may make you or your spouse subject to personal property taxes; active-duty personnel are generally exempt from payment of personal property taxes, so adding your spouse's name to an automobile title can cost you a lot of money.

INCOME TAXES

Military pay in general is subject to income tax. You do not pay tax on subsistence, quarters, and uniform allowances. Dislocation allowance, special duty pays, and hardship pay, however, are taxable.

Any nonmilitary earnings, including the pay received while employed during off-duty hours and the income of any of your dependents, are taxable. Military pay is excluded from federal income tax for service in any area that the president of the United States designates by executive order to be a combat zone. This exclusion is unlimited for enlisted members. If you spend a single qualifying day in the combat zone, your pay for the entire month is excluded from taxable income. Bonuses and special pays are also excluded from taxable income if within the previously stated limitations and earned in the same month in which you served in a combat zone.

The Servicemembers Civil Relief Act assures that a state in which a soldier is stationed but which is not the servicemember's legal residence cannot tax service pay. Legal residence is established at enlistment or thereafter when a soldier executes DD Form 2058, State of Legal Residence Certificate.

Alaska, Florida, Nevada, New Hampshire, South Dakota, Tennessee, Texas, Washington, and Wyoming do not withhold income tax from military pay. Kentucky, New Mexico, Minnesota, and Oklahoma instituted new tax guidelines in 2010 exempting certain military pay from state taxes for legal residents. Soldiers claiming legal residence in foreign countries or US territories are also exempt from paying state income taxes.

AGENCIES AND PEOPLE THAT CAN HELP

In addition to the quick overviews below, you can refer to the "Guide for Obtaining Information and Assistance" table or log in at Army Knowledge Online (https://www.us.army.mil), go to the Self-Service section at the top of the page and click on My Benefits. This Web page gives soldiers direct access to websites pertinent to all stages of the soldier life cycle, including recruiting, pay and retention, soldier family and well-being, transitioning, retirement, casualty affairs and survivor's assistance, and various calculators that assist in your economic decision-making.

Off Duty

Army Family and Morale, Welfare and Recreation (MWR) programs serve the needs and interests of each individual in the Army community for as long as he or she is associated with the Army, no matter where. This is another benefit that works to provide the Army family with the same quality of life afforded the society they protect.

Family and MWR programs include services and activities that help relieve stress, enrich the lives of servicemembers and their families, build strength and resilience, and help Army families stay physically, mentally, and financially fit. The following are examples of services offered:

- Child, youth, and school services.
- Soldier programs and community recreation.
- Family and MWR business initiatives.
- Armed Forces recreation centers.
- In-theater MWR facilities and supplies.

Army Community Services (ACS)

The Army Community Services (ACS) is an official Department of the Army organization established to provide information, aid, guidance, and referral services to military personnel and their families. ACS activities are monitored by the Army Adjutant General. The ACS webpage is www.myarmyone source.com.

The ACS provides a wide variety of services, including the following:

- Referrals for handicapped dependents.
- Family counseling services.
- Financial planning services.
- Lending services to provide bedding, linens, and housewares to military families until they can get settled at a new post.
- Volunteer services providing transportation for dependents when required.
- Child abuse information and referral.
- An emergency food locker from which needy families may draw supplies.

Army Emergency Relief (AER)

The Army Emergency Relief (AER) program operates in support of installation commanders by means of local officers and provides badly needed financial assistance to soldiers and their dependents. A local AER officer can authorize interest-free cash loans to soldiers and their family members. (Large loans must be approved by Headquarters, AER.) The AER website is www.aerhq.org.

AER loans may be approved for the following purposes:

- To defray living expenses because of nonreceipt of military pay.
- To provide money to help defray emergency travel expenses.
- To help pay rents, security deposits, and utilities.
- To help pay "essential POV [privately owned vehicle] expenses."
- To pay funeral expenses above and beyond those allowed by the government.

- To pay grants to the widows and orphans of deceased soldiers, in some cases.
- To provide cash to buy food when it is not available from the ACS food locker.
- To provide money to replace lost funds.

Soldiers (E-1–E-4) must apply for AER loans through their unit commanders by filling out DA Form 700, Application for AER Financial Assistance. The soldier must document his or her expenses or financial situation, and an allotment must be executed before the AER will disburse any money. Officers, including warrant and noncommissioned officers, are authorized to submit requests for AER financial assistance directly to the office nearest them.

Each year, AER disburses millions of dollars to help soldiers and their families. The only source for these funds is cash donations by Army members solicited annually during Army-wide fund-raising drives.

Army Family Action Plan (AFAP)

Today, more than half the Active Army Force is married. The Army now pays considerable attention to soldiers' families. The Army Family Action Plan (AFAP) provides a way for soldiers and family members to let Army leadership know what works, what doesn't, and what they think will fix it.

AFAP is the Army's way to support its families by giving commanders information on quality of life needs and expectations of soldiers and their families. Army installations conduct town halls and forums to learn about issues that are important to soldiers, families, retirees, and DA civilians within each community. Once validated, the issues are reviewed and prioritized by the command; if they cannot fix a problem or issue locally, they refer them to the annual Army AFAP conference.

The AFAP program starts locally when an annual symposium is held to examine issues of concern that unit-sponsored delegates believe need to be fixed. The volunteer delegates develop those issues through a series of workgroup discussions. They lay out the problems and inform the command of their ideas for solutions to resolve the issues. The top issues, as prioritized by the delegates, are briefed to leadership, who use the information to improve standards of living or to create or modify support programs. Since the first AFAP conference in 1983, many laws have been passed or amended to resolve more than a hundred quality-of-life issues affecting the Army family.

Army Family Covenant

In 2007 the Army announced the Army Family Covenant, its promise to provide soldiers and their families with a quality of life equal to their sacrifice to the nation. It commits the Army to improving family readiness by:

- Standardizing family programs and services.
- Increasing accessibility to health care.

- Improving soldier and family housing.
- Ensuring excellence in child, youth, and school services.
- Expanding education and employment opportunities for family members.

Better Opportunities for Single Soldiers (BOSS)

The goal of the Better Opportunities for Single Soldiers (BOSS) program is to enhance the morale and welfare of single soldiers to help sustain reenlistment rates and maintain combat readiness. BOSS serves as a representative of the single soldiers' community and transmits their issues to the chain of command. It can be a great tool for commanders to gauge morale regarding quality of life issues within their organization. BOSS also sponsors a number of activities for soldiers deployed or in garrison to improve morale.

The three BOSS core components are:

- *Quality of life*. This can be classified as the issues that soldiers can control to improve their morale, living environment, or personal growth and development. Unresolved issues identified during BOSS meetings will be channeled to the appropriate command or staff agency by the BOSS leadership. Army-wide issues are forwarded to the local AFAP conference for possible Army-level involvement.
- *Recreation and leisure*. Fun activities and entertainment requested by the single soldier community are planned by the BOSS council and typically coordinated with the installation MWR advisor and unit command sergeants major.
- *Community service*. BOSS members volunteer their off-duty time for community and on-post projects selected by the BOSS council.

Legal Assistance

A legal assistance officer will advise you on such matters as a will, power of attorney, divorce and separation actions, estates, tax problems, and other civil matters. The legal assistance officer can also provide you with a very useful "legal checkup," which is designed to identify any potential legal problems that you may have.

This officer is not normally permitted to represent you in civil court or to give you advice on matters of a criminal nature. Nor may he or she advise you about court-martial investigations or charges (a military counsel appointed by the Trial Defense Services office will assist you in such cases). If your problem requires the services of a civilian lawyer, the legal assistance officer can refer you, through cooperating bar associations, to civilian legal advisors or legal aid bureaus.

The *Servicemember's Legal Guide*, 5th Edition, published by Stackpole Books, provides comprehensive information on what soldiers and their families need to know about the law.

Chaplains

Chaplains are available to help soldiers, family members, and civilians with any type of concern they may have, be it spiritual, work related, or otherwise. Chaplains can offer counsel in areas ranging from marriage and family counseling to stress management and suicide prevention. Soldiers don't have to be churchgoers to use the chaplains to help them through the rough times. Lastly, Army chaplain regulations state that any communications to a chaplain acting as a spiritual advisor must be kept in confidence and cannot be told to anyone else without permission.

MEDICAL INSURANCE

Army health-care beneficiaries—you and your family—should take a long-term view toward medical and dental health. Eat foods that contribute to a longer life and exercise regularly. Rest properly. Brush and floss after meals. Get periodic physical and dental examinations. Follow the advice of doctors, dentists, and other Army health-care and medical care providers. Stay healthy to limit the effects of illness or disease. Beware of unsafe acts and conditions to avoid injury. When a person is ill or injured, nothing matters more than recovery.

When an active-duty soldier becomes sick or gets hurt, the Army direct care medical system provides care at no cost. In fact, AR 40-3, Medical, Dental, and Veterinary Care, prohibits active-duty soldiers, including active-duty Reserve Component soldiers, from seeking and obtaining medical and dental care from civilian sources without prior authorization from the local Army medical treatment facility commander. So while soldiers are on active duty, they do not need medical and dental insurance. But Army family members do—and they have it provided by TRICARE and the Dependent Dental Plan (offered through TRICARE).

Eligibility for TRICARE is determined by the Defense Enrollment Eligibility Reporting System (DEERS), a database of uniformed servicemembers (sponsors), family members, and others worldwide who are entitled under the law to TRICARE benefits. Active-duty and retired servicemembers are automatically registered in DEERS, but it is the sponsor's responsibility to ensure that his or her eligible family members are also registered correctly. All sponsors should ensure that their family members' status (marriage, divorce, new child, etc.), residential address, telephone numbers, and email address are current in DEERS so that TRICARE can send out information and have claims processed quickly and accurately.

TRICARE

TRICARE is a health-care program for members of the uniformed services and their families, and for survivors and retired members and their families. TRICARE combines the health-care resources of each of the military services and supplements them with a network of civilian health-care professionals to provide better access and high-quality service while maintaining the capability to support military operations. There are three TRICARE regions in the United States, each with an assigned lead agent who is responsible for the military health services system in that region.

Under TRICARE, family members have two basic choices for seeking medical care: Enrolled Choice (TRICARE Prime) and Non-Enrolled Choice (TRICARE Extra/TRICARE Standard). Active-duty members must enroll in TRICARE Prime and thus are not eligible for the Non-Enrolled Choice.

Members of the National Guard and Reserve and their family members are eligible for different TRICARE benefits depending on their status. If you are on military duty for thirty days or less and are activated in support of a contingency operation, you qualify for the same TRICARE benefits as an active-duty member.

Choice 1. Enrolled Choice (TRICARE Prime) provides the most comprehensive health-care benefits to the patient at the lowest cost. TRICARE Prime guarantees priority access to care at a military treatment facility (MTF) or, where available, an off-post, civilian, contracted doctor's office.

All active-duty military members must enroll in this choice and must use military facilities. Family members must also enroll to use this option. If you select the Enrolled Choice, you will be assigned to a primary care manager (PCM) whom you will see first for all of your medical needs. If necessary, your PCM will refer you to specialty medical care. There are no enrollment fees for active-duty families in TRICARE Prime.

Choice 2. The Non-Enrolled Choice (TRICARE Extra/TRICARE Standard) allows family members to seek medical care from any physician of their choice in the civilian community. The Non-Enrolled Choice is a more costly option than the Enrolled Choice. This choice incorporates two programs: TRICARE Extra and TRICARE Standard. Medical expenses are covered under these programs when family members are not enrolled in TRICARE Prime. A single deductible covers the use of either program.

Active enrollment and preauthorization are not required for your family to use the Non-Enrolled Choice, but a nonavailability statement must be obtained for civilian inpatient care. See your local health benefits advisor for more information.

TRICARE Standard is the basic TRICARE health-care program, offering comprehensive health-care coverage for people not enrolled in TRICARE Prime. (Active-duty servicemembers are automatically enrolled in Prime, and many other beneficiaries choose to enroll.) Standard does not require enrollment.

Fee-for-service flexibility. Standard is a fee-for-service plan that gives beneficiaries the option to see any TRICARE-certified/authorized provider (doctor, nurse practitioner, lab, clinic, etc.). Standard offers the greatest flexibility in choosing a provider, but it will also involve greater out-of-pocket expenses for you, the patient. You also may be required to file your own claims.

Costs. Standard requires that you satisfy a yearly deductible before TRICARE cost sharing begins, and you will be required to pay copayments or cost shares for outpatient care, medications, and inpatient care. A nonavailability statement for civilian inpatient care may be required for areas surrounding MTFs.

TRICARE Extra is an option that allows Standard beneficiaries to save money by making civilian doctors' appointments with doctors (nurse practitioners, labs, clinics, etc.) who are "participating" providers. Providers who participate in TRICARE agree to accept, as payment in full for services they render, the TRICARE maximum allowable charge (TMAC).

Nonparticipating providers may, by law, charge up to 15 percent above the TMAC for their services, and the TRICARE Standard beneficiary is responsible for the amount above the TMAC.

Participating providers will file claim forms for the TRICARE beneficiary. (Certified providers may or may not file claims on behalf of the Standard patient; the doctor may choose whether or not to do so on a case-by-case basis.)

Using the Non-Enrolled Choice allows family members the freedom to choose any civilian physician. Some physicians' services will be less costly than others. Your family members may continue to use military facilities on a space-available basis, but obtaining appointments will become very difficult.

TRICARE Pharmacy

Active-duty and retired military members have three options for filling their prescriptions: military pharmacies, the TRICARE Mail Order Pharmacy (TMOP) program, and the TRICARE Retail Pharmacy (TRRx). Prescriptions may be filled (up to a ninety-day supply for most medications) at an MTF pharmacy free of charge, although not all medications are available at these pharmacies. TMOP is available for prescriptions taken on a regular basis. You can receive up to a ninety-day supply (for most medications) of your prescription through the mail by using TMOP. Finally, prescription medications that your doctor requires you to start taking immediately can be obtained through a retail network pharmacy as part of the TRRx program.

TRICARE Costs

The charts below provide examples of cost shares for families using TRICARE. Health benefits advisors at MTFs or representatives at TRICARE Service Centers can assist you and your family in obtaining the medical care and services you need.

If you have questions about your military health-care benefits under TRICARE, there are many places to get answers. A member handbook may be obtained by visiting or calling your local TRICARE Service Center, by calling the health benefits advisor at your nearest military hospital or clinic, or by

ACTIVE-DUTY FAMILY MEMBERS

	TRICARE Prime E-1– E-4	TRICARE Prime E-5 and above	TRICARE Extra/Standard Families of E-4 and below	TRICARE Extra/Standard Families of E-5 and above
Annual Deductible (Individual/Family)	None	None	$50/$100	$150/$300
Civilian Outpatient Visit	$0	$0	Extra: 15% Standard: 20%	Extra: 15% Standard: 20%
Civilian Inpatient Admission	$0	$0	Greater of $25 or $15.15/day	Greater of $25 or $15.15/day
Civilian Inpatient Mental Health	$0	$0	$25 per day	$25 per day

visiting the website, www.tricare.mil. Each medical facility has a health benefits advisor, managed care office, or TRICARE Service Center. This should be your first contact for information. Additionally, below are telephone numbers for each region, where you can call and get information about TRICARE and your healthcare benefits.

TRICARE West
www.uhcmilitarywest.com
(877) 988-WEST (9378)
Alaska, Arizona, California, Colorado, Hawaii, Idaho, Iowa (except for the Rock Island Arsenal area), Kansas, Minnesota, Missouri (except for the St. Louis area), Montana, Nebraska, Nevada, New Mexico, North Dakota, Oregon, South Dakota, the extreme western portion of Texas, Utah, Washington, and Wyoming.

TRICARE North
www.hnfs.com
(877) TRICARE (874-2273)
Connecticut, Delaware, the District of Columbia, Illinois, Indiana, the Rock Island Arsenal area of Iowa, Kentucky, Maine, Maryland, Massachusetts, Michigan, the St. Louis area of Missouri, New Hampshire, New Jersey, New York, North Carolina, Ohio, Pennsylvania, Rhode Island, the Fort Campbell area of Tennessee, Vermont, Virginia, West Virginia, and Wisconsin.

TRICARE South

www.humana-military.com

(800) 444-5445

Alabama, Arkansas, Florida, Georgia, Louisiana, Mississippi, Oklahoma, South Carolina, most of Tennessee, and the eastern portion of Texas.

TRICARE Overseas

The TRICARE Overseas Program (TOP) is the DoD health-care program for soldiers and their families living outside of the United States. While similar to the stateside program, TOP has some differences.

The TRICARE overseas region has three areas:

- TRICARE Eurasia-Africa: Africa, Europe, and the Middle East.
- TRICARE Latin America and Canada: Canada, the Caribbean Basin, Central and South America, Puerto Rico, and the US Virgin Islands.
- TRICARE Pacific: Asia, Guam, India, Japan, Korea, New Zealand, and Western Pacific remote countries.

TOP has regional call centers to assist in coordinating care for TOP Prime and TOP Prime Remote beneficiaries. They also help coordinate emergency and urgent medical and dental care for active-duty servicemembers on temporary duty (TDY) or on leave overseas. If you are on TDY, you only need to provide a copy of your orders to the TOP call center for the area where you are located to coordinate for healthcare. Further information is available at the TOP website, www.tricare-overseas.com.

TRICARE *Prime* and TRICARE *Standard* are for active-duty servicemembers and their families. Only TRICARE Standard is for military retirees and their families who live overseas. Retirees cannot enroll in TRICARE Prime, but they can use TRICARE Standard.

TRICARE Reserve Select (TRS)

If in the Selected Reserve, you may qualify for and purchase TRICARE Reserve Select (TRS). This voluntary, premium-based health-care plan is only available when you are not eligible for any other non-premium-based TRICARE health coverage (like when serving on active duty or if covered under the Transitional Assistance Management Program TAMP). Family members are also eligible for TRS. If purchased, it is minimum essential coverage under the Affordable Care Act.

TRICARE for Life (TFL)

If you have both Medicare Part A and Part B, then TRICARE For Life (TFL) is your plan. Coverage is available worldwide, and you can see any provider you want. However, you will have greater out-of-pocket expenses if you get care from Veterans Administration providers or caregivers who opt-out of

Medicare, because they are not permitted to bill Medicare. TFL is Medicare wraparound coverage available to:

- Medicare-entitled uniformed service retirees, including retired guard members and reservists.
- Medicare-entitled family members and widows/widowers (dependent parents and parents-in-law are excluded).
- Medicare-entitled Congressional Medal of Honor recipients and their family members.
- Certain Medicare-entitled unremarried former spouses.

TFL pays the balance on the Medicare claim—what Medicare did not pay—for everything that is a TRICARE benefit.

TRICARE Young Adult (TYA)
TRICARE Young Adult (TYA) is a plan that qualified adult children can purchase once they are no longer eligible for cover under "regular" TRICARE, which ends when they turn twenty-one (or twenty-three if enrolled in college). It is only available for unmarried, adult children. The plan offers comprehensive medical and pharmacy benefits using one of the two different health plans available. If purchased, TYA is minimum essential coverage under the Affordable Care Act.

TRICARE Supplements
TRICARE supplements are not part of the TRICARE program. These different commercial plans are designed to be secondary coverage to TRICARE. Depending on the level of coverage, TRICARE supplements pay the cost share, deductible, and eligible excess charges under the Standard and Extra options so that on a combined basis eligible participants have 100 percent coverage in most cases. For more detailed information, check with any of the various associations representing the different members of the Armed Forces.

TRICARE Dental Program (TDP)
Active-duty soldiers receive all dental care, at no cost, from military dental treatment facilities and are therefore ineligible for the TRICARE Dental Program. The TDP is a voluntary dental plan open to families of all active-duty, selected Reserve, and individual Ready Reserve soldiers ordered to active duty for more than thirty consecutive days.

Sponsors must have at least twelve months remaining on their service commitments at the time of enrollment. After completing the initial twenty-four-month enrollment period, they may continue in the TDP on a month-by-month basis. Soldiers failing to pay premiums or who disenroll before completing the twenty-four-month lock-in are responsible for payment of all remaining premiums. Unless disenrolling for a valid reason, they are prohibited from reentering the program for twelve months.

Soldiers may disenroll from the TDP before completion of the mandatory twenty-four-month enrollment for the following reasons:
- When a sponsor or family member loses DEERS eligibility;
- When TDP enrolled members relocate outside the CONUS service area; or
- When an active-duty member transfers with enrolled family members to a duty station where space-available dental care for the enrolled members is readily available at the local uniformed services dental treatment facility.

Defense Health Agency (DHA)
On 1 October 2013, the DoD established the Defense Health Agency (DHA) to manage the Military Health System, including those previously managed by TRICARE Management Activity (TMA), which was disestablished on the same date.

Metropolitan Life Insurance Company (MetLife) administers for enrollment, claims processing, and customer service, and underwrites the TRICARE Dental Program. For further information, call the TRICARE Dental Program (MetLife) at (855) 638-8371 for CONUS and (855) 638-8372 for OCONUS. See also the MetLife website, http://mybenefits.metlife.com/tricare, or contact your nearest TRICARE Service Center, military dental treatment facility, or uniformed services personnel office.

LONG-TERM CARE
TRICARE and Medicare do not cover long-term care. The Federal Long-Term Care Insurance Program is an important benefit for members of the Army family, including retiree members and qualified relatives. It is insurance that helps you pay for care you need to perform daily activities if you have an ongoing illness or disability. It also includes the care you would need if you had a severe cognitive problem such as Alzheimer's disease: help with eating, bathing, dressing, transferring from a bed to a chair, toileting, continence, and similar areas. This type of care isn't received in a hospital and isn't intended to cure you. It is not acute care—it is chronic care that you might need for the rest of your life and that can be received in your own home, at a nursing home, or at another long-term care facility.

If you are younger than forty and healthy and you retire, the Federal Long-Term Care Insurance Program may not be the best deal. You may obtain comparable coverage at a lower monthly premium from one of the large companies that handle long-term care. Check the premiums calculator offered by the Office of Personnel Management online at https://www.ltcfeds.com/ltcWeb/do/assessing_your_needs/ratecalcOut for more information. To qualify, you must answer more questions about your health and habits than regular military personnel. Retirees can also call (800) 582-3337 Monday through Friday from 8 AM to 6 PM EST.

Warrior Transition Units (WTU)
Warrior Transition Units (WTU) are located at some major military installations where they provide support to wounded soldiers who require at least six months of rehabilitative care and complex medical management. A WTU closely resembles an operational Army unit, with a professional enlisted and officer cadre and operating procedures that build on the Army's model of unit cohesion and teamwork. This support network allows wounded soldiers to better focus on healing and more rapidly either transition back to the Army or civilian life.

Community Care Units (CCU)
A Community Care Unit (CCU) is similar to a WTU but is used by soldiers who receive medical care back home in their community through DoD, TRI-CARE, or Department of Veterans Affairs (VA) health-care facilities. The CCU mostly provides outpatient care management and transition services for soldiers who do not need day-to-day care provided by WTUs.

Soldier and Family Assistance Center (SFAC)
Soldier and Family Assistance Centers (SFACs) are typically located near a WTU to help injured and wounded soldiers. SFACs are coordinating offices that provide a number of centralized services to assist with administrative and personal needs of soldiers and their families during their stay at the WTU.

Most SFACs provide assistance with the following items:
- Logistics services.
- Financial services.
- Personnel services.
- Family assistance and support programs.
- Transition services.
- Army programs.
- Federal programs.
- State government services.

The Army Wounded Warrior Program (AW2)
The Army Wounded Warrior Program (AW2), formerly the Disabled Soldier Support System, serves the most severely wounded, injured, or ill soldiers and their families and helps them with their transition back into civilian or military life. AW2 has advocates located at major MTFs and VA medical centers

(VAMCs) that provide on-the-ground support to wounded, injured, or ill soldiers with disability ratings of 30 percent or more. AW2 serves soldiers and their families for however long it is needed. For more information, go to www.aw2.army.mil.

Wounded Soldier and Family Hotline
To support the unique needs and requirements of soldiers and their families, the Wounded Soldier and Family Hotline was established to provide personalized assistance. It can be reached twenty-four-seven at (800) 984-8523.

22

Separation, Discharge, and Retirement

SEPARATIONS

How and why a soldier leaves the Army depends on many factors, according to AR 635-200, Active Duty Enlisted Administrative Separations. Separation policies in AR 635-200 promote Army readiness by providing an orderly means to accomplish the following:

- Ensure that the Army is served by individuals capable of meeting required standards of duty performance and discipline.
- Maintain standards of performance and conduct through characterization of service in a system that emphasizes the importance of honorable service.
- Achieve authorized force levels and grade distribution.
- Provide for the orderly administrative separation of soldiers in a variety of circumstances.

The Army spends a substantial amount of money to recruit and train soldiers so that they are trained and ready for military service, so separating soldiers before they are able to complete their term is a huge waste of resources. Besides the hole each early separation causes in the ranks, it affects the Army and the units and leadership up and down the ranks, and the Army has to go out and recruit another person to fill that position.

AR 635-200 provides the authority for separation of soldiers upon expiration of term of service (ETS); the authority and general provisions governing the separation of soldiers before ETS; the procedures to implement laws and policies governing voluntary retirement of soldiers of the Army for length of service; and the criteria governing uncharacterized separations and the issuance of honorable, general, and under other than honorable conditions discharges.

The following selected entries are the authorized types of separations under the provisions of AR 635-200.

Chapter 4—Separation for Expiration of Service Obligation. A soldier will be separated upon expiration of enlistment or fulfillment of service obligation. Noncommissioned officers under the Indefinite Reenlistment Program can request separation from active duty at any time. Approval will be granted, however, only to those soldiers who have fulfilled their active-duty service obligation. Soldiers requesting voluntary separation in lieu of personnel change in status (PCS) must request separation within thirty days of being notified of the assignment. Soldiers will establish a separation date within six months from the date of application. Any separation date outside the six-month window must be fully justified.

Chapter 5—Separation for Convenience of the Government. A Chapter 5 separation covers the following: involuntary separation due to parenthood, lack of jurisdiction as ordered by a US court or judge thereof, aliens not lawfully admitted to the United States, personnel who did not meet procurement medical fitness standards, failure to qualify medically for flight training, personality disorders, concealment of arrest record, and failure to meet Army body composition and weight-control standards.

Chapter 6—Separation Because of Dependency or Hardship. Soldiers of the Active Army and the Reserve Components serving on active duty or active duty for training may be discharged or released because of genuine dependency or hardship. Dependency exists when death or disability of a soldier's (or spouse's) immediate family member causes the family or one of its members to rely upon the soldier for principal care or support. Hardship exists when—in circumstances not involving death or disability of a member of the soldier's (or spouse's) immediate family—separation from the service will materially affect the care or support of the family by alleviating undue and genuine hardship.

Chapter 7—Defective Enlistments, Reenlistments, and Extensions. This chapter provides the authority, criteria, and procedures for the separation of soldiers because of minority, erroneous enlistment or extension of enlistment, defective enlistment agreement, and fraudulent entry.

Chapter 8—Separation of Enlisted Women for Pregnancy. Chapter 8 provides authority for voluntary separation of enlisted women because of pregnancy. An enlisted woman who elects to remain on active duty when counseled may, if she is pregnant, subsequently request separation. Conversely, an enlisted woman who requested separation in writing may subsequently request withdrawal of the separation request.

Chapter 9—Alcohol or Other Drug Abuse Rehabilitation Failure. A soldier who is enrolled in the Army Substance Abuse Program (ASAP) for substance abuse may be separated because of inability or refusal to participate in, cooperate in, or successfully complete such a program.

Chapter 10—Discharge in Lieu of Trial by Court-Martial. A soldier who has committed an offense or offenses punishable by a bad conduct discharge or dishonorable discharge under the provisions of the UCMJ and the *Manual for Courts-Martial* may submit a request for discharge in lieu of trial by court-martial for the good of the service. The request does not prevent or suspend disciplinary proceedings. (See AR 635-200, pages 81–82 for details.)

Chapter 11—Entry-Level Status Performance and Conduct. This chapter provides guidance for the separation of personnel because of unsatisfactory performance or conduct (or both) while in entry-level status. It covers inability, lack of reasonable effort, or failure to adapt to the military environment.

Chapter 12—Retirement for Length of Service. A soldier who has completed twenty years' active federal service and who has completed all required service obligations is eligible to retire. Upon retirement, the soldier is transferred to the US Army Reserve Control Group (retired) and remains in that status until active service time plus control group time equals thirty years, and then is placed on the retired list. An Active Army soldier who has completed at least thirty years of active federal service will, upon request, be placed on the retired list.

Chapter 13—Separation for Unsatisfactory Performance. A soldier may be separated per this chapter when unqualified for further military service because of unsatisfactory performance, under the following circumstances: 1.) the soldier will not develop sufficiently, or 2.) the seriousness of the circumstance is such that retention would have an adverse impact on military discipline, good order, and morale, and 3.) it is likely that the soldier will be a disruptive influence, and 4.) it is likely that the circumstances will continue to recur, and 5.) the ability of the soldier to perform duties, including potential for advancement or leadership, is unlikely, and 6.) the soldier meets retention medical standards.

Chapter 14—Separation for Misconduct. This chapter establishes procedures for separating personnel for misconduct because of minor disciplinary infractions, a pattern of misconduct, commission of a serious offense, conviction by civil authorities, desertion, and absence without leave. A discharge under other than honorable conditions is normally appropriate for a soldier discharged under this chapter.

Chapter 19—Qualitative Selection Program (QSP). This chapter contains policies and procedures for voluntary and involuntary separation, for the convenience of the government, of active-duty NCOs and Army Reserve NCOs serving in Title 10 status, under the QSP. Soldiers separating under this chapter have their discharges characterized as honorable (see Chapter 14 for more on QSP).

DISCHARGES

For whatever reason, sooner or later each soldier must quit the service. In this section, we will consider the various types of discharges, the operation of the US Army transfer facilities, retirement, and veterans' rights.

Honorable Discharge

An honorable discharge is given when an individual is separated from the military service with honor. An honorable discharge cannot be denied to a person solely on the basis of convictions by courts-martial or actions under Article 15 of the UCMJ. Denial must be based on patterns of misbehavior and not isolated instances. An honorable discharge may be awarded when disqualifying entries in an individual's service record are outweighed by subsequent honorable and faithful service over a greater period of time during the current period of service.

Unless otherwise ineligible, a member may receive an honorable discharge if he or she has, during the current enlistment or extensions thereof, received a personal decoration or is separated by reason of disability incurred in the line of duty.

General Discharge

A general discharge is issued to an individual whose character of service has been satisfactory but not sufficiently meritorious to warrant an honorable discharge. Such persons would have, for example, frequent punishments under Article 15 of the UCMJ or be classified as general troublemakers.

Other than Honorable Discharge

Discharges that fall into the other than honorable discharge category are given for reasons of misconduct or security, or for the good of the service, and are covered by AR 635-200. No person shall receive a discharge under other than honorable conditions unless afforded the right to present his or her case before an administrative discharge board with the advice of legal counsel.

Bad Conduct or Dishonorable Discharge

A bad conduct discharge (BCD) is given by a court-martial, and only for punishment for enlisted soldiers. A soldier will be given a bad conduct discharge after an approved sentence by a general or special court-martial. In most cases, a BCD is after an individual serves time in a prison. A soldier who receives a BCD forfeits most veterans' benefits. A dishonorable discharge (DD) is the least desirable military discharge. It can only be imposed by a general court-martial, and then only if the *Manual for Courts-Martial* authorizes it. Murder and sexual assault are examples of the serious nature of the crimes which result in a dishonorable discharge.

Uncharacterized Separations

There are two types of uncharacterized separations: those given when a soldier is in entry-level status and those given because of void enlistments or inductions.

TRANSITION ACTIVITIES

US Army transfer facilities provide an informal, quiet atmosphere centrally located at a post where soldiers being separated may be processed within acceptable time limits. AR 635-10 prescribes that overseas returnees, except retirees, be separated on the first workday after their arrival at the separation transfer point, when possible. Personnel being released from active duty who are discharged before ETS or the period for which they are ordered to active duty are separated by the third workday after approved separation. All others are separated on their scheduled separation dates, except for those individuals who elect to be separated on the last workday before a weekend or a holiday.

Medical Examination

There is no statutory requirement for soldiers to undergo a medical exam incidental to separation, but they may schedule one if they desire. The Army requires a retirement physical no more than four months and no less than one month before retirement or start of transition leave if a soldier is being discharged or released and requests a medical examination; if review of the soldier's health record by a physician or physician's assistant warrants an exam; or if an examination is required by AR 40-501, Standards of Medical Fitness.

Veterans Compensation Program Physicals

Soldiers leaving the service who are or may consider filing a claim with the Veterans Affairs (VA) because of an illness or injury that happened due to their service can receive both the separation and VA compensation physical examination at the same time. This program reduced duplicate effort between the two agencies and has shortened the wait time for processing claims with the VA. It is important that soldiers start the exam process with enough time to complete it before leaving the service.

Soldiers can receive an exam:
- Up to six months before their ETS.
- Up to four months before retirement.
- Up to four months before transition leave (if requested).

Soldiers who are within forty-five days of terminal leave cannot participate in this program.

Each soldier undergoing separation processing will have his or her medical records screened by a physician, regardless of whether a separation physical has been requested. Advise your soldiers that a separation physical may be one of the most important medical examinations of their lives and the last record of active-duty health. Separation physicals end in a personal interview with a doctor. That interview is the proper time to bring up every single medical fact incident to military service. This interview substantiates service connection should a soldier, after discharge, request disability compensation from the Department of Veterans Affairs based on military service. Above all, each soldier being separated or retired from the service should make a copy of his or her medical and dental records and keep them after discharge.

Transition Assistance Program (TAP)

The DoD Transition Assistance Program (TAP) offers job assistance and separation counseling services for soldiers and their families as they leave the military. On Army posts, TAP services are delivered by transition assistance officers at Soldier for Life—Transition Assistance Program (SFL-TAP). Some of the services provided by TAP include pre-separation transition information and counseling, employment assistance, relocation, education and training, health and life insurance, finances, Reserve affiliation, disabled veterans, and retirement.

Soldier for Life Program

The newly created Soldier for Life program is the lead Army agency responsible for creating and monitoring programs and activities that assist soldiers and their families throughout their careers. This "life cycle" management begins when soldiers are first inducted, continues beyond their service, and is designed to help them stay connected to the Army.

Soldier for Life—Transition Assistance Program (SFL-TAP)

Your military service has earned you valuable services and benefits, but you can only take advantage of them if you understand which you're eligible for and how to get them. The Soldier for Life—Transition Assistance Program (SFL-TAP) is a transition and job assistance initiative located at military sites worldwide. If you are located too far from a listed SFL-TAP center, you may visit a Transition Assistance office at any other nearby installation, regardless of the service branch. Each SFL-TAP center includes a transition assistance job center, which is open to all active and Reserve component soldiers, Army civilians, and military and civilian family members. The SFL-TAP team provides eligible clients with transition advice and serves as a focal point for problems; it also provides clients with job search training, individual assistance and counseling, and a referral service. For more information go to https://www.SFL-TAP.army.mil.

On 21 November 2012 the Veterans Opportunity to Work (VOW) Act took effect and required every soldier to attend a pre-separation program before leaving the service. A mandatory five-day workshop was created and includes a pre-separation briefing on topics such as employment, education, and entrepreneurship opportunities for veterans.

Services typically provided by SFL-TAP centers include:
- *Pre-separation counseling.* As a soldier, your installation will not let you clear until you have received counseling. By law, soldiers must

receive required pre-separation counseling a minimum of ninety days before retirement or separation, and a completed DD Form 2648, the Pre-separation Counseling Checklist, is your proof that you have met this requirement. In counseling, you will receive information regarding available transition benefits and services as well as assistance in identifying your needs and developing an Individual Transition Plan (ITP).

- *Job assistance workshops.* These workshops provide you with the basic knowledge and skills necessary to plan and execute a successful job search.
- *Individual counseling.* Use the information discussed in the workshops to help you identify an objective, write résumés and cover letters, complete job applications, find job opportunities, prepare for interviews and job fairs, and negotiate salary and benefits.
- *Job search resources.* Available for your use, these include automated job listings such as the SFL-TAP Job Hot Leads, America's Job Bank, and the Transition Bulletin Board, which contains job listings and news regarding events such as job fairs, an automated résumé writer, Application for Federal Employment software, and a job assistance library.
- *Job assistance.* The SFL-TAP Center conducts individual, small-group, and large-group workshops to help you target your second career and prepare for interviews; find hidden job markets for your skills; evaluate job offers; build negotiating skills; dress for success; track job leads; evaluate employment agencies, job fairs, and automated résumé services; develop your résumé; and manage essential correspondence.

The Disabled Transition Assistance Program (DTAP) is a half-day seminar offered by the Department of Veterans Affairs, in conjunction with the three-day TAP. It is here that separating soldiers can learn about the Department of Veterans Affairs (VA) Vocational Rehabilitation Program and the application process for this possible benefit.

The law requires you to start the SFL-TAP process 180 days prior to your discharge date. You are eligible to be seen at the SFL-TAP office until you are discharged from the Army. For those retiring, SFL-TAP services can be maximized if begun two years prior to retirement. Services after retirement are available to Army retirees for life on a space-available basis. ID card-carrying family members are also eligible.

RETIREMENT

When you put the uniform into the closet for the last time, you do not have to stay in there with it. Those who do often pass quickly. You should begin early on in your career to think of retirement not as a thing that comes near the end of active life, but as the point of departure between the end of one exciting and fulfilling career and the beginning of another.

Making the Decision

You can request retirement from the Army when your active service—Active Duty for Training (ADT), Active Duty for Operational Support (ADOS), Active Duty for Special Work (ADSW), Temporary Tour of Active Duty (TTAD), Full-Time National Guard Duty (FTNGD), and Active Guard/Reserve (AGR)—totals twenty years. Army Reserve and National Guard soldiers may retire at twenty years of reserve duty and begin to draw retired pay at age sixty, or any date thereafter that they apply.

Unless you are at mandatory retirement, only you can make the decision to retire. If you are married, you will want to discuss the decision thoroughly with your spouse and family, but in the final analysis, it is you who must submit that application for retirement.

Army Retirement Services, Office of the Deputy Chief of Staff G-1, Headquarters, Department of the Army (HQDA), provides information on benefits and entitlements to active-duty personnel and families preparing for retirement. It also provides information to retirees and families through Army installation Retirement Services Offices (RSOs). The Retirement Services home page is located at www.armyg1.army.mil/rso.

Read the literature on retirement procedures at the MyArmyBenefits site, http://myarmybenefits.us.army.mil, and veterans' benefits at www.ebenefits .va.gov, so that when you arrive at the transition center for discharge, you will already know what to expect. Do not wait for someone else to tell you what your rights and benefits are. If you are to be retired at a post that does not have a transfer activity, your processing will be done at the local military personnel office. To an extent, you will be on your own there unless the personnel officer has people as experienced as the commander of a transfer activity in processing retirements.

Submission and Withdrawal of Retirement Applications

Any soldier who has completed nineteen or more years' service may apply for retirement. The request must be made up to one year prior but not less than nine months prior to the retirement date. Noncommissioned officers wishing to retire with less lead time should contact their military personnel directorate regarding exceptions to policy. Generally, to be eligible, all service obligations incurred as a result of schooling, promotion (unless a waiver is granted), and duty tours must be completed.

A retirement application cannot be withdrawn unless it is established that retaining the soldier concerned will be for the convenience or best interest of the government or will prevent an extreme hardship to either the soldier or his immediate family. The hardship must have been unforeseen at the time of the retirement application. Requests for withdrawal must be fully documented.

Transition Leave

Deciding whether or not to take terminal leave may not be an easy decision. The decision depends upon how much leave you have accrued at the time of retirement, how much leave you may have previously cashed in for pay, and what plans you may have for job-hunting activities, travel, or vacation.

If you take transition leave, you will be allowed to finish processing at the local transfer activity before departure on leave. Your DD Form 214 will be sent via registered mail. Arrangements to pick up retired ID cards may be made at any military installation.

Permissive TDY

Retiring soldiers may *with their commander's permission* take an additional twenty (or thirty) days leave to look for housing or a job in conjunction with retirement. This leave is called permissive TDY and is a nonchargeable, optional absence. You may not begin employment while in PTDY status (see AR 600-8-10, Personnel Absences, Leaves and Passes).

Allotments

Retirees are permitted up to six discretionary and nine nondiscretionary allotments, and may continue allotments that were in effect while on active duty with few exceptions.

You can start, stop, or change an allotment by letter, or online via myPay, using your Social Security number and personal identification number (PIN). More information on myPay is available at https://mypay.dfas.mil or through Army Knowledge Online (AKO). Mailed changes must include your signature and Social Security number.

Ceremonies

Each soldier who retires from the US Army is authorized to participate in a retirement review in honor of the occasion. These reviews are generally held on the last duty day of the month, and all personnel retiring from the service on that day at any specific post or installation are honored at the same special formation. You will be given the option to accept or decline a ceremony during your pre-retirement processing.

Pay

Every soldier has direct deposit while serving. Retirement should be no different, and you should continue to use electronic funds transfer (EFT, also called direct deposit) to a financial institution for your military retired pay. If your pay will continue to the same financial institution that you used on active duty, a new direct deposit form is not required; the DD Form 2656, Data for Retired Pay, will suffice. Changes to a financial institution *after* retirement require either an SF1199A (Direct Deposit Form) or an FMS 2231 (Fast Start Direct Deposit Form).

Discharge Certificates

Your DD Form 214, Certificate of Release or Discharge from Active Duty, is the most important of all the documents you will accumulate during your retirement processing; it is one of the most important documents you will ever receive during your military career. Ensure it is 100 percent correct before signing it. At the time of your separation or retirement, you will receive copy 1, the "short version," and copy 4, which lists the narrative reason for your discharge. File your copies and ensure your family knows how to access them. You may need them in the future to apply for Social Security benefits, or for your family to apply for your burial in a national or state veterans cemetery. *Do not file your DD Form 214 at a courthouse* unless they assure you that it will not be accessible as a matter of public records (due to increasing incidents of identity theft). If you are missing a previously issued DD Form 214, request a replacement from the National Personnel Records Center (NPRC) by completing the Standard Form 180 (SF 180), available at www.archives.gov/veterans/evetrecs/index.html.

Military Installation Privileges

Retired members, their dependents, and unmarried surviving spouses are authorized the use of various facilities on military installations when adequate facilities are available. This privilege includes commissary stores, post exchanges, Clothing Sales stores, laundry services, military theaters, Army recreation services facilities, clubs, and medical facilities.

Army regulations regarding exchange and commissary privileges for retired personnel apply overseas only to the extent agreed upon by the foreign governments concerned.

Mobilization Planning

All eligible retired Regular Army personnel are subject to mobilization, also known as a Retiree Recall tour. There are two programs for recalling retirees to active duty: Administrative, for non-contingency operations, and Overseas Contingency, for support of contingency operations. AR 601-10 Management and Recall to Active Duty of Retired Soldiers of the Army in Support of Mobilization and Peacetime Operations, governs the recall of retired soldiers who volunteer to return and serve an active-duty tour. All tours are approved by the Assistant Secretary of the Army.

If you are a retiree, make sure your mailing address and phone number are kept up to date with the Army Human Resources Command, as well as any changes to your physical condition. Ensure any written requests are signed and include your Social Security number. Call (800) 318-5298 or mail them to:

US Army Human Resources Command—Ft. Knox
ATTN: AHRC-PDR-RCR
1600 Spearhead Division Avenue, Dept. 420
Ft. Knox, KY 40122-5402

At the announcement of mobilization, retired personnel are ordered to active duty in their retired grade. Current medical fitness retention standards will apply until such time as the Secretary of the Army directs the application of mobilization standards.

Retired Pay

Following changes to the law, your military retirement plan will now be one of three possible versions. You determine your plan by the date that you *first* entered the military.

Final Pay used to be the most valuable retirement pay benefit but now it only applies to those who entered the service before 8 September 1980. Soldiers covered by the Final Basic Pay Plan who fail to complete their time-in-grade requirement (ranging from thirty days to three years, depending on grade) without an approved waiver will retire in the next lower grade and receive a percentage of the final basic pay for the next lower grade.

The High-3 retirement system is for soldiers who first entered service on or after 8 September 1980 and before 1 August 1986. High-3 also applies to members who first entered the service on or after 1 August 1986 and converted to the High-3 retirement plan by turning down the Career Status Bonus (CSB)/REDUX, an alternate option for soldiers who entered service after 31 July 1986.

If you are medically retired because of a disability incurred while on active duty, your retired pay is on your monthly active-duty pay multiplied by the percentage of disability.

The authority for nondisability retired pay, commonly known as length-of-service retired pay, is contained in Title 10, USC. Military retired pay is not based on financial need and is not a pension, but it is regarded as delayed compensation for completing twenty or more years of active military service. Nondisability retired pay falls under one of three different retirement systems:

- For those who entered active service before 8 September 1980, retirement pay base is computed using the highest grade satisfactorily held by the member.
- Those entering after 8 September 1980 fall under the High-3 system, where the retired pay is based on an amount equal to the total of the highest thirty-six months of active-duty basic pay, whether or not consecutive, divided by thirty-six. For the above two systems, each year of service is worth 2.5 percent toward the retirement multiplier. The longer a soldier is on active duty, the higher the multiplier and the higher the retirement pay, up to the maximum of 75 percent.

- Personnel who entered the service after 31 July 1986 may either select the High-3 system or elect to receive a one-time lump-sum career status bonus of $30,000. This option is called Career Status Bonus (CSB/REDUX). Soldiers with DIEMS dates on or after 1 August1986 receive a choice of retired pay plans as they approach their fifteenth year of active duty, provided they are not undergoing a separation or adverse action. These soldiers must choose either the High-3 pay plan or the CSB/REDUX plan. Under REDUX, a soldier retires at 40 percent of basic pay at twenty years' service, with this multiplier applied against the average basic pay, similar to the High-3 described above. At age sixty-two, two adjustments are made to the REDUX retiree's compensation. The first adjusts the multiplier to what it would have been under High-3. For example, a twenty-year retiree's multiplier would increase from 40 to 50 percent and a twenty-four-year retiree's multiplier to 60 percent. The second adjustment applies the full consumer price index (CPI) for every retirement year to this amount to compute a new base retirement salary, so that at age sixty-two, the REDUX and High-3 retirement salaries are equal. From this point on, REDUX cost-of-living allowances are again set at CPI minus 1 percent. CSB/REDUX is less generous than the Final Basic Pay or High-3 pay plans.

Social Security (FICA tax) *is not withheld from your military retired pay* because retired pay is not considered "earned income," but rather "deferred income." When eligible, you will draw full Social Security and full military retired pay. The receipt of one has no impact on the other, which is not the case with most private pensions!

Army retirees receive the *Army Echoes* newsletter (hard copies no longer mailed), retired pay statements, federal income tax statements (1099-R), and other correspondence originating from Defense Finance and Accounting Service (DFAS). To receive these important documents, you must keep your address up to date by writing to DFAS, US Military Retirement Pay, PO Box 7130, London, KY 40742-7130; faxing the change to (800) 469-6559; or entering the change of address at the myPay area of the DFAS website, www.dfas.mil. MyPay allows you to change your federal and state withholding taxes and exemption status; stop, start, or change allotments; change your correspondence address; update your financial institution EFT information; request a replacement IRS Form 1099R; and start, stop and change bonds. You can even opt to "turn off" hard-copy mailing of your annual retiree account statement.

Temporary Early Retirement Authority (TERA)

In 2012 the law changed to allow the Army and the other services to offer early retirement to servicemembers who have completed at least fifteen years of active service, should they choose to take this option. The law made it optional at the service's discretion; it is not an entitlement. As of this printing, the Army intends to use this limited program as part of its drawdown strategy to shape the force. It currently does not apply to ARNG and USAR soldiers.

Retired Personnel Records

Military personnel records for retired servicemembers discharged prior to World War I are on file at The National Personnel Records Center, Military Personnel Records (NPRC-MPR) in St. Louis, Missouri. Federal law requires that all requests for records and information be submitted in writing to 1 Archives Drive, St. Louis, MO 63138. Each request must be signed (in cursive) and dated within the last year.

Requests must contain enough information to identify the record among the more than 70 million on file. Certain basic information needed to locate military service records includes the veteran's complete name used while in service, service number, Social Security number, branch of service, and dates of service. Date and place of birth may also be helpful, especially if the service number is not known. You can fill out an online form at http://vetrecs.archives .gov, then print, sign, and send it to the above address.

Note: You should make copies of all the important documents in your military personnel file at some point before you retire. If you believe that an error or injustice has occurred and desire to request a review of your case by the Army Board for Correction of Military Records, you should apply in writing on DD Form 149, Application for Correction of Military or Naval Record. The application should be addressed to: Army Review Boards Agency, 251 18th Street South, Suite 385, Arlington, VA 22202-3531.

Survivor Benefit Program (SBP)

The Survivor Benefit Program (SBP) allows retired personnel to provide an annuity to certain designated survivors. Various amounts and types of coverage may be elected, with the maximum being 55 percent of the amount of a member's retired pay at the time of death. These persons may be the widow or widower, dependent children, or other persons with an insurable interest in a retired soldier. A detailed description of the SBP plan may be found at http://soldierforlife.army.mil/retirement.

Wearing the Uniform, Military Titles and Signatures, Awards, and Decorations

Wearing of the uniform by retired personnel is a privilege granted in recognition of faithful service to the country. Retired personnel may wear the uniform when such wear is considered appropriate.

Retired personnel wear the same uniform prescribed for active-duty personnel. Retirees not on active duty may wear the uniform with decorations and awards. The shoulder sleeve insignia for US Army retirees is authorized for wear on the left shoulder by retired personnel. The shoulder sleeve insignia of a former wartime unit may be worn on the right shoulder by retired personnel who served in the unit if wearing the Class A (green) uniform.

All retired personnel not on active duty are permitted to use their military titles socially and in connection with commercial enterprise. Such military titles must never be used in any manner that may bring discredit to the Army or in connection with commercial enterprises when such use, with or without the intent to mislead, gives rise to any appearance of sponsorship, sanction, endorsement, or approval by the Department of the Army or the Department of Defense.

Retired personnel who have not received the awards to which they are entitled or who desire replacement of items previously issued that were lost, destroyed, or are unfit for use without fault or neglect on the veteran's part may obtain them upon written application. Requests should be addressed to the US Army Human Resources Command, ATTN: AHRC-PDP-A, Dept. 480, 1600 Spearhead Division Avenue, Fort Knox, KY 40122-5408. Requests submitted to HRC can be sent in a letter or memorandum format, or by using the SF 180, Request Pertaining to Military Records. Requests must include a copy of the veteran's/retiree's separation or discharge paperwork DD Form 214 and any other supporting documentation to substantiate the request. The application should include a statement or explanation of the circumstances surrounding the loss or nonissue of the items concerned. Replacements are made at cost. No money should be mailed for replacements until you are instructed to do so.

Travel and Transportation Allowances
Soldiers are authorized travel allowances from their last duty station to their home. Shipment and storage of household goods incident to retirement is authorized on a one-time basis, subject to weight limitations and other controls. Specific information relative to shipment and storage of household goods is contained in DA Pam 55-2, Transportation and Travel: It's Your Move.

Retired soldiers are eligible for space-available travel, category VI, within the continental limits of the United States on DoD-owned or DoD-controlled aircraft. Eligible family members of retired soldiers who possess a valid military identification card can also fly when accompanied by the retiree.

VETERANS' RIGHTS AND BENEFITS
The benefits discussed in this section are available to all veterans regardless of status. All Department of Veterans Affairs (VA) benefits (with the exception of insurance and certain medical benefits) payable to veterans or their dependents require that the particular period of service upon which the entitlement is based be terminated under conditions other than dishonorable. Honorable and general discharges qualify the veteran as eligible for benefits. Dishonorable discharges and bad conduct discharges issued by general courts-martial are a bar to VA benefits. Other bad conduct discharges and discharges characterized as other

VETERANS' BENEFITS TIMETABLE

You Have *(after separation from service)*	Benefits	Where to Apply
Time varies	**GI Education:** The VA will pay you while you complete high school, go to college, or learn a trade, either on the job or in an apprenticeship program. Vocational and educational counseling is available.	Any VA office
10 years	**Veterans Educational Assistance Program:** The VA will provide financial assistance for the education and training of eligible participants under the voluntary contributory education program. Vocational and educational counseling is available upon request.	Any VA office
12 years, although extensions are possible under certain conditions	**Vocational Rehabilitation:** As part of a rehabilitation program, the VA will pay for tuition, books, tools, or other expenses and provide a monthly living allowance. Employment assistance is also available to help a rehabilitated veteran get a job. A seriously disabled veteran may be provided services and assistance to increase independence in daily living.	Any VA office
No time limit	**GI Loans:** The VA will guarantee your loan for the purchase of a home, manufactured home, or condominium; repair, alteration, or improvement of a home; or refinancing of an existing home loan.	Any VA office
No time limit	**Disability Compensation:** The VA pays compensation for disabilities incurred or aggravated during military service.	Any VA office
1 year from date of mailing of notice of initial determination	**Appeal to Board of Veterans Appeals:** Appellate review will be initiated by a notice of disagreement and completed by a substantive appeal after a statement of the case has been furnished.	VA office or hospital making the initial determination
No time limit	**Medical Care:** The VA provides hospital care covering the full range of medical services. Outpatient treatment is available to all service-connected conditions, or non-service-connected conditions in certain cases. Alcohol and drug dependence treatment is available.	Any VA office
Time varies	**Burial Benefits:** The VA provides certain burial benefits, including interment in a national cemetery and partial reimbursement for burial expense.	VA national cemetery having grave space, any VA office
No time limit	**Readjustment Counseling:** General or psychological counseling is provided to assist in readjusting to civilian life.	Any Vet Center, VA office, or hospital
Within 90 days of separation	**One-Time Dental Treatment:** The VA provides one-time dental care for certain service-connected dental conditions.	Any VA office or hospital
No time limit	**Dental Treatment:** Treatment for veterans with dental disabilities resulting from combat wounds or service injuries and certain POWs and other service-connected disabled veterans.	Any VA office or hospital
1 year from date of notice of VA disability rating	**GI Insurance:** Low-cost life insurance (up to $10,000) is available for veterans with service-connected disabilities. Veterans who are totally disabled may apply for a waiver of premiums on these policies.	Any VA office
120 days or 1 year beyond with evidence of insurability; or up to 1 year if totally disabled	**Veterans Group Life Insurance (VGLI):** SGLI may be converted to a 5-year nonrenewable term policy. At the end of the 5-year term, VGLI may be converted to an individual policy with a participating insurance company.	Office of Servicemember's Group Life Insurance, 213 Washington St., Newark, NJ 07102, or any VA office
No time limit	**Employment:** Assistance is available in finding employment in private industry, in federal service, and in local or state employment service.	Local or state employment service, U.S. Office of Personnel Management, Labor Department, any VA office
Limited time	**Unemployment Compensation:** The amount of benefit and payment period varies among states. Apply after separation.	State employment service
90 days	**Reemployment:** Apply to your former employer for employment.	Employer
30 days	**Selective Service:** Male veterans born in 1960 or later years must register.	At any U.S. post office; overseas at any U.S. embassy or consulate

than honorable may or may not qualify depending upon a special determination made by the VA, based on the facts of each case. To prove your eligibility for VA benefits, ensure that you keep a complete copy of your medical records and protect your DD Form 214, Discharge Certificate. For the most up-to-date information on the ever-changing suite of benefits veterans and retirees are entitled to the VA has published the *Federal Benefits for Veterans, Dependents and Survivors* handbook. They also maintain an online version at www.va.gov/opa/publications/benefits_book.asp.

Department of Veterans Affairs (Disability) Compensation

If you believe that you have a condition that may entitle you to VA compensation, file your claim at the time of separation. If the VA, upon reviewing your medical records, finds that you do have grounds for seeking compensation, an appointment for a physical exam will be made for you at the Department of Veterans Affairs hospital closest to your retirement home. Your claim will be processed based upon the examination results.

Disability Entitlements

Combat-Related Special Compensation (CRSC) and Concurrent Retirement Disability Pay (CRDP) are programs Congress created for military retirees. They allow eligible servicemembers to receive monthly entitlements along with their retired pay. CRSC is a special nontaxable compensation for disability and non-disability military retirees with combat-related disabilities; retirees must apply to HQDA to receive it.

To qualify for CRSC you must:
• Be receiving military retired pay.
• Have a disability rated at least 10 percent by Veterans Affairs (VA).
• Waive your VA pay from your retired pay.
• File a CRSC application with the Army.

Disabilities that may be considered combat related include injuries from armed conflict, hazardous duty, instrument of war (such as combat vehicles or weapons) and simulated war (such as training or exercises).

CRDP removes an unfair practice toward some military retirees that penalized retired pay for those with service-connected disabilities. Payment of benefits and retiree pay was prohibited until the CRDP program began 1 January 2004 but even now only affects a portion of retirees with service-connected disabilities. This pay is taxed the same way as retired pay and is normally considered taxable income. Eligible retirees receive CRDP automatically—there is no need to apply for this benefit, although you must be eligible for retirement pay to qualify. If you were placed on disability retirement and would be eligible for military retired pay without a disability, you may be entitled to receive CRDP. Under these rules, you may be entitled to CRDP if:

- You are a regular retiree with a VA disability rating of at least 50 percent.
- You are a reserve retiree with twenty qualifying years of service, a VA disability rating of at least 50 percent, and have reached retirement age.
- You are retired under the Temporary Early Retirement Act (TERA) and have a VA disability rating of at least 50 percent.
- You are a disability retiree who earned entitlement to retired pay under any provision of law other than disability and have a VA disability rating of at least 50. You might become eligible for CRDP at the same time you become eligible for retired pay.

Conversion of SGLI to Veterans Group Life Insurance (VGLI)

Veterans Group Life Insurance (VGLI) is a life insurance program that allows veterans to convert their full-time SGLI coverage to a lifetime renewable term insurance that you can keep for as long as you pay the premiums. A service-member has 240 days after separation to apply for VGLI, with no exam requirements. Beyond the 120 days, you have one year and 120 days to apply, but you must answer the health questions on the application and meet good health requirements. During the 120 days after separation, the SGLI coverage continues without premiums.

At any time, you may convert your VGLI coverage to an individual policy of life insurance with a commercial company that participates in the program at the company's standard premium rate, regardless of your health. No disability or other supplemental benefits will be provided on converted policies. You may convert up to the amount of VGLI coverage you hold. The VA website, http://benefits.va.gov/insurance/vgli.asp, provides information on how to convert to an individual policy and a list of participating companies.

SGLI Disability Extension

The SGLI Disability Extension allows soldiers who are totally disabled at time of discharge to keep the SGLI coverage they had in service at no cost for up to two years.

Service-Disabled Veterans Insurance (S-DVI)

The Service-Disabled Veterans Insurance (S-DVI) program was established in 1951 to meet the insurance needs of veterans with service-connected disabilities. Veterans have a number of options and policies to choose from. Policies are issued for $10,000; those who qualify for S-DVI may be eligible for Supplemental S-DVI, which has an amount up to $30,000.

Employment

Priority referral to job openings and training opportunities is given to eligible veterans, with preferential treatment for disabled veterans. Additionally, the job service assists veterans who are seeking employment by providing information about job marts, on-the-job training and apprenticeship training opportunities, and so on, in cooperation with VA regional offices and Veterans Outreach centers.

Veterans may seek employment with the federal government and receive some breaks when applying for federal employment:

- A 5-point preference is given to those who served during any war, in any campaign, in an expedition for which a campaign medal has been authorized, or for 180 consecutive days between 31 January 1955, and 15 October 1976.
- A 10-point preference is given to those who were awarded the Purple Heart, have a current service-connected disability, or are receiving compensation, disability retirement benefits, or pension from the VA.
- A veteran with a 30 percent or more disability may receive appointment without competitive examination with a right to be converted to career appointments and retention rights in reductions in force.

Veterans Recruitment Appointment (VRA)

Veterans Recruitment Appointment (VRA) policy allows federal agencies to hire eligible veterans direct to job vacancies without competition. You can be hired at any grade level up to and including a GS-11 or equivalent. After two successful years you will be converted to the competitive service, but veterans preference will still apply if you use the VRA authority.

Veterans Employment Opportunity Act (VEOA)

The Veterans Employment Opportunity Act (VEOA) is a competitive service hiring authority used to fill permanent positions in the federal government. It allows veterans to apply for jobs that are only open to "current competitive service employees." To be eligible for a VEOA appointment, your latest discharge must be issued under honorable conditions *and* you must be either a preference eligible *or* a veteran who finished three or more years of active service.

Education Benefits

There are many educational and skills development opportunities open to soldiers and veterans. These and other valuable benefits may also be open to spouses and children, as an estimated 25 percent or more of those benefitting from VA educational programs are nonveterans. It is important to know your benefits and which are best suited for you and your education and training goals.

Post-9/11 GI Bill

If you have at least ninety days of combined service after 10 September 2001 and are still on active duty, you may be eligible for up to thirty-six months of education benefits, generally payable for fifteen years, following your release from active duty. Also, some schools participate in the Yellow Ribbon Program and may make additional funds available for your education without any further charges to your GI Bill entitlement. The VA may offer you payments for a monthly housing allowance, a stipend for books and supplies, and a one-time rural benefit payment.

See your Army Continuing Education System (ACES) counselor for details on the GI Bill, the Veterans Educational Assistance Program (VEAP), and other education benefit programs. For more information, visit the GI Bill website, www.benefits.va.gov/gibill.

VA Home Loan Program

VA home loans may be used to buy a home; to buy a residential unit in certain condominium projects; to build a home; to repair, alter, or improve a home; to simultaneously purchase and improve a home; to refinance an existing home loan; to buy a manufactured home (with or without a lot); to buy a lot for a manufactured home that you already own; to purchase and simultaneously improve a home with energy-conserving measures; or to refinance a manufactured home loan in order to acquire a lot. Eligibility requirements vary based on period of service (except that all veterans, to be eligible, must have an other than dishonorable discharge certificate).

The loan terms are subject to negotiation between the veteran and the lender. The repayment period or maturity of GI home loans may be as long as thirty years and thirty-two days. Newly discharged veterans have certificates of eligibility mailed to their homes by the VA shortly after discharge. Other veterans may secure their certificates by sending VA Form 26-1880, Request for a Certificate of Eligibility, along with required supporting documents, to the VA regional office nearest them. Active-duty personnel may also take advantage of these loans.

You can also get your certificate of eligibility (COE) online at the VA eBenefits portal at www.ebenefits.va.gov. If you need assistance, call the eBenefits Help Desk at (800) 983-0937 on weekdays between 8 AM and 8 PM (EST).

One-time Dental Treatment

In addition to dental conditions that qualify for treatment because of service connection, veterans are entitled to a one-time dental treatment without review of service records to establish service connection. This treatment must be applied for within ninety days of separation. Do not fail to take advantage of this very important benefit. Contact the local VA office or go to the VA website https://www.1010ez.med.va.gov/sec/vha/1010ez/ and apply online.

TRICARE Retiree Dental Program (TRDP)

The TRICARE Retiree Dental Program (TRDP) is cost-effective dental coverage for retired soldiers and their eligible family members. This dental treatment plan typically covers some or all of the typical needs, and includes dental services like exams, cleanings, fillings, crowns, and surgeries. Like traditional dental plans, it requires enrollee-paid premiums.

Unemployment Compensation for Ex-Servicemembers (UCX)

The Unemployment Compensation for Ex-Servicemembers (UCX) program provides benefits for soldiers separated under honorable conditions. It is administered by the states (as agents of the Federal government). Because there is no payroll deduction from servicemembers' wages for unemployment insurance, benefits are paid for by the military branches.

Filing a Claim

You should contact your state workforce agency as soon as possible after you are discharged if you need to file a claim, as each state has its own policies. Be sure to have a copy of your discharge documents (DD-214 or similar form) when you open your claim. In many states, you may now file your claim by telephone or online.

VA Medical Benefits

The Department of Veterans Affairs provides a Medical Benefits Package, a standard enhanced health benefits plan available to all enrolled veterans. Through it, the VA offers the whole spectrum of medical benefits to qualified veterans: aids and services for the blind, alcohol treatment, domiciliary care, drug treatment, hospitalization care for dependents or survivors, nursing home care, outpatient dental treatment, outpatient medical treatment, and prosthetic appliances.

Just by your service you may qualify for VA health-care benefits as long as you were separated under any of the service classifications except a dishonorable discharge. Members of the ARNG or USAR who were called to and completed the full period of active duty may also be eligible for VA health benefits.

The VA maintains an annual enrollment system to manage the provision of quality hospital and outpatient medical care and treatment to all enrolled veterans. A priority system ensures that veterans with service-connected disabilities and those below the low-income threshold are able to be enrolled in the VA's health-care system. Veterans who are receiving compensation or who would be eligible to receive compensation (except for retirement pay) and need treatment for an ailment connected with their service are admitted as beds are available. Under certain circumstances, veterans who were not discharged or retired for disability or who are not receiving compensation and who apply for treatment of a non-service-connected disability may be admitted to a VA hospital. Any veteran with a service-connected disability may receive VA outpatient medical treatment.

There is no monthly premium to use VA healthcare; however, veterans may be required to make a co-payment. If a veteran has health insurance, it may cover the cost of co-pays. The VA will provide combat veterans with free medical care for any illness possibly associated with service during a period of hostility for five years from the veteran's release from active duty.

Veterans Crisis Line

The Veterans Crisis Line connects veterans, their families, and friends with a qualified, caring network of responders through a confidential toll-free hotline or online chat, or by text message. Veterans and their loved ones can call (800) 273-8255 and press 1. Those with computer access can chat online by visiting http://veteranscrisisline.net/ChatTermsOfService.aspx. They can also send a text message to 838255 to receive confidential support anytime. Support for deaf and hard-of-hearing individuals is available.

Vocational Rehabilitation

Generally, a veteran is eligible for vocational rehabilitation for twelve years following discharge or release from active service. A four-year extension is possible under certain circumstances, and further extensions may be granted for veterans who are seriously disabled when it is determined by the VA to be necessary because of disability and need for vocational rehabilitation.

Eligible disabled veterans may get training up to a total of four years or its equivalent in part-time or a combination of part-time and full-time training. Eligibility is determined by the VA.

VA Correspondence and Records

Keep a file of every paper the VA sends you. Your dealings with the VA will require patience and persistence; the required degree of each will depend to a large extent on how busy your local VA office is. Invariably, VA personnel are courteous, and they try to be helpful, but processing your claim may take some time.

VA Nursing Homes

The VA provides nursing home services to veterans through three national programs: VA-owned and -operated community living centers, state-owned and -operated veterans' homes, and through the Community Nursing Home program. Each of these programs has its own specific admission and eligibility criteria.

Burial

Burial is available to any deceased veteran of wartime or peacetime service (other than for training) who was discharged under conditions other than dishonorable at all national cemeteries having available grave space, except Arlington Cemetery.

Eligible veterans' dependents may receive a headstone or grave marker without charge, shipped to a designated consignee. The cost of placing the marker in a private ceremony must be borne by the applicant. The VA may pay an amount not to exceed the average actual cost of a government headstone or marker as a partial reimbursement for the cost incurred by the person acquiring a nongovernment headstone or marker for placement in a cemetery other than a national cemetery.

SOURCES

AR600-8-11, Reassignment
AR 614-30, Overseas Service
AR 635-10, Processing Personnel for Separation
AR 635-200, Active Duty Enlisted Administrative Separations
Retirement Services Office Handbook for Retired Soldiers and Family Members (2007)
Federal Benefits for Veterans, Dependents and Survivors
Army Retirement Services website, http://soldierforlife.army.mil/retirement
myArmyBenefits website, http://myarmybenefits.us.army.mil

Index

About the Author

CSM Dan Elder, USA (Ret.), served on active duty for twenty-six years in non-commissioned officer positions from squad leader to command sergeant major at the battalion, brigade, and nominative levels, culminating in his assignment as an Army Command senior enlisted leader. He served as a first sergeant, drill instructor, and senior instructor and on the staff of the US Army Sergeants Major Academy between operational assignments. His overseas assignments include Germany, Hungary, Bosnia-Herzegovina, and Iraq. He has received numerous awards and recognitions for his service. He lives in Texas.

STACKPOLE BOOKS

Military Professional Reference Library